CAMBRIDGE LATIN AMERICAN STUDIES

EDITORS

DAVID JOSLIN   JOHN STREET

IDEAS AND POLITICS OF CHILEAN INDEPENDENCE 1808–1833

THE SERIES

IDEAS AND POLITICS OF CHILEAN INDEPENDENCE
1808-1833

SIMON COLLIER, Ph.D.

School of Comparative Studies
University of Essex

CAMBRIDGE
AT THE UNIVERSITY PRESS
1967

Published by the Syndics of the Cambridge University Press
Bentley House, 200 Euston Road, London, N.W. 1
American Branch: 32 East 57th Street, New York, N.Y. 10022

Library of Congress Catalogue Card Number: 67–15395

Printed in Great Britain
at the University Printing House, Cambridge
(Brooke Crutchley, University Printer)

FOR

D.H.C. AND M.K.C.

in gratitude

The violent transition from darkness to noonday light—from rigid slavery to absolute liberty—is very critical.

RAMÓN FREIRE (1825)

CONTENTS

PREFACE

This book is an attempt to describe the nature of the political ideas and attitudes which informed the procedures of the revolutionary creole elite in Chile from the start of the Spanish imperial crisis in 1808 to the effective stabilization of the new Republic under Diego Portales in the early 1830s. In Part I, the growth of revolutionary ideals is considered, and I pay particular attention to the complex creole reaction to the crisis of 1808–10, which was the point from which the Chilean revolution—like all the Latin American revolutions—started out. Part II is devoted to a general description of the ideas and attitudes which were common to all sections of the revolutionary leadership and the creole intelligentsia and it covers the whole period from 1810 to 1833. In Part III I take up the story from the final liberation of Chile in 1817, and try to depict the shifting political moods which affected the life of the country until Portales and the conservatives imposed the durable and successful mould which was to give Chile (as far as the rest of Spanish America was concerned) an untypical history for the remainder of the nineteenth century.

Chile has always been a country where the study of history has flourished. In the nineteenth century, Jaime Eyzaguirre claims, 'to write history was a sign of intellectual quality',[1] and Chile produced an unexampled generation of laborious historical scholars. In 1910 the Peruvian José de la Riva Agüero was able to comment somewhat enviously on 'the multitudinous legion of historians which Chile—a country privileged in this—has engendered'.[2] The academic visitor from Europe is favourably impressed by the fact that Chile's most famous historians, no less than the most famous Chilean generals and statesmen, are well represented in the statuary of Santiago. It is hardly surprising, in these circumstances, that the crucial quarter-century that saw the birth of the Chilean republic should have been subjected to prolonged and scholarly inquiry. The great narrative historians of the nineteenth century—

[1] *Fisonomía histórica de Chile* (2nd edn. 1958), p. 131.
[2] *Historia en el Perú* (Lima, 1910), p. 544.

ix

Preface

I am thinking particularly of Diego Barros Arana, Miguel Luis Amunátegui, and Benjamín Vicuña Mackenna—have left us an incomparable and detailed account of the period of independence, and in the course of their work they naturally touched on the question of political ideas. In the present century, a number of excellent writers have come closer to an accurate assessment of the ideas of the revolution. Luis Galdames has written a massive and comprehensive treatise on the constitutional development of the period, a treatise whose range extends far beyond the boundaries of what is normally understood as constitutional history.[1] But the modern work which has most stood out, by its sheer volume and by the provocative and forcefully stated conclusions it contains, has been Francisco Antonio Encina's enormous *Historia de Chile desde la prehistoria hasta 1891*. Encina has called in question many of the most cherished interpretations of the great nineteenth-century scholars, and it is safe to say, I think, that no future history of Chile will wholly escape the influence of his monumental labour. Nevertheless, Encina's account of Chilean history has its faults. It can in no way be regarded as the equal of, for instance, Diego Barros Arana's. One is compelled to agree with Elías Almeyda Arroyo's contention that Encina 'arranges history to his taste and relates it as his prejudices dictate'.[2] These prejudices, I believe, are particularly serious as far as the independence period goes. Encina's marked hostility towards liberalism has led him to undervalue and even to distort the seriousness of purpose which characterized the activity of the Chilean liberals of the 1820s and 1830s. For Encina, the seven years of uncertainty (1823–30) that preceded what to him is the brilliant political epic of Diego Portales form a largely meaningless and discreditable interlude whose only purpose is to throw into sharp relief the creative achievement of his great hero. But despite these flaws, and despite the persistent intrusion of Spenglerian concepts (derived through Alberto Edwards) into his narrative, Encina must at least be credited with an imaginative historical intuition which has borne

---

[1] *Historia de Chile. La evolución constitucional desde 1810 hasta 1833* (1925).
[2] *La Historia de Chile de don Francisco Antonio Encina. Estudio crítico* (1952), p. 65. See also C.C. Griffin, 'Francisco Encina and Revisionism in Chilean History', *HAHR*, xxxvi (Durham, N.C., 1957), 1.

fruit, for instance, in his exposition of the revolutionary mystique.[1]
Encina may well have developed some of the themes of the
revolution in a tendentious and unacceptable way, and in support
of his generally anti-liberal viewpoint, yet one must also grant
that he was one of the first to detect the very existence of certain
themes.

'It is truly odd', wrote Sergio Villalobos R. in 1956, 'that,
confronted by the richness of the material accumulated...,
scholars have not felt themselves attracted to the theme of the
Independence of Chile, which demands to be taken up once
more.'[2] Since that date, there has in fact been something of a
revival of interest in the independence period. Sergio Villalobos R.
himself has provided us with a convincing reappraisal of the
origins of the revolution of 1810;[3] Hernán Ramírez Necochea
has re-examined the relatively little-known economic background;[4] and Néstor Meza Villalobos has reconsidered the period
between 1806 and 1810.[5] These are but three examples. Those
historians, however, who have dealt more specifically with the
question of political ideas have sometimes been less concerned with
the independence period itself than with previous or subsequent
historical developments leading into or out of the period. Thus
Jaime Eyzaguirre's *Ideario y ruta de la emancipación chilena* (1957),
which covers ideological history up to 1814, tries to connect the
1810 revolution with a broad Spanish tradition going back to St
Isidore. A second work which comes immediately to mind,
Ricardo Donoso's masterly *Las ideas políticas en Chile* (Mexico DF,
1946), starts with the end of the colonial era and proceeds to the
close of the nineteenth century, connecting the liberal struggles
of the independence period theme by theme with the anti-
aristocratic and secularist struggles of many years later. It can, I
think, be claimed that there has long been a need for an account
of the ideology of the independence period in Chile, and for a

[1] Encina, *Historia*, x, 51–77.
[2] *Indice a la Colección de Historiadores y de Documentos relativos a la independencia de Chile*
(1956), p. x.
[3] *Tradición y reforma en 1810* (1961), in my opinion the most distinguished work on the
background to the revolution of 1810 written by a Chilean this century.
[4] *Antecedentes económicos de la independencia de Chile* (1959).
[5] *La actividad política del Reino de Chile entre 1806 y 1810* (1958).

general re-examination of the interplay of ideas and politics which was a major characteristic of that time. There is one further point which I ought to make here. Two main interpretations of the independence period have been common amongst Chilean historians: the traditional nineteenth-century liberal view, which conceived the emancipation as a contest between light and darkness, and the conservative or Hispanist view, which has been concerned to devalue the liberalism that became orthodox after 1810 and to justify the conservative reaction of 1829 onwards.[1] It is perhaps useful that a foreigner should try to recross the battlefield and establish what may be regarded as a fresh view of the scene. I have therefore committed myself to no very definite verdict on the events of 1808–33. I present no general conclusions as to the worthiness or unworthiness of the various ideas which manifested themselves in Chile at that time. My only aim is to define and describe them more clearly.

It need hardly be added that in the course of this work I have noticed other themes which would be well worthy of sustained investigation. Of these, two seem to me to be of some importance for a better understanding of the course of Chilean history. The whole issue of political groupings, touched on so far in a rather cursory way by a few scholars,[2] still needs a thorough examination. There is also a striking need for an adequate description of the composition of the creole elite which carried through the revolution. The elite was aristocratic in nature; this is plain. But it would be interesting to learn the effect of regional and economic divisions within the aristocracy on the development of party politics in the 1820s and 1830s, and also the extent of foreign and non-aristocratic elements in the revolutionary leadership. These two matters are very much bound up with one another, and a detailed investigation of them would serve to illuminate many aspects of the revolutionary process and its outcome that still remain obscure or slightly puzzling.

While this book is primarily a humble contribution to the

---

[1] Broadly speaking, Amunátegui, Barros Arana and Vicuña Mackenna in the nineteenth century, and Donoso in the twentieth, can be classed as liberals. Edwards, Encina and Eyzaguirre may be regarded as conservatives.

[2] Edwards and Frei, pp. 16–32; Encina, *Historia*, x, 12–18.

historiography of the Chilean revolution, it also has a more general application. The study of the political ideas of independence in Latin America—indeed, of Latin American political ideas in general—has remained surprisingly backward, though there are indications that this state of affairs is gradually being remedied. Though the outstanding personalities of the period, such as Simón Bolívar, have understandably attracted a certain amount of attention, relatively little interest has been shown in the political ideas of individual countries, of lesser-known politicians, or indeed of political parties. This present description of ideas in Chile between 1808 and 1833 may therefore be regarded as something of a case-study. It is to be hoped that others will examine the experience of some of the other republics of Latin America. Only in this way can it be established whether or not there really was a common pattern of political ideas throughout the continent. It is widely assumed that a common pattern did prevail—and so far there seems no reason to reject this view—but documentary proof of the assertion is still needed, and, perhaps more important, some knowledge of local variations could be gained from further work.

The course of Chilean history itself has provided very convenient limits for my present study. The beginning of the *revolución de la independencia* is quite clearly marked by the Spanish imperial crisis of 1808. Its close is defined with similar clarity by the conservative rebellion of 1829, which brought to an abrupt end the period of political experiment and gave Chile a constitutional form which, however unsatisfactory, remained intact for over a generation. Can this twenty-five-year period be regarded as a legitimate unit of study? It could certainly be argued that many of the more important issues then in debate had been decided one way or another by 1823, the year when Bernando O'Higgins, having consolidated the independence of the republic, was forced into a premature retirement. Independence from the Empire, the liberal political philosophy, anti-colonialism—these were settled, as issues, by 1823. But in fact it took a further decade for certain other matters to be settled as firmly or as finally. The debates on federalism, on the right degree of executive authority, and on the organization of the Republic in general were all of them questions which remained undecided until after the *pro-nunciamiento* of 1829. All in all, it can hardly be contended that the Chilean revolution, considered as a domestic political process as well as a dispute with the transatlantic motherland, ended before Portales. Political ferment of a revolutionary sort continued un-abated up till then, after which it was rigidly suppressed and dis-couraged. I offer no apologies, therefore, for including the final phases of the independence period in this study, particularly since the interesting and important phase from 1823 to 1829 has long stood in need of reassessment.

Detailed narratives of the Chilean revolution are, naturally, available in Spanish,[1] and somewhat slenderer and less satisfactory versions in English as well.[2] For the convenience of the reader, however, I have incorporated a short narrative section into those chapters (2, 3, 6–9) which require this support. Without at least an outline of events—and this is all I pretend to supply here—the ideas discussed later on can become both vague and uninteresting. Only in Part II have I felt justified in abandoning a chronological scheme altogether, and for obvious reasons. It can hardly be denied that there was, during the revolutionary period, a basic stratum of political ideas together with a distinctive set of emo-tional attitudes, in short, a commonly accepted body of ideals. This body of doctrine, this ideology, can and should be treated analytically and separately, and this is what I have done in Part II. At the same time, there are many ideas and attitudes which cannot be considered except in relation to the events and moments which produced them. Thus the issue of independence, which to some

[1] Barros Arana, VIII–XVI, is the most detailed narrative of the period 1808–33. Encina, *Historia*, VI–X, provides an alternative. Domingo Amunátegui Solar, *Nacimiento de la República de Chile* (1930), is a useful one-volume summary. For a general reference book on specific events and characters, see Jordi Fuentes and Lía Cortés, *Diccionario histórico de Chile* (1965). The careers of individuals may be followed in Pedro Pablo Figueroa, *Diccionario biográfico general de Chile* (1st edn. 1887); 2nd edn. 1888; 3rd edn. 3 vols. 1897–1901); for foreigners, see the same author's *Diccionario biográfico de estranjeros en Chile* (1900); an alternative (in some respects less detailed) biographical dictionary is Virgilio Figueroa, *Diccionario histórico y biográfico de Chile* (4 vols. 1925–31).

[2] A. S. M. Chisholm, *The Independence of Chile* (London, 1912); Luis Galdames, *A History of Chile*, trans. I. J. Cox (Chapel Hill, N.C., 1941), pp. 141–243; Harry Bern-stein, *Modern and Contemporary Latin America* (Chicago, 1952), pp. 450–86; A. Curtis Wilgus, ed., *Argentina, Brazil and Chile since Independence* (Washington, D.C, 1935), p. 279–302.

extent dominated the '*Patria Vieja*', and the first years of the
O'Higgins regime, ceased to be a real talking-point after 1820
or so. The federalist movement, too, appeared and then disappeared within a circumscribed moment of time. To have forced
themes like these into a general analytical framework would, of
course, have been easy enough. But it would also have been
totally unacceptable to those who, like myself, see ideas as the
life-blood of political history and who believe that in nearly all
circumstances 'there is something in history to which justice can
be done only by the narrative method'.[1]

I was enabled to do the research on which my doctoral thesis
and this book are based thanks to the financial assistance of the
Department of Education and Science; Trinity Hall, Cambridge;
and the University of Chile. To these three bodies I express my
warmest thanks.

In the preparation of this book I have naturally incurred many
debts of a more personal nature, and it is proper and pleasant to
acknowledge these here. The chief of these debts, beyond all
question, is to Dr John Street, who supervised my postgraduate
work. To him I owe many hours of just criticism and balanced
advice, and it is true to say that without his constant and friendly
encouragement this book would not have been written in the first
place. His deep understanding of Latin American history and of its
distinctive problems has been invaluable throughout, though it is
only fair to add that he is in no way responsible for the mistakes
and errors of interpretation which may doubtless be found in
this study.

I must also most warmly thank Sr Sergio Villalobos R. for
the unfailing assistance he gave me during my stay in Chile in
1963, and similarly Professor Eugenio Pereira Salas, who did so
much to make that visit possible. I gratefully acknowledge the
help afforded me in Santiago de Chile by Don Guillermo Feliú
Cruz (Director), Sr Manuel Cifuentes, and Sr Ricardo Dartnell,
of the Biblioteca Nacional; and Don Juan Eyzaguirre (Director)
and Sra Nora Hansen of the Archivo Nacional. Many other kind

---

[1] Herbert Butterfield, *The Present State of Historical Scholarship: An Inaugural Lecture*
(Cambridge, 1965), p. 22.

Preface

Chilean friends, too numerous to mention individually, made my experience of their incomparable land a rich and varied one.

To those who helped to make my work in England a practical possibility, I owe an equal debt of gratitude: above all, Mr C. W. Crawley and Mr Graham Storey, of Trinity Hall. My colleagues Dr Gordon Brotherston and Mr Richard Ogle of the University of Essex have given freely of their advice on certain points of translation.

S.D.W.C.

The Old Rectory
Sutton, Bedfordshire
21 May 1966

ABBREVIATIONS

A.B.A.   Archivo de don Diego Barros Arana (Sala Medina, Biblioteca Nacional, Santiago).

A.M.I.   Archivo del Ministerio del Interior (Archivo Nacional, Santiago).

AR   L. Valencie Avaria, ed., *Anales de la República* (1951).

Arch.O'H.   *Archivo de don Bernardo O'Higgins.* In progress (1946–).

Arch.S.M.   *Documentos del Archivo de San Martín* (Buenos Aires, 1910–11).

AUC   *Anales de la Universidad de Chile.*

A.V.M.   Archivo de don Benjamín Vicuña Mackenna (Archivo Nacional, Santiago).

BACH   *Boletín de la Academia Chilena de Historia.*

CAPC   *Colección de antiguos periódicos chilenos.* In progress (1951–).

C.C.M.M.   Colección de copias de manuscritos de don José Toribio Medina (Sala Medina, Biblioteca Nacional).

CHDI   E. Matta Vial and G. Feliú Cruz, ed., *Colección de historiadores y de documentos relativos a la independencia de Chile* (1900–54).

F.O.   Foreign Office Papers (Public Record Office, London).

F.V.   Fondo Varios (Archivo Nacional).

HAHR   *Hispanic American Historical Review.*

RCHG   *Revista Chilena de Historia y Geografía.*

SCL   V. Letelier, ed., *Sesiones de los Cuerpos Lejislativos de la República de Chile, 1811–1845* (1887–1908).

NOTE

Books and articles cited in the footnotes are referred to by their author's name and, where necessary, by an abbreviated form of the title. The titles of a few newspapers are similarly abbreviated. Full details of all works so cited may be found in Sources B and C.

Books and articles of limited relevance to the subject of this study are cited in full in the footnotes. Unless otherwise stated, all works so cited were published in Santiago de Chile.

The author is responsible for all translations from Spanish sources, unless otherwise indicated.

S. D. W. C.

PART I
THE GROWTH OF THE REVOLUTION

I

BACKGROUND TO REVOLUTION

LATE-COLONIAL CHILE

Before considering the Chilean revolution itself, I must briefly set the scene.[1] At the end of the colonial period, the Captaincy-General, more formally known as the Kingdom, of Chile could still be regarded as one of the most distant outposts of European civilization. British colonization in the Antipodes had scarcely begun, while Chile was still the remotest of the dominions of the Spanish Crown in America. Nature had conferred on its territory a remarkable degree of isolation. To the North, the Captaincy-General was bordered by the Atacama Desert, whose immense riches were still largely unexploited. More permanent barriers— the Cordillera of the Andes and the Pacific Ocean—indicated the Eastern and Western boundaries of the province. Only to the South was there an element of doubt. Here the edge of Spanish settlement was roughly marked by the line of the River Bío-Bío, curving inland from Concepción. Beyond this line the Araucanian Indians preserved the separate way of life they had successfully defended against the Spanish Empire for two and a half centuries. The general situation along this Southern 'Frontier' was, by the eighteenth century, little more than a 'stalemate broken by brief flurries of warfare',[2] without the dramatic fluctuations in military fortunes that had characterized—and to some extent conditioned —Chilean history in the sixteenth and seventeenth centuries. Even so, the Indians were not to be underrated as a potential menace. As a member of the La Pérouse expedition observed, while on a visit to the South in 1786, one of the easiest ways for a foreign power to overcome Spanish Chile would be for it to conclude an

---

[1] For a full account of Chilean society at the end of the colonial period, see Barros Arana, VI, 311–576, and Encina, *Historia*, V, 107–680. The first section of this chapter is no more than a very short summary from these and other authorities.

[2] Louis de Armond, 'Frontier Warfare in Colonial Chile', *Pacific Historical Review*, XXIII (Berkeley, Calif., 1954), 132.

1-2

offensive alliance with the Araucanians. Such an alliance might well prove to be invincible.[1]

The total population of Chile at this period is difficult to estimate. The surveys undertaken in 1778 by Governor Jáuregui and in 1812 by the national Junta can hardly be regarded as comprehensive or particularly accurate even for the areas they affected to cover. It seems safest to say that the population around 1800 was well over half a million. If the Araucanians to the South of the Bío-Bío are taken into account, then it is entirely possible that there were roughly a million Chileans, of all varieties, at the time the revolution began.[2] Then, as now, the great majority lived in the rich and fertile Central Valley between Santiago and Concepción, though what is today referred to as the Norte Chico was also reasonably populated. It is worth remarking here that although Chile was long and narrow on the maps even in colonial times, its unusual degree of longitudinal extensiveness was not acquired until after independence, with the conquest of the Far North and the opening up of the Far South. In 1800, in fact, Chile was effectively no more than seven hundred miles long, less than a third of its present length.

Few Indians had survived North of the Bío-Bío. They had been assimilated by marriage, and an enormous class of *mestizos* had come into existence. *Mestizos* went to form well over half the total population of Chile in 1800. From their ranks were drawn the rural labourers, the itinerant workers on the land and in the mines, the peasant proprietors, the tenants of the big *haciendas*, and, not least, the sizable gangs of bandits, highwaymen and thieves. Most *mestizos* lived lives bounded by poverty and ignorance, though there was, perhaps, relatively little serious malnutrition in late-colonial Chile. Illiteracy, vagabondage, crime and drunkenness were widespread, and social evils such as these were

[1] Milet-Mureau, IV, 100–1.
[2] Barros Arana (VII, 315) claimed that the population in 1808 was 500,000. The leading Chileans of the time, except for Salas, general y used the round number of 1,000,000. Governor Jáuregui's survey only took in the Diocese of Santiago, and produced a total of 203,732. A very fragmentary survey of the Diocese of Concepción in 1791 resulted in a total of 105,114, certainly a gross underestimate. The patriot census of 1812, though defective, was more accurate. Its final total of just over 900,000 seems realistic. See Encina, *Historia*, v, 159–69, and x, 79–80.

denounced in vivid detail by the more enlightened Chilean thinkers of the time, notably Manuel de Salas.[1] In contrast to some of the other provinces of the Spanish American Empire, Chile had very few negro slaves Pure negroes were rare, and the total number of slaves at the start of the revolution did not exceed five thousand.[2] Nearly all of them werein domestic service, and the practice of manumission was fairly common. As for the Araucanian Indians South of the Frontier, they were to all intents and purposes a separate community. The missionary policy pursued by various religious Orders had been a conspicuous failure, and it was left to the Chileans of the second half of the nineteenth century to dispose of the 'Indian problem'.

The great mass of the population was dominated by a small oligarchy of creoles (and European Spaniards) consisting of upwards of two hundred families who regarded themselves (and were regarded) as noble. Many Chilean creoles had ancestries which contained more than one infusion of Indian blood, but not in sufficient quantities to render them *mestizos*. Originally, the aristocracy had been composed of the descendants of early settlers, but from the end of the seventeenth century onwards a substantial Basque element incorporated itself. Some of these newer members of the creole oligarchy had made their money in trade, but used it to acquire estates, land being the basis of all wealth in the colony. By and large, they were, to use Alberto Edwards' description, 'sensible, parsimonious, with regular and orderly habits'.[3] To the Basque-Castilian aristocracy there had also been added, in the early part of the eighteenth century, a barely noticeable but nonetheless important element of foreign blood, mainly French.[4] The family spirit of this Chilean oligarchy was particularly notable, and it would scarcely be an exaggeration to say that the country was dominated by a network of great

---

[1] Villalobos R., 'El bajo pueblo', p. 38. Manuel de Salas Corvalán (1754–1841). One of the outstanding figures of the period; syndic of the Consulado from its foundation; founder of the Academia de San Luis; member of the 1811 and 1823 Congresses; exiled to Juan Fernández, 1814–17.

[2] Feliú Cruz, *Abolición*, pp. 39–40; Encina, *Historia*, v, 162.

[3] *La fronda aristocrática*, p. 9. The Chilean aristocracy was less well off than its counterparts in Peru or Mexico: see Gómez de Vidaurre, II, 287.

[4] Fuenzalida Grandón, *Evolución social*, chs. 7–8.

families, the most widespread and powerful of which, the enormous Larraín clan, was to play a prominent part in the early development of the revolution.[1] The aim of the aristocracy was to ensure the permanence of its superior position in society by retaining control of its *haciendas* and by emphasizing its social leadership. This it did in two ways: by instituting *mayorazgos* (strict entails) and, where possible, by purchasing or otherwise acquiring Castilian titles. There were some fourteen *mayorazgos* at the end of the colonial period, seven of which had been created during the eighteenth century. There were some twelve Castilian titles in existence as well.[2] The *mayorazgo* and the title of nobility represented ideals of considerable importance to the Chilean aristocracy. Those who failed to secure either (and they were, of course, the majority), had to content themselves with becoming members of Orders of Chivalry or with making full use of any military rank they gained as a result of service in the local militias.[3]

The social structure of late-colonial Chile, then, was fairly simple. The creole aristocracy, with a small Peninsular Spanish element attached (there is no reason to differentiate between the two racial groups at this stage), was invested with social prestige and economic power. The creoles, it is true, lacked the additional advantage of possessing political control, and this, as will be seen, was one of their major grievances. Below the aristocracy in the social hierarchy was the vast lower class, either directly dependent on the aristocracy for its existence or eking out a precarious livelihood on its own abject *minifundia*. This basic division of Chilean society into two classes—leaving aside the Araucanians—was not complicated more than fractionally by the existence of a small creole and Peninsular Spanish 'middle class' of soldiers, lawyers, minor bureaucrats, small traders, and owners of such medium-sized rural properties as there were. The 'middle class' seems to have had largely aristocratic aspirations, and cannot be considered a potential third force.

With certain exceptions it was from the ranks of the creole

[1] See Amunátegui Solar, *Teatro político*, chs. 3–4.
[2] Amunátegui Solar, *La sociedad chilena*, contains detailed accounts of all the families which had *mayorazgos* and titles of nobility.
[3] Encina, *Historia*, v, 239–40 and 533–55.

aristocracy that the leadership of the Chilean revolution was later to be drawn. No picture of the revolution which ignores this basic fact can be said to be accurate. The creole leaders were to speak the language of the rights of man, of representative government, of popular sovereignty; and they meant what they said. But at the same time they did not—and could not—cease to be what they had been in the colonial period: aristocrats, landowners, the leaders of society. The effect of this on their political theory, and above all on the application of their political theory, was bound to be considerable. This is perhaps the place to observe that the great creole families who came to dominate the revolutionary process directly or indirectly, were a relatively close-knit and homogeneous group. Their economic interests were substantially similar. The geographical area they covered was by no means unmanageable. Chile never saw the dangerous racial rivalries or regional tensions that affected the post-revolutionary performances of some of the other American provinces. Chile in 1810 was socially and geographically compact, and this must help to account for the brevity of political disorder and the speedy transition to orderly government. It might almost be said that no other Latin American country possessed the advantages of geographical compactness and social homogeneity in the same measure as Chile. Chile was extremely well placed to achieve the stability and progress that *was* achieved after 1830.

The vast majority of Chileans, of whatever social class, lived in the countryside. The only city worthy of the name was Santiago, with a total population of rather more than thirty thousand in 1810. Architecturally, Santiago was recovering from the disastrous earthquake of 1730, and public works were carried out on a reasonable scale throughout the latter part of the eighteenth century, inspired or at least encouraged by such zealous Governors as Ambrosio O'Higgins. To some extent the Southern city of Concepción formed an alternative centre of power and influence in the Captaincy-General, but its population was little more than six thousand, much the same as that of La Serena, shortly to become the capital of the new Province of Coquimbo.[1]

[1] Created by the first national Congress on 23 September 1811.

7

Valparaíso, a fortress as well as a port, was still far from impressive as a town, though it was to expand dramatically during the revolution as a result of foreign trade. One other town may be briefly referred to here. Talca, with perhaps as many as six thousand inhabitants in 1810, was already showing signs of that civic spirit for which it has rightly become famous in Chile. In the last years of the colonial period, a group of cultivated creoles and foreigners was giving a notable stimulus to primary education there.[1] Urban life was characterized in general, Luis Galdames has written, by its 'rigidity and passiveness. An unalterable rhythm carried men and women day by day to their work or to their religious devotions.'[2] Public diversions of an elevating kind were virtually unknown, despite a few attempts to stage dramatic performances, though private celebrations were, if travellers' tales are to be believed, as gay as the naturally boisterous Chilean temperament permitted. Captain George Vancouver noted in Santiago: that 'Such a degree of levity is observable in the conduct of the *ladies*...as to give a stranger, and particularly an Englishman, no reason to entertain a very exalted opinion of their virtue, but rather to impress him with notions prejudicial to the female character.'[3] The sailors of the La Pérouse expedition found much the same thing to be true on a different social level in Concepción: 'Wine is very common in Chile; and...the women of the people are as complaisant there as they are in Tahiti.'[4]

The Catholic Church naturally wielded an enormous influence in the colony. Its established position reinforced the civil government, and it administered its own justice without interference from the secular courts or the Audiencia. By issuing *bandos* concerned with public morality, and complex regulations affecting saints' days and other festivals, the Church exercised a powerful control over much of the ceremonial of the time. Disputes between Bishop and Governor were as much a part of Chilean history as they were in other provinces of the Empire,[5] but in general these were on the wane in the eighteenth century.

[1] Encina, *Historia*, v, 214–17.   [2] Galdames, *Evolución constitucional*, p. 10.
[3] Vancouver, iii, 434–5.   [4] Milet-Mureau, ii, 70.
[5] See Amunátegui, *Precursores*, i, 159–225.

Though a majority of the Bishops of Santiago and Concepción in the final century of colonial rule were Spaniards or Peruvians, some, including the most illustrious (Manuel Alday of Santiago), were Chileans. The authority of the Inquisition, represented in Chile by a special commissioner, was still powerful, but less pervasive than in former times. While it continued to fulfil its major tasks—the eradication of superstition on the one hand, and the suppression of irreligious and subversive thought on the other —its position at the end of the eighteenth century was weakening considerably.

The role of the Church in such education as there was in Chile was especially notable. The majority of primary schools were run by the parishes, though a number of lay primary schools were set up in the eighteenth century. In 1803 there were some nine lay schools in Santiago alone, attended by nearly four hundred children,[1] not to mention the various church schools. Primary education was by no means non-existent but probably made little impression on the overwhelming mass of the population. The better creole families, of course, employed private tutors. Secondary and higher education was in a still more precarious state. There were only three establishments purveying secondary or higher learning: the Royal University of San Felipe, which had opened its doors in 1758; the Convictorio Carolino, established in 1778 as a replacement for the main Jesuit college in Chile; and finally the Academia de San Luis, founded in 1797. The University provided what Encina has described as 'a mediocre professional training enveloped in a semi-scholastic culture which was backward even in relation to its own time'.[2] The study of law and theology predominated. Of the 299 doctorates produced by the University up till 1810, the overwhelming majority were in these two subjects. It was Manuel de Salas who best appreciated the need for a new and more technical education in the Captaincy-General. He attempted to realize his vision in the Academia de San Luis, which was very largely his inspiration and which he helped

---

[1] Encina, *Historia*, v, 553.
[2] *Ibid.* 592–3. For the three institutions of higher education in general, see Barros Arana, VII, 494–502; Fuenzalida Grandón, *Desarrollo intelectual*, chs. 1–3; and Medina, *Historia de la Universidad*.

9

to sustain with his own funds.[1] Though the Academia was a failure, Salas did not abandon his educational idealism, and was given further opportunities to put it into operation during the revolution.

Chile was, for reasons of policy as well as of geography, essentially a 'closed' country, no more so in theory than the other American provinces, but perhaps slightly more so in practice. Foreigners were excluded, at any rate on paper. The strict regulations on this subject were, however, only fully enforced in time of war. At all other times foreigners (if they were lucky) could enter Chile, settle, marry Chilean girls, and win the approval of the local creole aristocracy. The well-known example of George Edwards, an English doctor who settled in La Serena just before the revolution, and who founded the distinguished Edwards family, amply illustrates this fact. Nevertheless, the total number of foreigners living in Chile at the start of the revolution was fairly small. When in 1809 Governor García Carrasco tried to round up all non-naturalized foreigners, he was only able to find some seventy-nine,[2] and while there were doubtless many more than this, his result is a fair indication of the real numbers involved.

Similar considerations applied to the Chilean economy. Agriculture and stock-raising were the dominant preoccupations of the creole oligarchy, together with a certain amount of mining in the North of the country, but such external trade as there was existed within an imperial framework. Chile traded either with the Spanish motherland or with the neighbouring provinces of the Empire. There were substantial commercial links with the River Plate, as well as the more voluminous and traditional commerce between Chile and the Viceroyalty of Peru to the North. The relaxation of trade restrictions inside the Spanish Empire which occurred under Charles III had a delayed effect in Chile, as a result of the War of American Independence. Eventually, however, there was a heavy importation of expensive consumer goods for which, in the last resort, Chile could not pay.

---

[1] Amunátegui, *Manuel de Salas*, I, 79-113.

[2] 21 Portuguese, 18 Italians, 10 North Americans, 9 French, 6 English, 4 Irish, 2 Swedish, 1 Russian, 1 German, 1 Maltese, 1 Austrian, 1 Dane, 1 Hungarian, 1 Scotsman, and 1 Netherlander (Amunátegui, *Crónica*, II, 333).

But, although the creoles were denied the right (except under special circumstances) of trading outside the Empire, they were able to indulge in contraband. Since smugglers do not normally publish statistics, it is impossible to say with any certainty what percentage of Chilean imports arrived illegally in this way. Contraband may have accounted for as much as twenty or even thirty per cent of all Chilean imports in a 'good' year—a year, that is, when fewer cargoes from Spain arrived than was usual—but, in reality, historians can do little more than speculate about the precise quantity. Contraband, however, was certainly a deeply rooted habit by the end of the colonial period. It involved many of the most respectable creoles from time to time, and it was organized on a highly businesslike basis.[1] Smuggling was a significant breach in the wall of Spanish exclusivism.

From the creole viewpoint Spanish exclusivism operated most forcibly in the domain of government and politics. By and large, Chile was very well governed at the end of the colonial era. It enjoyed the status of a Captaincy-General, administratively independent of Peru after 1798,[2] and subject to the immediate authority of a Governor and a Royal Audiencia. Under the reforms of Charles III, Chile was now divided into two Intendancies (Santiago and Concepción) as well as into twenty-two districts (*partidos*) presided over by a *subdelegado* or district governor. Though the machinery of colonial government worked with reasonable efficiency in the Chilean case, the most important political and administrative posts were still in the hands of Peninsular Spaniards. The creole aristocracy, possessing as it did a full measure of social and economic power, found it peculiarly galling to be excluded in this way from the higher levels of the government machine. Chile was, however, extremely fortunate in the quality of its late-colonial Governors. Agustín de Jáuregui (1773–80), Ambrosio de Benavides (1780–7), Ambrosio O'Higgins (1788–96), Gabriel Avilés (1796–9), and Luis Muñoz de Guzmán (1802–08) were all capable and intelligent administrators, well

[1] See pp. 36-F
[2] Peru had previously exercised certain limited powers of supervision. The administrative separation of 1798 was largely due to the economic conflict between the two provinces.

liked by the creole aristocracy, and eager to stimulate local progress in accordance with the latest enlightened ideas. The policies pursued by these zealous colonial functionaries seem to have ensured a high degree of harmony between creole aspirations and the smooth running of the government. The only institution through which the creole aristocracy *could* express its distinctive ambitions, the Cabildo or municipal council, was tactfully and cleverly enlisted on the Governor's side throughout. It is against this background that the furious creole reaction to the mishandled governorship of García Carrasco (1808–10) should be set.

If there is one purely political aspect of late-colonial life which must be singled out for special attention here, it is the fervent loyalism of Chilean creoles, and the affection in which they held the Spanish crown. It may well be the case, as Alberto Edwards suggested, that the majority of Spanish Americans obeyed their King without being aware of the fact that they were doing so—'some by habit, others by conviction, but most by the simple law of inertia'.[1] The fact remains that the members of the creole aristocracy who were capable of expressing an interest in politics at all were overwhelmingly and conscientiously loyal to the monarchy. A Chilean who was at Court in 1776 told the King that the creoles were 'more than your most faithful vassals; [we are] through a living love your willing slaves'.[2] And this loyalty, shared by creoles and Peninsular Spaniards alike, should always be borne in mind when the opening phases of the revolution are discussed. When, in 1808, Ignacio Torres emphasized to Napoleon that 'these Americas, which you wanted to seduce by treachery, are the patrimony of Ferdinand VII',[3] his sincerity was patent and absolute. Perhaps the most striking example of the depth of loyal feelings may be seen in the behaviour of the people of La Serena in 1809, when the municipality took possession of a portrait of Ferdinand VII. The district governor of Coquimbo

---

[1] *Organización política*, p. 23.
[2] 'Carta que un Chileno escribió...', p. 221. Sergio Villalobos R. convincingly ascribes this document to José Antonio de Rojas: 'José Antonio de Rojas, autor de una representación de los Españoles-Americanos', *RCHG*, no. 125 (1957), p. 152.
[3] *Proclama*, 19 October 1808, *CHDI*, VIII, 64.

ordered the people to celebrate as if the King himself, and not merely a pictorial representation of him, were arriving in the town: 'Noble and loyal Coquimbans!...Cover your walls with tapestries and the ground with flowers, so that this august person, the idol of our hearts, may pass by; and implore the God of Hosts to restore him as soon as possible to his royal throne.'[1] In fact, the portrait's triumphal entry into La Serena was even more splendid than the district governor could have expected. Cannons were sounded, triumphal arches were erected, processions and services were arranged, and the Cabildo turned out in force. The people, an eyewitness reported, were 'enthused and inflamed with the love by which they have wished and wish to mark themselvesout as the most faithful and most loyal vassals of the best and most benign of all the monarchs on earth'.[2]

There seems little doubt, therefore, that Manuel de Salas was right when he wrote, later on, that before 1810 the Chileans had wished only to be good Catholics and good Spaniards, 'qualities which they regarded as inseparable and as the two poles of their happiness'.[3] Governor García Carrasco, who was sometimes in-clined to take a sceptical view of the inhabitants of the Captaincy-General he governed so badly, could nevertheless write that he was fully 'persuaded of the honour and fidelity of the nobility and of the other classes in general'.[4] A distinguished foreigner who visited Concepción during the Spanish reconquest of Chile in 1816 recalled that he saw an old officer prostrate himself before a picture of the King and, with tears in his eyes, kiss its base.[5] Royalism, in creole and Peninsular Spaniard alike, was profound and sometimes fanatical. The plain fact is that during colonial times there existed, in Amunátegui's well-known phrase, a 'cult of the royal majesty', and that this was the most powerful of all political sentiments.[6]

Much of this feeling undoubtedly sprang from the ceremonial

[1] Joaquín Pérez de Uriondo, *Proclama*, 11 July 1809, Amunátegui, *Precursores*, I, 123.
[2] Ignacio Silva Borqués and Pedro Nolasco de las Peñas, *Testimonio*, 22 July 1809, *ibid.* I, 129.
[3] Letter of 28 August 1815 circulated secretly in Santiago (Salas, *Escritos*, II, 191).
[4] To Abascal, May 1810, *CHDI*, VIII, 265.
[5] Chamisso, p. 245. [6] Amunátegui, *Precursores*, I, 91–129.

importance of events in the life of the royal family, and, perhaps more significantly, from the maxims taught by Church and State alike. Francisco Antonio Pinto later recalled that, during his time as a student in the years before the revolution, it was clearly insisted that 'the authority of kings emanated from Heaven; and to resist it was to rebel against God'.[1] Even an enlightened thinker such as Manuel de Salas did not seriously question the fundamentals of divine right, not at any rate in public, though it is interesting to observe certain possible amendments to it which are implicit in his writings. Salas, it should be remembered, was the most enlightened and public-spirited Chilean of the time, the outstanding intellectual of the late-colonial period, and his political views are obviously of more than passing interest. 'Our august kings,' he wrote in 1801, 'knowing well that they are never such perfect images of Divinity as when they are doing good to men, base their greatness on public welfare.'[2] In other words, it could be argued, a king's divine right to govern depended to some extent at least on his willingness to do good. For Salas there was little doubt about this. Kings, he believed—and this he believed in public—should be like 'majestic rivers' pouring forth an endless stream of enlightenment and public works.[3] In a speech written for recital by one of his students at the Academia de San Luis, Salas expanded this view of monarchy. The King, he wrote, should undoubtedly wish to 'assure his own happiness through the happiness of the public'. He should therefore regard himself 'as a father rather than as the overlord' of his subjects. Above all, a king should appreciate that 'the great art of government, without which the great virtues of the heroes are as naught, consists in loving his subjects and in making himself loved by them'. Since Salas was, at the time, trying to drive home a specifically educational moral, he naturally linked the 'great art of government' to the need to improve public welfare, and linked public welfare to a reformed educational system.[4] Did this view imply some kind of limitation on royal power, perhaps even

---

[1] 'Apuntes autobiográficos', p. 70.   [2] Salas, *Escritos*, I, 625.
[3] *Ibid.*
[4] 'Discurso...por el alumno don Joaquín Campino', 29 April 1801 (Salas, *Escritos*, I, 602).

some element of contract? Elsewhere Salas spoke of Philip V as having been raised to the throne 'by Providence, his rights, and his virtues',[1] and it could be argued that this signified that virtue was an indispensable qualification for kingship. There was nothing new, of course, in this kind of theory of kingship, yet it was plainly different from the out-and-out regalism of many eighteenth-century Spanish thinkers. Whatever the nature of Salas' theoretical ideas about monarchy in general—and there are hardly enough of them to constitute a full-blown theory—one thing is clear: he saw the monarchy as the chief instrument of progress. A practical man as well as an idealist, Salas was concerned to work with and through the only instrument he and his contemporaries knew. In this, he was close to the great enlightened figures of eighteenth-century Spain. But if times changed, as they were indeed to change shortly afterwards, then enlightened reformers such as Salas would be inclined to back the new order that emerged in the hope that it might supply the much needed political dynamic for the execution of progressive schemes. These later developments were probably not foreseen, or even regarded as practical possibilities, by Salas and his contemporaries. Up to the time of the revolution, the creole reformers, whatever their innermost dreams, were not only prepared to work with the monarchy in stimulating the progress they all desired; they were enthusiastic to do so.

CREOLE GRIEVANCES

Many are the causes which have been assigned to explain the sudden independence of the Republics of Spanish America.[2] Doubtless it must be true that Napoleon's invasion of Spain in 1808 was the supreme and immediate cause. It certainly supplies the obvious reason for the striking parallelism in the course of events in the diverse American provinces after 1808, a parallelism it is hard to explain in terms of conspiracy. Yet 'colonies are like fruit; they fall when they are ripe'. So ran Turgot's famous dictum. Napoleon's invasion of Spain provided the occasion for

[1] *Memoria*, 12 January 1801, *Escritos*, I, 213.
[2] For a summary of these, see Humphreys and Lynch, pp. 3–27.

15

the revolution. It dictated the timing. But it did not, in the last analysis, cause the revolution. What factors, then, existed that were likely to transform a promising revolutionary situation—which Napoleon gratuitously handed the creoles in 1808—into a full-scale revolution for freedom? For it is clear that this is what happened in the Captaincy-General of Chile in the six years that followed Ferdinand VII's departure for Valençay. The 'Patria Vieja' (1810-14) in particular witnessed the transformation of the loyalist but ambiguous postures of 1810 into a real bid for national independence. While it is certain that some of the influences which forced this transformation sprang from immediate circumstances—the war of 1813-14 for instance—others had been latent previously. Chile was ripe for revolution, or at any rate ripening. What were the forces which ripened the fruit? In the remaining sections of the present chapter, I must briefly examine a series of factors which may form part of the answer. In the first place, a number of definite grievances and complaints on the part of the creoles should be mentioned. These alone would probably not have led to revolution, and certainly not in 1810. But, added to the powerful political momentum created by Napoleon, they played an important part in carrying the revolution beyond its original aims.

Chilean backwardness in certain matters was a grievance well to the fore in the minds of some of the men who have been called 'precursors' of the revolution. Chile was an underdeveloped colony, very much the poor relation of the Viceroyalty of Peru. The creoles, animated (as we shall see) by a sanguine view of Chilean potential, resented the fact that, for instance, the educational facilities of the Captaincy-General were so limited and so backward. José Antonio de Rojas[1] was considerably influenced in this respect by the example of Spain, which he visited in the 1770s. In Spain, Rojas saw a profusion of schools and academies, as well as the more traditional 'sights' of the Peninsula. Writing to a friend, he commented that if he had to choose between

[1] José Antonio de Rojas Urtuguren (1732-1817). One of the traditional 'precursors' of 1810; arrested, with Ovalle and Vera, on charges of subversion, May 1810; exiled to Juan Fernández, 1814.

carrying away one of the glories of the motherland and taking just one of the colleges back to Chile, he would choose the latter course without hesitation. 'But this is to daydream,' he added, not without a touch of sarcastic bitterness. 'The dawn of rationality has still to reach America.'[1] Rojas was impressed by educational advances in Spain, but not uncritically. He condemned the various impediments to free learning he found there, concluding that in Spain it was 'a crime to try to acquire knowledge'.[2] Rojas, it seems probable, was the author of a highly interesting list of complaints forwarded to José de Gálvez in February 1776. The fifth complaint of his list was a general statement of American educational grievances.

In many areas, and even in capital cities of America, education, universities and colleges are in a lamentable state of decay. Either through lack of application, or in order to save money, the measures which your Majesty disposed have not been taken... [There have only been] half-hearted measures which are insufficient to re-establish education following the expulsion of the Jesuits. This point is so important that, if Your Majesty does not remedy it, the youth of America will become completely ignorant, and education will disappear in those countries.[3]

An implied criticism of existing educational policy must also be seen in the numerous demands for improvement which Manuel de Salas and his colleagues made towards the end of the colonial period. It should also be remembered that Chile was without a proper printing press until 1811, though a small machine for turning out handbills and rough pamphlets had been introduced by the Bavarian Jesuit Haimhausen.[4] The Cabildo of Santiago made an effort to gain royal permission to install a press, but the petition drawn up for this purpose in 1789 was referred back to the Audiencia by the Crown, and the project seems to have been

[1] To Herrera, 7 June 1775, Amunátegui, *Crónica*, I, 40–1.
[2] To Monneron, 23 February 1775, *ibid.* II, 44.
[3] 'Carta que un Chileno escribió...', p. 221.
[4] Amunátegui Solar, *Jesuitas*, pp. 35–8; Medina, *Bibliografía*, pp. 3–18; Lawrence S. Thompson, *Printing in Colonial Hispanic America* (Hamden, Conn., 1962), pp. 87–93.

quietly forgotten,[1] an incident recalled in later years by at least one creole leader, Juan Egaña.[2]

Complaints of Chilean backwardness in the economic sphere, equally strong, will be considered presently in another context, but a grievance which was probably of even greater importance was the creole suspicion that equal rights were not being accorded to American Spaniards. This was another item in the list of complaints probably prepared by José Antonio de Rojas in 1776. In the matter of honours, Rojas claimed, a creole had to prove his ancestry back through eight generations—'in this', he asked, 'we beg to be put on the same footing as other Spaniards, whether from the Peninsula or the Canary Islands'.[3] Rojas also affirmed that creoles had to pay double for services rendered in connection with the acquisition of honours, and he urged that honours in general should be distributed far more evenly across the whole Empire.[4] This complaint can hardly be regarded as trifling. Honorary distinctions, as I have tried to make clear, played an important part in the life of the colony and ranked high in the scale of creole desiderata.

A more flagrant and serious example of pro-Peninsular and anti-creole discrimination was to be found in the system of appointments to high public office. This was later regarded by the creoles as a major cause of the revolution. A Chilean newspaper of the 1820s, in fact, blamed the independence movement on 'the brutal treatment which Spaniards accorded Americans, and the preference of the [Spanish] government for natives of its own territory to fill public positions in America'.[5] There were few evidences of 'brutal treatment' of creoles before the revolution in Chile, but the Spanish government's predilection for Spaniards in making high public appointments was clear and obvious enough to any creole with political or public ambitions. Striking evidence of the creole appreciation of this point was provided in a

---

[1] Amunátegui, *Precursores*, I, 244–5.
[2] Juan Egaña, *El chileno consolado*, II, 17. Juan Egaña y Risco (1768–1836). Born in Lima; member of the 1811 and 1823 Congresses; Senator, 1812 and 1824; exiled to Juan Fernández, 1814–17; a prolific writer. See chapter 7.
[3] 'Carta que un Chileno escribió...', p. 219.
[4] *Ibid.* p. 220.   [5] *Monitor Imparcial*, no. 28, 14 March 1828.

representation to the Crown drafted by a distinguished Chilean lawyer, Alonso de Guzmán.

> In the vast lands of the Indies [he wrote] Your Majesty owns the allegiance of innumerable young men of great loyalty and talent but stifled in their own country for lack of prospects; the dreary idleness to which they are condemned deprives them even of the consolation of travel, and their minds are empty of useful ideas. The status of the Creoles has thus become an enigma: they are neither foreigners nor nationals...and are honourable but hopeless, loyal but disinherited.[1]

The exclusion of creoles must, I believe, be accounted one of the primary causes of the revolution. As Richard Konetzke has shown, deliberate exclusion of creoles was never a part of the *law* of the Empire; but, nevertheless, it had come to form part of the imperial government's policy.[2] That this was a shortsighted and mistaken policy was seen by several intelligent Spaniards during the time of Charles III, but the measures proposed to remedy this state of affairs were never far-reaching and did not meet the creoles' basic demand: admission to high office.

The extent of the exclusion of the creoles from public office was probably exaggerated by some of the nineteenth-century liberal historians in Chile. It can hardly be denied, for example, that a number of important posts in the colonial bureaucracy at the end of the colonial period were in the hands of Chileans— though to adduce the example of Governor Mateo de Toro Zambrano, Conde de la Conquista, as does Jaime Eyzaguirre,[3] is to overstate the case; the Conde de la Conquista was, after all, the product of very exceptional circumstances, and, moreover, was legally nothing more than an interim Governor. The fact remains that the highest political posts were the virtual monopoly of Peninsular Spaniards, who could not be expected to have the same zeal for improving local conditions as native Chileans. Creole dissatisfaction over this issue went back a long way,[4] and was plainly quite marked by the first years of the nineteenth

---

[1] Quoted in Villalobos R., *Tradición y reforma*, p. 102. Translation from Humphreys and Lynch, p. 253.
[2] Konetzke, pp. 33–44.   [3] *Ideario y ruta*, p. 57.
[4] See Villalobos R., *Tradición y reforma*, pp. 100–1.

century. When William Shaler and Richard Cleveland conversed with creole families in Valparaíso in 1802, they found that a number of Chileans 'seemed generally to be awakening to a sense of the abject state of vassalage in which they were held by their European masters; the posts of honour and profit being exclusively in possession of Europeans, to the great annoyance of the Creoles'.[1] Creoles aspired not merely to high office in the administration—they sometimes achieved this in any case—but to the *important* offices, the decision-making posts. This was the substance of their grievance.

The creoles' desire to increase the degree of their participation in the tasks of government was heightened by the occasionally arrogant and superior attitude of European Spaniards themselves. The North American sailor Captain Amasa Delano noticed, during a visit to Chile at the start of the nineteenth century, that the Peninsular Spaniards he met held 'themselves much higher in their own estimation than the Chilian born',[2] scarcely a posture that would excite much sympathy when the course of events gave the upper hand to the creoles. Although it certainly cannot be argued that relations between creoles and Europeans were, in general, anything but very harmonious in the years prior to 1810,[3] there are one or two indications that the creoles were eager to assert their rights. Within the religious Orders, the system of the *alternativa* (by which creoles and Peninsular Spaniards held office in rotation) had been officially introduced as early as 1622; yet it was not until the start of the 1790s, following a lengthy controversy, that the system was finally established inside the Dominican Order in Chile.[4] It seems, too, that the Franciscans experienced a definite Chilean attempt to dominate certain high positions in the Order in 1802 and 1803, an attempt which caused a good deal of somewhat less than charitable wrangling.[5] But more serious than these incidents, perhaps, is the evidence that rivalry between creoles and Peninsular Spaniards

[1] Cleveland, I, 183–4.
[2] Amasa Delano, *A Narrative of Voyages and Travels in the Northern and Southern Hemispheres* (Boston, Mass., 1817), p. 291.
[3] See chapter 2, pp. 61–2.   [4] Amunátegui, *Precursores*, III, 48–57.
[5] *Ibid.* 57–9.

sometimes marked the proceedings of the Cabildo of Santiago. In 1788 the interim Governor of Chile found it necessary to intimate his intention of stopping 'the old and seditious effort sustained by a number of councillors' to exclude from municipal office 'natives of Spain, even though many of them were of notable distinction and were settled in the city'.[1] Again, in 1803, the Cabildo of Santiago firmly resisted attempts by the Peninsular *asesor letrado*, Pedro Díaz de Valdés, to interfere in the internal deliberations of the body. Díaz de Valdés presently complained of the 'contempt and aversion which the said Cabildo professes towards him on account of the circumstance or fact that he is not a creole'. The aim of the Cabildo, he added, was to make sure that 'there was no European at all on the body'.[2] These antecedents, scattered but well known, clearly indicate that rivalry between American and European Spaniards was far from absent in colonial Chile, and, more significantly, that it was the province's chief Cabildo that was most acutely conscious of the injustice of the creole position. The extent of creole awareness of the problem can be exaggerated, but it is fruitless to deny that it existed.

CREOLE PATRIOTISM

The creole grievances I have mentioned so far were the ones most definitely connected with the subsequent developments brought about by the revolution. There were, naturally enough, other grievances as well, which might, however, be thought to belong more properly to the normal life of the colony and which seem to have less relevance as far as the pre-revolutionary background goes: the creoles' persistent opposition to certain fiscal expedients of the Crown, for instance.[3] But the complaints, and the implied desires, already mentioned seem to have been related fairly closely to what must be regarded as one of the most significant of all late-colonial themes: the slow but certain growth of a sentiment of Chilean patriotism. Among the many factors which led to the

[1] Tomás Alvarez de Acevedo to the King, 29 April 1788, *ibid.* 94–5.
[2] Silvestre Collar to the Audiencia of Chile, 5 June 1808, referring to a letter from Díaz de Valdés dated 12 December 1803, *ibid.* 101.
[3] See Villalobos R., *Tradición y reforma*, pp. 89–100.

independence of Latin America, the Spanish historian Rafael Altamira once wrote, 'the substantial influence, undoubtedly, was the formation within the bosom of colonial society of a consciousness of its national personality'.[1] The growth of national awareness can nearly everywhere be ascribed to the effect of time and geography. The earliest Spanish settlers in the New World were Spaniards first, and Americans second. But their descendants grew increasingly conscious of their American origins. In the course of time they became Americans first and Spaniards second, while never ceasing to lay stress on their Spanishness. By the end of the eighteenth century, this process had clearly gone some way, to the extent that regional considerations sometimes supplanted considerations of social status. The Jesuit historian Gómez de Vidaurre reproached the Chilean aristocracy with preferring to marry off its daughters to Chileans rather than Spaniards, even when the Spaniards were of higher rank than their Chilean rivals.[2] Creole patriotism, then, was expressing itself in a fairly concrete manner, but despite this it remains an exceedingly difficult tendency to document adequately. In some ways, metropolitan Spaniards realized the dangers of local 'national' feeling earlier than did the creoles themselves, and this may well have led to the late-Bourbon policy of trying to draw the diverse units of the Empire closer together. As Campomanes and Floridablanca had observed some time before, the 'spirit of independence and aristocracy' could not be eradicated simply by chastising those who professed it. What was needed was a deliberate series of measures to unify the whole Empire and to prevent the American dominions from moving away from the motherland: 'those Provinces would be regarded as an essential part of the Monarchy, an idea which is not as well rooted now [1768] as it ought to be'.[3] The culmination of this trend of thought came in the manifestoes and decrees of the Central Junta and the Council of Regency in 1809 and 1810. By then, it was too late.

---

[1] *Resumen histórico de la independencia de la América Española* (Buenos Aires, 1910), p. 18. On this subject generally, see Belaunde, pp. 11–15, 38–40, and Humphreys and Lynch, pp. 287–300.

[2] Gómez de Vidaurre, II, 285–6.

[3] 'Dictamen de Moniño y Campomanes', 5 March 1768, Konetzke, pp. 45–7.

Background to Revolution

The origins of a local and distinctively Chilean patriotism must doubtless be sought in a period relatively soon after the Conquest itself.[1] The love of the Chilean soil and its many beauties achieved its first clear expression in the *Histórica relación del Reyno de Chile* of Father Alonso de Ovalle, published in Rome in 1646. Ovalle's book was, to use the words of Jaime Eyzaguirre, 'not a scientific work of erudition, but the poetic alleviation of a soul impregnated with nostalgia'.[2] But, whatever prefigurations of this type may be found and analysed, it was in the second half of the eighteenth century that the sentiment of affectionate patriotism became a regular characteristic of Chilean writings. The way in which it was expressed may be briefly summarized. The creole was defended against European innuendoes. The physical terrain and the economic potential of Chile were exalted and displayed. The world of the Araucanian Indian was reassessed in a new and more favourable light.

Intellectual doubts had been cast on the quality and capacity of the natives of America by Jan Cornelius de Pauw and other European writers. In Europe, the appearance of De Pauw's work was followed by a lengthy and vigorous polemic. There was also a forceful American reaction, as was only to be expected.[3] What the Mexican Jesuit Clavigero did for the incipient nationalism of Mexico,[4] Juan Ignacio Molina[5] did for Chile. Molina did not spare De Pauw. He accused him of making tendentious use of travel books, notably those of Frézier and Ulloa. De Pauw's work, he went on, was more 'a romance than a philosophical disquisition'. De Pauw, the now wrathful Molina gibed further, had never been to America, and, in short, he 'has made use of as much freedom with regard to America as if he had been writing

[1] See Meza Villalobos, *Conciencia política*, ch. 6; Eyzaguirre, *Ideario y ruta*, pp. 37–43; Villalobos R., *Tradición y reforma*, p. 55.

[2] *Ideario y ruta*, p. 38.

[3] For the views of De Pauw's *Recherches Philosophiques sur les Américains* (Berlin, 1768), see Gerbi, pp. 59–89, and for the European and American polemic, *ibid*. pp. 91–254.

[4] Gerbi, pp. 215–34; Luis González y González, 'El optimismo nacionalista como factor de la independencia de México', in *Estudios de Historiografía Americana* (Mexico DF, 1948), p 171.

[5] Juan Ignacio Molina González (1740–1829). Jesuit; after the Expulsion he spent the rest of his life in Italy, mainly at Bologna and Imola; the author of the finest and most famous of the eighteenth-century accounts of Chile.

upon the moon and its inhabitants'.[1] The backwardness of the creoles, claimed Molina, was certainly not due to their inherent incapacity or inferiority. It was merely a matter of lack of opportunity and education. The creoles, he wrote,

are generally possessed of good talents, and succeed in any of the arts to which they apply themselves. They should make as great progress in the useful sciences as they have done in metaphysics, if they had the same motives to stimulate them as are found in Europe. They do not readily imbibe prejudices, and are not tenacious in retaining them. As scientific books and instruments, however, are very scarce, or sold at an exorbitant price, their talents are either never developed, or are wholly employed on trifles. The expenses of printing are also so great as to discourage literary exertion, so that few aspire to the reputation of authors.[2]

Molina's compatriot and contemporary, Gómez de Vidaurre,[3] produced a similar verdict. He praised the creole mentality. Chileans were, he wrote, 'affable, humane, friendly towards foreigners,...generous,...valiant'.[4] Despite crippling educational disadvantages, there were nevertheless Chileans who knew, understood, and criticized the Newtonian and Cartesian systems.[5] The reaction to De Pauw was not confined to the exiled Jesuits. Manuel de Salas, too, extending his encomiastic embrace to all the inhabitants of America, denounced De Pauw as utterly ignorant of reality, and brought forward the names of Franklin, Peralta and Molina in evidence, adding: 'Can we not imitate them, and show that the lack was of teaching, not of aptitude?'[6]

Far stronger than this vindication of the creole reputation was a distinct *motif* of praise for the physical attributes of the Chilean homeland. Thus Molina could write that

Chile is one of the best countries in America. The beauty of its sky, the constant mildness of its climate, and its abundant fertility, render it, as

---

[1] Molina, I, xv–xvii.
[2] *Ibid.* II, 318.
[3] Felipe Gómez de Vidaurre (1739–1818). After the Expulsion he spent a number of years in Italy, but returned to Chile, probably in 1800.
[4] Gómez de Vidaurre, II, 290.
[5] *Ibid.* 296.   [6] Salas, *Escritos*, I, 608.

a place of residence, extremely agreeable; and with respect to its natural productions, it may be said, without exaggeration, not to be inferior to any portion of the globe.[1]

Juts as Italy was said to be the 'garden of Europe', so Chile was 'the garden of South America'.[2] Others, too, shared this genuine delight and lyrical admiration. Miguel de Lastarria[3] gloated over the fecundity of the Chilean soil: 'What stupendous fertility!... Here God chastises with abundance.'[4] Gómez de Vidaurre described his homeland as 'one of the most privileged countries',[5] and praised 'those delightful landscapes with their constant and perpetual greenness'.[6] Exile, perhaps inevitably, sharpened the appetite for Chile. On his death bed, in a delirious condition, Molina is said to have repeatedly clamoured for some fresh water from the Chilean Cordillera.[7] Another exiled Jesuit more famous for his religious millenarianism, Father Manuel Lacunza, wrote sadly in 1794 that 'only those who have lost Chile know what Chile is'.[8] José Antonio de Rojas, writing to his friend Manuel de Salas from Spain and telling him of his huge desire to return home, rotundly affirmed:

Friend, that is *the* country. I have always had this idea, and every day what little I see here confirms it. As you yourself say, Chileans do not need to do more than *want* to be happy for them effectively to be so. They have nothing to desire—Nature lavishes everything with open arms in that most beautiful of kingdoms.[9]

In dwelling on the beauties of the Chilean landscape, some writers became lyrical. As an example, here are the opening words of the

---

[1] Molina, I, 12.
[2] *Ibid.* I, ix. Gerbi (p. 240) refers to this side of Molina's writing as 'un nuovo sentimento d'attaccamento al proprio paese, qualcose come un embrionale e minuzioso patriottismo fisico'.
[3] Miguel de Lastarria (1759–1829). Born in Arequipa; arrived in Chile, 1777; moved to Buenos Aires, 1799, and to Spain, 1803; the grandfather of the great writer José Victorino Lastarria.
[4] 'Proyecto que se propone a la Suprema Junta de Real Hacienda del Reino de Chile en aumento del real erario...1793–5', in *Revista de Historia de América*, no. 46 (Mexico DF, 1958), p. 447.
[5] Gómez de Vidaurre, I, 3.
[6] *Ibid.* 20.
[7] Encina, *Historia*, v, 625.
[8] *Ibid.* 629.
[9] Rojas to Salas, 9 October 1774, Salas, *Escritos*, III, 360.

third Annual Report of José de Cos Iriberri to the Consulado of Santiago. It must be agreed that this is unusual terminology for an economic review.

On entering this Kingdom by any of its ports or by descending from the high Cordillera, what a delightful scene is presented by the multitude of streams and torrents, the verdure of the fields, the foliage of the trees, the alternating variation of valleys, hills and slopes, and the great herds of livestock which inhabit the landscape. What ideas of opulence and richness this agreeable sight stimulates![1]

And in Manuel de Salas we find a concise summary of this feeling when he describes the Kingdom of Chile as 'without contradiction the most fertile in America, and the most adequate for human happiness'.[2] There can be little doubt, then, that for a whole generation of alert and educated creoles, their country was, in Juan Egaña's words, 'the most precious portion of the earth and the most brilliant adornment of the Spanish crown'.[3] In 1804 Egaña paid tribute to his adopted country when he said: 'The idea of a city created for wisdom and peopled solely by philosophers, which has been the flattering dream of certain thinkers, could (were it practicable at all) be better carried out in Chile than in any other part of the world.'[4] Egaña's reasons were characteristic of the man. Chile, he went on to claim, was in possession of the human and natural resources needed for such a venture, and was conveniently remote from the centres of viciousness and intrigue in the world.

It is little wonder, then, that a departing Chilean Jesuit should lament, in 1767, his abrupt translation to 'foreign lands',[5] or that the agent of the Cabildo of Santiago in Cádiz in 1810 should write home that 'it can in truth be said that *there is no other*

[1] Cos Iriberri, *Tercera Memoria*, 30 September 1799, Cruchaga Tocornal, I, 309.
[2] *Representación hecha al Ministro de Hacienda don Diego de Gardoqui por el Síndico del Real Consulado de Santiago, sobre el estado de la agricultura, industria y comercio del Reino de Chile*, 10 January 1796, Salas, *Escritos*, I, 152. This document, Salas' masterpiece, is the classic description of the late-colonial Chilean economy.
[3] Speech, 15 November 1809, *CHDI*, XVIII, 17.
[4] 'Oración inaugural para la apertura de los estudios de la Real Universidad de San Felipe en el año de 1804' (Egaña, *Escritos inéditos*, p. 11).
[5] 'Despedida de la Compañía de Jesús al Reyno y Ciudad de Santiago de Chile', 1767 [verses] (F.V., vol. 259, pieza 6).

Chile but Chile'.[1] Patriotism may have emerged slowly, but its growth was sure. Néstor Meza Villalobos has shown that by 1810 the word *patria* had frequently come to mean Chile rather than the whole Empire (it was to preserve this double meaning in the early part of the revolution, too) and the word *patriota* a Chilean who loved his homeland.[2] The sense of the riches of Chile and the great opportunities for progress which existed there was becoming more and more deeply rooted by the time of the crisis of 1808–10. Some verses found amongst the papers of José Antonio de Rojas after his arrest in May 1810 contained the essence of the creoles' feeling. 'These kingdoms', ran the lines, 'are too great to be a bundle tied to Spain' any longer.[3]

A further indication of this rising patriotism, in my view, was an incipient tendency to idealize the Araucanian Indian, a feature which was later to become an important aspect of the mystique of the revolution.[4] Molina, in his painstaking and accurate account of Chilean history, gave prominence to the details of the Araucanian resistance to the Spanish advance.[5] Gómez de Vidaurre acknowledged that the Indians had their faults, but in general his description of them was complimentary,[6] and he made the point that he himself could—because of his own background—hardly be biased in their favour.[7] Elsewhere in his book, he praised other pre-Columbian civilizations in America, and wryly commented that 'the Spaniards found greater civility and better government in the vast Empires of Peru and Mexico than did the Phoenicians amongst the ancient inhabitants of Spain'.[8] But for those who wished to admire ancient Araucania, there was one work which provided them with their excuse more effectively than any mere history book: Alonso de Ercilla's epic poem *La Araucana*, 'the certificate of baptism of our nation', as its first Chilean editor, Abraham Koenig, wrote in 1888. *La Araucana* had gone through several editions between its first appearance in 1569 and 1632.

Fernández de Leiva to Rojas, 20 May 1810, Matta Vial, 'El diputado de Chile', p. 312.
[1] *Conciencia política*, pp. 247–9 and 259.
[2] 'Décimas', [1810], *Proceso seguido*, p. 60.
[34] See chapter 5, pp. 212–7.   [5] Molina, vol. II, books 3–4.
[6] Gómez de Vidaurre, II, 297–353.   [7] *Ibid.* II, 309–10.
[8] *Ibid.* I, 296.

The Growth of the Revolution

After 1632 there had been no further edition for a hundred years. In the eighteenth century, however, there was a revival of interest in the poem. The work was republished, in Europe, either wholly or partially, four times between 1733 and 1803. *La Araucana*, as Amunátegui once observed, had the merit of being one of the few national epics based roughly on hard fact.[1] In its pages, the Chileans could read an account of the heroic struggles which had accompanied the Conquest. And they could also identify themselves, to some extent at least, with the proud Indians defending Araucania against the might of Spain. Francisco Antonio Pinto has, happily, left us an invaluable description of the effect of the poem on the creole generation which was finishing its higher education in the first years of the nineteenth century.

It was at that time that I first read *La Araucana* by Ercilla, and we used to gather together in groups to savour the reading of it... It was a work that awoke in our hearts the love of our country, warlike sentiments, a thirst for glory, and a vague propensity for Independence. It was impossible to consider the great deeds of Caupolicán, Colo Colo, Lautaro and other giants of our history without feeling the heart burn with the desire to imitate them, and *to have a fatherland* to which we could consecrate our services.[2]

Chileans, at the end of the colonial period, could not only draw on their Spanish ancestry (which they did freely enough in search of titles and other honours). They could also look back to their Araucanian heritage. Chile had once been famous. Ercilla's epic had brought the heroism of Araucanian and Spaniard alike before the attention of the civilized world. As Juan Egaña wrote in 1804: 'The fame of the riches and fertility of Chile, and of the genius of its inhabitants, was resounding throughout Europe when the gross and uncivilized Russians were unknown even to their neighbours.'[3]

There was a moral in this observation of Egaña's, for, as he went on to point out, Russia had taken full advantage of the Enlightenment, while Chile had failed to do so. Alongside the

[1] *Precursores*, II, 500–1.
[2] 'Apuntes autobiográficos', pp. 77–8. (My italics.)
[3] Oración inaugural...1804', *Escritos inéditos*, p. 14.

28

creole exaltation of the homeland, in fact, there also existed a very strongly defined dissatisfaction with the late-colonial reality, and a desire for progress. Manuel de Salas, in the sentence in which he described Chile as the most fertile kingdom in America, affirmed that it was also 'the most wretched of the Spanish dominions'.[1] In his famous *Representación* of 1796, Salas painted a grim picture of misery and poverty, backwardness and economic failure, and recommended vigorous measures to combat these conditions. Gómez de Vidaurre wondered to what heights Chilean agriculture might not rise if it applied better methods of cultivation.[2] Cos Iriberri ascribed rural poverty to the concentration of land into an excessively small number of hands, and urged that a specific limit on land holdings should be enacted.[3] Anselmo de la Cruz,[4] another of the so-called 'precursors' of 1810, observed that the animal and vegetable kingdoms played their proper roles in Chile, but that Man lagged behind. To remedy this he demanded a full-scale system of popular education.[5] This is not the place to mention or elaborate all the various economic and social reforms suggested by men like Salas, Cruz and Cos Iriberri. But we must note that these reforms were considered to be urgent, and that they sprang from a sense of Chilean potential contrasted with Chilean reality. 'Chile could be the emporium of the earth,' Cruz wrote,[6] and yet the country was obviously a long way from fulfilling that destiny. The value of Chile was, as we have seen, exalted and praised. It was widely believed that Chile could make striking progress. The result of these reflections was a widespread dissatisfaction, and, as a consequence, the production of a definite reform programme. This reform programme was exclusively economic and social. It contained no political proposals, except, that is, the proposal that the monarchy should take a more active hand in affairs. But reform, it was felt, was urgently needed. Diego Barros Arana may be allowed to summarize this highly important

[1] *Representación*, 10 January 1796, *Escritos*, I, 152.
[2] Gómez de Vidaurre, I, 38–41.
[3] *Tercera Memoria*, 30 September 1799, Cruchaga Tocornal, I, 309–10.
[4] Anselmo de la Cruz Bahamonde (d. 1833). Later Finance Minister under O'Higgins, 1818–20.
[5] *Memoria Segunda*, 13 January 1808, Cruchaga Tocornal, I, 342.
[6] *Ibid.* 343.

aspect of the late-colonial scene. 'The most advanced men were persuaded', he wrote, 'that the reform of a few laws, the growth of population, and the diffusion of useful knowledge would make Chile a region privileged by her products and by the virile and enterprising character of her people.'[1] The economist-precursors in Chile retained their faith in 'enlightened despotism', but, like their counterparts in Europe, many of them were to become revolutionaries when the system of enlightened despotism broke down.

It is worth noting that Chilean judgements on these matters were corroborated by foreign visitors. When Juan Egaña described Chile in 1809 as 'the admiration of travellers',[2] he was not exaggerating. The La Pérouse expedition found that the fertility of the Chilean soil was well worthy of praise.[3] Captain Vancouver thought that Chile could fairly be considered 'one of the richest territories belonging to his Catholic Majesty'.[4] The Italian navigator Malaspina and his companions lauded the 'extreme fertility' and the 'almost inexhaustible soil' of the province.[5] The German Jesuit Bernard Havestadt, who had lived in Chile, devoted part of his later life to a copious study of the Indian language, claiming that in some ways it was superior to more fashionable tongues.[6] Chile, believed Father Havestadt, was outstanding for its climate, its soil, its abundance of foodstuffs— and was certainly better than Germany on all these counts.[7] It is noteworthy, too, that Malaspina, Vancouver, and La Pérouse all considered substantial reform a condition of any progress Chile might make in the future.[8]

[1] Barros Arana, VII, 439. For the ideas of the economist-precursors, see Ramírez Necochea, pp. 86–98.
[2] Speech, 15 November 1808, *CHDI*, XVIII, 19.
[3] Milet-Mureau, II, 60.
[4] Vancouver, III, 453.
[5] Malaspina, p. 610. Chilean and foreign estimates of the fertility of Chile were over-sanguine: see Encina, *Historia*, V, 101–3.
[6] Bernardus Havestadt, *Chilidúgu sive res chilenses vel descriptio status tum naturalis, tum civilis, cum moralis regni populique chilensis* (3 vols. 'Monasterii Westphaliae', 1777), II, 887–8.
[7] *Ibid.* III, 946.
[8] Malaspina, p. 610; Vancouver, III, 453–4; Milet-Mureau, II, 62.

DISRUPTIVE INFLUENCES

So far, I have tried to show that the creoles in Chile were conscious of certain grievances and also of the essential worth of their
country. These were obviously factors which might affect the
growth of any revolution that showed signs of becoming a
practical possibility. There were other factors as well, which
might well have helped to create a climate in which revolution
could develop if other circumstances were suitable. Until recently,
an important aspect of the pre-revolutionary scene—the economic
aspect—was largely unexplored. Now, however, the groundwork
for a proper study of the question has been carried out by Dr
Inge Wolff and Sr Hernán Ramírez Necochea. I must note,
however briefly, the sustained defence of Chilean economic
interests which had taken place through the eighteenth century,
and in particular the conflict which arose between Lima and
Santiago over the grain trade. Peruvian merchants were able, for a
number of reasons, to fix the price of Chilean grain to their own
advantage, and this state of affairs was denounced by more than
one creole leader in the late-colonial period. Chilean external
trade, Anselmo de la Cruz wrote, was 'groaning beneath the
Peruvian yoke'.[1] The tension between Lima and Santiago was
severe enough to lead to the creation, in 1795, of the Consulado
of Santiago[2], and was also a factor in the administrative separation of the Captaincy-General of Chile from the Viceroyalty
of Peru. The Peruvian determination to crush the Chilean revolution after 1812, and the Chilean resolutionto resist at all costs,
may well have owed a good deal to this background of rivalry
and resentment.

Whether Chile was or was not, in Ramírez's phrase,' a totally
constituted national economic unit' by 1810[3] is not a matter that
can be debated here. But it is clear that the small group of
economist-precursors already mentioned were analysing the
situation in largely Chilean terms, even if Salas, in his *Representación*

---

[1] To Governor Muñoz de Guzmán, 29 April 1806, quoted in Ramírez Necochea, p. 71.
For the grain trade conflict see Wolff, pp. 180–4.
[2] Wolff, pp. 186–7.   [3] Ramírez Necochea, p. 37.

of 1796, claimed that all he wanted was to make the Captaincy-General 'as useful to the metropolis as, hitherto, it has been useless'.[1] Ramírez has claimed that because of Chilean subjection to the economic policy of Spain and to the commercial interests of Peru, independence was rapidly becoming a necessity: 'the country needed to break out of its cloistered economic existence'.[2] But to what extent wider trading arrangements were ardently desired in Chile before 1810 is something of a puzzle. Cruz, who proposed a measure of open trade in his *Memoria* of 1809,[3] observed then that there was opposition to this on the grounds that religion and patriotism would be weakened by greater foreign contacts. In December 1810, it is worth recalling, the Consulado opposed anything more than a very limited extension of trading rights largely for reasons like these.[4] It was perhaps natural that the clamour for freer trade was less marked in Chile than in the River Plate, where mercantile activity was far greater in any case. It has also been claimed, by Sergio Villalobos R., that some Chileans were already enjoying a relatively unrestricted foreign trade before 1810,[5] though whether the January 1811 decree allowing *comercio libre* merely confirmed an existing situation, as he claims, is perhaps debatable.

The economic position of Chile at the end of the colonial period can fairly be called a disruptive influence. The effect of the expulsion of the Jesuits has also often been regarded as a factor which brought about the desire for some kind of change. It is worth outlining the ways in which this might have occurred. In Chile, as in the rest of the Empire, the Jesuits had played a notable part. They had known 'how to make themselves liked by everybody', as Marius André put it.[6] The Order had become immensely influential. It had accumulated over fifty *haciendas*, some of them the most fertile and productive in the Captaincy-General. The best Chilean wine of the period came from the Jesuit vine-

---

[1] *Escritos*, i, 178.
[2] Ramírez Necochea, p. 86.
[3] *Memoria Tercera*, 12 January 1809, Cruchaga Tocornal, i, 346.
[4] Barros Arana, viii, 271–4.
[5] Villalobos advances some interesting cases: 'El comercio extranjero', pp. 537–44.
[6] *La fin de l'empire espagnol d'Amérique* (Paris, 1922), p. 79.

yards. In education, too, the Jesuits had had an enormous influence, and, ironically enough, their zeal in this sphere was loudly commended to the Crown by the Chilean Audiencia on the eve of the expulsion.[1] There was a sense in which the Jesuits, to use Amunátegui Solar's words, 'came to be the true chiefs of society',[2] and it is certain that their abrupt removal caused shock and gloom amongst the people.[3] One of the expelled Jesuits referred to the act as 'the noisiest blow this vast Monarchy has ever heard'.[4] That this was not purely a Jesuit reaction is obvious. As Julio Alemparte has observed, any action of this sort taken against a religious Order was bound to be profoundly disconcerting in many ways.[5] The removal of the Jesuits had several important short-term effects in Chile. It caused a disruption of education from which Chile did not recover before the revolution, and thus added to the educational grievances felt by the creoles. It also strengthened the economic power of several creole families who were able to buy up Jesuit estates.[6]

Despite the active efforts of the imperial government to suppress certain dangerous features of the Jesuit ideology, particularly its ultramontanism, there is some evidence to suggest that some specific Jesuit ideas remained in circulation. In 1791, for instance, a member of the Mercedarian Order in Santiago made certain public statements which Governor O'Higgins interpreted as 'ascribing an abusive and illegal extensiveness to the authority of the Popes, to the prejudice of the independent and sovereign authority of Kings'.[7] But direct cases of subversive activity on the part of the exiled Jesuits were almost non-existent, though there was the highly interesting case of Juan José Godoy, a Chilean Jesuit who was in London in the early 1780s, apparently soliciting help from the British government for a plan to liberate Chile, Peru, Tucumán and Patagonia from Spanish rule.[8] Whether

---

[1] To the King, 28 April 1767, Amunátegui, *Precursores*, I, 225.
[2] *Historia social*, p. 118.
[3] Barros Arana, VI, 279–80.
[4] 'Despedida de la Compañia de Jesus...', F.V. vol. 259, pieza 6.
[5] *El Cabildo en Chile*, pp. 356–8.   [6] *Ibid.* pp. 358–9.
[7] Medina, *Historia de la Universidad*, I, 250.
[8] Batllori, pp. 58–61. For Godoy see José Toribio Medina, *Un precursor chileno de la revolución de la independencia de América* (1911).

Godoy was the same person as the mysterious 'Don Juan' who was engaged on a similar project at much the same time,[1] is less certain. Such activities had no bearing whatsoever on the development of the revolution inside Chile, though it is perhaps significant that in 1810 some four former Jesuits were to be found in the creole party agitating for a national Junta.[2] The greatest of the exiled fathers, Juan Ignacio Molina, was apparently a supporter of the revolution in his homeland. When in 1817 the O'Higgins regime confiscated an estate which he had inherited, Molina wrote from Italy that this action met with his entire approval. 'They could hardly have interpreted my own wishes better,' he is reported to have said.[3] The funds raised from the confiscation of Molina's property went to help build up the Chilean naval squadron.

The Jesuits' greatest contribution to the cause of independence lay, unwittingly, in their heightening of the sentiment of patriotism through intellectual activity.[4] How this operated in the case of Chile will by now have become obvious enough. The work of Molina and of Gómez de Vidaurre speaks for itself. Gómez de Vidaurre, it is interesting to note, hoped at one stage to set up a kind of research institute on Chilean affairs at Imola.[5] As for the magnificent contribution of Molina, whose work (in its Spanish translation) became available in Chile from the late 1790s, this was remembered with gratitude throughout the revolution, as a motion before the 1828 Congress testifies.[6] In ways such as these the Expulsion certainly contributed to loosening the emotional bonds which tied Chile to the motherland.

---

[1] Carlos Villanueva, *Napoleón y la independencia de América* (Paris [1911]), pp. 35–8.
[2] Eyzaguirre, 'La expulsión de los jesuitas', p. 181; Tocornal, p. 216.
[3] Encina, *Historia*, v, 624.
[4] *Batllori*, p. 171.
[5] Gómez de Vidaurre, I, 6.
[6] Session of 5 July 1828. *SCL*, XVI, 184. It was proposed that the port of Nueva Bilbao should be renamed 'Abate Molina' in honour of 'that wise and patriotic Chilean'. In the end, it was renamed 'Constitución' in honour of the work of the 1828 Congress.

Background to Revolution

The final aspect I must consider is the penetration of new ideas into Chile. Some of these ideas were harmless or neutral as far as the development of the revolutionary spirit was concerned. But certain political notions—the liberal formulations of the Enlightenment and the American and French Revolutions—might reasonably have been deemed subversive, and were in fact so deemed by the imperial government. How did such ideas enter Chile? In the first place, a number of creoles made the long, arduous and expensive journey to Europe, and acquired new concepts there. It is certain, for instance, that Manuel de Salas imbibed a good deal of practical learning from his stay in Spain, and returned to Chile impressed with the reforming activity of Charles III and his enlightened ministers. More interesting details, however, have been preserved of the visit made by José Antonio de Rojas between 1772 and 1777. Rojas acquired a sizable collection of books, came to dislike the atmosphere of the Court but to admire the educational improvements in Spain, entered into a correspondence with the historian William Robertson (though whether Robertson ever received or answered Rojas' letters is another matter), and gained a worldly and sceptical outlook.[1] While on a visit to Paris, Rojas appears to have made contact with Benjamin Franklin.[2] But by far the most important aspect of Rojas' stay in Europe, from my present point of view, is that he sent back a number of prohibited books to Chile, most of them under special licence. They filled sixteen boxes and included works by Rousseau, Montesquieu, Helvétius, d'Holbach, Raynal and Robertson.[3] Rojas apparently conceived a particular admiration for these last two names. A third creole visitor, this time to England as well as Spain, was Bernardo Riquelme, who, on return to Chile, was presently to assume his father's surname, O'Higgins, and become the leading hero in the struggle for independence. It was in London in 1798, on his own later admission,

---

[1] Amunátegui, *Crónica*, II, 21–97.   [2] Johnston, p. 141.
[3] Amunátegui, *Crónica*, II, 47–8. Rojas had two volumes of Robertson's *History of America* confiscated in Mendoza on his way back to Chile, Barros Arana, VII, 508 n.

that Bernardo O'Higgins was first inspired to join the separatist cause by Francisco de Miranda.[1] O'Higgins was, in point of fact, the only major Latin American liberator to have been influenced directly and personally by the great Venezuelan Precursor before the revolution. Whatever books or impressions the creoles might bring back from their travels, it is likely that the mere fact that they had been away at all was enough to arouse interest in Chile. As Miranda is supposed to have told O'Higgins: 'The Americans will impatiently and avidly demand from you a narrative of your travels and adventures.'[2]

Another source from which new ideas could have reached the Chileans was the extensive contraband trade which was carried on throughout the eighteenth century. At the start of the century, smuggling activity was very much the preserve of Frenchmen. As the French navigator Frézier observed, Frenchmen were sometimes badly treated in Santiago because of the unfavourable competition French contrabandists created for Chilean merchants in the capital.[3] Towards the end of the century, however, English and North American smuggling dominated the scene. As Governor García Carrasco later reported, Englishmen and North Americans could trade without much risk of discovery by the authorities; Chile was flooded with English goods 'imported' in this way; and many of the leading creoles were involved in the trade.[4] The sad case of the *Scorpion* in 1808 amply illustrates the procedures used by the contrabandists, and the extent of their influence.[5] The *Scorpion* was probably typical of the smuggling vessels that arrived off the Chilean coasts in the last years of the colony. It was owned and backed by 'sundry Merchants of the City of London'; and a locally resident Englishman or perhaps North American, a Mr Henry Faulkner, apparently advised the contrabandists on 'the State of the Markets' and 'the prospects of

---

[1] O'Higgins to Mackenna, 5 January 1811, Cruz, *Epistolario*, I, 27. See W. S. Robertson, *The Life of Miranda* (2 vols. Chapel Hill, N.C., 1929), I, 196–202.

[2] 'Consejos de un viejo sud-americano a un joven compatriota al regresar de Inglaterra a su país', [?1799], Vicuña Mackenna, *Vida de O'Higgins*, p. 63.

[3] Amédée Frézier, *Relation du voyage de la mer du Sud aux Côtes du Chili, de Pérou et du Brésil* (2 vols. Amsterdam, 1717), I, 169.

[4] García Carrasco to Pedro Zeballos, 20 December 1808, *CHDI*, VIII, 119–26.

[5] The fullest account is in Amunátegui, *Crónica*, I, 225–53.

making rapid sales'.[1] Smuggling was carried out in a highly businesslike way, and, as I have mentioned already, had become something of a habit in Chile. When the *Scorpion*'s captain was treacherously murdered on García Carrasco's orders, his creole friends, 'roved through the streets like madmen' in their anger and sorrow.[2] García Carrasco believed that it would be impossible to stop the contraband trade,[3] a view shared by his predecessor as Governor, Luis Muñoz de Guzmán, who felt (rightly) that geographical difficulties precluded complete vigilance on the part of the authorities.[4] But it was not only smuggling ships that troubled the sleep of colonial governors. Since the Convention of San Lorenzo (1790), the South Pacific was no longer a closed sea, and vessels which could now sail there legally were sometimes obliged to put in at Chilean ports. Governor O'Higgins had foreseen trouble on this score. Reporting the arrival of English, French and North American ships in 1792, he roundly affirmed that the San Lorenzo Convention 'inconveniences us on all sides, and will give us a good deal to do in the future'.[5] O'Higgins' forecast was entirely correct. By 1805 it was possible for the Governor to write that 'it is impossible to give a return of all foreign ships that are continually arriving in the Ports of this Kingdom, on account of their number'.[6]

Particular attention should be paid here to the North American vessels which touched at Chilean ports, for from such vessels a revolutionary doctrine could sometimes be passed on. There is no way of telling how many of the 257 North American ships which sailed in the coastal waters of Chile between 1788 and 1810[7]

---

[1] *Protest* of three captured members of the *Scorpion's* crew, dated 18 November 1809, A.B.A. vol. 25-2(3), fo. 379.

[2] Francisco Antonio de la Carrera to García Carrasco, 1 March 1809, A.B.A. vol. 25-2(3), fo. 276.

[3] *Representación* [1811], Vicuña Mackenna, *Coronel Figueroa*, Apéndice, p. 126.

[4] To M. C. Soler, October 1806, C.C.M.M. vol. 218, fo. 197–8. For an excellent description of the contraband trade, still regrettably unpublished, see Elizabeth Thiess P., 'El contrabando en Chile durante el siglo XVIII' (*Memoria de Prueba*, University of Chile, 1939). Thiess suggests that English smugglers must have been hampered by the language barrier in their contacts with creoles, but that they demonstrated the advantages of open trade in a concrete manner (p. 117).

[5] To Ambrosio Valdés, 19 September 1792, Amunátegui, *Precursores*, I, 315.

[6] To J. A. Caballero, 4 February 1805, C.C.M.M. vol. 218, fo. 1.

[7] For a list of these see Pereira Salas, *Buques norteamericanos*, pp. 13–44.

left any ideological as opposed to commercial impact behind them. Only some eighty or so are known to have called at Chilean ports. But some members of the various crews may have left medallions, watches and other items which could have borne propaganda emblems or messages.[1] And there is at least one case which shows that such behaviour was by no means uncongenial to the North American mariner. William Shaler and Richard Cleveland, owners of the *Lelia Byrd*, stayed some nine weeks at Valparaíso in 1802.[2] The notoriety they gained as a result of their various tussles with the colonial authorities soon made them well known in the port, and they were able to mix with several prominent creole families. Shaler and Cleveland gained some interesting impressions of colonial grievances from the creoles, and, in his memoirs, Cleveland recalled the 'bursts of indignation' with which the creoles expounded their complaints, 'which were generally accompanied with a hope that the period of emancipation was not very distant'. (Cleveland's memoirs were published in 1842 and he may perhaps have enriched the memory with a certain amount of ideological reflection.) Both Cleveland and Shaler were ardent apostles of the rational liberty being practised in the new republic to the North, and they took advantage of their unexpected opportunity to exploit the creole sense of grievance to the full.

Such sentiments were met by us with corresponding ones, by drawing a parallel between their country and ours, while each was under a colonial system of government, by adverting to the greater physical means in their possession to enable them to throw off the yoke, than was possessed by the Anglo-Americans, in the beginning of their Revolution, by demonstrating to them the greatly increased value of the products of their soil, and the diminished prices at which they would receive the manufactures of Europe, when their commerce should be freed from the shackles to which tyranny and folly had so long subjected it; and, finally, by remarking on the paralysing and debasing effects on the mind, which are inseparable from a protracted state of dependence and vassalage. For the better promotion of the

[1] Johnson, 'Early Relations', p. 265.
[2] For an account of their stay, see Nichols, pp. 59–65.

embryo cause, we gave them a copy of our Federal Constitution, and a translation into Spanish, of our Declaration of Independence.[1]

Shaler and Cleveland, it appears, deliberately carried copies of the Federal Constitution, the Declaration of Independence, and samples of various State constitutions.[2] Their intention to propagandize was evident from the start. It is, of course, impossible to say how much effect this sort of spontaneous propaganda work had in Chile, but it is almost inconceivable that it had no effect at all. Another case may also be mentioned here. Procopius Pollock of Baltimore, another North American citizen, was to be found in Chile at the time of Governor García Carrasco, who expelled him. Pollock's activities were construed as subversive, and he was apparently a friend of Juan Martínez de Rozas.[3] It may be concluded with some justification, I think, that the ideas of the American Revolution were being received in Chile, and these were bound to play a part in any subsequent developments in the Captaincy-General.

What effect had the French Revolution in Chile? Despite the remoteness of the province, revolutionary ideas from France managed to penetrate—and quite early on. Governor O' Higgins was plainly worried in 1795 by the appearance in Chile of certain documents 'which, for their style and contents, seemed to me to be more dangerous than any I had seen previously'.[4] The curious case of Dr Clemente Morán, a priest from Coquimbo, who advised his friends in the course of conversation to follow the example of the French Revolution, shows that new ideas from this source could somehow take root. Morán quickly became caught up in one of those lengthy (and tedious) jurisdictional quarrels between Church and State which so delighted the Spanish Empire in America, and the case was still unresolved at the time of his death in 1800.[5] It may well be true that Dr Morán was, to use Ricardo Donoso's phrase, one of the first upholders of republican ideals in Chile,[6] but it is equally true to say that he

---

[1] Cleveland, I, 184. [2] Nichols, p. 57.
[3] Eyzaguirre, 'Gacetas'; Pereira Salas, 'Influencia norteamericana', p. 60.
[4] To E. de Llaguno, 17 September 1795, Amunátegui, *Precursores*, I, 268.
[5] See Amunátegui, *Precursores*, III, 275–91; Villalobos R., *Tradición y reforma*, pp. 145–50.
[6] *Ideas políticas*, pp. 24–5.

was in every way an isolated and unimportant figure. The general creole reaction to the excesses of the French Revolution was one of horror: 'the worst scandal of all ages', as José Antonio de Rojas put it.[1] But this is hardly to say that even if the Terror was repudiated by good creoles, the ideas behind it did not achieve some publicity in Chile.[2]

In reality, evidence relating to the precise way in which new ideas were received is sparse. What can and must be emphasized here is that these ideas—from the Enlightenment in general and from the two Revolutions in particular—were fully present in Chile at the end of the colonial period, though necessarily only within a restricted group of creoles. Educated Chileans were aware of the great currents of enlightened thought. The small group of economist-precursors, as I have called them, displayed a clear knowledge of enlightened Spanish thinking on economic matters. Salas, Cruz, Cos Iriberri and their colleagues were considerably influenced by the neo-mercantilist arguments put forward by such figures as Count Campomanes, Bernardo Ward, and Joseph Campillo y Cosío.[3] Both Salas and Cruz enormously admired the work of Campomanes in particular.[4] Manuel de Salas and Juan Egaña showed that they were well acquainted with the names, though perhaps not the works, of the leading scientists and philosophers of the age.[5] And we know, too, that somewhat more contentious modern notions were circulating at the same time. At a university function in 1790, for instance, the divine origin of royal power was impugned with what Governor O'Higgins construed as 'excessive ardour'.[6] Knowledge of contemporary political and social theory was probably more widespread than has been generally supposed, and in the majority of cases it was undoubtedly harmless. Governor O'Higgins himself

[1] To Ambrosio O'Higgins, 17 July 1793, Eyzaguirre, *Ideario y ruta*, p. 77 n.
[2] Amongst Barros Arana's paper there is a handwritten translation of the *Déclaration des Droits de l'Homme*, dating from just prior to 1810, A.B.A. vol. 25-2(3), fo. 474. Other material, anti-revolutionary in tone, is in Archivo Eyzaguirre, vol. 27, pieza 9.
[3] See Will, pp. 2–3. Liberal economic ideas did not reach Chile until later.
[4] Cruchaga Tocornal, I, 346; Celis Muñoz, p. 53.
[5] Salas, *Escritos*, I, 578–9; Egaña, *Escritos inéditos*, p. 13.
[6] O'Higgins to the Rector of the University, 2 September 1790, Amunátegui, *Precursores*, I, 231.

was vaguely acquainted with the ideas of Rousseau, Buffon and Raynal, though he regarded most eighteenth-century thinkers as extravagant visionaries.[1] We have already seen how Rojas introduced prohibited books. There is some evidence to show that such books were freely lent round by Rojas, and passed through the hands of such men as Fray Francisco Javier Guzmán, Juan Antonio Ovalle, Juan Egaña and José Miguel Infante.[2] Juan Martínez de Rozas, the first outstanding leader of the revolution, plainly knew such works as Raynal's *Histoire Philosophique*, L. S. Mercier's *Histoire de l'An 2440*, Montesquieu's *Spirit of the Laws* and Rousseau's *Social Contract*. Some of these works he knew through his brother Ramón de Rozas, who was involved in a brush with the Inquisition in Lima in 1802 for being in possession of them.[3] As early as 1794 an enemy of the Rozas brothers had denounced them for behaving in accordance with 'the maxims of Voltaire and similar authors, whom they read with particular delight'.[4]

It was only a minority, and a very restricted minority at that, which indulged in the reading of prohibited texts, and even within that minority probably only a mere handful—the merest handful —would have been interested in politics of the revolutionary type. There cannot have been many who crossed the thin but perilous line separating reformist zeal from outright disloyalty. Were there any separatists at all in Chile before 1808? In Chapter 2 I shall consider some of the evidence relating to the men most likely to have been subversive in their aims during the crisis of 1808–10. But what of the period prior to 1808? Most Latin American republics can produce at least one or two pre-revolutionary conspiracies, nearly all of them speedily suppressed and achieving no local resonance whatsoever. Chile, however, can produce almost nothing. The curious conspiracy of Gramusset and Berney, two utopian (and possibly demented) Frenchmen who plotted

[1] Thomas, 'Los proyectos', pp. 132–3.   [2] Donoso, *Ideas políticas*, pp. 25–6.
[3] Medina, *Inquisición en Chile*, II, 530–40. These books had evidently been passing between Rozas, Camilo Henríquez and Baron Nordenflicht.
[4] Anonymous letter to the Duque de la Alcudia, 8 January 1794, Meza Villalobos, *Conciencia política*, p. 256. The best discussions of the penetration of new ideas in general are in Donoso, *Ideas políticas*, pp. 13–26, and Eyzaguirre, *Ideario y ruta*, pp. 71–84.

to set up a republic in Chile in 1780, can hardly be brought forward as evidence. It was a picturesque episode, though completely concealed from the vast majority of Chileans at the time. It was an isolated, ignored incident involving two eccentric foreigners and (probably) hardly anybody besides.[1] But even so, it is certain that there *were* separatists in Chile before the revolution, even if only the minutest handful. The case of Bernardo O'Higgins is well known, and it is more than probable that, under his influence, some of his friends came to believe in independence. But the extent to which separatist feeling was organized is difficult to say. There is virtually no evidence at all in the Chilean case to suggest a conspiracy. However, one particular piece of evidence demands a reference. On 2 January 1802, William Moulton, a North American sailor then visiting Talcahuano, noted in his diary that a Chilean 'military officer and learned man' had visited him secretly in his cabin. The unknown Chilean asserted that

the fire of liberty was enkindling thro' all the Spanish South-America; the people are forming select numbers of two, three or four in a club in every considerable town; they are confederated under certain injunctions, and communicate with each other... He declared that should they succeed in emancipating his country, it would not check his ardor were he assured that he must fall a sacrifice in the attempt... I charged my memory with what he said further on this subject. Should the kingdom of Spain be invaded by a neighbouring power, or should the security of the crown be threatened by the people, a revolution here would be the probable consequence.[2]

Even allowing for exaggeration on the part of the unknown informant and the North American, this points to the fact that there was a small group, necessarily very furtive, which was either actively working for independence or was at any rate eager for it, and prepared to wait for the moment when Spain's difficulty would provide America's opportunity.

Throughout this discussion it should be borne in mind that I have been considering the exceptions to the general rule of absolute obedience and loyalty. The various factors which were

[1] Amunátegui, *Precursores*, III, 179–255; Villalobos R., *Tradición y reforma*, pp. 129–39.
[2] Moulton, p. 83.

operating in the late-colonial period would not, in themselves, have brought about the independence which a minute number probably desired. Yet the creole sense of grievance, added to the growing number of those 'suggestions which in an imperceptible way were creating the atmosphere of nationality and the ideal of a fatherland',[1] would undoubtedly play some kind of part in shaping Chilean destiny if other, more immediate, factors brought about a revolutionary situation. It can perhaps be argued, too, that one condition for a successful revolution already existed: the small educated nucleus of potential leaders. Their influence in the years before 1808 was limited in the extreme. The ideal of reform, however, was certainly in the air in Chile, as elsewhere in the Empire, in the first years of the nineteenth century, even if the daring notion of political independence was still a rare flower. Provided the general structure of the Empire remained intact, political independence was a long way removed from the list of practical possibilities. But the structure did not remain intact, and, as a result, independence was closer than anyone would have dared to dream.

[1] Galdames, *Evolución constitucional*, p. 55.

2

THE MOVEMENT FOR HOME RULE
1808–1810

EVENTS: 1808–1810

At the start of the year 1808 few Spanish Americans could possibly have foreseen the coming of the wave of national Juntas which, two years later, marked the origins of their emancipation from the Spanish Empire. This is a measure of the abruptness of the happening. The Juntas of 1810 were not actively prepared for until the last moment. They did not represent the triumph of a carefully organized conspiracy. They sprang, in fact, from the confused nature of the times as a response to certain immediate dilemmas. The two most important features of the revolution of 1810 all over the continent were, first, that it asserted local creole rights to the full, stopping well short of total independence but nevertheless assuming a complete degree of autonomy and, second, that it was the work of minority elites which claimed to represent the vast mass of Spanish Americans who had no hand in the changes. Writing in 1813, Fray Camilo Henríquez observed that while most human revolutions were heralded by some general movement of opinion, this had never been true of Spanish America. Though there had been corruption and disorder under Charles IV, he added, 'those disorders did not prepare people's minds for the revolution to which they gave birth'.[1] The revolutions of 1810, therefore, were spontaneous events dictated largely by immediate circumstances. In Chile, almost exactly two years separated the reception of the news of Ferdinand VII's captivity from the installation of the national government. During those two years, the revolution was groped towards, prepared, and finally planned. The precise shape of the creoles' proposals only crystallized in the last six months.

The external events, the events of the European crisis, were of

[1] *Monitor Araucano*, tomo I, no. 86, 28 October 1813.

fundamental importance. The independence of Latin America began in Berlin. For it was there, in November 1806, that the Emperor Napoleon issued the first of his decrees setting up the Continental System, the economic blockade designed to defeat Great Britain. The refusal of Portugal to come to terms with the System obliged Napoleon to dispatch an army under Junot to force compliance. This led quickly to political complications in Spain, to the half-comic and half-tragic events at Bayonne in May 1808, and to the full-scale French involvement in the Peninsula which followed immediately. By deciding to impose his own government on the Spanish people Napoleon quite unintentionally triggered off the Spanish Empire's most convulsive period of disintegration. The huge drama of Spanish American emancipation which began in Berlin (or at least in Bayonne) ended sixteen years later with the victories of Bolívar and Sucre in the Peruvian highlands. News of the opening events of this drama reached the Captaincy-General of Chile in August and September 1808. August brought the news of the abdication (March 1808) of King Charles IV and the downfall of Manuel de Godoy, Prince of the Peace, and, at the same time, disturbing rumours began to spread about Napoleon's ultimate intentions towards the Spanish monarchy. September confirmed the creoles' worst fears. Ferdinand VII, it was then learned, had yielded up the Spanish throne at Bayonne, Joseph Bonaparte was to take on the unenviable role of crowned proconsul for his brother, and the Spanish people were resisting the French invader with obdurate heroism. In Chile, as elsewhere in the overseas Empire, the creoles became aware that their moment had come. Patriotic feelings which had been developing from early colonial times, together with political and economic aspirations which had taken shape more recently, were given an unexpected outlet, and the outlet was used.

An added local complication in Chile was the capricious and semi-despotic governorship of Francisco Antonio García Carrasco.[1] He had succeeded the well-loved Andalusian, Luis Muñoz

---

[1] Born in Ceuta 1743; died; 1812 arrived in Chile, 1796; by virtue of his senior military rank—and nothing else—he succeeded to the governorship in March 1808; deposed by the Audiencia, 16 July 1810.

de Guzmán, earlier in 1808. García Carrasco was hardly the man for the great emergency. In the course of two years he successfully alienated the Royal Audiencia, the Cabildo of Santiago, the University of San Felipe, and the creole aristocracy. He thus forfeited the only allies who could have helped him govern the Captaincy-General. His private implication in the brutal seizure of the English smuggling vessel *Scorpion* in October 1808, and the treacherous murder of its captain, Tristram Bunker, made the new Governor very unpopular. Had García Carrasco been personally more temperate in his attitude towards the creole aristocracy, he could conceivably have held Chile for Spain just as Abascal was to hold Peru. As it was, his misgovernment hastened the advent of a national Junta by generating a fierce current of political excitement. The structure of traditional authority would certainly have supported a bad Governor in normal times. But these were hardly normal times.

Already by the summer[1] of 1808-9 there were rumours in Santiago that a party of creoles wanted a Junta. Some were even supposed to be plotting total independence. Precise evidence as to the way in which new political ideas circulated is difficult to obtain, but it is clear that such ideas were fully discussed in a number of *tertulias* in Santiago and elsewhere. Most of the creole reformers were well known to each other, and the spread of autonomist proposals was largely by word of mouth; but political manuscripts plainly passed from hand to hand as well. It was not long before the reformers' discussions produced results. Towards the end of 1809 two men, Fray Rosauro Acuña and Pedro Arriagada (both, significantly, friends of Bernardo O'Higgins) were arrested for expressing subversive views, though, for reasons which remain obscure, they were not severely punished. In April 1810, however, the Viceroy of the River Plate informed García Carrasco that he had been assured by reliable sources of the existence in Chile of parties favouring independence from Spain. García Carrasco, who had issued a solemn precautionary admonition against subversion at the very end of 1809, did not

---

[1] The seasons of the Southern Hemisphere apply in all references to Chile. Summer runs from 21 December to 21 March.

hesitate to act on Cisneros' hint. On 18 May 1810 he ordered inquiries to be made into the conduct of three leading citizens of Santiago: José Antonio de Rojas, Juan Antonio Ovalle, and Bernardo de Vera y Pintado.[1] Rojas and Ovalle were elderly and respected patricians; Vera was much younger, but well known in the city. On 25 May the three men were arrested and sent to Valparaíso to await shipment to Lima for trial. An immediate public outcry prevented García Carrasco from sending the prisoners to Peru. A month later, however, Chile received the news of the May Revolution in Buenos Aires. García Carrasco interpreted the deposition of the Viceroy of the River Plate and the establishment of a national Junta as a fundamental threat to Ferdinand VII's sovereignty and continued Spanish hegemony in America. He had the three prisoners surreptitiously embarked at Valparaíso, though Vera, feigning illness, contrived to be left behind before the ship sailed. When the Governor's hasty action became known, the anger of the creole aristocracy in Santiago knew no bounds. The Cabildo plotted to overthrow the Governor by force and to set up a national government there and then,[2] while the Audiencia, spotting the danger, forestalled this drastic solution by deposing García Carrasco on its own initiative and replacing him by a well-liked octogenarian creole, Mateo de Toro Zambrano, Conde de la Conquista.[3] This last event (16 July 1810) had the immediate effect of calming political passions. 'The people showed extreme gladness and enthusiasm', wrote José Miguel Infante,[4] 'to see an American, whose bounteous character was widely known, at the head of the state.'[5] 'The sudden appearance of the sun', wrote Manuel de Salas more poetically, 'could not

[1] Bernardo de Vera y Pintado (1780–1827). Born in Veracruz, Mexico; brought up in Argentina; eventually naturalized as a Chilean; Argentine commissioner in Chile during part of the '*Patria Vieja*'; member of the 1824 Congress; one of the most active revolutionaries from 1808 onwards.
[2] 'Relación de los sucesos desarrollados en Santiago y que acarrearon la renuncia de presidente García Carrasco' [1810], *CHDI*, XVIII.
[3] His exact age at the time is uncertain; he was probably in his mid eighties.
[4] José Miguel Infante Rojas (1778–1844). Nephew of José Antonio de Rojas; *procurador* of the Cabildo of Santiago in 1810; member of the Congresses of 1811, 1824, 1826, and 1828; Senator, 1814; the most ardent promoter of federalist views in Chile.
[5] 'Relación de los sucesos desarrollados...', *CHDI*, XVIII, 40.

have dissipated the shadows with greater promptness.'[1] But the calm which followed the disappearance of García Carrasco was only an interlude. It soon became abundantly clear that creole agitation for a national government would continue.

Two issues appear to have been responsible for maintaining the political excitement at a high level: first, the question of whether or not to receive Francisco Javier Elío, who had by this time been appointed as the new permanent Governor of Chile, and, second, the issue of the Council of Regency, which had been set up in Spain as the successor to the Central Junta at the start of the year. The Conde de la Conquista's advanced age and his relative inactivity as Governor ensured that little could be done to prevent further creole discussion of these points. Elío's reputation as an uncompromising royalist did little to endear him to the creoles,[2] while the Conde de la Conquista appreciated that he himself stood to lose. The Cabildo of Santiago, meanwhile, was displaying a manifest unwillingness to recognize the authority of the Spanish Regency. Its young but vocal *procurador*, José Miguel Infante, stated the Cabildo's reservations in a wordy memorandum.[3] The Audiencia, however, was still powerful enough to force through a solemn public affirmation of support for the Regency, and the Cabildo had to accept the situation. By now it was clear that the agitation for a national government was mounting to a new climax. The news from Spain was growing gloomier and gloomier. The possibility of a complete victory by the French in Andalusia seemed weekly more credible. Finally, in the second week of September, the more active members of the Cabildo resolved to make another effort to secure a national Junta along the lines suggested by the example of Buenos Aires. After a brief struggle behind the scenes, with the Audiencia putting up a frosty resistance, the Governor agreed to summon a Cabildo Abierto—an open meeting of the chief notables of the city—on 18 September.

[1] 'Motivos que ocasionaron la instalación de la Junta de Gobierno de Chile' [1810], *CHDI*, xviii, 168.
[2] For Elío's activity in Montevideo, which gained him his reputation, see John Street, *Artigas and the Emancipation of Uruguay* (Cambridge University Press, 1959), pp. 94–110.
[3] *Representación*, 14 August 1810, Medina, *Actas*, p. 39.

The Movement for Home Rule

The creoles who had been agitating for a Junta throughout the winter were, it seems, largely responsible for arranging the business of the Cabildo Abierto in advance. At that assembly, with virtually no opposition, a national governing Junta was established, to be presided over by the Conde de la Conquista himself, and markedly respectable in character. The historic *Acta* of 18 September 1810 stated firmly that Chile would be preserved for King Ferdinand VII and defended against his enemies. The document contained little that seemed overtly subversive or revolutionary. It affirmed an intense loyalty to the monarch. Yet, at the same time, it represented a striking move towards autonomy within the Spanish Empire, and, still more significantly, it promised to summon a national congress.[1] Thus Santiago de Chile went through the same motions as Caracas, Buenos Aires, Bogotá, and other Spanish American cities, though in somewhat sedater fashion, and the first step towards independence was taken. The Cabildo Abierto of 18 September 1810 might well have led towards the kind of home rule most creoles wanted, without involving Chile in more extreme positions. As it was, later events made it merely the first of a series of stepping-stones which led, just over seven years later, to Chile's final separation from the Spanish motherland. It is for this reason that the Chilean instinct to celebrate 18 September as the republic's main national holiday is fully justified.

THE CONSTITUTIONAL DILEMMA

The initial reaction in Chile to the news of Ferdinand VII's captivity was one of intense, even fanatical loyalism. This loyalism remained a basic feature of the creole movement for home rule through the months that followed. 'Today', wrote Manuel de Salas in 1815, 'nobody is ignorant of the fact—though there are some who affect to doubt it—that the first movements in Chile, which were impelled by the movements in Spain, were in agreement with the Spanish cause and on its behalf.'[2] The first

---

[1] The *Acta* of 18 September 1810 is printed in *SCL*, I, 3; Medina, *Actas*, pp. 60–2; and no less than four times in *CHDI* (VIII, 358; IX, 70; XVIII, 206; XXIX, 85). A facsimile may be found in Medina, *Actas*, between pp. 60 and 61.

[2] 'Explicación de su conducta política durante la revolución', Salas, *Escritos*, I, 100.

utterances of the Cabildo of Santiago in the crisis were full of glowing allusions to the 'constant fidelity which animates this people towards its beloved and august sovereign'.[1] Prominent creoles such as the Conde de la Conquista wrote in private letters of their willingness to sacrifice their sons in defence of the great patriotic cause.[2] Ignacio Torres, who was soon to become an ardent advocate of the Junta and later an equally ardent patriot, invoked the remote and captive monarch in lyrical tones:

O Prince who is worthy to rule all kingdoms! Trust in God, Who is a just judge and Who will not leave the insolence of your oppressor unpunished. In the meantime, count on the loyalty of your Spaniards, your Americans, and especially your Chileans. All of them love you, all venerate you with the greatest tenderness.[3]

This intense feeling of loyalism quickly erupted into a series of proclamations issued by the Cabildo of Santiago.[4] On 19 September 1808, barely a week after the first full confirmation of the Bayonne news, the Cabildo affirmed that Chile was anxious to do what she could for the monarchy in its hour of danger.

The loyalty of the inhabitants of Chile has in no wise degenerated from that of their forefathers who, at the cost of their heroic blood, drew this country from out of the state of barbarism in which it had previously existed, and, by joining it to the Spanish Empire, civilized it, peopled it, and christianized it... All we want is to be Spaniards; all we want is the rule of our incomparable King.[5]

The Cabildo's enthusiastic loyalism persisted in this form into 1809. It protested to the new Central Junta in Spain that Chile was showing a 'blind obedience' to the motherland, that respect for the lawful authorities was absolute, and that 'there is no Spanish province where the love of the King and of the metropolis has been so clearly and uninterruptedly maintained'.[6] There

---

[1] *Proclama*, 17 September 1808, Amunátegui, *Crónica*, I, 195.
[2] See Conde de la Conquista to José Gorbea y Vadillo, 13 September 1808, in Jaime Eyzaguirre, *El Conde de la Conquista* (1951), p. 177.
[3] Torres, *Advertencias*, p. 41.
[4] See the *acuerdos* of 8 October and 2 December 1808, Amunátegui, *Crónica*, I, 217, 222.
[5] *Acta* of 19 September 1808, Meza Villalobos, *Actividad política*, pp. 45–6.
[6] To the Central Junta, 4 February 1809, *ibid*. p. 157.

seems no reason whatever to doubt that statements like these were perfectly sincere, particularly in view of the background of extreme loyalty discussed briefly in chapter 1. The sense of shock produced by Napoleon's brusque disposal of Ferdinand VII and the knowledge that the Spanish Peninsula was now the scene of a life-and-death struggle was deep and wounding. 'Our enthusiasm for the Spanish cause was sincere,' wrote Francisco Antonio Pinto[1] many years later, recalling the creole reaction to the crisis of 1808 through a rich haze of revolutionary memories. He remembered, too, how he and his young friends wore badges in their hats, bearing Ferdinand's portrait.[2] For the overwhelming majority of creoles, therefore, there can be small doubt that the Spanish cause was the right cause. Its justice was patent and absolute. From every part of America, Chile included, money poured into Spain to back up the armed struggle of the motherland, and creoles illustrated the loyalty of the colonies by fighting in the Peninsula themselves. To take but two well-known examples, both José de San Martín and José Miguel Carrera served in the Spanish army against the French before they turned their attention to liberating their American homelands from Spain.

As time went by, however, it became clear that Ferdinand's captivity had raised thorny constitutional problems for Chile and the other component provinces of the American Empire. The question posed was a simple one: 'Now that our King has been made captive through Napoleon's infamous treachery, and without having named a regent for the Kingdom, what ought the the Nation to do?[3] How, for instance, ought the Chileans to regard the new, spontaneous authorities which were rising in the Peninsula? In the first glow of pro-Spanish enthusiasm, it was thought by some, perhaps most, that the new Juntas which had been set up in Spain following the French invasion should be accepted unquestioningly as the natural government of the

---

[1] Born 1775, died 1858; Chilean envoy in Buenos Aires, 1811, and London, 1813–14; Minister of Government, 1824–5; Intendant of Coquimbo, 1825–7; acting President of the Republic, 1827–9; a tolerant and humane liberal whose administration was in many ways a model.

[2] 'Apuntes autobiográficos', pp. 93–5.

[3] Infante, *Representación*, 14 August 1810, Medina, *Actas*, p. 36.

Empire. This was the view of Ignacio Torres in September 1808. 'Supreme Junta of Seville!' he wrote; 'communicate your orders to us! We shall obey them as though they were letters and instructions from Ferdinand VII, whom you represent.'[1] The final phrase of Torres' injunction is of considerable interest. In Torres' view, the Junta of Seville had now become the authority where 'the representative sovereignty of our Ferdinand is deposited'.[2] The sovereignty of the monarch, he held, had been transferred to the spontaneously generated body which now governed what was left of the Spanish Peninsula. Those who doubted the essential legitimacy of the position of the Junta of Seville were to be despised as 'traitors, and unworthy of the name of Spaniard'.[3] This view was, of course, by no means dissimilar to that of orthodox royalists, who believed that the Peninsula—and men of Peninsular origin—had absolute rights of government over the Americas, whatever form Peninsular authority might or might not take. This doctrinaire royalist position was stated, somewhat negatively, by Father José María Romo in his famous and controversial sermon of 29 August 1810,[4] which incited an instant protest from the Cabildo of Santiago. But nowhere in Chile was it stated as extremely and as forcibly as it was by Bishop Lué at the Cabildo Abierto of 22 May 1810 in Buenos Aires.[5]

Despite Torres' assertion that the legitimate government of Chile was still located in Spain, the constitutional problem remained grave. In 1809 it could be held, in Britain, that 'Spanish America is, virtually, independent at this moment,'[6] and here lay the crux of the matter. With the removal of Ferdinand VII, the traditional structure of the Empire had collapsed. Its keystone had vanished. Means had to be found, sooner or later, to bring order into a constitutional situation which had become intolerably puzzling. It was inevitable that a debate should spring up over the question of sovereignty and its precise location in the new set

---

[1] *Advertencias*, p. 41.   [2] *Ibid.* p. 40.
[3] *Ibid.*   [4] *CHDI*, XVIII, 103–12.
[5] See *Los sucesos de mayo contados por sus actores, Cornelio Saavedra, Manuel Belgrano, Martín Rodríguez y Tomás Guido* (Buenos Aires, 1928), p. 65.
[6] William Burke, *Letters on the Affairs of Spain and Spanish America* (London, 1809), p. 30.

of circumstances. The solution argued by Torres (in his first phase) and the royalists was simple enough: Peninsular leadership and guidance should be accepted without question and without complaint. But this answer did not appeal to everybody. Already, in September 1808, if we are to believe Torres, there were creoles asking the question, 'Who has authorized that Junta to govern the Nation?' And still others were urging restraint on the amount of financial help which Chile was sending to the motherland: 'Our resources are scanty,' it was being said, 'and if we take away any part of them, we weaken ourselves and will be unable to resist the enemy if he comes to invade us.'[1] Torres himself, in a lengthy report to the Crown, stated that he had heard José María de Rozas[2] (nephew of Juan Martínez de Rozas) question the legality of the Junta of Seville,[3] and a day or two later the same man had expressed the view that Chileans should swear allegiance only to the King, and not to any intermediate body in Spain.[4] Juan Martínez de Rozas,[5] too, was heard telling José Antonio de Rojas on 27 January 1809 that the people of Chile had no need to obey the Central Junta if they felt otherwise inclined.[6]

If certain doubts about the right of the new Spanish Juntas to rule Chile were expressed as early as the end of 1808, these doubts had hardened into unalterable conviction by the time the Central Junta was succeeded by the Council of Regency at the start of 1810. José Miguel Infante, *procurador* of the Cabildo of Santiago, impugned the legitimacy of the Regency in a long

[1] *Advertencias*, p. 42.

[2] José María de Rozas Lima y Melo (1776-1847). Member of the 1811, 1823, and 1829 Congresses; Senator, 1818-22 and 1834-7; a conservative in the 1820s and later.

[3] *Informe*, p. 8. In the first months after the crisis, there was often some confusion as to which Spanish Junta was which. See Sigfrido Radaelli, 'Las Juntas Españolas de 1808 y su repercusión en el Río de la Plata', *Revista de Historia de América*, no. 49 (Mexico DF, 1960), p. 181. For the Spanish Juntas and Regency in general see Raymond Carr, *Spain 1808-1939* (Oxford, 1966), pp. 90-92.

[4] *Informe*, p. 9.

[5] Juan Martínez de Rozas Correa (1759-1813). Born in Mendoza; *asesor* to the Intendancies of Santiago and Concepción, 1790-1804; his marriage to the daughter of the shipping magnate José Urrutia y Mendiburu (1746-1804) made him one of the most influential creoles in the South; secretary to García Carrasco's government, 1808-9; member of the Junta, 1810-11, the 1811 Congress, and the Concepción Provincial Junta, 1811-12; exiled to Mendoza, 1812; one of the indisputable heroes of the revolution.

[6] *Informe*, p. 32.

memorandum on 14 August 1810. The Central Junta, he then claimed, had never had the right to nominate its own successor. Nor did the way in which the Regency had assumed control bear all the signs of constitutional propriety.[1] Though, in the end, the Cabildo agreed to recognize the authority of the Regency in a public ceremony, it never officially swore allegiance.

The Spanish authorities, then, were unable to count on an automatic obedience from the Chileans. But by their very existence they were able to suggest to the creoles that there was a constitutionally acceptable solution to the great dilemma. The crumbling of the traditional structure of authority, after all, had worked its effects in Spain as well as America. If the Spaniards were able to set up governing Juntas, why should not Americans be able to do the same? It seems quite clear that the notion of establishing a local or national Junta in Chile came directly from the recent Peninsular precedents. Infante put this in perspective when he addressed the historic Cabildo Abierto of 18 September 1810.

In a case like the present one, Ley 3, Tít. 15, Part 2 provides for the establishment of a Governing Junta, to be composed of members nominated by 'the great ones of the kingdom, together with the prelates, the rich men, and other good and honourable men from the towns'. As soon as it knew of the captivity of its monarch, the Spanish nation established the Supreme Junta of Seville, then the Central Junta, and finally the supreme council of Regency; and despite the fact that the sovereign authority was deposited in these Juntas and in the Regency, several provincial Juntas subordinate to the Supreme Junta were established as well.[2]

This was an important assertion. Not merely did Infante justify the general principle of all Juntas by reference to the *Siete Partidas*, but he also affirmed the right of any of the Spanish provinces to set up local Juntas under the supreme authority. By September 1810, of course, several of the American provinces had already done this. For the Chileans, the example of Buenos Aires was

[1] Medina, *Actas*, p. 39.
[2] *CHDI*, xviii, 222–3. The law cited by Infante may be consulted in *Los códigos espanoles* (12 vols. Madrid, 1847–51), ii, 420, and it will be seen that Infante's use of it was questionable. But it obviously did not appear to be at the time.

particularly compelling, and, while they probably did not know of the revolutions in northern South America, they were well aware of the various movements which took place abortively in 1809.[1] That the Spanish precedent for Juntas was considered important is also shown by a brief passage from the anonymously circulated *Catecismo político cristiano* of 1810, a document whose general significance I shall discuss later in the present chapter. 'The Americans can and should establish their own provincial Juntas,' claimed the *Catecismo*, 'even as the provinces of Spain have formed theirs, which are dependent on the general Junta on which their delegates sit.'[2] Neither Infante nor the anonymous political catechist, it should be noted, held that a local Chilean Junta should be unrelated, constitutionally, to the Central Junta in Spain.

There was, however, one serious drawback to this view. Royalist and Peninsular elements could easily maintain that what was acceptable in Spain was unacceptable in the colonies. Could the establishment of a Junta in Chile take place without the specific authorization of the Spanish government? 'What is certain', said Father Romo in his contentious sermon of 29 August 1810, 'is that we have no order from the Peninsula for a change of such consequence.'[3] It is true that the Spanish Regency had not issued definite instructions to the creoles to form their own governments, but the whole tenor of Spanish orders, manifestoes and proclamations from the start of 1809 onwards could easily be interpreted— and obviously was interpreted—as an explicit encouragement in that direction. The upsurge of liberalism in Spain in 1808, 1809 and 1810 was accompanied by a generous and expansive new attitude towards the American colonies. An *oficio* from the Central Junta in January 1809 expressed the pious hope that relations between Spain and America would soon be placed on a more equitable basis, and defined the Junta's aims asbeing 'to reform abuses, ameliorate institutions, remove restrictions, and establish the relations between metropolis and colonies on a true basis of justice'.[4] The famous decree of 22 January 1809 called for

[1] See pp. 79, 90.
[2] Amor de la Patria, p. 102.
[3] *CHDI*, xviii, 106.
[4] Amunátegui, *Crónica*, i, 299.

American participation in the Central Junta and for the dispatch of representatives. The Spanish dominions in the New World were no longer 'colonies or factories' but 'an essential and integral part of the Spanish monarchy'.[1] The equally famous decree of 14 February 1810, drawn up by the perfervid liberal poet Manuel José de Quintana and accompanied by a stirring proclamation, announced the installation of the Cortes in the near future and the need for America to send deputies. The colonial era, proclaimed Quintana, was at an end: 'your fate no longer depends on ministers, viceroys or governors—it is in your own hands'.[2] The American colonies were once again described as an essential part of the Empire, and the creoles were told: 'From this moment...you are raised to the dignity of free men.'[3]

The substance of these various decrees and proclamations had two effects. First, the creole sense of grievance was heightened, as will be seen presently, by the metropolitan admission that the American dominions had received something less than equitable treatment in the past. Second, the ground was to some extent cut from under the feet of those who might be disposed to rely on the Peninsula for comprehensive political direction. Legally speaking, these new doctrines of liberation broadcast from Spain gave the Chilean creoles a suitable argument with which to justify their establishment of a Junta. As Infante put it, in his speech to the Cabildo Abierto of 18 September,

> If it has been declared that the peoples of America form an integral part of the monarchy, if it has been recognized that they have the same rights and privileges as the peoples of the Peninsula, who have established provincial Juntas—then ought we not to establish provincial Juntas ourselves?[4]

Furthermore, as Infante noted on the same occasion, the proclamation setting up the Regency had recommended the Junta of Cádiz as a model for those who wished to found other local governments, while the decree of 10 May 1810, denying Ameri-

---

[1] Conde de Toreno, *Historia del levantamiento, guerra y revolución de Espana* (5 vols. Madrid, 1835), II, Apéndice, pp. 32–4.
[2] García Huidobro, 'Las Cortes de Cádiz', p. 336.
[3] *Ibid*.   [4] *CHDI*, XVIII, 223.

cans the right to submit matters of '*gracia y justicia*' to the Regency for the time being, was a further encouragement to form just such a government.[1] The Spanish precedents and the implied Spanish encouragement were of great importance for the Chileans, as they were for other Spanish Americans. The enthusiastic propaganda of the Spanish liberals was not only imbibed. It was reinterpreted to mean that local Juntas in America were necessary and essential. As the Venezuelan writer Manuel Palacio Fajardo later put it, 'it was not extraordinary that the South Americans listened with avidity to these doctrines, or that they should determine to avail themselves of the first opportunity to put them into practice'.[2]

LOCAL NEEDS AND PRESSURES

The idea of a national Junta was a definite response to the constitutional dilemma imposed by outside events, but it was also at any rate in part the logical outcome of certain needs and pressures which exerted themselves inside the Captaincy-General of Chile. Among the most important of these local processes was the rise of the Cabildo of Santiago to a position of power and influence. In a very real sense the Cabildo won the political initiative between October 1808 and September 1810, and became the instrument of the revolution. At the beginning of the year 1808 the Cabildo, whatever its previous role at certain periods during the colony, was largely uninfluential and inactive as a body. It was composed of minor and unimportant figures. This state of affairs altered with the growth of tension in the international crisis. In July 1808 García Carrasco agreed to the appointment of twelve 'auxiliary councillors'. These included José Antonio de Rojas, Manuel de Salas, Ignacio Carrera, and (as secretary) Bernardo de Vera y Pintado—all of them men who at that stage could have been described as reformers and who later became ardent 'patriots'. The result of this measure was a sudden and striking increase in Cabildo activity. It was the Cabildo that led the demonstrations of support for the imprisoned Ferdinand, and

[1] *CHDI*, XVIII, 223.
[2] Palacio Fajardo, *Outline of the Revolution in Spanish America* (London, 1817), pp. 354–5.

which took in hand an impressive review of defence arrangements, proposing a large number of changes.[1] As a result, the Cabildo quickly gained in public esteem. 'According to the general opinion', an agent of the Central Junta reported, 'this has been the body that has acquired most credit in the present circumstances.'[2]

The most significant aspect of this is that the Santiago Cabildo was, in effect, playing an exaggerated and 'national' role. It was attempting to run the affairs of the entire country, and it is hard to disagree with Amunátegui's assertion that this feverish burst of activity sheltered nothing less than 'the aspiration to constitute a national assembly'.[3] Certainly it is the case, as Amunátegui also noticed, that the Cabildo totally ignored the rights and duties of both the Royal Audiencia and the other Cabildos in Chile.[4] It also insisted that, in some sense, it now represented the whole people of the Captaincy-General, and that it had the natural right to pronounce on 'things important to the homeland and the common welfare'.[5] Infante, while discussing the Regency issue in August 1810, told the members of the Cabildo that 'each one of you is constituted a father of the fatherland,...and...gathered together, you have the power of the whole people'.[6] Later in the same year Infante asserted that the Cabildo was 'invested with the representation of all the people'.[7] By its increased activity in all spheres, and by its assertion of a representative capacity, the Cabildo plainly put itself forward as a contender for power within the Captaincy-General.

In the view of Julio Alemparte, the supreme function of all leading Spanish American Cabildos in 1808–10 was 'to act as bridges for the revolution'.[8] It is clear that in the Chilean case this is exactly what happened. The creole reformers gained control of the Cabildo from an early stage, and through it they

[1] Amunátegui Solar, *Teatro político*, ch. 5; *adem*, 'Noticias inéditas', p. 27; for the defence changes see Amunátegui, *Crónica*, I, 198.
[2] José Santiago Luco to the Supreme Junta, 9 December 1808, *CHDI*, VIII, 178.
[3] *Crónica*, I, 209.   [4] *Ibid*. 210.
[5] Petition to the Central Junta, 7 November 1809, Meza Villalobos, *Actividad política*, p. 94.
[6] *Representación*, 14 August, 1810, Medina, *Actas*, p. 36.
[7] *Representación*, 6 November 1810, *ibid*. p. 72.
[8] *El cabildo en Chile*, p. 405.

conducted their campaign for a national Junta. Infante, in an extremely interesting account of the circumstances leading up to the deposition of García Carrasco in July 1810, gives a particularly revealing glimpse of the lengths to which the Cabildo was prepared to go in securing its main aims. On 15 July, Infante relates, a meeting was held at the house of one of the principal *cabildantes* to plan the immediate campaign against the Governor.

It was agreed that on the following night, the eve of the day designated for the change in the Spanish government [of Chile], the two *alcades* and the *procurador* would meet to decide on a place where the Cabildo could be defended and could operate freely. Secondly, they would order the convocation of its members...The Cabildo's first dispositions would be to intimate to the Governor that his rule had ended, and that it would be assumed by the Cabildo for five days, during which time the people would be summoned...to name a provisional government until the meeting of a Congress of deputies elected by all the towns in the state. Such were the fundamentals.[1]

This was, when all is said and done, an extremist plan. There was no hint of any projected collaboration with the Audiencia or any other formal body in the province. The Cabildo was quite prepared to act alone and to proceed almost immediately to the appointment of a national government. In the event, as we have seen, the Audiencia acted faster than the Cabildo, and disposed of García Carrasco on its own initiative, after which the Cabildo's tactics had to be more discreet. The Cabildo's clear intention to ride to power on the wave of creole indignation at García Carrasco's dispatch of Rojas and Ovalle to Lima was, as it turned out, a miscalculation. Nevertheless, the Cabildo remained the focus of agitation for a Junta, and it was responsible for initiating the decisive negotiations with the Governor which eventually resulted in the achievement of its aim on 18 September. The Cabildo's decisive role in the revolution of 1810 was admitted soon afterwards by Infante. 'It is well known to everybody', he told his fellow councillors in November, 'that it was you who, with indefatigable zeal and constancy, worked for the installation of a Junta, overcoming the arduous and serious

[1] 'Relación de los sucesos desarrollados...', *CHDI*, XVIII, 39.

difficulties which are the consequence of any proposal to change the government.'[1] By November 1810, in fact, the Cabildo's exalted notion of its own importance had led it into an attempt to keep the new Junta under its control, in the matter of the timing of the congressional elections. This was a natural outcome of the Cabildo's role in the movement for home rule. For the Junta was nothing if not the child of the Cabildo.

A second local factor which hastened the advent of the Junta was, as we have seen, the ill-fated governorship of Francisco Antonio García Carrasco. To judge from the hyperbole employed by his many enemies, García Carrasco might be thought to have been one of the nastiest tyrants of history. Such a verdict would, of course, be absurd—there is little evidence to suggest that he was anything but amiable personally.[2] But there can be small doubt that the Chileans came to regard their Governor with bitter disdain and contempt. Manuel de Salas, in more than one graphically phrased document, contrasted García Carrasco's rule with that of his efficient predecessors, 'the active O'Higgins, the just and benevolent Avilés, the wise, noble and virtuous Muñoz de Guzmán', with whose departure from the scene, Salas added, 'the happy tranquillity of Chile vanished, as did the liberty of Rome on the death of Pompey and Caesar'.[3] Certainly García Carrasco managed to mishandle virtually every issue with which he was confronted. He came to power in the first instance by insisting on his technical and legal right to do so—apparently at the behest of Juan Martínez de Rozas—though this was against the wishes of the Audiencia, which had an alternative candidate (from its own ranks) for the interim governorship. Within a month or two of this initial disagreement, García Carrasco alienated the University of San Felipe.[4] At first, however, he enjoyed the confidence of the Cabildo of Santiago, which in August 1808 petitioned for his appointment as Governor to be made permanent.[5] These good relations broke down towards the

[1] *Representación*, 6 November 1810, Medina, *Actas*, p. 72.
[2] Villalobos R., *Tradición y reforma*, pp. 158, 206 n.
[3] 'Motivos que ocasionaron la instalación...', *CHDI*, XVIII, 153.
[4] Amunátegui, *Cronica*, I, chs. 1–2.
[5] Barros Arana, VIII, 75.

end of the year,[1] and the Governor's private involvement in the brutal affair of the *Scorpion* lowered his standing even further, to such an extent that one of his loyal subordinates informed him frankly that 'a great revolution has taken place in the minds, interests and pretensions of a great part of the inhabitants of Chile'.[2] It was even hinted by some that the Governor was disloyal to the Crown,[3] perhaps because of his association with Rozas, but this accusation was swiftly belied by his inquisitorial attitude towards those who professed support for a national Junta. The sudden arrest of Rojas, Ovalle and Vera in May 1810 brought matters, as we have seen, to a head. Creole fury against García Carrasco reached a final spasm. The *óidor* Manuel de Irigoyen made it clear to the unfortunate Governor, at the time the Audiencia deposed him, that there was now 'general discontent' throughout Chile as a result of his misgovernment.[4] García Carrasco's mishandling of the Chilean situation was unquestionably a major cause of the political excitement which led to the creation of the Junta. An interesting confirmation of this point is that a formal justification for the Junta, written by Manuel de Salas for publication in Spain, was almost completely taken up with an account of García Carrasco's misdeeds (picturesquely presented) rather than with the type of arguments so successfully employed, for instance, by Infante in his speech on 18 September.[5] It would be interesting to speculate what would have happened in Chile had a more tactful and conciliatory Governor been in command during the crisis.

Accompanying this theme of rising discontent with the government went an alarming growth of bad feeling between the creoles and Peninsular Spaniards. That relations between the two racial groups had hitherto been good is strongly testified in several documents by Manuel de Salas. Chile, he recalled in 1815, had been one of the few places in Spanish America where 'that

---

[1] See Meza Villalobos, *Actividad política*, pp. 57–9.
[2] Francisco Antonio de la Carrera to García Carrasco, 1 March 1809, A.B.A. vol. 25-2(3), fo. 275.
[3] Meza Villalobos, *Actividad política*, pp. 66–7.
[4] Talavera, p.16.
[5] 'Motivos que ocasionaron la instalación...', *CHDI*, XVIII, 151–169.

dismal rivalry' between them was unknown.[1] Francisco Antonio Pinto, in his autobiographical fragment, also left a picture of this aspect of colonial life. 'The most complete harmony reigned between Chileans', he wrote, 'and even with the Spaniards.'[2] These good relations suffered a noticeable deterioration after the events of 1808. Ignacio Torres then maintained that a few 'traitors' were in fact trying to introduce 'discord between Europeans and Creoles, attempting to persuade them that they are divided into parties, which is false, since such parties do not exist'.[3] Manuel de Salas noted down on a scrap of paper some time in this period that a manuscript 'letter...against the Europeans in America' was circulating. 'It is good,' he added, evidently with some glee.[4] The division seems to have deepened as the proposal to establish a Junta gained ground amongst the creoles. At all events, by April or May 1810, José Antonio de Rojas was heard defining his political aims, somewhat brusquely, as 'independence—and finish with all the Europeans'.[5] As the tense winter of 1810 wore on, the division became still deeper, the racial cleavage running along political lines as well. '*All* the Europeans,' ran a letter written in August, 'together with the wisest and soundest Chileans, are against those who favour the Junta plan.'[6] By September relations had reached a point of acute crisis. During the hurried consultations that resulted in the Cabildo Abierto of 18 September, the Cabildo, after discussing the matter with the Governor, agreed to attempt to pacify the populace, but was obliged to do this along racial lines, entrusting the creoles to one man and the Peninsular Spaniards to another.[7] At much the same moment the Audiencia observed that widespread 'uneasiness and anxiety' had developed.[8] José Miguel Infante, in his speech on 18 September, mentioned that tension had been increasing steadily: 'hatred and aversion between the two factions mounted day by day, until they menaced each other

---

[1] Letter of 28 August 1815 circulated secretly in Santiago, Salas, *Escritos*, II, 191. Cf. 'Motivos que ocasionaron...', *CHDI*, XVIII, 152.
[2] 'Apuntes autobiográficos', p. 87.   [3] *Informe*, p. 27.
[4] 'Anónimo', n.d., Salas, *Escritos*, III, 378.   [5] *Proceso seguido*, p. 15.
[6] J. J. Rodríguez Zorrilla to Fray Diego Rodríguez, 26 August 1810, *CHDI*, IX, 47–8.
[7] *Acta* of 13 September 1810, Medina, *Actas*, p. 47.
[8] *Oficio* of 13 September 1810, *ibid.* p. 49.

with extermination'.[1] The historic *Acta* which recorded the creation of the Junta made mention of this factor, and Agustín Eyzaguirre,[2] one of the chief agitators for a change, saw the restoration of peace as a main aim of the Cabildo Abierto.[3] And in a sermon preached soon afterwards, a Dominican father rejoiced over the ending of what he called 'a tempest of afflictions, frights and fears'.[4] It is plain, then, that the situation in August and September 1810 had shown signs of becoming unmanageable. The uncertainty could only be ended by a clear decision either for or against a Junta.

There remains one final local aspect to be considered: the efforts of the Junta of Buenos Aires to influence the course of events in Chile. The May Revolution in Buenos Aires was not only a living example to Chileans who supported the notion of a national government; it was in itself ideologically expansionist. The extensive trade links between Santiago and the Argentine capital were an advantage from the viewpoint of the Argentine Junta, as the Viceroy of Peru was to note later on.[5] The presence in Chile of Argentine or pro-Argentine figures such as Juan Martínez de Rozas, Juan Pablo Fretes,[6] Bernardo de Vera y Pintado and Manuel Dorrego (who was later to make a tragic appearance in the history of his own country) was an added assistance. In August 1810, the Buenos Aires government sent a letter to Santiago urging the organization of a 'legitimate representative authority' in Chile.[7] Alvarez Jonte, the first Argentine commissioner to Chile, was given specific propaganda tasks to this end even before the Chilean Junta was set up,[8] though he did not arrive in Santiago until after that event. A natural

---

[1] *CHDI*, xviii, 221.

[2] Agustín Eyzaguirre Arechavala (1766–1837). Member of the 1811 Congress and the 1813–14 Junta; exiled to Juan Fernández, 1814–17; Senator, 1824; Acting President of the Republic, 1826–7.

[3] To Manuel Romero, 30 September 1810, Eyzaguirre, *Archivo epistolar*, p. 235.

[4] Fr Antonio Guerrero on 11 October 1810, *CHDI*, xviii, 339.

[5] Abascal, ii, 160.

[6] An Argentine priest resident in Chile at this time; a close friend of Bernardo O'Higgins; member of the 1811 Congress.

[7] To the Cabildo of Santiago, 30 August 1810, Mitre, i, 305. Mariano Moreno wrote to the Governor of Chile on the same day, offering to support him in the event of an attack by Peru, Levene, p. 137.   [8] Alvarez Jonte, p. 46.

target for the efforts of Buenos Aires was Juan Martínez de Rozas, whose sympathies were not merely revolutionary but also decidedly pro-Argentine. A secret agent, Gregorio Gómez, was sent to Chile with an encouraging letter for Rozas from the Argentine leaders Belgrano and Castelli, but he was arrested at the frontier on his arrival in the Captaincy-General at the end of July 1810. Despite this, three members of the Junta party (José Gregorio Argomedo, Bernardo de Vera y Pintado, and Gaspar Marín) managed to gain access to Gómez and the letter was probably passed on to Rozas.[1] Gómez was certainly not the only Argentine agent in Chile in the period between the May and September revolutions, but it is likely that the active intervention of such agents counted for less than propaganda and example in general. A certain amount, perhaps even a good deal, of patriot propaganda reached Chile from the far side of the Cordillera after May. The royalist writer Manuel Antonio Talavera, an eye-witness of the first stages of the Chilean revolution, referred in August 1810 to 'all the poison and venom in the public papers' coming from Argentina.[2] He was later to characterize the Chilean Junta as 'the legitimate daughter of the Junta of Buenos Aires'.[3]

THE CREOLE PROGRAMME

The September Junta was the creole response to a number of dilemmas. Yet it would be wrong to assume that these local needs and pressures together with the constitutional problem provided the main motive force which created the political initiative of 18 September 1810. The creoles had a programme. The Junta was seen as the essential first step on the path towards the fulfilment of this programme. The creole leaders had specific political reforms in mind, and a set of basic theoretical ideas with which to justify their revolution. By 1814, when much had altered in Spanish America, it seemed obvious to Fray Camilo Henríquez that

the real motives which occasioned the setting up of Juntas were... equality of rights, open trade, internal government in the hands of

---

[1] Tocornal, pp. 178–81. [2] Talavera, p. 35. [3] *Ibid.* p. 318.

friends of the country who would stimulate its welfare, and the apportionment of public positions amongst its inhabitants, to well-deserving citizens.[1]

The movement for a Junta was something more, in fact, than a legalistic concern to settle constitutional problems, important as these were. The various local processes I have described were symptoms, not merely causes. This was a movement for what, referring to the tradition of Anglo-Irish history, we must call Home Rule. At first it represented little more than the fear that Napoleon's massive armies would overcome what was left of free Spain—a prospect which seemed entirely possible in the Chilean winter of 1810—and the natural desire to assure a government in Chile which would not be subordinate to the Corsican 'usurper'. Francisco Antonio Pinto recalled in later years how he had first heard Manuel de Cotapos, a prominent creole leader, express the view in 1809 that Chile should try to set up a government that would inspire confidence and which would not betray the province to the enemy.[2] The example of certain highly placed Spanish leaders—Infante named them in his memorandum to the Cabildo on the Regency issue[3]—was a sobering one. If *they* could commit high treason, who could guarantee the Chileans that their own Spanish Governor would not follow suit at some stage? Over and above this, there was the whole question of defence and the need to make more efficient arrangements in this sphere. Chileans had been anxious about the state of military preparedness in the colony ever since the English Invasions in the River Plate in 1806 and 1807. Juan Martínez de Rozas made the point well in a letter to his friend José Antonio de Rojas: 'We can do little here to help our motherland, unless it be with money, which we have done already. But we can do a great deal to help ourselves.'[4]

This particular motive—the creoles' desire to be the masters of their own house at a time of imperial emergency—cannot be regarded as trifling. But the reformers wanted more. Agustín Eyzaguirre, contemplating the possibility of a national Congress

[1] *Carta a Don Pacifico Rufino de San Pedro por H.V.*, 25 May 1814, reprinted in *Arch.O'H.* II, 254. [2] 'Apuntes autobiográficos', p. 96.
[3] *Representación*, 14 August 1810, Medina, *Actas*, p. 38
[4] Letter of 3 September 1809, *Proceso seguido*, p. 29.

soon after the installation of the September Junta, believed that such a body would work 'to make a firm and stable government, and form laws to assure our liberty'.[1] What did he mean by 'liberty' in this context? He himself provides the answer in a letter he wrote soon afterwards: 'a wise constitution which will deliver us from despotism and arbitrary rule in the future'.[2] The agitation for the Junta, therefore, implied the demand for a measure of political reform. It also implied the demand for a measure of social and economic reform. This became evident from the first moments of the crisis. The Cabildo of Santiago, when naming its agent to go to Spain, expressed the hope of Spanish 'benevolence' towards the Chilean economy.[3] 'We believe the era of this country's prosperity has arrived,' the Cabildo told the Central Junta on 4 February 1809, and it hoped then that the Central Junta would listen carefully and sympathetically to the 'frank representations' of its 'well-deserving vassals'.[4] A particularly interesting expression of this theme is to be found in a speech written by Juan Egaña for a university function at which García Carrasco was honoured in November 1809. Chileans, said Egaña, were 'full of hope in the regeneration of the monarchy', but there were many important reforms which needed to be carried out. 'Agriculture and trade, which form the real wealth of the people,' cried out to be 'stimulated, well directed, and freed from the impediments which hinder their advance'. Education was backward, Egaña admitted sadly, but such was the character of the Chilean people that a strong hand could create great currents of progress. Egaña concluded that the chief problem lay in a considerable 'want of resources', and that this want was 'principally due to the lack of a good political organization'.[5] These were remarkably frank words, even though they were set in the middle of a hypocritical paean of praise for García Carrasco.

It seems profitless to deny, therefore, that the 'very pro-

[1] To Miguel Eyzaguirre, 26 November 1810, Eyzaguirre, *Archivo epistolar*, p. 238.
[2] To Juan Ruiz, 4 January 1811, *ibid.* p. 243.
[3] *Acta* of 2 December 1808, Amunátegui, *Crónica*, I, 222.
[4] Meza Villalobos, *Actividad política*, p. 157.
[5] Speech of 15 November 1809, *CHDI*, XVIII, 19–21.

nounced desire for social betterment' which Amunátegui noticed amongst the first Cabildo statements after the start of the crisis[1] became deeper as time went on. One of the verses found amongst the papers of José Antonio de Rojas after his arrest in May 1810 put the point clearly enough: 'Sure of her rights, America demands trade, markets, highways, factories, and agriculture.'[2] There was an important element in the revolutionary programme which was concerned with the redress of past grievances, both political and social. At first it seems to have been assumed that the remedy for Chile's ills—and it should not be forgotten that these had been expounded in some detail by Salas and other precursors before 1810—was to come from a regenerated Spain. Presently, however, it became clear that only a local Chilean government could set about the task in a conscientious and clear-sighted manner. Only two months after the creation of the Junta, Infante dwelt on the work of the promised national Congress in one of his memoranda. 'And after two hundred years of a government which has been in no way propitious for the Americas...', he asked, 'what injuries will [the deputies] *not* have to protest against?'[3]

Grievances there certainly had been, and these demanded swift action, but outwardly at least the Junta was set up to preserve the rights of Ferdinand VII. The Kingdom of Chile remained (at least on paper) 'ever loving, ever loyal,...one of the most precious jewels that embellish the diadem of the Adorable Ferdinand'.[4] But it was now made clear that Chile owed allegiance to the King rather than to Spain. 'We are vassals of the King of Spain, but not of Spain without her King,' wrote Manuel de Salas in the *Diálogo de los porteros* of 1811, one of the classic statements of the case for a Junta.[5] This was, certainly, one of the fundamental justifications for home rule. It was repeated over and over again: 'we swear allegiance to the King, not Spain'.[6] The unknown author of the *Catecismo político cristiano* put it more formally:

[1] *Crónica*, I, 223.   [2] 'Décimas', n.d., *Proceso seguido*, p. 57.
[3] *Representación*, 14 December 1810, Medina, *Actas*, p. 85.
[4] Junta to the Spanish Ambassador, Rio de Janeiro, 2 October 1810,, *CHDI*, xxv, 317–18.
[5] *Diálogo de los porteros*, p. 177.
[6] 'Décimas', n.d., *Proceso seguido*, p. 59.

The inhabitants and provinces of America have sworn fidelity to the Kings of Spain alone...They have not sworn fidelity to, nor are they vassals and dependents of, the inhabitants and provinces of Spain. The inhabitants and provinces of Spain do not, therefore, possess authority, jurisdiction or command over the inhabitants and provinces of America.[1]

Juan Egaña, who submitted a lengthy doctrinal statement about the position of the 1810 revolution some five years later when in exile on Juan Fernández, asserted that Chile was 'united to the nation solely by the link of the monarch', and that it had the same rights as any other kingdom of the Empire.[2]

This was a highly important point—and strictly justifiable in relation to the pre-Bourbon Spanish theory of empire—but the political programme of the creole reformers did not stop there. It implied a very definite proposal of restraint on the powers of the King. One of Bernardo de Vera y Pintado's manuscript proclamations of 1808–9 contained the principle that 'the people confer the crown on the man best capable of upholding its welfare; the people will never grant its power in order to be made unhappy'.[3] Hence there was a great need for some kind of constitution which would delineate the exact rights and obligations of both monarch and people. The author of the *Catecismo político cristiano*, examining a series of possible future developments in the imperial crisis, laid down a rule for the relationship between King and creoles.

If by some happy occurrence [Ferdinand] breaks the heavy chains he bears and takes refuge amongst his children in America, then you, Americans, will deliver up to him these precious remnants of his dominions;... but taught by the experience of all ages, you will also form a constitution which will be impregnable...to the abuses of despotism and arbitrary power, and which will assure your liberty, your dignity, your rights and prerogatives as men and as citizens.[4]

Such a constitution, it was widely agreed, could only be framed and sanctioned by a nationally elected Congress. The Junta, when chosen, could never be more than a provisional authority, en-

---

[1] Amor de la Patria, p. 106.
[2] 'Memorial escrito en el presidio para dirigirse al Rey Fernando vii', *El Chileno consolado*, ii, 8–9.   [3] Arcos, p. 337.   [4] Amor de la Patria, p. 106.

trusted with the day-to-day administration and with the specific task of summoning a Congress. It is clear...', said Infante, 'that the people...should elect their representatives so that, gathered in a general Congress, they can determine the sort of government that is to operate until the sovereign is restored to his throne.'[1] The promise to hold a Congress was formally embodied in the *Acta* of 18 September 1810, but the idea itself was common property to all the revolutions of 1810.[2] It derived from the political liberalism of the American and French Revolutions and also, perhaps more forcibly, from the more recent example of the summoning of the Spanish Cortes. 'Summon the Cortes!' had been a persistent battle-cry of the Spanish liberals, and it is hardly surprising that the Spanish Americans, as well as their cousins in Spain, took the hint. Although the American dominions had had the right to hold their own Cortes,[3] it had never been fully exercised and it can hardly be argued that the notion of a national Congress in 1810 was descended from this shadowy fiction.

Underlying the whole of the creole programme was a theory of popular sovereignty which, though never formally expressed at length, nevertheless informed all the procedures of the patriots of 1810. From what source, it was asked, did the power of the King originally emanate? Manuel de Salas provided the answer in his *Diálogo de los porteros*: 'Kings come from God by the hand of the people, and to serve the people's welfare.'[4] The author of the *Catecismó político cristiano* went into the matter at greater length. Was the people, he asked, able to depose its King?

The people, which has conferred the right of command on the King, can, like any constituent party, revoke its powers and name other guardians who better correspond to the public good. This has been the opinion— or to put it better, this has been the established doctrine—of the saints, philosophers, and wise men of antiquity; but the kings have proscribed it in the territories of their Empire.[5]

The monarch, therefore, possessed power in order to preserve the public welfare, and it was the people, the community as a whole,

[1] *Representación*, 14 December 1810, Medina, *Actas*, p. 84.
[2] See Belaunde, p. 142.   [3] Walton, *Exposé*, p. 23.
[4] *Diálogo de los porteros*, pp. 180–1.   [5] *Amor de la Patira*, p. 100.

which conferred power in the first instance. The corollary of this doctrine could be stated very briefly.

Question. And if the government is dissolved by the death or captivity of the King and all his family, to whom does authority return, and who can organize it anew?
Answer. Authority returns to the people from whom it came forth.[1]

This theory was full of the most significant possibilities for the Chileans and Spanish Americans in general. It gave them a complete justification for the provisional governments they wished to set up in response to both their circumstances and their aspirations. But much more than this, it gave them a weighty theoretical argument with which to justify any *future* changes in government they might wish to make. In this sense, despite the fulsome references to the Adorable Ferdinand which appear in their public documents, the men of 1810 were stating a decidedly revolutionary position, and this position seems the more revolutionary the more the colonial background of passive obedience to Peninsular direction is considered. For the patriots of 1810, the monarch was no longer able to exercise sovereignty. The people had reassumed it. The people was now able to bestow to in some new authority. This was the line taken by Infante in August 1810 when he asserted that if the King 'at any time abdicates his throne, it passes by law to his nearest relative, and if there is none, the people reassumes, *jure devoluto*, the power to choose a King'.[2] According to Infante, this was what happened in the case of Ferdinand VII, whose detention in France ranked as 'civil death', equivalent to abdication in its effects.[3] In 1811 José Miguel Carrera referred to this as the commonly held explanation of the political changes of 1810. 'It is certain', he wrote, 'that with the King in captivity and having resigned the throne, the peoples of the Spanish monarchy reassumed the possession of the sovereignty they had deposited there.'[4] The Junta itself, in a letter to Lord Strangford,[5] stated the doctrine in slightly more modern language.

[1] *Amor de la Patria*, p. 100.   [2] *Representación*, 14 August 1810, Medina, *Actas*, p. 39.
[3] *Representación*, 14 December 1810, *ibid.* p. 84.
[4] *Manifesto*, 4 December 1811, *SCL*, I, 197.
[5] British Ambassador at Rio de Janeiro.

The captivity of Ferdinand VII, it affirmed, 'has put into operation the people's imprescriptible right to choose a representative government worthy of its confidence, and this capital, using the faculties granted by the metropolis, has installed the provisional Junta'.[1] One or two subsidiary points connected with the basic core of doctrine may be mentioned briefly at this juncture. Infante held that, even though in normal times the monarch held sovereign power, the people had never conferred it on him absolutely. 'When the people bestowed all its authority on the King,' he wrote, 'it reserved certain points by which it could assure its own security and the preservation of its rights, by establishing Cabildos to which it conferred all its powers in order that the Cabildos might represent it.'[2] It did not matter to Infante that this supposition bore little relation to recent historical reality. In fact, this could be explained away in somewhat sinister terms, and a moral could be drawn. Referring to the various 'faculties reserved' by the Cabildos, Infante noted:

With the design of furthering despotism, there has always been a constant effort to suppress these faculties, and it is for this reason that the Cabildos have so little authority—to the great prejudice of the people they represent. However, since non-usage is not sufficient to invalidate laws,...Chileans should resume their rights and put them into operation.[3]

Here Infante, like the liberals in Spain, looked back beyond the era of Bourbon regalism to the decay of municipal liberties under the Hapsburgs. He instinctively shared the Peninsular liberal view of the pristine perfection of the late-medieval Spanish constitution.[4]

In one way and another, therefore, the basic theory behind the creation of the Junta of 1810 was concerned with the sovereignty of the community, and the return of sovereignty to the people as a result of the 'civil death' of Ferdinand VII. A tenuous form of social contract, of the ruler–people type, was clearly implicit.

[1] Letter of 2 October 1810, *CHDI*, xxv, 320.
[2] *Representación*, 6 November 1810, Medina, *Actas*, p 73.   [3] *Ibid.* pp. 73–4.
[4] For this interpretation of history as a background to Spanish liberalism see Richard Herr, *The Eighteenth Century Revolution in Spain* (Princeton, N.J., 1958), pp. 337–47.

On the surface of things, it might seem that the framework of ideas used by the Chileans in 1810 stemmed from an essentially Spanish tradition, according to which power originated with God, passing from Him through the people to the sovereign.[1] And yet while much of the thought of 1810 is 'populist' in this sense, its main impulse seems to me to have been liberal. Certainly the political ideas expressed lacked the coherence and firmness of the revolutionary ideology which was so soon to be shaped. But some of the main elements in that ideology were already discernibly present: popular sovereignty, a system of rights, the idea of a representative assembly, the need for a constitution, and so forth. Spanish legal precedents were rightly regarded as important, which is why José Miguel Infante, on the night of the arrest of Rojas, Ovalle and Vera, was searching through his law-books to find a clear-cut justification of the Junta principle.[2] Yet at the same time, the patriots of 1810, like their counterparts in Spain itself, were eager to establish limitations on royal authority—in fact, to bring about a constitutional monarchy. This is apparent from the early demands for a Congress and constitution. The Chileans of 1810 were not merely demanding (and attaining) home rule for themselves. They were also rejecting absolutism.

THE MASK OF FERDINAND VII

The September Junta represented the triumph of autonomist hopes. It protested its fervent loyalty to Ferdinand VII. Though the political doctrine which underscored its installation was revolutionary, this was probably not noticed by more than a handful of people, for only an educated minority of creoles and Peninsular Spaniards were capable of reasoning in this way. To the majority of unlettered Chileans, the new Junta was, as the Cabildo of San Felipe put it, 'the representative of [Ferdinand's] royal person and the other legitimate authorities'.[3] The district governor of Copiapó could write that 'far from inspiring senti-

[1] Giménez Fernández, pp. 13–15. For these ideas elsewhere in America, see Belaunde, ch. vii. For the sixteenth-century background, consult Bernice Hamilton, *Political Thought in Sixteenth Century Spain* (Oxford, 1963), chs. 2–3.
[2] Zapiola, p. 177.　　　[3] *Acta* of 5 October 1810, *CHDI*, xviii, 258.

ments of novelty in the people, this wise and proper measure, laid down by God Himself, has drawn forth sweet and joyful "*vivas*" from the innermost depths of the heart, as much from the common people as from the aristocracy'.[1] The strongly loyalist tone of the governor's communication may be taken as typical of the general provincial reaction—unanimously favourable—to the news of the creation of the Junta.[2] It is also worth mentioning at this point that the Junta presented so legal an appearance that it actually succeeded in gaining recognition by the Council of Regency in Spain;[3] 'this was the only Junta the government of Spain ever acknowledged'.[4] The facts seem to speak for themselves. The Chileans went about the task of securing an autonomous regime with such delicacy that the Peninsular authorities accepted the fact without demur.

It is impossible to leave the matter there. The Junta issued no flamboyant declaration of independence, but by its very existence it went some way towards this. 'We Americans', wrote Vera in 1813, 'named our own government; that was already a *de facto* emancipation.'[5] The historian's curiosity compels him to ask whether the loyalty so evident on the surface did not conceal some deeper purpose: the purpose of total independence rather than home rule. It has sometimes been supposed that the creoles used loyalty to the King as a tactic rather than out of conviction, and that they assumed what has been called 'the mask of Ferdinand VII' to hide their real aims. The creole movement was autonomist; that much is certain. But was there an element within the movement which had separatist aims going far beyond autonomism? Perhaps no final answer can be given to this question in the case of Chile, but there is at least some evidence that can be brought to bear on this most fascinating of the enigmas of 1810. What grounds, first of all, are there for supposing that the creole home-rule movement included a separatist element?

I have already mentioned the heightening of discords between creoles and Peninsular Spaniards in the winter of 1810. This was

[1] Juan Bautista Cortés to the Junta, 22 October 1810, *CHDI*, xviii, 227.
[2] For examples of this, see *CHDI*, xviii, 226–336.
[3] Real Orden, 14 April 1811, Matta Vial, 'La Junta de Gobierno de 1810', p. 59.
[4] Walton, *Exposé*, p. 98. [5] *Semanario Republicano*, no. 4, 28 August 1813.

accompanied, intellectually, by an anti-Spanish feeling which prefigured the full-scale *leyenda negra* of the revolutionary ideology a few years later.[1] This feeling expressed itself in two ways: first, in a clearly enunciated hope that Spain would be defeated in the war with France, and second, in a catalogue of the iniquities and injustices of the colonial era. Ignacio Torres noted that as soon as news of the royal journey to the French frontier reached Chile prophets of gloom began to abound.[2] José María de Rozas greeted the news of military disasters in the Peninsula with a joy which Torres found incomprehensible and disgraceful.[3] In 1810 José Antonio de Rojas was accused of having put forward the view that Spain was lost 'with demonstrations of joyfulness'.[4] More significant, than this, however, is Torres' assertion that a group of prominent creoles (including José María de Rozas, Manuel de Salas, Bernardo de Vera y Pintado, Carlos Correa, and sometimes Juan Martínez de Rozas) had been discussing ways and means of discrediting news of any Spanish victories that might come through.[5] When news of some successes arrived on 3 October 1808, Vera apparently replied to critics of his unpatriotic viewpoint that a Spanish victory over the French would be 'the final misfortune for the Americas'.[6] In 1810 Vera was supposed to have said that 'America would never be content if it remained under the domination of Spain'.[7] Remarks such as these, if they were made at all, must certainly temper any uncritical acceptance of the creoles' effusions of loyalty to Ferdinand VII.

Alongside these statements there went the first frank expressions of an anti-Spanish 'black legend'. Vera, in his legal defence against the charge of subversion in 1810, spoke of the 'excesses of that base, sordid and cowardly policy under which, by the lowest means and dispositions, Americans have been regarded as real slaves, obliged to suffer every sort of outrage in silence'.[8] The unknown author of the *Catecismo político cristiano* went much further than this. Half-way through the work comes an eruption of wrathful indignation.

[1] See chapter 5, pp.   . [2] *Informe*, p. 4. [3] *Ibid.* p. 6.
[4] *Proceso seguido*, p. 11. [5] *Informe*, p. 22. [6] *Ibid.* p. 18.
[7] *Proceso seguido*, p. 13. [8] *Ibid.* p. 321.

Unfortunate Americans, you are treated like slaves. The oppression in which you have lived, and the tyranny and despotism of your governors, have eradicated or suffocated the seeds of heroism and liberty in your hearts. European governors, oppressor-tyrants, inhuman barbarians, tremble!...Tremble, I repeat, for even now a terrible sword of vengeance hangs over your heads. Cruel usurpers of the authority of the people...[1]

Later on, the same writer showed clearly that the creoles resented the implications of some of the nobly phrased decrees from the Central Junta and Regency in Spain.

Americans, restrain the irritation within your breasts. In another age, the declaration of a pontiff was necessary for the primitive inhabitants of America to be taken for rational beings. Today, the declaration of a government is needed for you to be reputed an integral and essential part of the Spanish Empire, for you to be considered as raised to the high dignity of free men, for you to cease being what you have been in the past—that is, miserable slaves.[2]

Almost in the same breath the unknown catechist commented: 'You have been colonists, and your Provinces have been miserable colonies and factories;...this infamous quality cannot be wiped out by fine words.'[3] This last sentence recalls Juan Martínez de Rozas' reaction to the Central Junta's high-minded promises. To Rozas the Central Junta was nothing more than 'a college of philosopher kings', generally untrustworthy from the American viewpoint. Despite the Junta's fulsome declarations, thought Rozas, there was always a real chance that the American dominions would again become 'what they have always been: colonies and factories in every sense of the word'.[4] This emphasis on the evils of the past was soon to become a cardinal feature of the revolutionary mystique in Chile. Significantly, it is in the *Catecismo político cristiano* that we meet, for the first time, a detailed list of Spanish iniquities—the commercial monopoly, excessive taxation, the lack of educational progress, and so on—which afterwards became almost a standard way of denouncing the motherland.

[1] *Amor de la Patria*, p. 102.   [2] *Ibid.* p. 107.   [3] *Ibid.*
[4] To José Antonio de Rojas, 24 July 1809, *Proceso seguido*, p. 25.

75

Political separation cannot be conclusively deduced from statements like these, although it is probable that the men who had debeloped this anti-Spanish viewpoint would be thinking almost automatically about the possibility of independence. I must next examine a series of statements made by royalists in Chile, consisting of vague suspicions that something untoward was occurring beneath the surface of events. In 1808, for instance, Ignacio Torres claimed that a handful of 'traitors' was trying to dampen down enthusiasm for Ferdinand and the Spanish cause.[1] The traitors he thus accused were some ten or so leading creoles, some of whom were almost certainly not separatists. At the same time, Torres limited his accusations of really serious treachery to four men: 'four wretched agitators are promoting novel ideas of independence', he wrote.[2] The identity of these four men is debatable, but Juan Martínez de Rozas was amongst them, and evidently their leader.[3] Torres' evidence, however, is of particular interest because he himself soon became a supporter of the scheme for a Junta. Not that he exaggerated the importance of the 'four wretched agitators'. He devoted a good deal of time and energy to denouncing their activities and documenting his suspicions, yet they were not, in the end, to be regarded as more than a few 'factious men who, taking advantage of the inactivity of the government, which is in the power of their leader Dr Juan [Martínez de] Rozas, could perhaps cause a certain amount of harm'.[4]

Torres was by no means alone in his suspicions. The royalist Juan José Jiménez de Guerra reported to the Supreme Junta of Cadiz in November 1808: 'This capital city of Santiago..., though inhabited by many loyal men, unfortunately contains a rabble of traitors who...are...trying to seduce men with the ideas of independence and insubordination towards the Supreme Junta.'[5] Jiménez de Guerra also affirmed that the Cabildo of Santiago was sending out dubious propaganda to other Chilean Cabildos, and even to the Cabildo of Buenos Aires.[6] There is some

---

[1] *Informe*, p. 27.
[2] To Francisco de Saavedra, 7 November 1808, *CHDI*, VIII, vii.   [3] *Ibid.*
[4] *Ibid.*   [5] Letter of 9 November 1808, C.C.M.M. vol. 219, fo. 228.   [6] *Ibid.*

evidence that this had been going on over the previous months.[1] Jiménez de Guerra was disposed to take a more serious view of the situation than Torres.

The confidence the generosity of our spirit inspires in us [he wrote] has often been—and is even more today—the cause of the tragedies we deplore; and it is this confidence that is dissuading this Capital from curbing evil defamers with an exemplary punishment, on the vain pretext that it is nothing; they are only talkers; they are incapable of carrying out their ideas. It is not borne in mind that, with similar reasoning and unfounded confidence, the warnings from Peru were ignored back in 1779. What happened then was that Túpac Amaru caused great disasters which could have been prevented if the help demanded early on had been sent more quickly.[2]

It could well be that Jiménez de Guerra had a lively imagination, and yet something had obviously occurred to set his mind working in this direction, and the reference to the insurrection of Túpac Amaru indicates the seriousness of his reading of events. Just over a month later Jiménez de Guerra informed the Supreme Junta that in the 'disloyal Capital of Chile' there was 'a complete lack of love for our King'. All that good Spaniards and royalists could hope for, he added, was the dispatch of a strong-minded Governor who could deal with 'so faithless a people'.[3]

Governor García Carrasco himself maintained a suspicious attitude towards the creole reformers, particularly in the latter half of his short period of government. In mid 1809, in a letter to Spain, he referred briefly to a separatist conspiracy headed by the *regidor* Nicolás Matorras, though he admitted that his evidence was insufficient to warrant a prosecution.[4] García Carrasco was informed that the Matorras conspiracy was the work of dissident elements known as 'free-masons' and united together in a 'pernicious congregation' which styled itself the 'Republican Junta'.[5] Thereafter the Governor grew increasingly inclined to discover conspirators at every turn. Early in 1810, on receiving the

[1] See two letters from Buenos Aires to Santiago at this time: J. Merino to M. J. Semir, 16 September 1808, and M. de Alzaga to A. J. García, same date, *CHDI*, VIII, 50–3.
[2] C.C.M.M. vol. 219, fo. 230.
[3] Letter of 12 December 1808, C.C.M.M. vol. 219, fo. 237–42.
[4] García Carrasco to the King, June 1809, *CHDI*, VIII, xvii–xxi.
[5] Auto [1809], *CHDI*, VIII, 88.

newly elected *alcaldes* of the Cabildo of Santiago, he behaved with extreme discourtesy by accusing them of disloyalty and by describing the Cabildo as 'insubordinate' and as 'notoriously aspiring to independence'.[1] By May 1810 García Carrasco certainly believed that Rojas, Ovalle and Vera were the 'principal promoters of a republican establishment'.[2] And he was convinced that the Cabildo agitation at the time of his deposition in July was disloyal in its aims: 'The main object was independence,' he afterwards wrote, 'and to achieve it the destruction of the government was necessary.'[3] To García Carrasco, the proceedings of the 18 September were a solemn and disgraceful hypocrisy: 'That Junta... by shaking off the yoke of subordination, constituted itself absolute and independent, despite the fact that it recognized the sovereign authority of King Ferdinand VII as legitimate. But this was a chimera with which the traitors thought to hide their treachery at that time.'[4] Other royalists also thought that the publicly expressed loyalism of the 18 September was little more than a mask. In 1813 one of the expelled *óidores* of the Royal Audiencia observed, in a lengthy memoir, that the 'convulsions of the Capital' in 1810 had all been 'premeditated',[5] and that a profound degree of hypocrisy had characterized the Cabildo Abierto of 18 September. 'A distance as enormous as that between Heaven and earth', he wrote, separated 'what the *Acta* referred to and the reality of the event'.[6]

Before discussing the relevance of suspicions like these, I must first turn to the actual official accusations of separatism that were made in 1809 and 1810. The first case to be investigated was that of the two *chillanejos*, Pedro Arriagada and Fray Rosauro Acuña. Arriagada, it was claimed, had said that

there was no longer a King in Spain; that Joseph Bonaparte was sworn and crowned as such... That the Central Junta was composed of

---

[1] 'Carta de Santiago Leal a Patricio Español' [1810], *CHDI*, VIII, 229.
[2] To the King, 27 August 1810, *CHDI*, IX, 10.   [3] *Ibid. CHDI*, IX, 15.
[4] *Representación* [1811?], Vicuña Mackenna, *Coronel Figueroa*, Apéndice, p. 131.
[5] 'Manifiesto documentado que hace don José de Santiago Concha Jiménez Lobatión del Consejo de S. Magd. Oidor Decano de la Real Auda. de Chile, de su conducta en el tiempo de la revolución de dicho Reino. Stgo, 21 abril de 1813', C.C.M.M. vol. 224, fo. 297.
[6] *Ibid.* fo. 314.

usurpers...to whom subordination need not be rendered;...that what was best for the people was to seek to be independent of all nations and to shake off the Spanish yoke, becoming republicans; that this kingdom did not need a King.[1]

Acuña, it was alleged, had made similarly subversive statements, and had further admitted that several other people in Chillán were of the same opinion and were saying so openly.[2] Acuña and Arriagada were not punished severely (if at all) for having expressed these views, but, as I will show presently, there is good reason to assume that they meant what they said.[3]

On 17 April 1810 the Viceroy of the River Plate, Baltasar Hidalgo de Cisneros, informed Governor García Carrasco that he had heard of the existence in Chile of several subversive political groups, 'one advocating independence, another proposing subjection to foreign domination, but all of them determined to remove themselves from the rule of our august sovereign lord, Ferdinand VII'.[4] On 24 May, as a result of this communication from Cisneros, García Carrasco issued a statement which declared that certain parties were expressing opinions 'in favour of independence and liberty', and were trying to instil a spirit of 'insubordination and freedom', following 'the bad examples which the cities of La Paz and Quito, and Charcas, have given'.[5] The following day saw the arrest of Rojas, Ovalle and Vera, and evidence was quickly brought forward to show that these three men had all been making separatist and anti-Spanish statements of the sort already quoted, and that they were actively interested in plotting against the state.[6] Certain suggestive papers were found in possession of both Rojas and Vera, though nothing which could be described as openly subversive. Later, when the case was heard again, after García Carrasco had left the scene, several witnesses withdrew their allegations against the three men.

The standard defence consistently adopted by Rojas, Ovalle, and Vera was that while they honestly admitted having talked

---

[1] García Carrasco to Manuel de Irigoyen, 1 November 1809, Amunátegui, *Precursores*, III, 513.
[2] *Ibid.* III, 514.   [3] See note.   [4] *CHDI*, VIII, 260–1.
[5] Auto publicado por bando, 24 May 1810, *Proceso seguido*, pp. 242–3.
[6] Depositions of several witnesses, *Proceso seguido*, pp. 4–15.

about independence, they had never meant total separation from the Spanish Empire. Ovalle put this point with particular force.

What is understood by independence? Separation from the metropolis? That is not lawful, and I have always been heard to say that there is no justification for it...Now then, if the French conquer Spain (and God forbid that they should), ought we to be dependent on the French? Anybody who says 'yes' deserves to be hung, the same as anybody who says that we should subject ourselves to the English. So independence from these is both just and necessary.[1]

Later, in a letter urging the establishment of a national Junta as soon as possible, Ovalle asserted that he for one had never spoken of 'absolute independence',[2] and the vehemence of his denials is striking. For his part, Vera made a well-documented statement of an identical position when he came to defend himself against García Carrasco's charges later in the year.[3] And in a latter to the Bishop of Santiago he maintained firmly that Chile should 'stay independent for the sovereign while he still lives and for whoever succeeds him in the event of his death'.[4]

Two things are clear from these various accusations and defences: first, the term 'independence' was in use amongst creole reformers in 1809 and 1810, and second, there were degrees of independence being considered. Independence from France, if France overran Spain, or independence from the temporary and provisional governments of the Peninsula did not mean the same thing as total separation from the Empire, though the authorities may perhaps be pardoned for having supposed, as they obviously did, that the difference was not particularly significant. But plainly the search for a separatist element cannot be allowed to rest purely on the evidence provided by royalist suspicions, interesting and perhaps accurate as some of these were.

Domingo Amunátegui Solar affirmed on one occasion that there were only two men in Chile in 1810 who really believed in total independence from Spain: José Antonio de Rojas and

---

[1] *Representación*, Valparaíso, 28 May 1810, *CHDI*, VIII, 322–3.
[2] To the Cabildo of Santiago, 2 July 1810, *CHDI*, VIII, 325.
[3] 'Solicitud y defensa', October 1810, *Proceso seguido*, p. 316.
[4] To J. S. Rodríguez Zorrilla, 13 June 1810, Vicuña Mackenna, *Coronel Figueroa*, Apéndice, p. 137.

Bernardo O'Higgins.[1] It seems likely that the bulk of the Chilean creole elite did not want more than home rule, but even so this is carrying matters altogether too far. Separatist ideas and aims can reasonably be attributed to others beside Rojas and O'Higgins, and I must now review some of the evidence relating to the creole leaders most likely to have been less loyal to Ferdinand VII than the majority of their fellows. No final or conclusive list of the separatists in Chile can ever be drawn up, and the extent of the republican and anti-Spanish tendency will always be difficult to assess. Even so, there were some men working for complete independence within the home-rule movement, and some of them gave themselves away. It is convenient to divide the possible separatists into two groups: the nucleus of plotters based on Santiago, and the 'Southern' party centring on Concepción and Chillán.

A number of creole leaders in Santiago must be regarded as having been likely separatists in 1810. Bernardo de Vera y Pintado seems a fairly clear-cut case. Ignacio Torres numbered him amongst the 'factious men' he suspected of disloyalty in September 1808, and reported that he was one of the handful who tried to discredit the news of Spanish military successes.[2] At much the same period, Vera was drawing up manuscript proclamations and manifestos for hand-to-hand circulation amongst the creole reformers, and this seems to have been a fairly intensive activity.[3] He was also very active in the Cabildo's plan to depose García Carrasco,[4] and, at a banquet given on 31 July 1810 in honour of the newly appointed Governor, the Conde de la Conquista, he apparently created something of a stir by his 'indirect barbs against the monarchy,...and satires against the leaders of the royalist party'.[5] But most suggestive of all was his defence against the accusation of treason levelled against him by García Carrasco. Vera expressed the orthodox view already described—that 'independence' was not the same as 'absolute independence'—yet oddly enough one of the chief points of his case was that a man could not be punished for holding private opinions of this sort

---

[1] 'El principio de la revolución de 1810', *CHDI*, xxx, li.   [2] *Informe*, p. 22.
[3] Arcos, p. 337.   [4] *Ibid.*   [5] Gay, v, 112.

in any case. 'Neither philosophy nor morality', he wrote, 'has taught that *to long for independence* is a crime.'[1] It was on the basis of this point that Vera was presently found to be innocent.[2] Why should he have chosen to include it in his defence? Was it an implied admission that he himself *had* longed for independence? His later role in the '*Patria Vieja*', as one of the most ardent of the revolutionaries, also indicates that his agitation for a Junta in 1810 concealed a deeper end.

The evidence concerning José Antonio de Rojas, who has traditionally been regarded as a separatist and conspirator by Chilean historians, is somewhat scantier. He was already an old man by 1810. Whether or not he had been involved in the abortive 'conspiracy of the three Antonios' in 1780 is uncertain.[3] Though he was watched over by the authorities thereafter,[4] a point recalled by García Carrasco,[5] there is a possibility that this was as much for personal reasons as for any other.[6] Nevertheless, Rojas was a sceptical personality, and was not inclined to take a very favourable view of the colonial order. He was certainly at the heart of political discussions in late 1808 and early 1809, and was in continuous correspondence with Juan Martínez de Rozas. Late in 1808 he had been heard to say: 'It is now time to think of setting up a republic in Chile.'[7] It is hard not to conclude that Rojas deserved the honourable reputation for separation he acquired later on.

What of other possible separatists in the capital, apart from Rojas and Vera? Nicolás Matorras, a prominent member of the Cabildo, was classed by Torres amongst the 'suspicious subjects' of late 1808,[8] and was, as we have seen, thought by García Carrasco to have been at the head of a plot on behalf of independence in 1809.[9] Matorras was certainly a leading Cabildo

---

[1] *Proceso seguido*, p. 324.
[2] Dr Sánchez, *Vista fiscal*, 11 October 1810, *ibid.* p. 365.
[3] Amunátegui, *Precursores*, III, 202; Villalobos R., *Tradición y reforma*, pp. 143–5. The conspiracy is traditionally called 'the three Antonios' because the Frenchmen Gramusset and Berney were both Antoines, and Rojas' implication has often been assumed, though Villalobos R.'s evidence on this point is telling.
[4] Amunátegui, *Crónica*, II, 101–2.   [5] To the King, 27 August 1810, *CHDI*, IX, 10.
[6] See Amunátegui Solar, *La sociedad chilena*, II, 383–4.
[7] Torres, *Informe*, p. 17.   [8] *Ibid.* p. 6.   [9] See pp.   , nn.,   .

agitator and a firm advocate of the Junta. The case of Manuel de Salas is more obscure. His somewhat erratic political posturings between 1810 and 1815 make any final judgment or supposition in his case extremely difficult. Yet he was involved in the conversations of 1808–9 which Torres found so disturbing,[1] and was always a strong supporter of the Junta. If there were other separatists in the capital—and it seems at least probable that Carlos Correa[2] and Gaspar Marín[3] can be placed on any tentative list—they would certainly have been included in the circle around José Antonio de Rojas. I shall consider some further possibilities presently.

We are on much surer ground when dealing with the 'Southern' group of conspirators, based on Concepción and Chillán. The pivotal personality in the South was Bernardo O'Higgins. O'Higgins' influence during the period of the crisis was very far from being extensive, but he was closely connected with men whose political standing was more considerable than his own. In 1812, O'Higgins told his Argentine patriot friend Juan Florencio Terrada:

Since the 25th May [1810] you have had no other object in view than independence from Spain and the adoption of republican institutions, but in Chile neither your uncle [Juan Pablo Fretes],[4] nor Rozas nor I have dared declare openly that this has been our *true aim since the beginning of our revolution.*[5]

This sentence on its own would go a long way towards establishing O'Higgins' separatist intentions—and those of Rozas and Fretes—were these really in doubt. But they are not. All that is known of O'Higgins' background—conversion to the separatist cause by Miranda,[6] secret meetings with Fretes and José Cortés

---

[1] *Informe*, pp. 6, 17, 22.
[2] Carlos José Correa de Saa Lazón. Member of the 1811 Congress; exiled to Juan Fernández, 1814–17; his house appears to have been a major focus of revolutionary activity at this time.
[3] José Gaspar Marín Esquivel (1772–1839). Secretary of the Junta, 1810–11; member of the Congresses of 1811, 1825, 1828, 1831,–4; Senator, 1812–14 and 1829.
[4] Fretes' separatism is almost indubitable. He had met O'Higgins at Cadiz in 1802.
[5] Letter of June 1812, Vicuña Mackenna, *Vida de O'Higgins*, p. 129 n.
[6] O'Higgins to Mackenna, 5 January 1811, Cruz, *Epistolario*, I, 27.

The Growth of the Revolution

Madariaga[1] in Cádiz in 1802,[2] correspondence with Terrada and other Argentine patriots before 1810, which attracted the attention of the Intend ant of Concepción[3]—confirms abundantly that Bernardo O'Higgins, for one, was a separatist and a conspirator well before the revolution of 1810.

From O'Higgins separatist influence flowed in several directions. Most notable amos gst his fellow-thinkers was Juan Martínez de Rozas, who, according to Juan Mackenna,[4] recognized in O'Higgins his best friend and the only man in whom he could confide.[5] Rozas was twenty years older than O'Higgins, but their friendship seems to have been deep and lasting. A relative of O'Higgins who answered questions put by the historian Barros Arana in 1854 claimed that the two men first discussed the possibility of liberating Chile from Spanish rule soon after O'Higgins' return from a visit to Peru in 1804.[6] This is a more reasonable view than the supposition that Rozas was suddenly converted to separatism after his withdrawal from García Carrasco's administration in 1809. Ignacio Torres, as we have seen, believed that 'Don Juan Rozas and his followers are the authors of the plan of rebellion and independence against our legitimate sovereigns'.[7] If this is accepted, it can only be assumed that Rozas, by winning García Carrasco's confidence early in 1808 and acting for a while as his chief adviser, was attempting to manipulate the Governor for his own purposes. As José Santiago Luco reported to Spain, Rozas had 'sought means to delude this Governor'.[8] Rozas had to retire from the government after the *Scorpion* affair, from which he seems to have benefited financially.[9] Later on, in October 1809,

---

[1] José Joaquín Cortés Madariaga (1786–   ). Chilean priest who played a leading part in the installation of the Junta of Caracas, 19 April 1810.

[2] Vicuña Mackenna, *Vida de O'Higgins*, p. 60.

[3] O'Higgins to Mackenna, 5 January 1811, Cruz, *Epistolario*, I, 26.

[4] Juan Mackenna O'Reilly (1771–1814). Born in Ireland; appointed by Governor Ambrosio O'Higgins to supervise the resettlement of the town of Osorno; Governor of Valparaíso, 1811; served in the campaigns of 1813–14; shot in a duel in Buenos Aires by Luis Carrera; evidently a patriot from the start of the revolution.

[5] Mackenna to O'Higgins, 20 February 1811, *Arch.O'H.* I, 71.

[6] Manuel Riquelme to Barros Arana, 14 September 1854, A.B.A. vol. 25-2(9), fo. 2.

[7] *Informe*, p. 28.

[8] To the Supreme Junta (Cadiz), 9 December 1808, *CHDI*, VIII, 196.

[9] Amunátegui Solar, *Jesuitas*, pp. 85–6.

an agent of the Central Junta warned the Intendant of Concepción to watch over Rozas' conduct and also that of Rozas' brother-in-law Antonio Urrutia Manzano, one of the most powerful creoles in Concepción.[1] The case of Juan Martínez de Rozas is not an altogether easy one to discuss. He was an odd combination of idealist and opportunist. It may well be that whatever his inner sentiments—and I for one do not doubt that these were separatist and revolutionary—he was content to play a somewhat cautious and wary role in the crisis of 1808–10, but later, when he dominated the Junta and tried to spur on the revolution, he proved himself capable of decisive action. He was certainly an ambitious man, and personal interest never seems to have been far from his political calculations. As his great opponent José Miguel Carrera wrote, 'he wanted to be another Washington, but lacked the valour and the virtues which adorned that great man'.[2] Rozas did not in fact lack courage, as his composure during the Figueroa insurrection of 1 April 1811 shows very clearly, and his part in the revolution from the moment the Junta was set up was crucially important, even if tragically abbreviated. But, although his ultimate contribution to the development of the revolution was necessarily slight, Rozas, like Mariano Moreno in the River Plate, deserves to rank high among the fathers of the Chilean fatherland.

Associated with O'Higgins and Rozas in the South (bearing in mind that Rozas was absent from the South from early 1808 to early 1809) were such figures as Fray Rosauro Acuña and Pedro Arriagada, whose arrest on charges of subversion I have already mentioned. O'Higgins referred to these two men as his 'decided political disciples',[3] and this strongly suggests that their various expressions of dissident opinion in 1809 were sincere. Another Southern figure who almost certainly held similar views—though he did not live to see the Junta—was José Antonio Prieto. The French scholar Claude Gay was later told that Prieto and Rozas had discussed independence 'well before 1810'.[4] On his deathbed,

---

[1] Joaquín Molina to the Central Junta, Lima, 18 October 1809, quoted in Amunátegui, *Crónica*, I, 389.
[2] *Diario militar*, CHDI, I, 33. [3] To Mackenna, 5 January 1811, Cruz, *Epistolario*, I, 26.
[4] 'Sur l'histoire du Chili et la révolution' (notes), Archivo Gay-Morla, vol. 52, pieza 73, fo. 393.

in 1809, Prieto 'never ceased talking about independence...and kindled a great anger against the Spaniards'.[1] Whether other members of the Rozas–O'Higgins circle—Luis de la Cruz, the Spaniard Carlos Spano, Esteban Manzano, etc.—were separatists or not is less certain. Some members of the group may have been influenced in that direction.[2]

It seems highly probable, therefore, that there did exist two groups, one based on Santiago and the other in the South, both of which contained a hard core of extremists. The precise extent of their influence must, as I have said, remain uncertain. The two groups were almost certainly in contact with one another, and may well have embraced a number of other creole leaders whose general position in 1810 is a lot less clear. What, for instance, can be said of José Miguel Infante, the young *procurador* of the Cabildo of Santiago who, more than anyone else, gave ideological content to the movement for home rule? There is no evidence directly linking him to disloyalty, unless through his close association with the three arrested men of May 1810, and yet, some twenty years later, in his federalist newspaper, he made the following comment about the Junta of 1810: 'The Junta was obliged to swear that it would defend and preserve the kingdom for Ferdinand VII, just as the Junta of Buenos Aires was. Without this, the opposition of people acclimatized to servitude would have been irresistible.'[3] It is by no means easy to say how accurate a sentence such as this may be. It may mean either that Infante himself recalled having taken part in an elaborate hypocrisy in September 1810, or that he was recollecting the true nature of events through the rose-coloured spectacles of the revolutionary mystique. If indeed Infante's memory was substantially correct, then the extent of genuinely subversive influence must have been very much greater than I find it possible to suggest here. This may have been the case, but it is not something that can safely be asserted on the basis of available evidence. If Infante and his colleagues on the Cabildo really were separatists, then they kept their secret

---

[1] 'Sur l'histoire du Chili et la révolution' (notes), Archivo Gay-Morla, vol. 52, pieza 73, fo. 394.
[2] Vicuña Mackenna thinks they were (*Vida de O'Higgins*, pp. 104–7).
[3] *Valdiviano Federal*, no. 47, 11 October 1831, p. 2.

very well indeed—almost, it is fair to say, too well. It seems in-conceivable that a widespread separatist and republican conspiracy would not have left more traces than are in fact apparent. On the other hand, it is true to say that in the twenty years that separated the events of 1810 and the statement by Infante I have just quoted, the whole political outlook had altered profoundly, and this alteration was bound to have its effects on the creole inter-pretation of recent history. The alternatives must be stated and the matter has to be left there. The case of Manuel José Gandaril-las,[1] a vocal separatist in the '*Patria Vieja*', presents us with similar issues. In 1834 he asserted in print that the Cabildo Abierto of 18 September 1810, 'though disguised with the appearances of obedience and love towards Ferdinand VII, was in reality the establishment of the republican system in Chile and the complete shaking off of the colonial chains'.[2] Again, it is difficult not to detect the operation of the revolutionary mystipue in a statement like this. The Revolution of 1810 *may* have been the establishment of the republican system in Chile, but if so, it was a remarkably discreet and cautious establishment, and it does not look like one to the historian. Men hardly set up republics and throw off their colonial chains by asserting their profound loyalty to the King and their constitutional dependence on the metropolitan authorities, even if the King happens to be com-fortably remote from his kingdom and the metropolitan authori-ties on the verge of defeat.

Juan Egaña, a man who was to play an important part at every subsequent stage of the Chilean revolution, is another whose position in 1810 demands to be made clear. In a letter to José Miguel Carrera in 1813, Egaña boasted of his love for 'a system that delighted my heart long before there were Frenchmen in Spain';[3] yet it is not certain how far Egaña's own system was separatist even in the '*Patria Vieja*'.[4] The borderline between

---

[1] Manuel José Gandarillas Guzmán (1788–1842). Editorial assistant to Camilo Henríquez in the '*Patria Vieja*'; a strong *carrerino*, he remained away from Chile from 1814 to 1823; member of the Congresses of 1824–8; Minister of Finance, 1825–6 and of the Interior, 1826–7; later a supporter of Portales.

[2] Gandarillas, p. 12. [3] Letter of 17 February 1813, Egaña, *Escritos inéditos*, p. 126.

[4] See Eyzaguirre, *Ideario y ruta*, pp. 138–40.

autonomism and separatism in his various writings between 1810 and 1814—and there is no shortage of these—is imprecise. By 1813, when he drew up the diplomatic instructions for Francisco Antonio Pinto's mission to London,[1] he seems to have been separatist, but in his earlier 'Declaration of the Rights of the Chilean People',[2] he seems equally to have accepted some form of association with the Spanish Empire. Like Manuel de Salas, Juan Egaña could prove ideologically erratic. Both Salas and Egaña, when in exile on Juan Fernández during the Spanish reconquest, reverted (for the purposes of the Spanish government, at any rate) to the official Chilean line taken in 1810. Both men conveniently forgot that they had taken more extreme positions at one time or another between 1810 and 1814.

I have dwelt at some length on the evidence relating to at least a few of the personalities of 1810, because it seems important to identify the probable supporters of independence, where this is possible, and to establish that the political current which was ultimately victorious had its advocates even in 1810. But there are other hints of separatist feeling, quite apart from what is known or what can reasonably be supposed about individual cases. Some of these hints are to be found in the pages of the *Catecismo político cristiano*, a work which I have several times quoted in the course of the present chapter. The *Catecismo* was written (this now seems certain) partly in Upper Peru and partly in Chile between July and September 1810.[3] It contains strong suggestions of republicanism. The republican form of government is exalted as the most perfect on earth from the viewpoint of the people,[4] while monarchy is frequently condemned as unlawful and oppressive.[5] Though it is clearly stated that the Chileans' first duty is to agitate for a national Junta, there is also the recommendation that new forms of government should be considered in the event of Ferdinand's failure to return. 'Time and the circumstances will then become the rule of your conduct.'[6] The

---

[1] Egaña, *Escritos inéditos*, p. 136.   [2] As on p.   .
[3] Almeyda Arroyo, p. 219. Almeyda Arroyo is wrong, in my view, to deny the probability of Upper Peruvian authorship of part of the *Catecismo* (pp. 236–7). In exhorting Goyeneche, the unknown author says: 'huid de *esta* tierra'.
Amor de la Patria, pp. 96–7.   [5] *Ibid.* pp. 96–8.   [6] *Ibid.* p. 106.

Catecismo also contains a lengthy section denouncing the Spanish colonial order, and casts an envious glance at the North Americans, 'enjoying all the advantages of an honest liberty'.[1] These are strange sentiments to be met with in such profusion in a supposedly loyalist document. The *Catecismo*'s importance for the home-rule movement has been the subject of differing opnions. Francisco Antonio Encina regards it as 'totally alien to that movement',[2] while Jaime Eyzaguirre considers that it 'defined in a masterly way the doctrinal and juridical conception that dominated in those moments'.[3] Of these two views, the latter is the more likely to be accurate. The main points of political doctrine embodied in the *Catecismo* are in surprising agreement with the notions being put forward by José Miguel Infante in his various *Representaciones* of 1810, which are as faithful an indication of the main creole doctrines of the moment as can be found. It is clear that the manuscript did circulate within the little circle of the creole leaders,[4] and, though its authorship remains a baffling mystery,[5] the document plainly represented an important body of ideas then current. It should, however, be emphasized that these ideas, which could only have been passed on by word of mouth or in manuscript, were confined to a very small minority.

Added to this, there are one or two indications that a few creoles were conscious that great events awaited Chile and Spanish America in the immediate future. In a letter to José Antonio de Rojas in 1809, Esteban Manzano wrote that he was glad to hear that Rojas was in good health, for 'the great day, as events are showing, is very close at hand, and it would be very sad to die without the consolation of seeing and experiencing the advantageousness of what we desire'.[6] An anonymous proclamation found amongst Vera's papers after his arrest contained similar language: 'the tremendous day which will decide our fate is approaching'.[7] There is nothing at all explicit in such statements.

---

[1] *Amor de la Patria*, p. 106.   [2] *Historia*, VI, 156.   [3] *Ideario y ruta*, p. 109.
[4] Almeyda Arroyo, pp. 226–7. There may have been a copy in Concepción.
[5] Almeyda Arroyo's suggestion that Vera was the author of the Chilean section (pp. 238–43) is convincingly argued. Traditionally, the book has been ascribed to Juan Martínez de Rozas.
[6] Letter, n.d., *Proceso seguido*, p. 38.   [7] 'Rasgo patriótico', n.d., *Proceso seguido*, p. 61.

Manzano tried to explain away his phrase by asserting that his 'great day' referred to the great day when the French would be expelled from Spain,[1] and Rojas lyoally confirmed that this was the true meaning, but neither argument sounds convincing in the general context. One can only speculate. Did the 'great day' mean the revolution?

The majority of the members of the movement for home rule in Chile acted loyally and conscientiously in 1810, even though they constantly bore their own interests in mind and had a definite and innovatory political programme as well. But in addition, it is impossible to escape the conclusion that there was a small group which was prepared to carry its demands for reform much further. It is known, for instance, that the events of 1809 in Quito, La Paz, and Chuquisaca aroused different reactions within the pro-Junta movement in Chile. Some claimed to support these insurrections,[2] while others—Agustín Eyzaguirre, for instance[3]—condemned them as subversive of good order. This division of opinion may well have reflected the borderline between creoles whose basic aim was autonomy within the Empire and those who were eager to look for a more radical solution.

The small separatist group was incapable of colouring the whole movement, and by working in collaboration with the autonomists it acted realistically. Yet it can hardly be emphasized too forcibly or too frequently that autonomy in itself was a revolutionary concept, and a concept, moreover, which opened the gateway to further political changes. One of the first to appreciate this was the royalist chronicler Manuel Antonio Talavera, who observed the events leading up to the installation of the Junta at first hand. In a series of 'thirteen reflections' written in his diary on 18 September 1810, he asked himself a pointed question.

Will it not be their expedient to instal this sort of government now, and another sort later on, availing themselves of the same method? Will they not be able to shake off the yoke of subordination with a system of independence?[4]

---

[1] *Proceso seguido*, pp. 69, 134.　　　[2] Pinto, 'Apuntes autobiográficos', p. 96.
[3] Agustín Eyzaguirre to Bernardo Solar, 19 January 1810, Eyzaguirre, *Archivo epistolar*, p. 231.　　　[4] Talavera, pp. 99–100.

Later on, when the change was accomplished, Talavera noted the numerous apparently suspicious proceedings of the new government, including its willingness to tolerate a 'free and general licence to write and spread propositions of independence',[1] and he suggested that, whatever the appearances, disloyalty had been in the air when the Junta was created. Even allowing for royalist bias, for misinterpretation of what may have been innocent happenings in themselves, and for a loyal chronicler's natural anxiety to present an attractive narrative to the King, it is hard not to see in Talavera's words the hint that the Junta was consciously a preparation for something more than home rule within the Empire. Many of the men who planned the Junta and who attended the triumphant Cabildo Abierto of 18 September 1810[2] were loyal, and devotedly loyal, to Ferdinand VII. Probably most of them were. It is equally certain that some of them were not.

[1] Talavera, p. 142.

[2] The names of the chief leaders of the movement for home rule in Chile can be found in two interesting lists: (1) Names of some fifty agitators sent by García Carrasco to the King on 27 August 1810 (*CHDI*, IX, 23–6). (2) 'Principales patriotas que contribuyeron a la instalacion de la junta gubernativa', a roll drawn up by the survivors of the 1810 movement in 1847 (*CHDI*, XVIII, 352–60). Those who attended the Cabildo Abierto have not been recorded. For a list of those who probably attended, see Rául Silva Castro, *Asistentes al Cabildo Abierto de 18 de setiembre de 1810* (2nd edn. 1960), pp. 21–88. For the hurried consultations that led up to the Cabildo Abierto, see Medina *Actas*, pp. 44–59, and also José Gregorio Argomedo, 'Diario de los sucesos ocurridos en Santiago de Chile desde el 10 hasta el 22 de septiembre de 1810', in *CHDI*, XIX, 1.

3

THE 'PATRIA VIEJA'
1810–1814

All over Spanish America, the years immediately following 1810 were marked by an acute crisis of ideological definition in those provinces which had set up national Juntas. Creole leaders struggled amongst themselves to promote or restrain the separatist revolution which was developing. In Venezuela the fervent republicanism of the revolutionary leadership prompted an early declaration of independence, while in the River Plate the issue remained formally undecided for the time being. Quite apart from their ideological preoccupations, the creole revolutionaries soon found that they faced a mounting tide of royalist reaction both from within and without. The royalists, by and large, had tolerated the creation of Juntas, but were unwilling to allow any further moves away from the traditional imperial framework. In Chile, problems of ideological definition were mingled with disastrous personal and family rivalries, and the tide of royalist reaction, promoted by the strenuous activity of the authoritarian Viceroys of Peru, ultimately cracked the fragile edifice of rational liberty. And yet, at the same time, the four years between the creation of the first national and autonomous government and the overthrow of the patriot army at Rancagua were essentially years of creation. The Captaincy-General of Chile became the State of Chile, loosening its connection with the Empire in a constantly maintained movement despite the continued absence of a formal declaration of independence. Representative government was tried for the first time. New institutions were developed. And above all, the 'Patria Vieja', as this four-year period is styled by historians, saw the first full elaboration of the new political ideas and patriotic emotional attitudes which went to make up the ideology of the revolution. This ideology was to operate in all the subsequent phases of revolutionary activity. Its emergence during the 'Patria Vieja' was a fact of the profoundest importance. This was, in nearly every respect, the formative period of the Chilean revolution.

The national Junta set up on 18 September 1810 adopted a set of politicies which were both liberal and cautious at one and the same time. The defence system was reviewed, consolidated, and built up. Ports were thrown open to international trade by the famous decree of January 1811. A sense of solidarity with the Junta of Buenos Aires was carefully fostered. Outwardly at least, there was little yet that boded ill for Chile's traditional relationship with the Spanish Empire. The name of Ferdinand VII was still invoked at regular intervals. The guiding hand which directed the Junta imperceptibly towards more radical postures was that of Juan Martínez de Rozas, the most extreme creole member of the new government. Rozas had been appointed to the Junta on 18 September because of his influence in the South. He soon came to dominate the Junta. The Conde de la Conquista, whose appointment as chairman had been a prestige measure more than anything else, no longer took much part in proceedings. He frequently fell asleep at meetings, and died in March 1811. By this time the Junta's promises of support to Buenos Aires—now engaged in a conflict with the Viceroyalty of Peru—were provoking serious doubts in royalist circles, and prompted a royalist insurrection on 1 April 1811, headed by Colonel Tomás de Figueroa. Figueroa may have imagined himself as a Chilean General Monk, restoring the kingdom to its lawful obedience,[1] but his movement came to nothing, and he himself was rapidly brought before a firing squad. The main result of this incident was the dissolution of the Royal Audiencia. The Audiencia had icily but unsuccessfully resisted the political changes of September 1810, and represented an older order which was becoming increasingly unfashionable. Moreover, it seems to have been implicated in the Figueroa mutiny, and, under strong pressure from the government, it disintegrated in the weeks that followed.

[1] For a full account of the origins, course and outcome of this insurrection—the baptism of fire of the Chilean revolution—see Vicuña Mackenna, *Coronel Figueroa*.

Meanwhile the municipalities of Chile had been electing the deputies to serve in the promised national Congress. Rozas had insisted on the holding of the Congress, despite opposition from within the Junta, and against his own inner inclinations.[1] When Congress met, on 4 July 1811 (a date rich in revolutionary associations), it became obvious that its composition was cautious and conservative in character and that henceforth the revolution would move only slowly towards the destination Rozas and his separatist friends had in mind. Rozas' own group of *exaltados* was confined to twelve deputies, and Rozas' political ascendancy was seen to be fading fast. Tension between the radical and conservative elements in Congress mounted quickly. The major bone of contention was the size of the Santiago delegation. Earlier in the year the Cabildo of Santiago had solicited and secured the right to send twelve deputies to Congress, a total which seemed excessive to provincial deputies in general and to Rozas' group in particular. Santiago's obdurate resolve to have a really substantial delegation seemed a deliberate manoeuvre to increase the size of the moderate contingent in Congress. On 9 August, after a number of intemperate sessions, Rozas withdrew from Congress in disgust, taking his radical phalanx with him. He retired to Concepción, his own traditional base, set up an independently minded Provincial Junta (5 September) and left the remaining deputies in the Congress to their fate.

Their fate was, in fact, embodied in the person of a dashing young soldier who had just returned to Chile from gallant service in the Peninsular War. His name was José Carrera.[2] Aided by his equally energetic brothers Juan José and Luis,[3] José Miguel lost no time in involving himself in politics. In September 1811 he assisted in a purge of deputies from the Congress, and, two

[1] O'Higgins to Mackenna, 5 January 1811, Cruz, *Epistolario*, I, 37.
[2] José Miguel Carrera Verdugo (1785–1821). After his service in Spain, he returned to Chile in July 1811; became dictator by his coup of November 1811; commanded the patriot forces in the South from April to November 1813; was captured by royalists in March 1814; escaped in May 1814 and re-established himself as dictator, 23 July; did not return to Chile until 1817. For his erratic later career and execution, see Benjamín Vicuña Mackenna, *El ostracismo de los Carrera* (1886).
[3] Juan José Carrera Verdugo (1782–1818) and Luis Carrera Verdugo (1791–1818). Both executed at Mendoza. The remains of the three Carrera brothers were taken back to Chile in 1828.

months later, on 15 November, he headed a *coup d'état* which resulted in his assumption of personal power and the dissolution of Congress altogether. These proceedings were viewed with distaste by Rozas and his followers in the South, and the Provincial Junta of Concepción resisted Carrera's pretensions with vigorous manifestos and an implied threat of civil war. Rozas warned Carrera that praetorianism was no substitute for orderly civil government. It is quite clear from the evidence that Rozas was prepared at this point to detach the province of Concepción from any relationship with Santiago and to join it to Buenos Aires.[1] Such an arrangement would have been unworkable, even had the Argentine government been willing to countenance it, but it was a fair measure of Rozas' general frustration at the time.

The first four months of 1812 saw several attempts to paper over the ugly cracks which now lay between the two provinces. On 12 January, Bernardo O'Higgins (representing Santiago at Carrera's personal request) and Manuel Vásquez de Novoa (representing Concepción) signed a draft agreement to put an end to the quarrel. This was almost immediately ratified at Concepción, but was rejected by Carrera. Troops of the rival parties began to concentrate on opposite banks of the River Maule, the provincial border. On 25 April, Rozas and Carrera met nearby in an attempt to settle their differences by personal contact. Their conversations were cordial but unproductive. By mid May it was clear that further negotiations had failed between the two sides, but the troops were gradually withdrawn from the Maule, and the danger of civil war was averted. Rozas' position at Concepción soon became precarious in the extreme. He ran short of money, appealed urgently to Buenos Aires for a loan, but was suddenly unseated by a military rising on 8 July. Carrera deported him to his birthplace (Mendoza) where he died soon afterwards. With Concepción brought to heel, and the only alternative *caudillo* disposed of, Carrera found himself undisputed master of the country. Under his aegis, a number of revolutionary reforms were enacted and the momentum of the revolution was regained.

It was during Carrera's relatively brief period of government

---

[1] Talavera, p. 505.

that a number of new and important influences began to operate in favour of the revolution. Of these the most significant was plainly the printing press. For the first time in Chilean history, ideas could be printed and distributed on a reasonably large scale within the nation. The Carrera regime, committed somewhat vaguely and incoherently to a revolutionary programme, was quick to understand the uses to which a printing press could be put. A constant deluge of decrees, proclamatios, manifestoes and similar documents poured from the small team of North American type-setters who operated the machinery. An embryonic journalism arose with the foundation of the first Chilean newspaper, *La Aurora de Chile*, which, together with its successor, *El Monitor Araucano*, was a government-backed publication. The third of the newspapers of the '*Patria Vieja*', *El Semanario Republicano*, first edited by Antonio José de Irisarri,[1] advocated a separatist republicanism more coherently and intelligently than its predecessors.[2]

With these new facilities at their disposal, a small group of patriot writers began to exercise its literary talent to an extent naturally undreamed of in the past. The members of this group included Irisarri, Vera, Gandarillas, Salas, Juan Egaña and others. But by far the most outstanding personality of the period in this respect was a newcomer, Fray Camilo Henríquez,[3] a Chilean who had served something of a revolutionary apprenticeship in Quito and who returned to his native land at the end of 1810, 'bringing the lava of Chimborazo with him', to use Vicuña Mackenna's phrase.[4] Placed in charge of *La Aurora de Chile*, Henríquez used the newspaper to spread knowledge of his revolutionary ideals and also the 'feeling' of the new era he passionately believed had

---

[1] Antonio José de Irisarri Alonso (1786–1868). Born in Guatemala; arrived in Chile 1809; interim Supreme Director of Chile in March 1814; Chilean representative in London 1818–24; Intendant of San Fernando 1836–7; a restless individual with a strong gift for polemical writing.

[2] For the introduction of the printing press into Chile see Medina, *Bibliografía*, pp. xxvii–xxviii, and Lawrence S. Thompson, *Printing in Colonial Hispanic America* (Hamden, Conn., 1962) pp. 87–93.

[3] Camilo Henríquez González (1769–1825). Born in Valdivia; educated in Lima; lived in Buenos Aires 1814–22; the most ardent revolutionary propagandist of the period; the father of Chilean journalism. His best articles have been conveniently anthologized in Silva Castro, *Escritos políticos*, pp. 60–182.

[4] *Coronel Figueroa*, p. 110.

come to Chile. The opening words of the prospectus of *La Aurora* show with some clarity Henríquez' aims and purposes as far as the press was concerned.

We now have in our possession the great and precious instrument of universal enlightenment, the printing press...After the sad and insufferable silence of three centuries—centuries of infamy and lamentation!—the voice of reason and truth will be heard amongst us...[1]

These resonant words opened the history of Chilean journalism. With his *Aurora*, Henríquez provided a classic vehicle of revolutionary propaganda. He considered himself as an educator, trying to spread correct principles amongst people generally unacquainted with advanced notions. He believed himself to be 'a free citizen,...a philosopher who finds his homeland wherever he finds freedom, and who everywhere promotes enlightenment'.[2] The pages of *La Aurora de Chile* and *El Monitor Araucano* do not leave us in doubt for long as to what Henríquez thought to be enlightenment. As the French scholar Claude Gay noted, he 'speaks of nothing except political principles'.[3] The nature of these principles was revolutionary. In his years in Peru before the revolution of 1810, Henríquez had read widely. He had been caught up in more than one brush with the Inquisition for being in possession of prohibited books, including the works of Raynal, Rousseau's *Social Contract*, and Mercier's *Histoire de l'An 2440*.[4]

Added to these leaders of the intellectual revolution there was a less vocal but nonetheless vital group of foreigners who were also actively promoting the ends of reform and independence. Among others, there was Mateo Arnaldo Hoevel, a Swedish North American, who imported the first printing press at the behest of the government. There was Jaime Zudáñez, a patriot lawyer from Chuquisaca, who became a government secretary and attended the peace negotiations at Lircay in 1814. And most notable of all, there was Joel Roberts Poinsett. Poinsett represented the United States in Chile, became an intimate friend of the Carreras, presented a

---

[1] *Aurora de Chile*, prospecto, p. 1.
[2] To the Junta, 1 October 1813, quoted in Barros Arana, IX, 250 n.
[3] 'Notes sur le journal la Aurora', n.d., F.V. vol. 697.
[4] Medina, *Inquisición en Chile*, II, 539–42.

draft constitution, and accompanied the patriot troops in their first campaign against the royalists.[1] Poinsett's influence on Carrera aroused suspicion not only amongst Spaniards and royalists, but also amongst English observers in the River Plate. 'That Firebrand Mr Poinsett', one of them wrote home, 'is as busy as a Fiend in contaminating the whole population on that side of the continent.'[2]

The increased revolutionary momentum of 1812 soon produced a disastrous effect outside Chile. Relations with the Viceroyalty of Peru had been deteriorating for some time. Peru, the focus and centre of Spanish power in South America, had failed to develop a successful movement for home rule in 1810, and was now locked in a harsh conflict with the government of the River Plate. The clever and astute Viceroy, José Fernando de Abascal y Sousa, was deeply suspicious of the Juntas of 1810, and he interpreted developments in Chile as signifying a march towards total independence. At the beginning of 1813 Abascal dispatched a small task-force under Brigadier Pareja to crush the Chilean revolution. Under Pareja a nucleus of troops established itself in the South, took Concepción, and started to advance up the Central Valley. Tactically and logistically, this was the easiest approach to the Chilean heartland, and it was to be the standard Peruvian strategy until the final royalist failure in 1818. Carrera's response to the military threat was commendably energetic. He rode South from Santiago immediately, leaving the government in the hands of a newly appointed Junta, and devoted his best efforts to neutralizing the royalist advance. Royalist numbers, meanwhile, had been vastly increased by the accretion of numerous Chilean sympathizers. The ensuing conflict had something of the character of a civil war.

The royalists were unable to make very much headway. After the battle of San Carlos (14 and 15 April 1813) they found

---

[1] Collier and Feliú Cruz, *passim*. See also J. Fred Rippy, *Joel R. Poinsett, Versatile American* (Durham, N.C., 1935), pp. 41–55.

[2] Captain Peter Heywood to Viscount Melville, 4 December 1812, F.O. 72/152, p. 299. An edited version of this long letter may be found in Edward Tagart, *A Memoir of Peter Heywood* (London, 1832), pp. 245–61, but it omits such phrases as 'that Firebrand' and 'as a Fiend'.

themselves obliged to seek the relatively inexpugnable safety of the town of Chillán. Carrera invested the town in June, but despite valiant efforts the patriots were unable to dislodge the royalists. The war quickly reached a condition of stalemate. By now the Junta which had taken over the government from Carrera in Santiago was consciously opposed to his war leadership. In October 1813 the Junta moved South to Talca, to mount a brief and fruitless peace initiative and to take charge of the military situation in general. On 27 November it decreed Carrera's dismissal from the post of patriot commander-in-chief, and replaced him by Bernardo O'Higgins, who had built up a solid reputation for tactical skill and personal valour during the preceding campaigns. Carrera resisted this move, and O'Higgins hesitated before assuming his new command. This untimely vacillation also marked the origins of the split between Carrera and O'Higgins, a split which was presently to have disastrous consequences. On 1 February 1814, however, Carrera finally came round to the view that national unity was more important than personal strife, and he ordered his troops to support O'Higgins as commander-in-chief.

Carrera's action was far from precipitate, and O'Higgins' own lack of decision weakened the general position of the patriots. A second task-force from Peru, commanded by General Gavino Gainza, entered Chile at the start of 1814 and soon caused considerable alarm among the patriots. Gainza's initial successes were considerable. The Junta beat a hasty retreat from its temporary capital at Talca, and a Cabildo Abierto in Santiago vested supreme power in Francisco de la Lastra,[1] with the title of Supreme Director, on 7 March. Lastra as Supreme Director and O'Higgins as commander-in-chief were hard put to it to prevent sweeping royalist successes. Gainza's troops captured Talca, but his way North to Santiago was barred by O'Higgins. By now, however, the patriots were exhausted and disorganized. The royalists, too, were badly placed to strike a decisive blow. The need for some

[1] Francisco de la Lastra de la Sotta (1777–1852). Served in the Navy in Spain 1793–1803; member of the 1811 Congress; Governor of Valparaíso 1811–14, 1818–22, and 1825–9; Supreme Director of Chile, March to July 1814; one of the senior liberal officers cashiered in 1830.

sort of accommodation between the two armies was apparent. Through the mediation of an English naval officer, Captain James Hillyar (later Rear-Admiral Sir James Hillyar), a treaty of peace between patriot and royalist armies was negotiated and concluded on the banks of the River Lircay near Talca on 3 May 1814. Under this agreement Chile was to continue to enjoy substantial autonomy, along with open trade, but was to accept the Spanish Constitution of 1812, the sovereignty of Ferdinand VII, and an end to the use of the distinctive national flag which the Carrera government had introduced. Neither O'Higgins nor Gainza really believed that this fragile armistice would last, and they kept wary eyes on each other's activities.

Carrera, meanwhile, had been absent from the scene, having been made prisoner by the royalists soon after O'Higgins' assumption of the military leadership. Perhaps with royalist connivance, he was able to escape and to make his way back to Santiago, where, on 23 July, he overthrew Lastra's government and re-established himself as dictator. O'Higgins, still in command of much of the patriot army, instantly repudiated the authority of the new regime, and the first clashes of an inevitable civil war took place. These were, fortunately, restricted in the amount of damage they caused to either side, but the conflict diverted attention from more serious tasks. 'Chile's ruin was sealed,' Carrera was later to write.[1] His assessment was correct. By this time the Viceroy of Peru had refused to give his sanction to the Treaty of Lircay, and a third invasion of Chile had been mounted under General Mariano Osorio.

O'Higgins and Carrera sensed the need to end their differences. O'Higgins generously rode into Santiago to offer his services to his former rival without conditions. Osorio, however, had advanced a long way up-country before the patriots had time to reconcentrate their forces and confront him. The viceregal strategy of the two previous campaigns was repeated, but this time with success. Uncertainty over tactics and an unhappy lack of co-ordination between O'Higgins and the Carrera brothers gave Osorio an added advantage. Finally, O'Higgins took the

[1] *Diario militar, CHDI*, I, 352.

decision to defend the town of Rancagua, fifty miles South of Santiago, in a last-ditch effort to stem the royalist tide. After a heroic battle (1 and 2 October 1814) the gamble was lost. Rancagua fell, and with it the 'Patria Vieja'. Both Carrera and O'Higgins fled across the Cordillera of the Andes to Mendoza, accompanied by a tragic host of political refugees. Osorio entered Santiago in triumph and set about restoring the old order as it had existed before 1810. Carrera eventually reached the United States, and began the erratic existence which ended before a firing squad in Mendoza on 4 September 1821. O'Higgins, for his part, was to cement his new friendship with José de San Martín, and together with him to plan the great movement of final liberation which, under the most heroic auspices, was to usher in the 'Patria Nueva'.

The experiences of the Chilean people during the four years of the 'Patria Vieja' were far from happy. The outcome of the first representative assembly was negative. A bitter undercurrent of rivalry between the Carreras and the Larraín family (and its many associates) tinged many of the political struggles of the period with an unnecessary harshness. The patriot campaigns against Pareja, Gainza and Osorio were often mismanaged. The failure of liberal institutions and the prevalence of a pattern of instability in the period have led many writers to question whether the Chileans were ready for the sort of revolutionary doctrines propagated between 1810 and 1814. The idea of independence, as will be seen, did not command universal support. The end of the colonial era was sudden in the extreme, and the difficulties of the transition to liberalism were bound to be testing and severe. There were some Chileans who saw this clearly even before 1814. Juan Martínez de Rozas, for instance, was worried by the possibility that the first Congress would produce utopianism and foolishness. O'Higgins, in a conversation with Rozas just before the latter went to Santiago to take up his position on the Junta, managed to convince him that it was 'necessary to start somewhere',[1] and Rozas finally agreed. Juan Mackenna, too, believed that the Congress would be a failure. It

---

[1] O'Higgins to Mackenna, 5 January 1811, Cruz, *Epistolario*, I, 37.

might, he wrote, remind him of scenes he had witnessed as a schoolboy in Ireland: 'everyone wants to talk, nobody to listen; everyone wants to command, nobody to obey'.[1] Bernardo de Vera y Pintado, downhearted after the Carrera *coup d'état*, reported to Buenos Aires that the 'civic virtues' necessary for the revolution were entirely lacking in Chile, and that the 'egoism and ambition' of Chileans were 'incompatible with popular government'.[2] The mercantile oligarchy of Buenos Aires, though it tried hard to influence the situation in Chile throughout the period, saw the existence of a powerful landowning aristocracy in Chile as a major impediment to revolution. 'A salutary Democracy', wrote Hipólito Vieytes, 'will never be established in Chile.'[3]

These comments were to some extent justified. There was a good deal of uncertainty in the air during the '*Patria Vieja*'. It may well be true, as Encina has suggested, that none of the governments of the time really knew what they wanted, and that their political aims were confused.[4] Yet the patriots were confronted by truly immense difficulties. They lacked experience, and they had the gargantuan task of creating revolutionary sentiment where none had existed previously. Nevertheless, despite an element of timidity, they set about their tasks with energy and confidence. Their mistakes were the mistakes of passionate men, and the revolution they brought into existence was to win eventual acceptance despite all the setbacks and frustrations. The cause which lost at Rancagua was to triumph for ever at Chacabuco.

THE MOVEMENT AWAY FROM SPAIN

The principal theme of the political activity of the '*Patria Vieja*', leaving aside the elaboration of the revolutionary ideology and the expressions of nationalist emotion, was the movement away from Spain. Whether the agitation for a national Junta in 1808–10 concealed proposals for total independence from the Spanish

[1] Mackenna to O'Higgins, 20 February 1811, *Arch.O'H.* I, 73.
[2] Letter of 9 December 1811, *CHDI*, xx, 353.
[3] Vieytes to Alvarez Jonte, 28 March 1811, Alvarez Jonte, p. 143.
[4] Encina, *Historia*, VII, 8–9.

Empire is a matter I have already considered in Chapter 2. But it is clear, at all events, that many Chileans soon began to consider the establishment of the Junta of September 1810 as an event of considerable, indeed of revolutionary significance. Less emphasis was now placed on the protection of the rights of Ferdinand VII, and more on home rule. It had been the other way round, in public at least, between 1808 and 1810. One unknown writer was now able to regard Chile and Buenos Aires as 'peoples which have known how to break the chains of their servitude',[1] while another interpreted the creation of the Junta in the following way:

A free and enlightened people establishing and ratifying a system of government which it had maturely considered, examined and approved! That was the spectacle you gathered to celebrate on that memorable 18 September...[2]

The same writer urged that those Chileans about to be elected to the first Congress should be drawn from the ranks of 'lovers of the liberty of the homeland'.[3] Fray Camilo Henríquez, in his first public pronouncement after returning to Chile, rejoiced that his people had at last taken 'a great and unexpected movement towards its freedom, towards that single and sublime desire of all strong spirits'.[4] Henríquez expatiated on the glorious future which awaited those who embraced the cause of freedom, citing as his main example the experience of the United States. 'The inevitable course of events, O people of Chile,' he wrote, 'summons you to participate in this destiny'[5] At much the same time, the start of 1811, yet another writer saw the 18 September 1810 as a moment of great and dramatic change: 'You thought to be free; and in a single instant you converted the wretched condition of slavery into the glorious hierarchy of heroism.'[6] Thus, even before the

---

[1] 'Sobre la necesidad Justicia y conveniencia de cortar todas las relaciones mercantiles con Lima y sus dependencias. A los habitantes de Chile un patriota' [MS manifesto, ?February 1811], A.B.A. vol. 25–2(3), fo. 759.
[2] 'Discurso patriotico dedicado à la memoria del dia 18 de Septiembre de 1810' (MS manifesto, early 1811), A.B.A. vol. 25–2(3), fo. 783.
[3] *Ibid.* fo. 789.
[4] 'Proclama de Quirino Lemachez', Silva Castro, *Escritos políticos*, p. 45.   [5] *Ibid.*
[6] 'Chilenos, permitid que un compatriota...' (MS manifesto, ?March 1811), A.B.A. vol. 25–2(3), fo. 801.

opening of the first Congress in July 1811, there were Chileans who saw their new political status as something more than a re-affirmation of loyalty to Ferdinand VII, and who regarded the installation of the Junta as an act of decisive importance.

It is difficult to say with any certainty whether statements like these indicated a desire for complete independence. Certainly Camilo Henríquez seems to have had this in mind from the start, but there was still a strong current of autonomism in Chile, and the use of the word 'liberty' need not show more than that. Yet autonomists and separatists—and there must have been many who sat on the fence between the two positions—agreed now that 1810 marked a point from which there could be no going back. 'It was necessary', wrote Manuel de Salas, 'that things should change.'[1] And, at this point, some new terminology began to appear. The imperial crisis and the creation of the Junta were now being interpreted as the breakdown and renovation of the social contract. As Irisarri observed in 1812: 'The social pact which we had previously has been dissolved, and the people must gather together to form it anew.'[2] If the King of Spain were to be party to any renovated 'pact' then certain changes would have to be made clear to him. As Henríquez put it, in his sermon before the installation of Congress on 4 July 1811, 'if Divine Providence restored Ferdinand VII. . .to Spain, or conducted him to one of the regions of America', he would be welcomed back to his dominions, but only under 'the fundamental pact of our con-stitution'.[3] There would in fact (as Henríquez made clear on the same occasion) have to be a much more equitable balance between King and parliament in any new political order. Less than a year later, Henríquez made his first unequivocally clear call for total independence, and it is likely that this represented no sudden change of heart on his part. Manuel de Salas, however, was more consistent at this stage in advocating a continued link (however tenuous) with the monarchy, though he demanded a definite change of heart: 'Let us open our eyes. . .and work to make sure that our allegiance to Ferdinand VII and Spain is the effect of our

---

[1] *Diálogo de los porteros*, p. 172.
[2] *Aurora de Chile*, tomo I, no. 38, 29 October 1812, p. 158.   [3] *SCL*, I, 36.

own free will, a deliberate decision rather than blind deference to men who...will deliver us, like beasts, to Bonaparte.'[1]

This feeling, expressed in several ways, was the underlying note of the sermons and speeches delivered at the opening of the first national Congress. Thus Juan Martínez de Rozas insisted that 'with one voice the inhabitants of Chile protest that they will obey nobody but Ferdinand, that they are resolved to free themselves at all costs from the chance of being ruled by anyone else, and to preserve these dominions for him'.[2] Yet, almost in the same breath, Rozas hinted at the conditions this well loved monarch would have to observe in the event of his restoration.

The good Spaniards...are preparing to present him on his return with a constitution...which will avoid the repetition of those horrors into which the abuse of power has plunged the nation, and which will restore the nation to the enjoyment of those inalienable rights of which it has been deprived.[3]

Rozas then added that the Americans had been summoned to the Spanish Cortes in an insulting manner and would not, therefore, be able to attend. Rozas' speech, by laying stress on the need for a constitution and on popular sovereignty, certainly shows that his subtle mind had already leapt far beyond the theoretical rights of Ferdinand VII. 'In the only possible and legal manner', he said, 'the Chilean people is here congregated *for the first time*,'[4] thus clearly hinting that in his opinion all previous constitutional arrangements had smacked of illegality.

The occasion of the installation of the Congress of 1811, then, was not used to express an open desire for separation, even if Vera, in a poem to commemorate the event, exulted that 'Liberty, Heaven's sweet gift, is our consolation today',[5] and looked forward to the advent of prosperity for Chile 'through its worthy deputies'.[6] On the first anniversary of the 18 September 1810, which followed soon afterwards, Vera displayed another of his political poems in front of the government palace, beneath

---

[1] *Diálogo de los porteros*, pp. 173-4.   [2] *SCL*, I, 39.
[3] *SCL*, I, 40.   [4] *SCL*, I, 38. (My italics.)
[5] 'Un ciudadano de Chile a la solemne apertura del Congreso', F.V. vol. 244, pieza 71 (copy).   [6] *Ibid.*

an allegorical picture of the defeat of tyranny. In one stanza he exhorted his readers to contemplate the experience of a single year in which 'the despotism of three hundred' had been destroyed. The political system regenerating Chile, he added, ran 'like the sun in its career'.[1] It was absurd, of course, to suggest that the habits and institutions of three centuries had collapsed overnight. They had not. But a verse like Vera's showed the dramatic way in which some patriots wanted to interpret and celebrate the change. What is more, the language being used by Vera and men like him was now strikingly different from the language of 1810.

The first Junta, as we have seen, came into existence legally, and it took its stand on traditional Spanish rights and, to a lesser extent, on specific concessions of the Peninsular government. Not for some while did the Junta or its successor authorities abandon the convention (hypocritical or not) that it ruled in the name of and on behalf of Ferdinand VII. Not until the end of April 1813, in fact, did the government drop the King's name from the preambles to official decrees—an obvious and immediate consequence of the outbreak of war.[2] But long before April 1813 the government had already given certain indications of the underlying drift of its policies. It is particularly instructive to compare two documents issued within a very short time of each other towards the end of 1811. The first is a manifesto issued by the Junta (which at that stage was completely subservient to Congress) on 15 October. It opens with the following stirring paragraph:

Citizens! After three hundred years, during which time you have listened to that well-sustained maxim from the code of oppression that sovereigns are accountable only to God, hear now for the first time the law of reason, and the homage which your representatives render to the sacred rights of the people.[3]

All classes of society—but in particular slaves, businessmen, litigants and farmers—were invited to appreciate the virtues of the new 'system', but throughout the rhetorical paragraphs there was no mention of the Adorable Ferdinand whatsoever. Nevertheless,

---

[1] Amunátegui, *Alborada poética*, p. 270.
[2] A decree dated 6 May 1813 was headed (for the first time) 'The Governing Junta of Chile, representing the national sovereignty', with no mention of Ferdinand (*CHDI*, XXVII, 96).   [3] *SCL*, I, 138.

on 6 November the national Congress dispatched a letter to the Viceroy of Peru, informing him that Chile's 'adherence to the motherland is based on unalterable principles which everybody knows and feels'. The great aims of 1810, said this letter, had been 'to preserve the order and tranquillity of this kingdom, and to maintain it faithful and submissive to our sovereign lord King Ferdinand VII and the legitimate authorities which govern his dominions during his absence and captivity'.[1] Doubtless part of the tone of this letter can be attributed to the need to preserve good relations with the Viceroyalty of Peru—relations had been deteriorating over the preceding months. But the plain fact remains that the Santiago government was adopting a different language when dealing with its own citizens, and that the usual references to Ferdinand were being reserved for touchy outsiders like Abascal.

At the beginning of 1812, when the rivalry between Rozas and Carrera was reaching its height, further indications of the new Chilean attitude were made manifest. The draft agreement signed by Bernardo O'Higgins and Manuel Vásquez de Novoa on 12 January 1812 contained some important principles. According to this treaty, Chile was to remain without a formal constitution until such time as France finally overran Spain, 'or if for just and necessary motives it proved necessary to declare independence before this'.[2] Emphasis was added to this point by an express determination not to recognize any Spanish government as legal until Ferdinand's return, and this was plainly an unwelcome prospect, for

if this is the case, and independence is not declared, the kingdom will enter into negotiations...to obtain open trade and manufactures, to provide that natives of the country shall be given public offices, and to ensure that the government, if it takes on another form, is not exposed to the horrors of arbitrariness and despotism as in the past.[3]

Here then, independence was seen as a decided possibility in the immediate future, and, even if independence did not come, autonomist rights were to be constantly affirmed. The agreement

[1] *SCL*, I, 171.   [2] Convention of 12 January 1812, art. 3, *Arch.O'H.* I, 182.
[3] Art. 11, *Arch.O'H.* I, 183–4.

between O'Higgins and Vásquez de Novoa did not fail to arouse the suspicions of royalist elements in Chile. The ecclesiastical Cabildo of Santiago claimed that the article quoted above was 'in contradiction to the often repeated oath of loyalty to our beloved sovereign', and that the Junta of 1810 had been set up to preserve that oath.[1]

It is obvious that by the start of 1812 the Chilean government had gone beyond formal protestations of loyalty to the King and was placing far more emphasis on the positive aspects of home rule. Ferdinand's name was mentioned in a casual way throughout the '*Patria Vieja*', but with less evident sincerity as time went on. In an interesting article written in November 1812, Manuel de Salas affirmed roundly that the 'System consists of Governing ourselves by ourselves alone.'[2] He announced that Chile's pact with Ferdinand VII was no longer valid, since in Canon Law both parties had to be in a position to fulfil the terms of a contract, and Ferdinand was manifestly no longer able to do so.

What laws, what reforms, can he send us from the Castle of Valensey [*sic*]? Ah! If by some chance the unfortunate young man is already dead, how great will be our shame when...we see that we have been conducting our affairs *in the name of an imaginary and non-existent being*![3]

Yet even while making this sharp point, Salas remained vaguely in favour of the link with the Crown. Ferdinand, he wrote, would continue to be King at least until another Congress—a second Congress was a recurrent dream between 1812 and 1814—fixed the country's political course more clearly and explicitly.[4]

The feeling contained in Salas' article was reflected, too, in the provisional 'constitution' of 1812. Its famous fifth article stated, baldly enough, that 'no decree, provision or ordinance which emanates from any authority or tribunal outside the territory of Chile will have any effect, and those who try to give effect to such orders will be punished as offenders against the state'.[5] Yet this provision was placed alongside a deferential bow to Ferdinand,

---

[1] Ecclesiastical Cabildo to the Junta, 3 February 1812, Varas Velásquez, 'Reglamento constitucional', p. 125.
[2] 'Discurso sobre el sistema', *Aurora de Chile*, tomo I, no. 39, 5 November 1812, p. 161.
[3] *Ibid.* p. 162.   [4] *Ibid.*   [5] Reglamento Constitucional, *SCL*, I, 260.

who was still to be accepted, nominally at least, as King.[1] Samuel Burr Johnston, a North American typographer resident in Chile for much of this period, believed that this latter provision was a deliberately hypocritical measure designed to buy time for the revolution.[2] But neither the first nor the second Carrera government proceeded to the step of making a formal declaration of independence, even after the war against the royalists heightened the anti-Spanish feeling in the country. Indeed, at the very end of the 'Patria Vieja', with General Osorio's army advancing up-country towards the capital, Carrera justified his resistance in the name of Ferdinand VII. Osorio came brandishing the Spanish Constitution of 1812, and demanded Chile's conformity with its provisions. Carrera, however, had already heard of Ferdinand's release from captivity and his suppression of the 1812 Constitution, and taunted Osorio with the King's words that all who upheld the document were traitors.[3] Outwardly at least, both sides in the final campaigh of 1814 fought for Ferdinand VII.

Thus it would seem that, as far as the various governments of 1810–14 were concerned, total independence from Spain was never a publicly expressed policy. The creole leaders conducted an opportunist approach, waiting to see how far events would play into their hands. They did not decide to strike out on their own, as the Venezuelans had done—and the Venezuelan declaration of independence was printed in the seventh issue of *La Aurora*, on 26 March 1812—and in this they were no doubt influenced by the equally uncertain attitude of the government in Buenos Aires. This is hardly to say that no demands for total independence were made during this period. Quite the contrary is true. Camilo Henríquez was the first to issue such a demand, in open and unequivocal fashion, in a famous editorial in his *Aurora*.[4] Vera, in some verses for the second anniversary of the September Junta, proclaimed for all to hear that Chile was 'hastening at a rapid pace towards the great day of its independence'.[5] Soon afterwards Henríquez, in another editorial for *La Aurora de Chile*, stated

---

[1] *Ibid.* art. 3,   [2] Johnston, p. 65.
[3] *Monitor Araucano*, tomo 2, nos. 75–9, 2–16 September 1814.
[4] Tomo 1, no. 17, 4 June 1812. Henríquez quoted parts of Thomas Paine's *Common Sense*.   [5] *Aurora de Chile*, tomo 1, no. 34, 1 October 1812, p. 143.

forthrightly: 'The prosperity of America is incompatible with the old order of things; and the current circumstances are the favourable moment offered us by Providence to attain our liberty.'[1] He noted at the same time that whatever might be generally believed, Great Britian was unlikely to assist the cause, since Spain would probably confer trade privileges on Britain in any case, were America to remain under Spanish rule.

The Viceroy of Peru, interpreting the actions of the Carrera government as a straightforward advance towards independence,[2] finally decided at the end of 1812 that the Chilean revolution had to be crushed by force of arms. The dispatch of the Peruvian task-force and the subsequent military campaigns in the South certainly strengthened separatist feelings in Chile, quite apart from stimulating more directly anti-Spanish feelings. In the opening issue of his independent newspaper *El Semanario Republicano*, Irisarri dedicated several paragraphs to considering government policy, and took the opportunity to recommend a greater degree of frankness about its true aims.

We must become independent if we do not wish to fall back into a slavery even more fearful and cruel than in the past...We lose nothing by proclaiming our independence from Ferdinand, who exists only to devastate his dominions...The only King we possess is the Sovereign People...We cannot advance further with a hypocritical policy.[3]

Several issues later Irisarri returned to the theme and argued that, whatever the appearances might lead one to suppose, the true aim of all the new American governments was the winning of freedom. 'Everything the Americans are doing today', he wrote, 'is directed towards their independence; and, if...they are not displaying their ideas with complete clarity, this is, and can only be, for fear of the consequences, a fear conditioned by the weakness we acquired in servitude.'[4] Irisarri, at least, had no doubts about the inner direction of patriot policy. For him, and he was by no means alone, there were now only two possibilities: the Chileans could either move ahead to full independence, or they could

---

[1] *Aurora de Chile*, tomo I, no. 35, 8 October 1812, p. 145.
[2] Abascal, I, 4–5.   [3] *Semanario Republicano*, no. I, 7 August 1813.
[4] *Ibid.* no. 5, 4 September 1813.

return to the servitude of the old order as it had existed prior to 1810. The Treaty of Lircay in May 1814, which appeared to have brought the struggle against the royalists to an end, was condemned in some circles because it appeared to close the gateway to complete liberty and independence. A vigorous public polemic brought separatist feelings to the surface with a vengeance. For, as Manuel José de Gandarillas admonished an opponent: 'It is clear that America cannot and should not attain her prosperity in pious brotherhood with Spain. Undeceive yourself, and firmly believe that America will gain her longed-for freedom by force of arms.'[1]

Despite these open calls for full independence from nearly all the leading (or most active) creole intellectuals during the *'Patria Vieja'*, no government, as we have seen, proceeded to the final step of issuing a formal declaration. What was the reason for this failure? In the first place, it seems certain that the progress of the revolution was hampered by the notorious personal rivalries between the two factions generally referred to as the Carreras and the Larraíns, the 'Guelphs and the Ghibellines of the revolution', as Vicuña Mackenna called them.[2] These internal dissensions of the ruling elite impeded any clear agreement on policy. Samuel Burr Johnston believed (in October 1812) that, had these dissensions been absent, independence would already have become an accomplished fact.[3]

But quite apart from these political difficulties, the chief problem so far as any patriot government was concerned lay in the immense dead weight of indifferent or even hostile opinion with which the revolution had to contend. Irisarri could woefully lament the fact that of the 'million inconveniences' working against the patriotic cause, public opinion was the greatest.[4] It was not so much that the royalists used every conceivable trick to damage the spread of revolutionary propaganda, including disguising themselves as ghosts to play on the superstitious fears of the population.[5] This, after all, was only to be expected. But it was

---

[1] *Carta de dos amigos a don Firmiano Roca*, June 1814, *Arch.O'H.* II, 294–5.
[2] *Vida de O'Higgins*, p. 109.   [3] Johnston, p. 61.
[4] *Semanario Republicano*, Extraordinario, 5 February 1814.
[5] The friars at Chillán did this, representing the patriots' souls in Hell (*Década Araucana*, no. 4, 20 August 1825, p. 60).

sometimes hard to convince Chileans that the new political ideals were practical. In 1813, for instance, it was reported that several soldiers in the South wished to surrender to the royalist forces, giving as their reason that 'there will never be a Republican Government in America; that the best Government is Despotic or Purely military'.[1] Here, if one is to accept the account, was a clear rejection of patriot principles by patriot soldiers. But, generally speaking, such principles were far from widely known. Vera believed that the Chilean revolution owed a good deal to the spirit of imitation, 'before the principles that justified the movement had been made generally known'.[2] Even Bernardo O'Higgins admitted to his Argentine friend Terrada that there were probably more republicans in a single street in Buenos Aires than there were in the entire Kingdom of Chile.[3] Manuel de Salas, to take a third example, enjoined on Joel Roberts Poinsett the need for caution when drafting a new constitution for Chile. 'He read my project', wrote Poinsett, 'and told me that the advanced ideas proposed therein would go down badly in the country.'[4] Manuel José de Gandarillas, recalling the 'Patria Vieja' from the vantage point of twenty years afterwards, described its major fault as 'ignorance of political principles, and an absence of knowledge of the rights of man'.[5]

One must accept, therefore, that enthusiasm for the patriot cause was far from universal. The revolution had to face indifference and misunderstanding. And, in addition, the national difficulties which resulted from the outbreak of war in 1813 soon made themselves widely felt. The political tensions behind the legacy of the Carrera regime threatened to drag Chile down to defeat. 'Our beloved Chile has lately become worse than poor Buenos Aires,' wrote one patriot. 'The evils which have oppressed Buenos Aires and almost drawn her over the precipice are the ones I observe here.'[6] The pressure of war soon threatened

---

[1] J. M. Zorrilla to Antonio Ermida, Arauco, 25 August 1813, Archivo Eyzaguirre, vol. 35, pieza 31.
[2] To the Government of Buenos Aires, 8 April 1813, Márquez de la Plata, p. 108.
[3] Letter of June 1812, Vicuña Mackenna, *Vida de O'Higgins*, p. 129 n.
[4] To Vera, n.d., Collier and Feliú Cruz, p .90.   [5] Gandarillas, p. 13.
[6] 'D. J. B.' to A. N. de Orjera, Concepción, 30 September 1813, Archivo Eyzaguirre, vol. 20, pieza 40.

to bring patriot Chile to the point of exhaustion. Military and financial inadequacies mounted in the early months of 1814. Captain James Hillyar saw the situation as it was on his arrival in Chile in the following way:

The wealthy are deprived of their property to support the war, the poor are becoming discontented from the total stagnation of commerce, and consequent want of employment, and I believe a very great majority would prefer a return to the old system, bad as it was, to the continuance of the present.[1]

There were good reasons, even in 1814, to be cautious in stating the aim of total independence. The revolutionaries wanted it, but they were uncertain of the final authority they now invoked—the general will.

POSSIBILITIES OF RECONCILIATION

Although Chile's movement away from the Spanish motherland was constantly maintained between Septembr 1810 and October 1814, there was, as we have now seen, a certain unreadiness to cut the final link. The more moderate revolutionaries had, all along, been concerned to retain at least a token association with the Empire. The virtues of home rule were not a subject for debate, but the *degree* of home rule was still a major preoccupation. Until the outbreak of war at the start of 1813 an optimistic assessment of the possibilities of reconciliation with Spain was sometimes expressed. In 1811, for instance, Manuel de Salas even went so far as to imagine the details of such a reconciliation, although in a somewhat fanciful and unrealistic manner. In his *Diálogo de los porteros*, he described how the restored Ferdinand VII would receive a Chilean deputation. The leader of the deputation would tell the adored monarch how his Chilean subjects had suffered 'a most insulting policy for the space of three centuries', how the creoles had been deprived of public office, forced to endure a purely passive role even in commerce, and how a 'favourite of your own father' pillaged the Empire for his own benefit. After further tearful descriptions of Chilean grievances, the leader of the

---

[1] To J. W. Croker, Valparaíso, 12 April 1814, F.O. 72/169, p. 43.

delegation would explain how the Juntas had been set up to take on the responsibility of self-government in Ferdinand's absence. 'If, Desired Ferdinand,' he would say, 'your distant vassals erred in their methods, their aims were praiseworthy.' Ferdinand would listen patiently and sympathetically, taking in the creoles' points one by one, and his reaction would be fully worthy of the great and magnanimous monarch Salas mistakenly supposed him to be. The final scene of the reconciliation would consist of a complete vindication of the creoles' course of action, and a repudiation of the authoritarian behaviour of the royalist viceroys and governors who had opposed the revolution.

I seemed to see Ferdinand the Good, his eyes brimming over with sweet tears, descend from his throne and embrace those who preserved the New World with the same majesty as Ferdinand the Catholic displayed in removing the chains from the man who discovered it... [I seemed to see him] showing the same horror towards the Abascals, Elíos and Cisneros as that other Ferdinand showed towards the Bobadillas, Aguados and Cañetes, etc...[1]

Salas knew little or nothing of Ferdinand VII, and was certainly not to know how completely misplaced his touching confidence was. Yet these pages from the *Diálogo de los porteros* are worth mentioning if only to demonstrate that a final break with the monarchy was regarded as inconceivable in some circles, and that Manuel de Salas, the most edcuated Chilean of the day, could still envisage a joyful reconciliation despite his consciousness of creole grievances.

Salas, to do him justice, was consistent in trying to maintain good relations with the Viceroyalty of Peru, whatever his own inner position. As he wrote in exile in 1815,

Chile could not become separated from a protector nation in Europe to which she was bound by as many links as convenience, justice and reason could establish...Three times I believed that the time had come to re-establish harmony with the Lima government. I urged my case effectively, but I was repulsed.[2]

---

[1] *Diálogo de los porteros*, pp. 196–200.
[2] To Osorio, 14 February 1815, Salas, *Escritos*, I, 66–7.

The 'Patria Vieja'

Extreme patriots like Bernardo O'Higgins, on the other hand, realized from the start that Peru represented the most serious threat to the cause of revolution in South America, and that Abascal would attempt to crush any new form of government in Chile. Referring to the examples of Quito and La Paz, he wrote (in the first week of 1811) that he was 'convinced that, as soon as he finds the right occasion, Abascal will treat us in the same way, and will employ all his efforts to destroy us'.[1] This forecast was, of course, proved correct by the events themselves. But it should not, perhaps, be forgotten that when the war finally came, many patriots felt very strongly that it was a struggle against Lima rather than against Spain. Spain was, after all, a great distance away, and, moreover, was supposed to be liberal, while Lima and Abascal were very much closer. The Viceroy himself could be considered as a visible representation of what the creole leaders now thought of as despotism and tyranny. Abascal, even as early as the start of 1811, was one of those

monsters who, in the guise of superiors, become the scourge and horror of mankind. Such phenomena are ferocious beasts, which it is necessary to cleanse from the earth...and the kingdom of Chile will deserve history's apotheosis if it helps to exterminate the monsters who are pillaging Peru.[2]

The Junta of 1813 was able to define the war as 'the war with the Viceroy of Lima',[3] and the Cabildo of Santiago could use the term 'Invading Army from Lima' to describe the enemy.[4] I have already mentioned how, at the very end of the 'Patria Vieja', Carrera taunted Osorio with the incorrectness of Peru's constitutional position, and, at that late stage, the patriots could claim, with some semblance of justification, that all Osorio was attacking Chile for was 'his income and his rank'.[5] Lima, it was felt by

[1] To Mackenna, 5 January 1811, Cruz, *Epistolario*, I, 25.
[2] 'Sobre la necesidad Justicia y conveniencia...', A.B.A. vol. 25-2(3), fo. 760.
[3] *Manifiesto del Gobierno de Chile a las Naciones de América y Europa* (30 May 1813), CHDI, XXIV, 314–15.
[4] *Acta*, 16 May 1814, Medina, *Actas*, p. 317. The enemy could also be termed 'Concepción' (*ibid.* pp. 204, 206), since the invasion forces recruited much of their strength in the South.
[5] *Monitor Araucano*, tomo 2, no. 75, 2 September 1814.

some, was attempting to crush the revolution for largely economic reasons.[1] The military confrontation of 1813–14, therefore, was not necessarily conceived of as a direct struggle between Chile and the motherland. It could be regarded either as a straightforward conflict with a bullying neighbour or, at the very least, as an assertion of local rights against the motherland at one remove. The fact that it was Peru rather than the Peninsula which had taken the anti-revolutionary initiative prevented the creoles from venting all their pent-up fury on Spain.

In spite of the growth of separatism, was there still a chance of reconciliation with Spain? In Buenos Aires in 1812, Captain Peter Heywood of the Royal Navy gained the impression from a conversation with Manuel Bulnes[2] that 'the People of Chile...might with no very great difficulty, be prevailed upon to accept the new Constitution for Spain under the Guaranty of our Government'.[3] The Junta, in October 1813, seemed almost disposed to come to terms with the royalists. In an abortive peace initiative, it contacted the royalist commander and urged him to negotiate on the grounds, first, of Chilean military superiority, and, secondly, of humanity: 'we are fighting against Americans, against the inhabitants of the same state'.[4] In February 1814 the Junta informed Captain Hillyar (who had already discussed the question of peace terms with Abascal in Lima) that its true aim was 'to consolidate the Spanish Nation in an equal and just manner'.[5] In April of the same year the new regime of Francisco de la Lastra, confronted by Hillyar's evident willingness to mediate between the two sides in the war, firmly denied that total independence had ever been an object of the revolution, and somewhat uncharitably blamed any tendency towards separatism on the Carreras.

During the time of that despotism, all plans were altered, and hints were made alluding to an independence which [the Carreras] could

---

[1] *Monitor Araucano*, tomo 2, no. 80, 20 September 1814.

[2] Manuel Bulnes Prieto (d. 1866) was not openly separatist at this period though his allegiance after 1817 was fervent; he became commander of the Chilean army in Peru, 1838; gained glory as the victor of Yungay (20 January 1839), on the strength of which he became President of the Republic 1841–51.

[3] Heywood to Melville, 4 December 1812, F.O. 72/152, p. 299.

[4] To General J. F. Sánchez, Talca, 22 October 1813, A.B.A. vol. 25-2(4), fo. 404.

[5] To Hillyar, 24 February 1814, F.O. 72/169, p. 50.

not declare because they were uncertain of the general will. Without doubt, it was that anarchy, and those unconsidered steps, which moved the Viceroy of Lima to carry a destructive war to these territories.[1]

The government, 'wishing to elect a government concordant with the general ideas of the monarchy,'[2] and hoping to restore matters to the state in which they had been before the Carreras took power, dispatched Hillyar to arrange meetings between the patriots and the new royalist commander General Gainza. Hillyar was successful in this mission, though he had nothing to do with the substance of the agreement[3] embodied in the form of the Treaty of Lircay.[4] The Treaty gave Chile its autonomy for the time being, and provided for the sending of Chilean deputies to the Cortes in Spain. In return the Chilean government was to make a number of concessions such as the abolition of the national flag (which it did). International trade was to continue. These—and several stipulations about the withdrawal of royalist military units—were the main points of the agreement reached.

The Treaty of Lircay provided the excuse for a considerable amount of public debate on the progress of the revolution. Some creoles appeared to welcome the Treaty as a genuine accommodation with the motherland, while other sopposed it on the ground that the way forward to independence was now barred. Lastra, the Supreme Director, justified the Treaty by referring to the substantial gains it incorporated. The government had conceded something, he admitted, but the advantages outweighed the effect of this.

Local self-government, command of the armed forces, possession of public offices, open trade—these are the fruits of our transaction with General Gainza. What country, even after a thousand victories, has gained so many advantages from a war?[5]

[1] *Acta* of Supreme Director and Senate, 19 April 1814, *SCL*, I, 338.
[2] *Ibid.*
[3] This is made clear in Captain M. H. Dixon to J. W. Croker, Buenos Aires, 3 June 1814, F.O. 72/169, p. 205. Cf. Graham and Humphreys, pp. 143–5.
[4] Printed in *SCL*, I, 340–1.
[5] *Manifesto*, April 1814, *Arch.O'H.* II, 162. The whole of the public polemic on the Lircay issue is printed in *Arch.O'H.* II, 245–302.

Even Bernardo O'Higgins, many years later, did not feel ashamed of having put his signature to a document which, as he wrote, 'would have saved torrents of blood, and much human misery'.[1] On the face of it, the Treaty of Lircay represented a real attempt to adjust the differences between Chile and the metropolis through the Viceroy of Peru. But, as it happened, the Viceroy himself was bound to disapprove of what his commander in the field had done. Abascal's own terms for a settlement, as expressed to Captain Hillyar in Lima, 'comprised in substance a return to the former System',[2] while, under the Treaty, Chile was left with a considerable degree of autonomy. On the Chilean side, there is good reason to doubt whether the government was really sincere in its ratification of the Treaty. The Argentine commissioner in Santiago believed that Lastra and his colleagues had agreed to the Treaty only as a means of buying time,[3] and from Lastra himself there is evidence that this was indeed the case and that his true aims were not those achieved at Lircay. Writing to the Chilean emissary in Europe, Lastra told him that Chile would not succumb,

that she is resolved to be free at any cost, that the more she knows her rights the more she hates slavery, that she has completely forgotten the old system, that she wants a liberal system which will provide this part of America—the most abandoned and downtrodden part—those advantages which until now it has not experienced. These are the true and intimate sentiments of Chile. These are the liberal principles for which Chile has proposed to defend herself. If at any time in the official correspondence you notice any expressions which indicate another sense, you must believe that the variation is accidental and that the circumstances...demand it. But in substance the opinion is, and will remain, what I have told you.[4]

The fact remains, however, that the Treaty of Lircay could have supplied a reasonable basis for reconciliation if both sides had been

[1] To an unnamed correspondent [in English], 3 May 1838 (*borrador*), F.V. vol. 645, fo. 18.
[2] Hillyar to Croker, 12 April 1814, F.O. 72/169, p. 43.
[3] Juan José del Pazo to the Supreme Director of the United Provinces, 2 July 1814, A.B.A. vol. 25-2(5), fo. 363.
[4] Lastra to Pinto, 27 May 1814, *CHDI*, IV, 194 n.

prepared to accept its terms. Neither side, however, was in a reasonable mood in 1814. On the one hand, Abascal's insistence that Chile return to the old order as it had existed prior to 1810 meant, in practice, that no concessions to local autonomy could be made. On the other, the inner direction of Chilean policy was now sufficiently separatist to prevent the possibility of any lasting reconciliation with Spain.

One suggestion—a highly interesting suggestion—made during this period was that the Spanish Empire should be reorganized within a new framework. Schemes of Spanish American federation were not unknown during the revolution, as will be made clear in chapter 5. The earliest such schemes envisaged continued collaboration between the colonies and the Spanish Crown, or at the very least a defensive alliance to protect what was left of the Spanish Empire. Juan Egaña's *Plan de Gobierno* of August 1810 suggested a Chilean initiative to summon a conference to arrange a defensive federation of the American colonies,[1] and this appears to have been the first Chilean scheme. Camilo Henríquez also seems to have shown some interest in this idea, and it made a shadowy appearance in his sermon before the installation of the 1811 Congress.[2] But it was Egaña's *Declaración de los Derechos del Pueblo de Chile*, written in 1811 or 1812 and printed in a modified and more patriotic form in 1813, which provides the best illustration of this theme.[3] Under Egaña's scheme, Chile was to enjoy complete home rule, but was to be associated externally with 'the Spanish peoples' through a general congress. Ferdinand VII was to be recognized as the constitutional head of the whole imperial Spanish nation (though the 1813 version admitted as an alternative anybody else nominated by the general congress). That Juan Egaña's aim in this scheme was a reorganization of the Empire rather than a federation of independent republics is clearly indicated by his later description of it as 'the fundamental basis of a General Confederation of the Spanish Empire'.[4] Those writers (and I am not amongst them) who still regard the independence of

---

[1] *CHDI*, XIX, 108.   [2] *SCL*, I, 36.   [3] Printed in *SCL*, I, 209–11.
[4] 'Memoria de los servicios públicos del dr. dn. Juan Egaña', *RCHG*, tomo XXVII, no. 31 (1918), p. 18.

The Growth of the Revolution

Spanish America as an unmitigated tragedy would perhaps be justified in regarding Egaña's grandiose vision of a Spanish Commonwealth of Nations as an acceptable solution to the imperial dilemma which might have stood some chance of operating had not the attitude of the Spanish government itself been so obdurately illiberal and anti-creole. The suppression of the revolutionary governments by force of arms signified a certain end to any such hopes as far as Egaña himself was concerned.

While some minds may have contemplated, in a visionary way, the ideal of a revived and perfected relationship with Spain, it cannot seriously be doubted that by 1814 most of the leaders of the Chilean revolution were separatists in the full sense of the word. 'The affections of the larger part of the community', Captain Hillyar observed in a report to London, 'are almost weaned from the parent community.'[1] The shock of war had braced Chilean nerves, even if it had also created discontent. Bernardo de Vera y Pintado thought that 1814 would mark the first real year of the Chilean revolution.[2] It was Captain Hillyar, though, who saw as clearly as anyone else the probable *dénouement* of the struggle.

The troops under the General of Lima, I think will eventually be successful, and the Spaniards of course regain their wonted ascendant; but unless a more liberal policy is adopted than heretofore, and they endeavour to conciliate instead of irritating and oppressing the Creoles; unless they allow them a fair proportion of the higher Offices and all other employments of the State; and a real not nominal participation of the equal rights of all Spanish Subjects, it will only last until the oppressed can find assistants to shake off the yoke.[3]

The policy recommended by Hillyar was never carried out. Even f Osorio, the victorious conqueror, would himself have wished to attempt conciliation, as seems probable, his brutal successor as Governor of Chile, Francisco Casimiro Marcó del Pont, preferred to rule the Captaincy-General by means of atrocities and chastisements. But there was no lack of 'assistants' to throw off the

[1] To Croker, 12 April 1814, F.O. 72/169, p. 44.
[2] To the Government of the United Provinces, 1 October 1813, Márquez de la Plata, p. 134.   [3] To Croker, 12 April 1814, F.O. 72/169, p. 44.

newly imposed colonial tutelage. When O'Higgins returned in triumph in 1817, he would first consolidate, and then declare, the independence which had become the only solution to the imperial dilemma.

THE DICTATORSHIP OF JOSÉ MIGUEL CARRERA

No description of Chilean ideas and politics during the four years of the 'Patria Vieja' would be complete without a discussion, however brief, of the figure who dominated the course of Chilean history in that period. Handsome, personable and youthful, the extraordinary personality of José Miguel Carrera has, thanks to the efforts of generations of hagiographers, become a romantic hero of the first order. Carrera was the stormy petrel of the Chilean revolution. He destroyed the first national Congress. He sponsored a set of radical reforms which opened the way for Peruvian military intervention. He overthrew the Lastra regime in time to bring about the conquest of patriot Chile by Osorio. These are the facts of history, and they must be disentangled from the legend.

Though Carrera's government was military and absolute, he could rely on a considerable measure of popular support. This seems certain. 'His party amongst all classes of people', wrote one patriot, 'is considerable.'[1] The North American typographer Samuel Burr Johnston was of similar opinion. Though the Carreras were usurpers, he concluded, they were by no means despots. They gained power by force, but retained it by conquering the affections of the people.[2] In this, at least, Carrera was successful. In 1817, when San Martín and Pueyrredón were planning the liberation of Chile, they had to take into account the public feeling for Carrera, who had, as Pueyrredón expressed it, 'the affection of the common people'.[3] Carrera himself was fully aware of the fact. 'If I sustained myself in power by bayonets alone,' he asked later, 'why did I work so much with the people?'[4]

[1] J. M. Pérez de Cotapos to Narciso Pérez, 19 October 1813, Archivo Eyzaguirre, vol. 35, pieza 28.
[2] Johnston, p. 34.   [3] Pueyrredón, Campana de los Andes, facsimile 10.
[4] Diario militar, CHDI, I, 230.

But did this respect for the people include an attachment to the constitutional forms which would have created popular government? According to Luis Carrera, José Miguel did not intend to maintain his military dictatorship indefinitely, and it was only 'the unexpected invasion of the Lima army' which 'frustrated the plans, which had already been made, to give the people the free use of their rights'.[1]

What were Carrera's aims? If one is to believe his long manifesto of 4 December 1811, in which he attempted to justify his *coup d'état* of the previous month,[2] he intended to give a decided impulse to the revolution and to destroy the lethargy into which (so he said) its leaders had fallen. He criticized the immaturity of political ideas in Chile, the inadequacy of the Congress, and the division of sovereignty that had taken place. 'Tyranny has to end,' he wrote. 'We must be zealous to bring freedom into being.'[3] There seems little doubt that Carrera wanted independence, despite the vacillations of his policy in this respect. 'Oh, that we might have the glory of seeing the Chilean state free,' he wrote to Poinsett'.[4] But beyond this, his political aims remain vague in the extreme. He gave little indication of the form he wanted freedom to take. It is perhaps easiest to regard him as a personalist leader—in a sense O'Higgins never was—whose main motive was private glory and an intense disdain for the Larraín family and its many political associates. It was, it seems, a typical piece of Larraín boastfulness that decided him to overthrow the congressional regime of September 1811. During a walk with Carrera, Fray Joaquín Larraín arrogantly claimed that his family now had all the most important offices in the state—he had the presidency of the Congress, his brother-in-law the presidency of the Executive, and his cousin the presidency of the supreme court. Carrera, or so he relates in his diary, was extremely irritated by this remark, and in return asked Larraín who had the presidency of the bayonets.[5] Not long afterwards Carrera used

---

[1] *Manifiesto que hace a los pueblos el comandante general de artillería don Luis de Carrera*, n.d., CHDI, XXIV, 365.

[2] *SCL*, I, 197-9.

[3] *Ibid.* I, 199.   [4] Concepción, 24 January 1814, Collier and Feliú Cruz, p. 168.

[5] *Diario militar*, CHDI, I, 37.

the bayonets at his command to overthrow the Larraín-dominated Congress.

It is, unfortunately, impossible to escape the conclusion that one of the most notable characteristics in Carrera's make-up was arrogance. He could write of his enemies that 'by destroying *my* fortune they destroyed the State's'.[1] And the postures to which his personal ambition took him were amply illustrated by his conduct after 1817, when he actively attempted to undermine the O'Higgins regime for reasons, as far as one can see, of pure spite. The United States envoy H. M. Brackenridge, who met Carrera at Montevideo in 1818, unfavourably summed him up as 'likely to turn his sword against his country for the gratification of revenge'.[2] A year earlier, when news had arrived of the liberation of Chile by O'Higgins and San Martín, Carrera's 'rage and disappointment knew no bounds'.[3] This makes unhappy reading, and it certainly calls in question Carrera's degree of patriotism.

Carrera's high-handed treatment of some of his political opponents during the '*Patria Vieja*' naturally led to opposition and resistance, though his behaviour in this respect was perhaps no worse than O'Higgins' later. Juan Martínez de Rozas warned the new dictator that 'Rome began to fall from the time the Praetorian guards usurped the power of electing and deposing their high magistrates'.[4] The Junta which dismissed Carrera from the post of commander-in-chief in 1813 described his regime, somewhat exaggeratedly, as a more fearful despotism than the one which had ruled Chile over the previous three centuries.[5] The brief provisional 'constitution' which Carrera introduced in 1812 to sanction his dictatorship also came under attack, once Carrera was in the South and conveniently far away from the capital. The constitution, alleged Irisarri, was invalid. It failed to take the general will of the people into account. Its proponents had themselves illegally superseded the lawful representative assembly of the previous year. Nor had the constitution itself been introduced in an appropriate manner.

---

[1] Carrera, 'Borrador de un manifiesto', p. 266.   [2] Brackenridge, I, 235.
[3] *Ibid.* 268.
[4] Concepción Provincial Junta to the Junta of Santiago, 10 December 1811, *SCL*, I, 206.
[5] *Bando (borrador)* [December 1813/January 1814], *Arch.O'H.* I, 306.

Everybody knows that on 27th October 1812, in the hall of the Consulado, there appeared a large piece of paper to which citizens of the capital had to put their names, unless they wished to expose themselves to the resentment of the soldiers.[1]

In a later article, Irisarri attacked the foundations of the Carrera regime by criticizing the view that the *coup* of 15 November 1811 could in any way be said to represent the voice of the people.

The voice of the people is not the voice of four friends who plan to indulge their passions by staging a little scene of revolution. The 'people' I saw on 15th November 1811 could only be called 'people' by a very knavish sort of irony.[2]

Irisarri, connected as he was with the Larraín family, might well have been accused of political bias. Juan Egaña, on the other hand, was rather less committed to the anti-Carrera movement, yet he too openly urged the dictator to resign and to re-establish 'the political liberty of the kingdom'.[3]

The legend of José Miguel Carrera is best left as a legend. The belief that he was in some way more 'radical' than his opponents cannot ultimately be substantiated. Indeed, in 1818 he went so far as to criticize O'Higgins for abolishing titles of nobility, on the ground that this was an imprudent political move.[4] The supposition that Carrera was 'republican' and pro-North American, while O'Higgins was 'monarchist' and pro-English is similarly unfounded. As Carrera's close friend Joel Roberts Poinsett wrote in 1817,

Ohiggins [sic] is not an Englishman in his politics and is easily led and most firmly attached to republican principles, more so than our friend C[arrera]. The latter possesses more intellect & more vigour of Character and I think is the only man I know there capable of carrying the revolution to a successful termination, but his Republicanism was due to my ascendant over him & I found on that subject he was difficult to govern.[5]

---

[1] *Semanario Republicano*, no. 10, 9 October 1813.   [2] *Ibid.* 19 February 1814.
[3] To Carrera, 17 February 1813, Egaña, *Escritos inéditos*, p. 133.
[4] *Manifiesto que hace a los pueblos de Chile el ciudadano José Miguel Carrera* (4 March 1818), *CHDI*, VII, 63 n.
[5] To an unknown correspondent, Charleston, 31 October 1817, *HAHR*, XLIII (1963), p. 407. See Alemparte, *Carrera y Freire*, pp. 8–10 and 133–311, where Carrera's republi-

The 'Patria Vieja'

Bartolomé Mitre's well known judgement that Carrera possessed all the vices of Alcibiades and none of his virtues[1] is perhaps a little harsh. Nevertheless, it must be stated that Carrera seems, on the face of things, to have been motivated largely by personal ambition, while his regime represented, to use Encina's words 'a movement destitute of any political significance'.[2] His intervention in the politics of the 'Patria Vieja' was a disaster, and his final reappearance in July 1814 was, in all probability, one of the major causes of the downfall of patriot Chile and the triumph of Spanish arms. Yet there is one definite sense in which Carrera deserves his legend. His reforms[3] and his sponsorship of revolutionary propaganda made possible the elaboration of the revolutionary ideology, which was by far the most important intellectual activity of the 'Patria Vieja'. By 1814 the revolution was well under way. Though it met with disaster at Rancagua, the subsequent royalist attempt to restore the old order was short-lived. The fact that the cause of independence was able to return to the struggle was in large measure due to the heightening of ideological activity which Carrera permitted and actively encouraged. This was his chief contribution to the development of his homeland.

can integrity is contrasted with O'Higgins' 'compromising' attitude to monarchism. But there is no real evidence that can turn O'Higgins into a monarchist—see chapter 6, pp. .

[1] Mitre, I, 326.   [2] Historia, VII, 23.

[3] These are concisely listed in Manuel G. Balbontín, *Epopeya de los húsares* (2nd edn. 1963), 37–43. (Balbontín is one of the latest recruits to the army of *carrerino* writers). The struggle between Carrera and O'Higgins went on long after they were both dead. For their supporters' more modern battles (mainly over the siting of statues and the nomenclature of hotels) see Alemparte, *Carrera y Freire*, pp. 13–18.

PART II

THE REVOLUTIONARY IDEOLOGY

4

FUNDAMENTAL POLITICAL IDEAS

THE FORMULATION OF THE NEW IDEOLOGY

During the four troubled years of the *'Patria Vieja'* the political consciousness of the ruling creole elite in Chile was largely transformed. Certainly there remained sections of the aristocracy which paid only lip service to the new ideals, and which did not find it particularly inconvenient to have to live under the restored colonial regime between October 1814 and February 1817. Total acceptance of the ideology of the revolution came later, after the victories of the Army of the Andes and the formal establishment of full independence. By 1830, the old orthodoxy based on loyalty to the Crown and obedience to the Peninsular authorities had been replaced by the contemporary orthodoxy of individualist liberalism. Chileans no longer regarded themselves as subjects of the Spanish Empire, but as citizens of a sovereign independent community with all the attributes of a nation state. The concept of rights conceded by a near-absolute monarchy had vanished. In its place was the notion that rights were in some sense natural and inalienable. It is the purpose of the present chapter, and of the chapter which follows, to describe and define the fundamental elements of this new body of ideas and attitudes.

Before considering the political ideas of the revolution, I must first indicate how these were formulated in the first place. It should never be forgotten that political theory was almost invariably indulged in for practical purposes in Chile between 1810 and 1833. It was used to justify national moves against Spain or Peru, or alternatively to give substance to internal political initiatives. More often than not, political theory was an arm of propaganda, directed either against the external enemy or against political opponents within Chile. It was not looked upon as an activity in its own right. There was no real attempt by any Chilean of the period to arrive at the fundamental principles of politics, in the manner of Plato or Rousseau. The revolution produced no *Republic*, no *Social Contract*. The exponents of the revolutionary ideology were patriotic propagandists rather than speculative thinkers, but even on this level the Chileans produced nothing to compare with *Common Sense* or *The Federalist*. An exception in some respects to this general tendency—as to so many others—was Juan Egaña. Though much of Egaña's writing was a justification of a few basic doctrines, these doctrines represented an original attempt to reach a fundamentally correct political position. Egaña's theory was, on many points, strikingly different from the common revolutionary ideology, and it deserves separate treatment (in chapter 7) for this reason.

The revolutionary ideology was elaborated in three successive phases. The formative period of the process was, as I have already indicated, the '*Patria Vieja*', when the introduction of the printing press and the foundation of a handful of newspapers permitted the publication and dissemination of political ideas on a wider scale than ever before. As a result of the fervent publicism of Henríquez and his colleagues, the main lines of the revolutionary ideology were fully developed by 1814. The second phase of the process roughly coincided with the government of Bernardo O'Higgins (1817–23). It saw a renewed attack on the main problems of revolutionary thought after the parenthetical silence of the Spanish reconquest. As in the '*Patria Vieja*', most of the political literature of the O'Higgins period was strictly practical in its intention. The preoccupations of the small Chilean intelligentsia were much the same as they had been during the '*Patria Vieja*', though certain themes—the justification for independence, the systematic denigration of Spain, and so on—made their appearance more strongly than before. After the fall of O'Higgins in January 1823, a third phase of ideological development set in. The multiplication of newspapers, many of them highly political as far as their contents went, made the elaboration of diverse points of view not only possible but extremely popular. The numerous changes of the later 1820s encouraged the discussion of a wide variety of specific constitutional points and political prescriptions. In a purely quantitative sense, this third phase was the richest and most fecund of the three. Yet the basic doctrines then appealed to had already been enunciated in the '*Patria Vieja*' and under O'Higgins.

It is fair to say that the Chilean revolution produced no really original political theorist, though the figure of Juan Egaña must certainly rank high in the general Latin American panorama of the period. Men like Egaña and Camilo Henríquez were prolific writers, and both deserve attention in their own right. But the formulation of the revolutionary ideology was not the work of one man but of many, though Henríquez merits the honour of having been the first and in some ways the most constant of the political thinkers of the time. The small educated nucleus of Chileans (and by Chileans one must include foreigners like Egaña and Vera who regarded themselves as such) provided the basic writings, mainly through the pages of newspapers. This small creole intelligentsia included the writers already mentioned as having dominated the '*Patria Vieja*': Vera, Irisarri, Egaña, Salas, Gandarillas, etc. These intellectuals continued their work for the revolution after the reconquest. Henríquez was active from his return to Chile in 1822 until his death in 1825. Vera was prominent under O'Higgins and, to a lesser extent, until his death in 1827. Irisiarri re-emerged as a powerful political journalist for a brief period in 1818, before departing for London, where he continued his polemical career in a more general way. Egaña and Salas worked right through until the end of the revolution. They were, of course, joined by others. Gandarillas, who had served something of an apprenticeship during the '*Patria Vieja*', returned to Chile after the fall of O'Higgins and once more became an influential political writer at certain periods. Some of the best journalism of the 1820s came from men who were actively enagaged in the polemical struggles of the time: Diego José Benavente, José Miguel Infante, Melchor José Ramos, and the indefatigable popular-liberals Manuel Magallanes and Nicolás Pradel. It would, in fact, be impossible to draw up a truly comprehensive list of all the personalities involved—not, at any rate, a list which did full justice to all the political intellectuals who played some part, however momentary, in the exposition of the basic ideas first introduced in the 'Patria Vieja'. It would, however, be wrong to ignore the contribution of a number of itinerant foreigners, the most distinguished of whom, the Spanish man of letters José Joaquín de Mora, exercised a considerable influence in Chile at the end of the 1820s. Other foreigners who appeared on the scene at various points included Bernardo Monteagudo, for a brief period during O'Higgins' government, and the Frenchman Dauxion Lavaysse, who engaged in the polemics of the 1820s with a gusto that made him highly unpopular in certain circles.

'Politics', wrote Irisarri, 'is the noblest of sciences, and teaches us the true interests of the people.'[1] But despite this the revolution produced no single systematic treatise on politics which can be regarded as a faithful expression of the revolutionary ideology. Such treatises and pamphlets as were written—occasional works such as Dauxion Lavaysse's denunciation of federalism (1823) or Egaña's discussion of religious toleration (1826)—were usually concerned with specific issues rather than with a broad view. Even Juan Egaña, the most voluminous writer of the revolution, never composed a comprehensive political treatise, and this is surprising. His justification of the 1823 Constitution (1824), or his collection of articles on federalism (1825), hardly merits this description. It is not to this type of work that we must turn in our search for the revolutionary ideology, but to a wide diversity of different sources. Some of these ought to be mentioned here.

What may loosely be termed official sources often provide interesting insights into the political mentality of the period. Official manifestos were usually issued to justify the Chilean revolution to the world and to the republics of America, or sometimes to add weight to a particular action on the part of the government of the day. Hints of certain underlying political premises can sometimes be discerned, too, in state decrees. The texts of the various presidential messages to Congress, and of the congressional debates themselves, are also valuable in this respect. Thanks to the magnificent compilation of Valentín Letelier, the proceedings of the Congresses of the revolution have been

---

[1] 'Sobre las consecuencias que debe traernos la independencia', Semanario Republicano, 4 September 1813.

recorded with a reasonable degree of comprehensiveness. By no means all the meetings of the different legislatures left behind full descriptions of debates—as often as not, a bare and uninformative *Acta* was the sole product of each day's session—but for certain crucial periods, notably the federalist ascendancy, verbatim reports of deputies' speeches have been preserved. Even though many of these speeches were concerned with trivial issues of a procedural or even personal nature, they remain an important source of information.

If governmental and parliamentary sources are valuable, the private correspondence of public figures—where this is available —is more disappointing. The letters of Bernardo O'Higgins and Diego Portales, to take the two most important examples, reveal relatively little in the way of political reflection. Here again, however, the Egaña family creates an exception. The correspondence between Juan Egaña and his son Mariano, which somewhat onesidedly illuminates the political processes of the later 1820s, contains a wealth of commentary on the important issues of the day and is an indispensable aid to the study of the liberal and federalist period.

All these sources—the occasional book or pamphlet, official and parliamentary papers, and private correspondence—play their part, but ultimately it is from the newspapers of the period that the richest impression of the political thought of the revolution can be gained. Chilean journalism, as we have seen in the case of *La Aurora de Chile*, began with an honourable record of political activity, and politics continued to be its main subject-matter until the time of Diego Portales. The main concern of newspapers, particularly in the 1820s, was the development of the revolution and the various struggles which followed on the abdication of O'Higgins. Editorials often commented rather too fulsomely on passing phases of the political struggle and minor events which have little relevance to the general point of view I am pursuing here. Nevertheless, the average Chilean newspaper between 1812 and 1830 conceived its function as partly educative. Long articles, often in serial form, repeatedly expounded the progress of the revolutionary cause in Chile and America, the most suitable form of government, aspects of the latest constitution, and the general principles of politics. Some journals, appearing monthly, provided an even weightier contribution to political discussion. Outstanding in this respect were Henríquez' *Mercurio de Chile* (1822–3) and Mora's *Mercurio Chileno* (1828–9). Towards the end of the 1820s, however, the tone of Chilean journalism was to some extent altered, or at any rate complemented. A new style of newspaper put in its appearance, concentrating on news rather than views. The most famous example was *El Mercurio de Valparaíso*, founded in 1827 and still being published every day. Originally a liberal newspaper, it nevertheless adopted a realistic and objective style which enabled it to survive the abrupt decline in journalistic activity which set in under Portales. It was with the growth of *El Mercurio* and the government-backed *El Araucano* (founded in 1830), not to mention a number of less famous newspapers with more exclusively mercantile interests, that Chilean journalism began to lose its revolutionary flavour and to become more like journalism as we know it today.

FIRST PRINCIPLES

'What is liberty if it does not base its gentle rule on diamond foundations: a generous, wise and equal law concordant with the eternal law?'[1] José Joaquín de Mora asked the question in 1828, but it represented a fundamental preoccupation of the creole intelligentsia. How could liberty be given an institutional form which would guarantee its survival in a world where social conditions made for perpetual instability? The answer seemed fairly simple. The law which created a suitable framework for the operation of liberty had to be as 'natural' as possible. It had to be consonant with the eternal yardstick of the Natural Law. Natural Law, to the Chileans, was fixed in a permanent and unshakable position in the universe. It was, as Camilo Henríquez put it, 'an immutable and immortal justice, anterior to all empires'.[2] It was impossible to escape it or to oppose it indefinitely.

---

[1] Mora, 'Al Dieziocho de Setiembre de 1828', Amunátegui, *J. J. de Mora*, p. 127.
[2] Sermon of 4 July 1811, *SCL*, I, 34.

Fundamental Political Ideas

'We could not', affirmed O'Higgins, 'elude that ancient law of nature which fixes the order all beings must follow in their physical and moral organization.'[1] Thus natural law was the regulating mechanism of the universe and of human life. It stood parallel to, and was in some ways connected with, the fundamental laws of human society. As a newspaper in 1827 expressed it: 'Necessary laws direct all the beings of nature, and constitute, for us, the order of the universe; and natural laws, equally necessary, direct mankind and maintain order in society.'[2] It would be an error to suppose that this notion played a prominent part in the general ideology of the revolution, but it can nevertheless be said that at the back of many Chileans' minds there did exist a comforting feeling that there was a supreme law with which all human laws must, ultimately, be concordant. This 'order which rules the world naturally'[3] was also, in an indefinable manner, the source of human rights which, as will be seen, were regarded as natural and inalienable. It was also, in a sense, the archetype of all lesser legislation. 'Natural law is the mother of all positive laws.'[4]

Human society was completely in accordance with this natural order. It existed for certain set purposes. As the Concepción Provincial Assembly declared in 1826:

The origin of society was to seek that welfare which men were unable to find in the solitary life. Men accepted one necessary evil [government] in order to avoid greater evils. So it is that the association has as its object the welfare of the associates.[5]

It will be seen from this statement that a 'state of nature'—'the solitary life'—was automatically assumed, and also that the origins of society had to involve a certain measure of agreement between equals, since society was described as an association. No Chilean seems to have been prepared to elaborate on the question of the state of nature, though the popular–liberal Manuel

[1] *Manifiesto*, 5 May 1818, *Arch.S.M.* XI, 61.
[2] *Patriota Chileno*, tomo 3, no. 17, 13 January 1827, p. 70.
[3] *El Araucano*, no. 15, 25 December 1830, p. 4.
[4] *Ilustración Araucana*, no. 1, 6 September 1813.
[5] To the Congress, 8 August 1826, *Patriota Chileno*, tomo 2, no. 51, 6 September 1826, p. 214.

Magallanes,[1] in his inaugural oration to the short-lived Society of the Friends of the Human Race in 1826, tried to draw a brief picture of 'that state of imperfection'.[2] On the other hand, whatever the degree of theorizing about the state of nature, it seemed evident to everyone that, to use the words of the constitutional commission of 1823, 'there is no society without contract'.[3]

This notion of contract was highly important to the revolutionaries, and it must be considered here with extreme care. 'Men are born free and equal in their rights', stated a newspaper of 1823, 'and by their nature they aspire to happiness.'[4] Society, it was held, was the only framework which could give men happiness. The same writer commented, with disarming frankness, 'We do not possess documents relating to the great primitive societies,' but he assumed that a number of factors had combined to bring them into existence in the first place: the need to escape some local tyrant, the 'chance gathering together' of separate tribes and families, and so forth.[5] Society, however, needed regulation, and hence the social contract. Since man had been born free and equal, it stood to reason that he could only submit to regulation by an act of his own free will. As Henríquez put it, in the first of his many pronouncements on the subject: 'Nature made us equal, and only by virtue of a freely, spontaneously, and willingly concluded pact can another man exercise a just, legitimate and reasonable authority over us.'[6] By and large, the revolutionary ideology did not regard the contract as having taken place at the beginning of society, but at some stage shortly afterwards—though there was a certain amount of confusion on this point. The social pact was a pact between society and its rulers, and it was unthinkable that society could function properly without rulers. The working of the social contract could be illustrated in many ways. Here, for example, we see the principles behind taxation being explained in terms of the contract.

[1] Manuel Magallanes Otero; prominent popular-liberal politician of the 1820s; member of the 1828 Congress; a tireless journalist.
[2] *Volcán Chileno*, tomo 1, no. 2, 4 May 1826, p. 7.
[3]
[4] *Tizón Republicano*, no. 2, 3 March 1823, p. 5.   [5] *Ibid.*
[6] 'Proclama de Quirino Lemachez', Silva Castro, *Escritos políticos*, p. 46.

There are various rules established to preserve order in society, which are called the social contract. This contract is between society and its government; and amongst the articles of which it consists is this one: that the citizen gives to or deposits with his Government a very small part of what he possesses so that with it the Government can assure to him the peaceful possession of what he has left.[1]

It seems, therefore, that the creole intelligentsia had a fairly clear idea of what it meant by the social contract. It was an agreement under which society transferred the function of regulation to a government. It was a simple idea, and old-fashioned even at the time it was elaborated, but it served the Chileans' purpose.

But how far could this contract be said to be binding? The answer was that it was by no means binding. It could be modified or improved. 'No people', asserted Manuel de Salas in 1811, 'can renounce the power to improve its social pact.'[2] This implied that there were certain conditions under which the contract could be broken. If, indeed, a government failed to observe the stipulations of the original contract, then the people who had concluded the pact with the government had the right, if not the duty, to revolt. 'A man must fulfil the conditions of the pact he has made with authority', it was stated in 1829; 'but if this authority violates these conditions, it is just and necessary to punish the violation with insurrection.'[3] The newspaper *El Insurgente Araucano* put this doctrine even more specifically: 'The people should only tolerate a government while it fulfils the contract to secure its welfare; in the event of any failure to do so, the people no longer has any obligation towards the ruler.'[4] It is clear here that the term 'social pact' or 'contract' was being equated with the written constitution, an equation which was also indicated at much the same time by Francisco Antonio Pinto's reference to the 1828 *carta* as 'the sacred pact' binding all members of society.[5] A violated constitution, it was held, automatically lost all validity. Thus, during the first months of the Portales regime, there were several references in the press to the fact that

[1] *Avisador Chileno*, no. 13, 30 November 1824, p. 107.
[2] *Diálogo de los porteros*, p. 191.
[3] *Espectador Chilean*, no. 1, 21 August 1829, p. 3.   [4] No. 1, 10 February 1827, p. 6.
[5] Speech of 31 January 1829, SCL, XVI, 590.

the 1828 Constitution had been 'annulled by the infractions of those who signed it'.[1] 'The effects of the Constitution have been suspended,' claimed the short-lived Junta of 1829–30, 'as a precise consequence of its infractions.'[2] The crisis of 1829 was referred to on at least one occasion as 'the dissolution of the social pact'.[3] This, of course, had been a standard interpretation of the imperial crisis of 1808–10.

But the breakdown of the social contract, when this occurred, did not mean that society itself had dissolved. Bernardo de Vera y Pintado, commenting on the collapse of the 'pact' between Chile and Ferdinand VII, wrote that

in this situation each man considers himself to be in that state anterior to the social pact from which all obligations between king and vassals originate. Thies does not mean that those vassals are reduced to the wandering life that precedes the formation of societies. A people is a people before it gives itself a King.[4]

What, then, held individuals together in such a situation? Henríquez gave the most convincing and realistic answer. A people without a constitution, he believed, 'is an association of men between whom may be perceived no other link than those relations maintained by custom'.[5] It is quite plain from these references and from others that some Chileans, at any rate, thought of the social contract in historical terms.

Connected very intimately with the doctrine of contract was, as might be expected, the idea of popular sovereignty, 'the American dogma', as Joaquín Campino[6] called it.[7] What was sovereignty? Why was it 'popular'?

Sovereignty is a power superior to all the other powers in society. Considered at its root, the term can only correspond to a power anterior to all others, a power which constituted all others, which is to say the

[1] *La Opinión*, no. 23, 27 February 1831, p. 3.   [2] *Documentos Oficiales*, no. 2, n. d.
[3] *La Opinión*, no. 29, 8 April 1831, p. 4.
[4] *Monitor Araucano*, tomo I, no. 97, 23 November 1813.
[5] *Ibid.* tomo 2, no. 69, 12 August 1814.
[6] Joaquín Campino Salamanca. Member of the 1824 and 1826 Congresses; an outstanding liberal; in the opinion of Vicuña Mackenna, the only man on the liberal side who would have rivalled Portales (*Diego Portales*, I, 20).
[7] *Monitor Imparcial*, no. 7, 22 September 1827.

power that created the social pact or constitution; and nobody doubts that this primitive and inalienable power, independent of all forms of government, resides in the community.[1]

Henríquez, the author of this passage, had earlier laid down the doctrine in simple form in his *Catecismo de los patriotas*: 'Sovereignty resides in the people; it is one and indivisible, indispensable and inalienable.'[2]

Whatever the theoretical location of sovereignty, it had to be used. Sovereignty had to be delegated to a power which could legally and properly employ it. 'Ultimately, it is a principle in a representative regime that the exercise of sovereignty does not reside in the nation, but in the persons to whom the nation has delegated it.'[3] José Miguel Infante, in the Congress of 1824, tried to define the constitutional position of the deputies in accordance with this principle.

Sovereignty resides in the people. It is intransmissible. [The people] can never be rid of it. We for our part are simply a few commissioners, entrusted with making laws...We do not possess more than this power, which is a part of the delegated sovereignty.[4]

As will be seen, representative government was thought to be the only valid mechanism through which sovereignty could be delegated. It is worth noting that every Chilean constitution of the period contained an express declaration of the doctrine of popular sovereignty, and we may take as typical the clear and concise formulation of the Constitution of 1833: 'Sovereignty resides essentially in the nation, which delegates its exercise to the authorities which this Constitution establishes.'[5]

'The sovereignty of the people', claimed a newspaper of 1827, 'consists of giving ourselves laws, and nominating deputies to express the general will.'[6] What, it might be asked, was the general will? There was little inclination in Chile to follow or to reinterpret Rousseau's unsatisfactory (or at any rate difficult)

[1] Henríquez, '¿Qué es el Pueblo en los Gobiernos Representativos?' *Mercurio de Chile*, no. 10, 31 August 1822.
[2] *Catecismo de los patriotas*, p. 149.
[3] *Mercurio de Chile*, no. 10, 31 August 1822, *CAPC*, IX, 310.
[4] Session of 11 December 1824, *SCL*, X, 119.   [5] Art. 4, *AR*
[6] *Miscelanea política y literaria*, no. 2, 6 August 1827, p. 14.   , I, 161.

conception. Indeed it is safe to say that no Chilean of the time attempted to state the doctrine in Rousseau's terms at all, preferring to rely on the simple formula of the will of the majority—which is what 'general will' signified in most political writings of the Enlightenment apart from those of Rousseau. Hence 'the general will... is the will of the majority'.[1] In the Congress of 1824, Manuel José de Gandarillas spoke of the way in which the general will could be made known. 'The minority must subject itself to the decision of the majority,' he then said. 'This is what is known as the declaration of the general will.'[2] In most ways this was the safest and simplest conception. When José Miguel Carrera proclaimed in 1812 that his regime was showing its 'conformity with the general will through public opinion',[3] he was using a hypocritical form of words rather than expressing a different view of the matter. And such forms of words could be used with dangerous ease by any *caudillo* who chose, as the history of Latin America in the nineteenth century abundantly illustrates.

The corollary of the doctrines of the social contract and of popular sovereignty was government by consent of the governed. This, of course, was merely a statement of the same basic principles in another way. 'Since the public authority is exercised over men who are free by nature', wrote Henríquez, 'the rights of sovereignty, in order to be legitimate, have to be based on the free consent of the people.'[4] Here was a clear test by which the legality of any given government could be measured. Most governments in human history, it was felt, would have failed the test. 'The great majority of governments', wrote a patriot in 1811, 'have been the product of force and terror; we should not compare ourselves with these.'[5] The Greek and Roman regimes, he went on, had been guilty in this respect. The English Constitution, too, could hardly be said to agree with the true criterion of popular consent: 'That constitution is nothing more than an agreement

[1] *Miscelánea política y literaria*, no. 2, 6 August 1827, p. 14.
[2] ...ion of 31 December 1824, *SCL*, X, 202.
[3] Pream... ..le, 'Reglamento Constitucional', 1812, *SCL*, I, 259.
...ly 1811, *SCL*, I, 36.
[4] Sermon, 4 Ju..., ...dedicado à la memoria del día 18 de Septiembre de 1810' [early 1811], A.B.A. vol. 25-2(3), ...
[5] 'Discurso patriotico ...' fo. 784.

between the followers of William I (*sic*) and James II; it is the effect of circumstances and not the choice of a free people.'[1] It should in fairness be added that, whatever its accuracy on questions of English history, a statement like this reflected a minority viewpoint. Most creole writers and politicians admired the 'classical' English Constitution with a passion that can only be described as extraordinary.[2]

Naturally, the role of government in society was considered to be of paramount importance, whatever the circumstances of its origin. 'Governments', wrote Henríquez, echoing the U.S. Declaration of Independence, 'have been instituted to preserve men in the enjoyment of their natural and eternal rights.'[3] What these natural and eternal rights were will be considered presently. On its own, however, this was a negative definition. O'Higgins in 1818 implied a further purpose for which governments had been instituted: 'to provide men with an aid to their security and to the prosperity of the association'.[4] Governments, of course, had a direct responsibility for the regulation of society and the maintenance of order. As Henríquez put it, government was 'the central force, guarded by the public will, to regulate all the actions of all members of society and to oblige them to contribute to the object of the association'.[5] Beyond a few statements like these, it is difficult to say whether a truly common notion of the nature and function of government existed in revolutionary Chile. Henríquez, for instance, seems to have looked on government as an agency of national formation. In an article written in 1813, he condemned Montesquieu for assuming that climate was the major influence on mankind, and ascribed an important role to the work of governments. 'If it is government, then, that forms men, then a government of regeneration is needed to make them republicans and generous defenders of their rights and freedoms.'[6] This phrase 'government of regeneration'—also used by Henríquez in the prospectus for *La Aurora de Chile*—seems to imply a view of

---

[1] Concepción Provincial Assembly, Manifesto, 6 October 1826, *SCL*, XII, 30.
[2] See chapter 5, pp. .   [3] *Catecismo de los patriotas*, p. 148.
[4] *Manifiesto que hace a las naciones...1818*, p. 19.
[5] Sermon of 4 July 1811, *SCL*, I, 37.
[6] *Semanario Republicano*, Continuación, Extraordinario, 10 November 1813.

government entailing vast functions. Authority, in Henríquez' view, should not merely answer to the general will; it should itself set out to mould the general will. 'It is very difficult', he said in 1811, 'to establish the best laws without previously preparing the spirit of the people for them. It seems that not everyone is worthy of being free.'[1] O'Higgins, for his part, once described the Junta of 1813–14 as 'a truly paternal government',[2] and this, to judge from his own period of rule, may well have represented his personal ideal. The liberals of the 1820s, in their turn, while agreeing with the regulative element in government, were chiefly concerned to pare its functions down to a minimum. In the 1830s, with the conservative reaction, emphasis was once more placed on the need for strong, centralized government. There was, then, no common viewpoint as to the degree of government needed to carry through the revolution. And this was, in fact, one of the chief points of divergence between the different political groups of the 1820s and 1830s. The debate on government and the functions it had to fulfil was to continue right up to the end of the revolution. But the first principles which lay behind the institution of government—its dependence on popular consent and its contractual relationship with society—were never in dispute.

FORMS OF GOVERNMENT

Formal surveys of the diverse types of government, in the manner first popularized by Aristotle, were rare during the revolution, and, moreover, there was nothing speculative or objective about the one or two attempts that were made. The discussion of different forms of government had one aim: to demonstrate the immense superiority of the republican form. In his *Aurora de Chile*, Henríquez divided governments into three types: Democracy, Aristocracy and Monarchy. Of these, Henríquez believed, Democracy was the oldest and purest form. It was usually followed by Aristocracy, and eventually degenerated into Monarchy. Henríquez viewed political history as a more or less continuous oscillation.

[1] *SCL*, I, 37. [2] Proclamation, January 1814, *Arch.O'H.* II, 36.

Fundamental Political Ideas

History shows us states passing in alternation from democracy to monarchy, from monarchy to democracy, with aristocracy occupying the interregnum between these two forms...It seems that lack of education and virtue has originated the overthrow of governments, and that passion has always been the sole cause of political revolutions.[1]

In his *Catecismo de los patriotas*, Henríquez omitted the aristocratic category from his classification, referring only to the monarchic and republican forms of government, representing tyranny and despotism (sometimes regarded as distinct types in themselves) as attributes capable of being developed by either form.[2] Henríquez, it is plain, used the term 'republican' in the same sense as the term 'democratic'. In the *Catecismo político cristiano* of 1810 there was a clearer division of forms. Its unknown author mentioned three basic types of government: the Monarchic, which consisted of rule by one man within a framework of law, the Despotic, where one man ruled without legal restraints of any sort, and finally the Republican. The Republican form was divided into two categories: the Aristocratic Republican, defined as the rule of the nobility alone, and the Democratic Republican, defined as the rule of the whole people through its representatives. The analysis of forms in the *Catecismo* remained unsurpassed in other writings of the time.[3]

When it came to discussing which of the various forms of government was preferable to the others, there was virtual unanimity. Monarchy (except at certain periods of the revolution) was rejected outright, while a republican government, sometimes styled a democratic government, was regarded as the most consistent with the first principles enunciated above. Was it possible, asked Irisarri, that there could be a government in which the people received less consideration than in a monarchy?[4] (Ironically, Irisarri himself was by no means free of monarchist sympathies later on.) Arguments against monarchy were grave in the extreme. It stood condemned by its own origins, for most kings came to power as a result of a state of disorder or through

[1] *Aurora de Chile*, tomo I, no. 16, 28 May 1812, p. 65.
[2] *Catecismo de los patriotas*, pp. 152–4.   [3] *Amor de la Patria*, pp. 96–100.
[4] 'Sobre el origen y naturaleza de las monarquías', *Semanario Republicano*, no. 7, 18 September 1813.

elaborate confidence tricks.[1] Violence was usually employed, as had been the case both with the Roman Empire and with the kingdoms that succeeded it.[2] While it might be true that monarchy sometimes submitted to legal constraints, it was far more probable that the regime would degenerate into despotism. It was axiomatic that monarchy had a built-in tendency towards tyranny.[3] 'The King', wrote the author of the *Catecismo político cristiano*, 'is known as "the boss", and he demands that people should address him on their knees, as if men were debased animals of another species.'[4]

The commonest device used by monarchs to cement their growing despotism, it was held, was the doctrine of divine right. This was ardently condemned by the creole intelligentsia. It is worth mentioning here that much of the discussion on the question of divine right was conducted in the earlier years of the revolution, when most minds were doubtless prompted by living issues rather than by an abstract desire to establish theoretical principles. Irisarri wrote in 1813 that kings 'persuade men that they are sent by the Eternal Being to rule over mortals; and nobody then dares to ask, with Rousseau, "Where are the warrants that justify that wonderful origin?"'[5] Henríquez was equally emphatic on this point.

Princes have worked ingeniously to…make men believe that their authority was not only independent of the consent and will of the people, but was by its very nature supreme and sacred, as though celestial.[6]

Henríquez, by no means uncharacteristically, also rejected the dogma of divine right on religious grounds. 'God wishes men to have some sort of government, but He does not say that this man or that man should be the ruler.'[7] It was true that Saul and David had been chosen by God, 'but that was only for the Jews,'[8] a

---

[1] 'Sobre el origen y naturaleza de las monarquías', *Semanario Republicano*, no. 6, 11 September 1813.

[2] Amor de la Patria, p. 99.

[3] *Ibid.* Cf. *Monitor Araucano*, tomo 2, no. 3, 10 December 1813, and *Semanario Republicano*, no. 6, 11 September 1813.

[4] Amor de la Patria, p. 97.   [5] *Semanario Republicano*, no. 6, 11 September 1813.

[6] *Catecismo de los patriotas*, p. 154.   [7] *Ibid.* p. 153.   [8] *Ibid.*

somewhat lame argument. Other writers, however, persisted on the religious aspect, and it was observed that despite the case of Saul and David the Divine opinion had tended to condemn monarchy,[1] and could almost be said to prefer the republican form.

In addition, there were certain inherent disadvantages in a monarchy, which the author of the *Catecismo político cristiano* went to some pains to point out. If the monarch were elected, then the state ran the risk of political convulsions at every election. On the other hand, if succession were by hereditary right, there was the equally unhappy possibility that the kingdom might fall into the hands of a tyrant or an imbecile.[2] This was standard reasoning in many political treatises of the eighteenth century. Of course, there was always the argument that a monarch could be restrained by a framework of fundamental or constitutional law, but Irisarri impatiently condemned this view as unrealistic. 'Do we wish to make [the king] dependent on the laws when his power is such that he can break them with impunity? Miserable theories, contradicted by the experience of all peoples and all ages.'[3] As Irisarri remarked in the course of the same article, Spain had once been the most moderate monarchy in Europe, but was now the most despotic. Monarchy, then, was to be rejected. In practical terms, anti-royal propaganda was reasonably efficient. We know from Fray Juan Ramón's description of the revolution as it affected Chillán that 'nothing was more hateful to the insurgents than the name of *the King* and of his sovereign authority'.[4]

So the form of government most favoured by the Chilean revolution was to be republican. This was a term which was virtually interchangeable with 'democratic' or 'popular', depending on the author and the circumstances. The advantages of republican government seemed patent and obvious.

Republican democratic government, in which the people rules through the deputies or representatives it elects, is the only one which preserves

---

[1] Amor de la Patria, p. 96. He based his argument on the admittedly somewhat damaging Divine pronouncement in 1 Samuel viii. 7–18.

[2] *Ibid.* pp. 96–7. Cf. Rousseau, *Social Contract*, book III, ch. 6.

[3] *Semanario Republicano*, no. 7, 18 September 1813.

[4] 'Relación de la conducta observada por los padres misioneros del colegio de la propaganda fide de la ciudad de Chillán', *CHDI*, IV, 20.

the dignity and majesty of the people, which draws man closest to and least separates him from the primitive equality in which God Almighty created him; it is the least exposed to the horrors of despotism and arbitrariness; it is the smoothest, most moderate, freest, and is, by consequence, the best for making rational beings happy.[1]

Irisarri, too, was lyrical about the republican form. 'In the civil order', he wrote, 'there is no word as sweet or as sonorous as Republic... [by which] we visualize a state wisely ruled by the general will, where just laws protect the rights of man... To say Republic is to say happiness.'[2] It was argued by Henríquez that God Himself favoured republics, since this was the way in which the Israelites had been governed before they debased themselves and accepted kings.[3] But far more important than this, a republic was the only form of government which allowed the sovereignty of the people a just and legitimate representation. The great dangers of republican government, it was thought, lay in its dependence on a minimum of public enlightenment and civic virtue. Historically, Irisarri averred, Athens had succumbed to Pisistratus, Genoa to the Podestàs, Venice to the Doges and the Council of Ten, and Florence to the oligarchic power of the Medicis. Of the old republics of Italy, he maintained, only San Marino had retained any semblance of its pristine republican virtue.[4] It was difficult, if not impossible, to establish republican governments among peoples which had long been politically depraved. Irisarri advanced the case of France and Napoleon to add weight to this last point.[6] Republican government was the exception rather than the rule in history. Its repeated failures made melancholy reading. Was there any chance at all that the Chileans could succeed where so many had failed? By and large, the answer to this question was confident and affirmative. Enlightenment and virtue were considered indispensable instruments, and the revolutionaries hoped and believed that these commodities could be rapidly and successfully introduced. This whole question of neces-

---

[1] *Amor de la Patria*, p. 96.
[2] 'Sobre los gobiernos republicanos', *Semanario Republicano*, no. 8, 25 September 1813.
[3] *Monitor Araucano*, tomo 2, no. 3, 10 December 1813.
[4] *Semanario Republicano*, no. 8, 25 September 1813.   [5] *Ibid.*

sary virtue was extremely important to the creole leaders, and it will be considered in its proper place presently.

Republican government, in the Chilean concept, amounted to representative government. Representation was the logical solution to certain dilemmas implied by the first principles already described: the need to delegate sovereignty, and the equally severe need to prevent the advance of despotism on the one hand and the inevitable chaos, on the other, which would be caused by direct democracy in the Aristotelian sense of the word.[1] There was no argument about the general principle, but the actual mechanisms of representation naturally aroused a good deal of discussion throughout the revolution. It was taken for granted that some kind of popular election was necessary—not even Juan Egaña completely abandoned this idea. Henríquez strongly argued in favour of direct elections, rejecting electoral colleagues as an 'invention of tyrants'.[2] There was, perhaps, substantial agreement on this point. José Miguel Infante characterized the right to elect as sacred in the extreme, since it was 'the only one where each citizen exercises for himself that part of sovereignty which corresponds to him'.[3] Whether popular elections should be overfrequent was, however, another matter. Henríquez, even in his most revolutionary moments, was inclined to follow conservative opinion and to pronounce against elections held too often. These, he affirmed, would lead to instability in the state through the constant variation of factions in power.[4] Against this, Infante argued that frequent elections were a good way of allowing popular agitation a legitimate outlet.[5]

If popular elections were a cardinal element in the new philosophy of representative government, universal suffrage was not. The 'people', on the whole, did not in practice mean much more than the creole aristocracy and intelligentsia. There were many sections of the population, it was held, which were incapable of voting properly. 'No form of government demands from a man

[1] 'Representación', *Observador Chileno*, no. 5, 28 October 1822.
[2] *Mercurio de Chile*, no. 20, 6 February 1823, *CAPC*, IX, 431.
[3] *Valdiviano Federal*, no. 68, 1 April 1833, p. 1.
[4] *Monitor Araucano*, tomo 2, no. 10, 11 January 1814.
[5] *Valdiviano Federal*, no. 68, 1 April 1833, p. 2.

so high an appreciation of his rights as does the popular representative form',[1] and it was a mistake to assume that everyone possessed such an appreciation. As Infante put it, in the debate on the election of provincial governors in the 1826 Congress, 'in the states where democracy has been best perfected, a child is not permitted to act as legislator, nor as elector, since he does not possess discernment'.[2] There were a good many political 'children' in Chile, it was thought. The following year, the Provincial Assembly of Santiago laid down its criteria for judging which sorts of men should vote on the future form of government for Chile. It claimed that there were two types:

(1) proprietors, who are the men exclusively affected, and so linked to the fate of the Republic that they lose everything in the event of disorder and gain everything in the event of tranquillity and prosperity; (2) men who have some instruction in the basis of government.[3]

It need not surprise one, therefore, that in practice suffrage was limited to a fairly small section of the total population of Chile. The revolution was liberal in nature, and virtually no stream of liberalism in the world at that period fully accepted universal suffrage even as a principle. Domingo Amunátegui Solar has shown that all the many electoral laws in Chile at this time (those of 1810, 1813, 1823–8, 1831 and 1833) demanded literacy and property qualifications which effectively debarred the great mass of the people from voting in elections.[4]

As a logical extension of this, it was also generally thought that the legislatures chosen by the 'people' should be composed of the more reliable elements in society. It was deemed important that the people should be represented by 'prudent organs which should speak on its behalf'.[5] These 'prudent organs' ought to consist of members of the aristocracy.

Who are those who most naturally have the right to represent the nation? They are the citizens who are in the best position to

[1] *Correo mercantil, diario comercial y político*, no. 308, 25 April 1833.
[2] Session of 13 July 1826, *SCL*, XII, 128.
[3] To the Comisión Nacional, 14 August 1827, *SCL*, XV, 65.
[4] *Democracia en Chile*, pp. 16–72.
[5] 'Del Pueblo', *Correo de Arauco*, no. 42, 14 January 1825, p. 187.

know the nation's needs, its conditions and its rights, the citizens who are most interested in the public welfare, in short, the land-owners.[1]

A remark like this illustrates with supreme clarity the aristocratic nature of the Chilean revolution. José Joaquín de Mora, however, was prepared to spread his net a little wider in the search for ideal representative classes: 'rich farmers..., industrious capitalists,...active bankers,...clever manufacturers'.[2] This was not to say, however, that legislative bodies should comprise men who always thought alike on every issue or whose interests were identical. The need for political parties was appreciated. Agitation of a peaceful kind was always desirable in a truly representative system. There should always be 'a party which watches over and censures the operations of the government. In free states, the object of an opposition is to defend the Constitution and preserve liberty.'[3] Partisan feeling and the rise and fall of different political groups should be welcomed as a sign of political health. 'There is not, and never will be', asserted the newspaper *El Insurgente Araucano*, 'a republic or free people which has not had parties and continual upsets. These are created by opinion and circumstances, which raise up one party while destroying its opponents.'[4]

A final point on the question of representation should be made here. Representation, it was held, had to be fair. In other words, it was plainly inconsistent in a republican system to allow one area of the country a disproportionately powerful voice in public affairs. This point was ventilated most thoroughly with the rise of the federalist movement in the 1820s, which was (or appears to have been) far more concerned with abstract principles than with genuinely divergent local interests. The first moment in the revolution when equal representation for equal areas was argued convincingly was in 1811, when Santiago obtained the right to send an excessive number of deputies to the first national Congress.

---

[1] 'De los representantes de una Nación', *Correo de Arauco*, no. 43, 26 January 1825, p. 191.
[2] *Mercurio Chileno*, no. VI, 1 September 1828, p. 284.
[3] *El Fanal*, no. I, 24 March 1829. Cf. *Paz Perpetua á los chilenos*, no. 2, 13 April 1836, p. 12.
[4] *Insurgente Araucano*, no. 3, 19 February 1827, pp. 21–2.

Manuel de Salas, protesting against this, asserted that if one province were over-represented, other provinces would be deprived of their legitimate rights.[1] Bernardo O'Higgins, at much the same moment, observed that Santiago's claim to twelve seats in Congress was patently unjust and absurd, 'for no capital of a republican government—not even London, with a million inhabitants represented by only two deputies—has ever attained so prodigious a number'.[2]

CONSTITUTIONALISM AND THE BALANCE OF POWERS

These basic principles of popular sovereignty and representative government had, naturally enough, to be stated publicly in the form of a written constitution, a document which would also contain many prescriptions for the successful regulation of society. The semi-miraculous powers ascribed to constitutional and legal documents in general will be considered in chapter 5. For the moment, what must be considered is the set of criteria by which constitutions had to be judged and the principles which had to be borne in mind when they were framed. The Chileans held that a constitution was of fundamental importance to society, and that to some extent it could be said to embody the social contract itself. President Pinto hinted at this in 1829 when he told Congress that, by framing the Constitution of the previous year, it had given Chile

the vital condition of its being, the fundamental aid to its consistency, the sacred pact which binds all its members, the inestimable rights which guarantee public order, which constitute liberty, and which convert the masses into a society and force into the mainspring of protection and security.[3]

A document which embodied so cardinal a feature of life and which had to fulfil such important tasks obviously had to be

[1] 'Representación', 27 July 1811, F.V. vol. 812, pieza 4.
[2] To the people of Los Angeles, n.d., *Arch.O'H.* I, 118. Cf. the protest of other *exaltado* deputies dated 24 June 1811, which claimed that unequal representation contradicted the 'general will of the kingdom' (*Arch.O'H.* I, 113). Few Chileans would have been suprised at O'Higgins' description of London as the capital of a 'republican' government.   [3] Dissolution speech, 31 January 1829, *SCL*, XVI, 590.

drafted with the greatest care. For, as Henríquez put it, in a somewhat exaggerated way, 'the making of a constitution is the masterpiece of great geniuses; it demands a profound philosophy, a consummate prudence, and a vast knowledge of history'.[1] Juan Martínez de Rozas, in his speech at the opening of the 1811 Congress, played down this notion that constitution-makers should be demi-gods. Constitutions, he claimed, should be based on 'the torches of reason and nature',[2] and should be drawn up with specific reference to the country concerned, 'observing its inclinations, resources, situation, nature and other circumstances'.[3] This view—that a constitution should be basically in accordance with the nation for which it was designed—was a common one, and not even Juan Egaña departed from it,[4] whatever the appearances to the contrary. 'What political system is the best?' asked Henríquez, and concluded: 'This is an insoluble problem, for the system should accommodate itself to the current circumstances of the people.'[5] Later on, Henríquez wrote that the defects of a government generally sprang from the disagreement between its constitution and the character and conditions of the country.[6] No constitution which failed to bear this principle in mind could possibly endure for long.

It would be vain to establish the most beautiful form of government and to issue the best laws if customs were not in consequence with them, for they would be nothing more than a statute built on air, which would be destroyed by the slightest shaking.[7]

Some writers also urged that constitutions should not be too complicated. Rozas warned against complexity in his speech to the 1811 Congress, one of his all-too-few pronouncements on such matters. 'Learned Greece, the studious Germans, the profound Britons', he said, 'have never had constitutions as adequate as poor Helvetia or the descendants of the companions of the simple Penn.'[8] In O'Higgins' time, as might be expected, this

---

[1] *Aurora de Chile*, tomo I, no. 16, 28 May 1812, p. 66.
[2] *SCL*, I, 40.   [3] *Ibid.*   [4] See chapter 7, p.   .
[5] *Aurora de Chile*, tomo I, no. 2, 20 February 1812, p. 6.
[6] *Ibid.* tomo I, no. 16, 28 May 1812, p. 66.
[7] *Observador Chileno*, no. 6, 6 November 1822.   [8] *SCL*, I, 40.

demand for a 'simple' constitution enjoyed a certain currency, largely as a justification of the very simple Constitution of 1818. Bernardo Monteagudo, in his brief incursion into the field of Chilean journalism, warned loudly against 'premature constitutions', and suggested that Chile, with its provisional charter of only a few articles, was better placed than Argentina in this respect.[1] Flowery theories, it was held, were best avoided when framing constitutional laws,[2] and in the 1820s, when experience had embittered a number of people, a coolly realistic tone was once again applied to the discussion of the problem. *El Monitor Imparcial* criticized the French Constitution of 1791, the Spanish Constitution of 1812, and the Chilean Constitution of 1823 for their complete lack of realism, and proposed that all that was needed was a 'basis for a constitution' rather than an elaborate and extensive document.[3] This idea appealed, somewhat paradoxically, to Juan Egaña in his declining years, and bore fruit in his *Carta Constitucional*, which he defined as a 'basic interim charter'.[4]

When it came down to constitutional arrangements, the Chileans—with the notable exception of Egaña—did not depart radically (or indeed at all) from the traditional framework laid down by the United States Constitution or the Spanish Constitution of 1812. The influence of these two documents was everywhere apparent, though the Chileans never tried to copy the unicameral element in the Spanish document. The fundamental *motif* of the constitutional theory of the revolution was the balance of powers. It was not to be expected that any original viewpoints on this well worn notion would emerge. Irisarri laid down that there had to be three powers in every republic:

The law, which regulates the internal and external affairs of the State; the execution of that law; and the administration of the same in civil or domestic matters—these are the three parts of a Republican government, the three powers which must balance the propensity of some towards despotism and of others towards anarchy.[5]

[1] *Censor de la Revolución*, no. 3, 10 May 1820.
[2] *El Argos de Chile*, no. 2, 4 June 1818.   [3] No. 1, 18 August 1827, pp. 1–2.
[4] Egaña, *Colección*, II, 89. After the experience of 1823–4, nobody took any notice of the scheme.
[5] *Semanario Republicano*, no. 9, 2 October 1813.

Fundamental Political Ideas

As to the relations between these three powers, opinions varied. By many, if not most, it was held that each power had to be independent of the others, and that it was the balance between them that guaranteed liberty. Hence the importance of assigning a definite sphere of activity to each of the powers. The Congress of 1811 was 'intimately convinced not only of the need to divide the powers, but also of the importance of fixing the limits of each of them'.[1] A clash between the powers was to be avoided; so was the possibility of any collusion between them. They had to be kept independent and balanced. 'Independence is the essential character of power,' claimed a newspaper of 1823, 'and the expression "dependent power" is as absurd as "circular triangle".'[2] The notion of balance was sacred. 'The powers balance their forces in equal equilibrium,' wrote José Joaquín de Mora. 'The balance does not incline to the ruler, or to the senate. Laws, and their execution—these are the two poles between which the social machine runs and rests.'[3] Another writer affirmed that the balance of power was a true reflection of the natural order, for 'the movement of the planets is governed (if I may use the expression) by constitutional combinations'.[4] The idea of balance was written into all the constitutions of the period, with varying degrees of specificity. The clearest definition of the concept appeared in the 1828 document: 'The exercise of sovereignty, delegated by the Nation, . . . is divided between three powers, the Legislative, the Executive, and the Judicial, which shall be exercised separately, never in any case coming together.'[5] This meant, of course, not merely a balance of powers but also an actual separation of powers—a common but misguided development from the original formulation of Montesquieu. Despite its symmetry and attractiveness, the notion of separation was not shared by everyone. Juan Egaña rejected it outright, as will be seen. Even the generally *exaltado* Henríquez, who could usually be relied on to support any piece of abstract liberal theorizing, seems

[1] Reglamento de la Autoridad Ejecutiva, 8 August 1811, *SCL*, I, 49.
[2] 'División de poderes', *El Liberal*, no. 9, 26 September 1823, p. 73.
[3] Verses on the 1828 Constitution, Amunátegui, *J. J. de Mora*, p. 130.
[4] *El Independiente*, tomo I, no. 5, 24 October 1827, p. 19.
[5] Art. 22, *AR*, I, 144.

to have recognized that the separation of powers, while acceptable as a decorative piece of democratic theory, led to certain disadvantages in practice. The example of other countries, he asserted, condemned the idea. 'The Executive power is essentially legislative,' he wrote, 'and in all civilized countries it assists in the formation of the laws, as we see in England, France, Spain, Portugal, the United States, etc.'[1]

The question of the Executive power was one which was accorded different treatment at different stages of the revolution, and will be considered chronologically. The Chileans' first attempt to regulate the functions of the Executive, in the standing orders for the conduct of the Executive power enacted by Congress on 8 August 1811, resulted in an effective congressional supremacy. Later on, O'Higgins regarded a strong Executive as supremely valuable. The liberals and federalists of the later 1820s tended to annul the Executive on principle, and after the conservative reaction the pendulum swung back to strong centralized government. The extent of the Executive's powers, therefore, and the exact ceremonial status this was to be accorded, were issues in continual debate throughout the revolution.

As far as the Legislative branch was concerned, there was a certain amount of abstract discussion. It was automatically and unquestioningly accepted that a legislature had to be divided.[2] Henríquez, making liberal use of the writings of Jean Louis de Lolme and other thinkers, argued that a constitution should not only establish checks on the Executive power but that it should also limit the influence of the legislature. Without such limitations, he believed, the Legislative power would 'alter the laws, and the Constitution, in the way God created light'.[3] In addition, a unicameral legislature would be excessively open to irresponsible behaviour by intriguers and factions, and the whole country would suffer. As a writer of some eighteen years later put it, a bicameral system assured

---

[1] Session of 17 August 1822, *SCL*, VI, 77.
[2] I have not noticed a single proposal for a unicameral legislature in Chile at this period, except for the nominated Senates created by the constitutions of 1812 and 1818, which were not, in any case, elected bodies.
[3] *Aurora de Chile*, tomo 2, no. 5, 4 February 1813.

greater circumspection and maturity in the formation of laws, and greater difficulty for partisan eloquence or the ardour of enthusiasts to overcome what sound reason and experience dictate.[1]

There were, in short, too many dangers in allowing the legislative power to be united.

The real problem in a bicameral system was the nature of the second or upper chamber. Henríquez asserted that the upper house should, ideally, act as a buffer between the people, represented in the lower house, and the Executive, protecting both parties from each other. This, he assumed, was the function of the United States Senate and of the English House of Lords. A solidly aristocratic upper house, however, was open to the objection that it could easily turn despotic. Therefore an elected senate, with perhaps a designated number of aristocrats, was perhaps the best answer.[2] In practice, of course, the various Senates which were created in Chile were of three sorts: first, those which were elected, usually on a provincial basis; second, those which were nominated (Carrera's and O'Higgins' fell into this category); and third, the Senate or *Censura* envisaged by Juan Egaña.

NATURAL RIGHTS

A fundamental position in the ideology of the revolution was occupied by the notion of natural rights. These were intimately bound up with the natural law which, as we have seen, lay behind all theories of politics. Henríquez, in his sermon on 4 July 1811, had referred to 'an immutable and immortal justice, anterior to all empires', and he then went on to affirm that

the oracles of this justice, promulgated by reason and written in human hearts, invest us with eternal rights. These rights are, principally, the power to defend and sustain the liberty of our nation, the permanence of the religion of our fathers and the property and honour of families.[3]

Natural rights were, in fact, divided into two types: national and individual. National rights were, inevitably, the first to be

---

[1] *El Araucano*, no. 41, 25 June 1831, p. 4.
[2] *Aurora de Chile*, tomo 2, no. 5, 4 February 1813.   [3] *SCL*, I, 34.

principle that 'the first thing, in any state, is the inviolability of property'.[1] By some it was held that property itself, and not merely the right to property, was part of the natural order: 'A man's property is not dependent on the law; it is anterior to the law.'[2] Though the holding of property conferred certain privileges, it also imposed certain duties—the alleviation of poverty, and the responsibility of helping the state in times of difficulty.[3] Naturally enough, the conditions of the social contract might occasionally demand sacrifices on the part of the owner of property, both as regards his person and his goods:

Nobody can take these away from him arbitrarily; only the law, which a man has imposed on himself for his own welfare, has the right to take away something from everyone and dispose of a man's person: but if the needs of the community demand this, it will never be done *unequally*.[4]

The right to hold property, then, was fundamental, even though the state could legitimately take away part of it in the form of taxation.

Along with security and property went *equality*, and, in order to understand precisely what this signified to the leaders of the Chilean revolution, it is necessary to discard most of the modern implications of the word. A newspaper of 1823 pointed out that nature itself seemed to have conferred a fair measure of *in*equality on mankind. Natural inequality was so great that

pretensions to any equality other than that which we enjoy before the law are purely ideal. Doubtless the great perfection of the social pact consists of destroying the effect of those differences; yet it is necessary to admit that...there will always be men of talent, energy and virtue in the midst of others who lack such qualities completely.[5]

Legal equality did not mean, affirmed *El Popular* in 1830, that everybody had equal rights to 'consider themselves qualified to preside over public affairs'.[6] Social classes were unanimously

---

[1] Session of 19 January 1825, *SCL*, x, 299.
[2] *El Liberal*, no. 3, 15 August 1823, p. 27.
[3] See *Gazeta Ministerial de Chile*, 19 June 1810, *CAPC*, VI, 259.
[4] *Registro público*, tomo I, no. 4, 21 April 1826, p. 45.
[5] *El Apagador*, no. I, 3 June 1823, pp. 8–9.   [6] No. 20, 16 August 1830, p. 3.

agreed to be necessary—and, as we have seen already, there was little doubt as to which class should be entrusted with the reins of government. Some believed that a balance of classes was necessary for the welfare of the state: 'It is necessary that the different classes should balance each other, no class gaining too notable an ascendancy.'[1] This, however, was more a decorous piece of theorizing than a deeply held belief. The Chilean revolution was aristocratic; it was hardly in its interest to attempt to formalize any abstract 'balance' of classes. Equality, then, was tempered by the natural order and by a social stratification believed to be inevitable. It had to be reduced to the simple formula of equality before the law, and this, and nothing more, was the true meaning of the term throughout the period. 'Equality of legal rights'[2] was the furthest anybody could go in defining equality. 'All men are born equal and independent', wrote Henríquez, 'and ought to be equal in the eyes of the law, whether it protects or punishes.'[3] 'Equality', wrote Ignacio Torres, 'is the right to invoke the law...whether one is rich or poor, great or humble.'[4] The different legal codes which were applied to soldiers, priests, civilians and children were not basically a contradiction of this legal equality, though Torres' argument on this point was specious in the extreme. The different hierarchies in society, he claimed, actually preserved equality, for 'since there can be no order without them, and no society without order, it is a consequence that they lead to legal equality'. But, added Torres, the same offences should always receive the same punishment, irrespective of a man's position. The old regime would have executed a plebeian fire-raiser while merely exiling an aristocratic one. The laws of an independent Chile, he claimed, would be based on very different principles.[5]

I come lastly to the question of *liberty*. Perhaps the nicest definition and discussion of the problem was presented by Irisarri in his newspaper *El Duende de Santiago* in 1818. The

[1] *Correo de Arauco*, no. 43, 26 January 1825, p. 191.
[2] 'Proyecto de Acta Constitutiva de la Federación Chilena', art. 25.
[3] *Catecismo de los patriotas*, p. 148. Cf. Declaration of the Rights of Man, art. VI.
[4] *Gazeta Ministerial de Chile*, 19 June 1819, *CAPC*, VI, 260.
[5] *Ibid.* VI, 261.

freedom gained through national independence, he asserted, was not what some people apparently believed it to be.

If we only called 'liberty' that state of absolute independence in which men have never found themselves and which, in fact, could only be imagined by certain philosophers of our time,...then of course we will admit that we have not gained liberty, and that we never shall gain it, for it is an impossibility.[1]

The 'primitive freedom' enjoyed by man in the state of nature, thought Irisarri, was almost certainly a chimera. But at all events, society by common agreement represented an improvement on nature, and society was composed of human beings. Human beings had neither the right nor the liberty to break rules. In both Irisarri's view, and in the view of other writers, liberty was therefore of two types: 'natural' liberty, and 'civil' (sometimes called 'rational') liberty. Natural liberty, a writer affirmed in 1833, meant allowing the will to express itself in any direction without restriction. It was plainly an absurdity, though perhaps a man's private thoughts partook, to some extent, of natural freedom. Civil liberty, the freedom of man in society, was of quite a different order, he added.[2] Civil liberty could best be defined as the freedom to 'work and do freely anything that does not prejudice another man',[3] or, in Irisarri's more formal terminology, 'that faculty to do for our own benefit anything that does not offend the rights of others'.[4] Henríquez, not untypically, combined both the law of nature and the precepts of his religion in discussing the matter. After defining freedom in much the same terms as Irisarri, he went on:

Liberty is founded on nature; its rule is justice, and its safeguard and bulwark the law. The limits of liberty are comprehended in this maxim of Our Lord Jesus Christ: Do not do unto others what you would they should not do unto you.[5]

[1] 'Libertad', *Duende de Santiago*, no. 1, 22 June 1818, p. 1.
[2] *El Cosmopólitan*, no. 2, 1 May 1833.
[3] *Registro público*, tomo 1, no. 4, 21 April 1826, p. 44.
[4] *Duende de Santiago*, no. 1, 22 June 1818, p. 3.
[5] *Catecismo de los patriotas*, p. 148. Cf. 1818 Constitution, tít. 1, art. 4; Egaña's draft constitution of 1813, art. 23; French Constitution of 1795.

This, broadly speaking, is what liberty meant to the creole intelligentsia. Plainly, however, there were certain aspects of liberty—some specific freedoms, in fact—which demanded special emphasis, and of these none was more important than freedom of thought, opinion and expression. For 'without the freedom to think about political matters and the great circle of human knowledge, man is a slave even at the centre of his being'.[1] Obviously a man's thoughts were his own affair, but a more delicate problem was posed by the extent to which he wished to express them in public. Thus Domingo Salamanca, who had written a scathing private letter on the subject of the Carrera regime, defended his right to do so when charged with subversion. Part of his legal defence went into the question.

Freedom to think is invulnerable. It is born of a Law of nature, which does not recognize any higher law. Irons, chains, and even death itself have no power to destroy it...Man, who in order to live in society deposits a part of his natural independence, cannot be punished at the whim of that society...Thus, human laws do not punish a man's opinion whilst it remains in the Sphere of private thought, but only when it is made public and becomes a suggestion containing ideas subversive of good order, public tranquillity, and respect to the magistrates—a suggestion capable of inducing others to think badly of the State, and so to make opponents of the Government.[2]

Salamanca claimed that by writing a letter to a personal friend, he was not necessarily attempting to subvert the state.

The main problem raised by the doctrine of freedom of expression in this period was, undoubtedly, the position of the press in a republican society. The invention of the printing press was rightly considered to have been a fundamental cause of human progress. 'Without Gutemberg', Henríquez wrote, 'mankind would have groaned in eternal slavery.'[3] The extraordinary influence of the press was everywhere acknowledged; it could be used as 'a method of insurrection unknown to Antiquity'.[4] Used responsibly, the press had a duty to censor the acts of government

[1] *Nuevo Corresponsal*, no. 1, [1823], p. 7.
[2] Defence, dated 20 January 1812, A.B.A. vol. 25-2(3), fo. 645-6.
[3] *Mercurio de Chile*, no. 23, 13 March 1823, *CAPC*, IX, 465.
[4] *El Sol de Chile*, no. 1, 3 July 1818, pp. 4-5.

The Revolutionary Ideology

and to enlighten society at one and the same time. In the 1820s, when newspapers became a prominent feature of the Chilean scene, this aspect naturally received a good deal of emphasis. 'Tyrants are born out of the silence in which we leave their first arbitrary acts,' proclaimed *El Tizón Republicano*, adding that the chief role of newspapers was to keep watch over all the activities of the government,[1] and in particular to 'combat public abuses and bad conduct on the part of magistrates'.[2]

It was essential, therefore, that the press should be left free to fulfil these important functions. Infante, not unexpectedly, put freedom of the press in a commanding position in his semi-libertarian federalist philosophy:

Without the free and expeditious use of the press there can be no public spirit, no opinion, no freedom; and without laws that destroy the influence of power and its satellites...the free use [of the press] will be obstructed by diverse means.[3]

In short, freedom of the press was 'the guarantee of all the freedoms'.[4] It had to be carefully cultivated and zealously protected. Some journalists became almost lyrical when expounding this theme. *El Liberal*, which printed Jefferson's famous sentence on the subject[5] at the head of each issue, once printed a poem extolling the virtues of an unrestricted newspaper press: 'Oh, second Sun of the World, oh Freedom of the Press!'[6] Another paper of extreme liberal sympathies expressed itself in much the same way: 'Oh, delightful Freedom of the Press! All the Journalists of the earth will charge, in pitiless war, against the cruel Despot who destroys you!'[7] Nobody, with the possible exception of Juan Egaña and his son Mariano, seriously doubted that the press should be free as of right. Nevertheless, it was sometimes felt, the press could never be granted complete licence. Even the press law of 1828, the most liberal of any in the period, conceded that there were at least four crimes which could be committed

[1] No. 1 [24 February 1823], p. 2.   [2] *Ibid*, no. 17, 28 July 1823, p. 195.
[3] 'Libertad de imprenta', *Valdiviano Federal*, no. 71, 1 August 1833.
[4] *Clamor de la Patria*, no. 3, 4 April 1823, p. 6.
[5] 'Error of opinion may be tolerated where reason is free to combat it.'
[6] No. 26, 17 August 1824, p. 1.
[7] *Despertador Araucano*, no. 2, 17 May 1823, pp. 11–12.

162

through the medium of the printed word: blasphemy, immorality, sedition and private injury.[1] In order to control such excesses as might occur, the most popular expedient was the institution of a special press committee or *jurado de imprenta*, before which all cases concerned with infractions of the law could be brought.[2]

Religious freedom, however, was not a matter on which Chilean opinion was unanimous. The revolutionary period saw only the beginnings of a struggle on this issue which was to last until the close of the nineteenth century.[3] Most of the constitutions of the time established Roman Catholicism as the official religion of the state. There were, even so, one or two indications of a more tolerant attitude in certain circles. Bernardo O'Higgins, for instance, seems to have wanted freedom of belief in Chile, even if he felt himself unable to offer Protestants the privilege of public worship.[4] His 1818 Constitution made the Catholic Church official and prohibited other denominations from exercising their faith in public,[5] though this latter provision was absent from the 1822 Constitution, where the installation of Catholicism as the state religion was reiterated.[6] The 1828 Constitution also made the Catholic Church official and established, but added a significant article which declared that 'nobody will be persecuted or molested on account of his private opinions',[7] a humane provision absent from the Constitution of 1833. In general, it cannot be said that there was a very strong demand for religious liberty during the revolution, even though intolerance and fanaticism were attacked by the small group of passionate anticlericals in the 1820s and 1830s.[8] The opponents of religious freedom were, if anything,

---

[1] Proyecto de Ley de Imprenta, art. 11, *SCL*, XVI, 396.

[2] For an examination of the press laws see Eduardo Naveas Echiburu, 'La legislación y los juicios de imprenta en Chile, 1812–72' (unpublished *Memoria de prueba*, University of Chile, 1956), and also Donoso, *Ideas políticas*, pp. 344–54. Ultimately the *jurado de imprenta* was a failure and was omitted from the Constitution of 1925.

[3] The best description of the attitude of the 1810–33 period is in Donoso, *Ideas políticas*, pp. 174–90. My own short paragraph does not pretend to replace Donoso's full account, but to mention a few further aspects.

[4] See Jaime Eyzaguirre, *La actitud religiosa de don Bernardo O'Higgins* (1961), pp. 20–5.

[5] Tít. 2, cap. único.   [6] Arts. 10–11.

[7] Art. 4. See *El Constituyente*, no. 1, 3 June 1828, attacking this article.

[8] A good example is the article 'Intolerancia', *El Liberal*, no. 37, 11 November 1824. Varying degrees of anticlericalism may be observed in *El Cometa*, *El Espectador*, *El Philopolita* and other papers.

more vociferous than the apostles of tolerance, as the cases of Juan Egaña and Fray Tadeo Silva tend to indicate. Even Camilo Henríquez argued on one occasion that Chileans should adopt the cause of independence from Spain because this would enhance the purity of religion—Spain, he claimed, had suffered greatly from excessive contact with impious countries such as England and France.[1] Whether Henríquez seriously believed this, or was merely using the argument as another means of stimulating patriot enthusiasm, is another matter. By and large, however, informed liberal opinion was content to allow religious liberty a few decades before being introduced into Chile. 'Later there will come a day', wrote Juan García del Río, '(yes, I perceive it there in the darkness of the centuries) when these matters can be safely discussed in Chile.'[2]

VIRTUE AND ENLIGHTENMENT

Individual rights, which the Chileans regarded as 'a free man's noblest possession',[3] were recognized, along with the establishment of national freedom, as the chief advantage of the new political order. Added together and allied to a 'republican' constitution, they signified as much civil liberty as was compatible with the existence of society. Yet the creole intelligentsia was very well aware that freedom brought dangers as well as opportunities. 'It is not only necessary that men should be free in order to be happy,' wrote Gandarillas, '...but it is also necessary to know how to use liberty in order to give happiness a proper domicile.'[4] If liberty were not to be used correctly, it was widely felt, then the state rank the risk of descending into anarchy. This was a constant fear. Freedom could only survive if the country steered the uneasy course between the Scylla of despotism and the Charybdis of democracy.

In a republican government like ours, we should try to evade the two extremes: the power of the aristocracy, which leads us to oligarchy, and the power of the plebeians, which will precipitate us into anarchy.[5]

---

[1] *Semanario Republicano*, no. 7, 11 December 1813.
[2] *El Telégrafo*, no. 72, 24 March 1820.
[3] Introduction to the draft of the 1828 Constitution, 20 May 1828, *SCL*, xvi, 17.
[4] *Carta de dos amigos a don Firmiano Roca*, 7 June 1814, *Arch.O'H*. ii, 295–6.
[5] *La Ley y la Justicia*, no. 2 [1829].

For, as Bernardo Monteagudo remarked, Spanish Americans had quickly come to 'fear the tyranny of the people when infatuated with deliriums'.[1]

What was the solution to this problem? Despotic government had to be tamed, but an overdose of liberty could lead to anarchy. How could liberty be assured? Irisarri gave the standard answer in 1818: 'I repeat once and a thousand times over that the ruin of social liberty has always been occasioned by licence...If we wish to be free, *let us be virtuous*: let us imitate the Anglo-Americans.'[2] 'Virtue is the sole support of freedom,' affirmed a newspaper of 1829.[3] Republican institutions, in short, could only operate successfully if accompanied by public virtue. 'In general', declared a conservative newspaper of 1833, 'a nation's prosperity and tranquillity depend on the quantity of moral virtues in its people.'[4] Virtue was one of the keystones of the social and political order, therefore, and it had to be stimulated by every means within the power of the government. 'The basis of politics should be to cultivate the virtues and to establish them amongst all classes of society.'[5] Juan Egaña, as will be seen, took this principle and made the inculcation of virtuous national morality the fundamental theme of his own distinctive political theory. No other Chilean writer went this far, yet the idea of virtue as an indispensable foundation for stable and harmonious political life was very deeply rooted.

If most Chilean writers avoided Juan Egaña's complicated methods of inculcating virtue, it was because they had a simple and optimistic answer: education. Education was the proper means of introducing virtue. The official gazette was able, in 1819, to describe the reopening of the Instituto Nacional as 'the foundation stone of our welfare',[6] and there was an intense optimism about the results of education.[7] It was widely felt that

---

[1] *El Censor de la Revolución*, no. 1, 20 April 1820.
[2] *Duende de Santiago*, no. 3, 6 July 1818, p. 6.
[3] *Espectador Chileno*, no. 1, 21 August 1829, p. 1.
[4] *El Cosmopólita*, no. 1, 30 April 1833, p. 2.
[5] *Patriota Chileno*, tomo 1, no. 11, 23 February 1826, p. 142.
[6] *Gaceta Ministerial de Chile*, tomo 2, no. 3, 31 July 1819.
[7] See the speech by Joaquín Campino in *Redactor de la Educación*, no. 4, 1 February 1825, p. 111.

education would moderate natural passions and control the innate tendency of men to seek licence. 'We must admit', wrote García del Río, 'that ignorance and error are the cause of all the evils which afflict society.'[1] 'Education', believed *El Correo de Arauco*, 'will always make a people moderate.'[2] 'The stability of popular governments', it could be claimed, 'depends entirely on the education of their peoples.'[3] Yet if education prevented mankind from falling into the error of licence, it also fore-armed mankind against the other great threat: despotism. Despots, it was agreed, could best be undermined by the diffusion of solid political principles. 'The monarchs of Europe trembled when they saw that the principles of Voltaire, Rousseau, Montesquieu, Mably and other sublime geniuses had been disseminated.'[4] There was a natural contradiction between tyranny and enlightenment. 'Despots oppose the enlightenment of their people, for they want to rule over blind men and barbarians in order to oppress them better.'[5] Education went with freedom, ignorance with tyranny. As Henríquez put it, 'liberty presupposes a great mass of enlightenment spread out amongst the multitudes, while on the other hand tyranny reigns amidst darkness and error'.[6] Looking back at their own educational history, the Chileans felt that they were correct in accusing the Spanish regimes of having adopted a deliberate policy of ignorance with this precise end in view.

Education, then, was a guarantee of freedom. This was recognized by the citizens of La Serena when they founded an educational institute in that town as a direct result of their 'recently acquired liberty, and the desire to propagate learning without which this liberty could not survive'.[7] Education, however, had to be linked closely to virtue, for unless virtue were somehow implanted, freedom would perish. The Junta of 1813, when setting up an educational commission, observed that

[1] *El Sol de Chile*, no. 10, 18 September 1818, p. 1.
[2] No. 42, 14 January 1825, p. 187.
[3] *Mercurio de Valparaíso*, tomo I, no. 27, 12 December 1827, p. 105.
[4] *Argos de Chile*, no. 4, 18 June 1818.
[5] *Correo de Arauco*, no. 42, 14 January 1825, p. 187.
[6] *Catecismo de los patriotas*, p. 152.
[7] Victorino Garrido to the Minister of the Interior, 27 October 1830, A.M.I. vol. 59, fo. 24.

all States degenerate and perish in proportion to their neglect of national education...If it is necessary to form character, and inspire in the People a certain type of morality analogous to their circumstances and constitution, then it is doubly necessary in an infant State.[1]

Since the Chilean revolution had taken the road of representative government, the education of the vast number of illiterates in the country was a prime necessity. Without the eradication of illiteracy, it was held, 'the representative system cannot be solidly established amongst us; it cannot be said, in the meantime, that we have more than a few forms of government sustained by the will of a few people'.[2] But, looking beyond these obvious political needs, there was also the importance of education in preparing man to enjoy the happiness freedom conferred on him. As Henríquez expressed it: 'To make people happy, it is necessary to educate them.'[3]

It followed from this that education was to be regarded as a primary task of republican government. It was to be 'one of the principal duties of the social pact'.[4] A representative government, wrote Manuel de Salas, 'must always work to propagate sound and solid knowledge of all kinds, and it cannot survive if these do nor prevail'.[5] This is why educational policies and improvements were followed with such enormous interest and enthusiasm by the creole intelligentsia. A comment by one newspaper on the attempt to introduce the Lancasterian System into Chile may be taken as typical of an almost universal attitude.

Yes, the new system of education that is being propagated will give being to a new and better order of things; instruction will replace ignorance, and attract a new age of moral felicity;...and societies will then be based on unshakable foundations.[6]

It was not given to the governments of the revolution to do all, or indeed anything like all, that they wanted to do in the field of

---

[1] Decree of 1 June 1813, *CHDI*, xxvi, 205.
[2] *Correo Mercantil*, tomo 2, no. 308, 25 April 1833.
[3] *Aurora de Chile*, tomo i, no. 13, 7 May 1812, p. 56.
[4] Educational Committee of Congress, *Informe* of 15 October 1823, *SCL*, viii, 316.
[5] Salas, *Escritos*, iii, 37.   [6] *El Amigo de la Verdad*, no. 4, 14 June 1823, p. 37.

education. Yet their faith in its power to transform society, and above all to establish the virtue which underpinned political liberty, was a fundamental link in the chain of their political theory.

SOURCES OF THE REVOLUTIONARY THEORY

It will by now have become clear that the main political ideas of the Chilean revolution were liberal and individualist in character, and that they stemmed from the diverse currents of late eighteenth-century and early nineteenth-century liberalism: from the encyclopaedist tradition, with its rational emphasis on a universal natural order and its hope that infallible rules for the conduct of society could be found; from the deepening of some of those themes in the French Revolution; and from the moderate but parallel ideology of the independence movement in the Thirteen Colonies. It is difficult to claim that traditional Spanish elements found much of a place in this new system of thought. The sovereignty of the community had certainly been a theme expounded by Suárez and other distinguished sixteenth-century Spanish jurists; yet it can hardly be allowed that their particular expression of it influenced the Chileans to any marked degree, except perhaps somewhat vaguely during the crisis of 1810, when some elementary 'populist' notions were evidently in circulation. It may very well be that the Spanish tradition, which in many ways was a less coherent prefiguration of some of the main themes of eighteenth-century liberal political thought, made the adoption of the new ideas easier for the creole intelligentsia, but what cannot be doubted is that the 'modern' principles elaborated by the great Enlightened and Revolutionary thinkers on both sides of the Atlantic formed the main source from which the creole generation of 1810–33 drew its inspiration. The Chileans revealed an enormous and fervent admiration for those thinkers and of the European Enlightenment in general. Saluting 'that brilliant constellation of geniuses', Monteagudo affirmed that 'the history of the eighteenth century, compared with that of previous ages, displays human enterprise in a light of intrepidness and perseverance of which no other example can be found, even in the ages of fable'.[1] Juan Egaña expressed a similar admiration for the 'delicate enlightenment and sublime politics of happy and cultured Europe, whose progress in the present era will be the wonder of all ages'.[2] Chileans were acutely conscious of 'that torrent of enlightenment which, emanating from cultured Europe, is now embracing America'.[3] Chile became, overnight, a 'people thirsting for useful knowledge';[4] and the press gave evidence of this, for, in addition to their interminable production of articles on the day-to-day political situation, it produced numerous accounts of new inventions, scientific theories, and other miscellaneous pieces of information.[5]

It is easier to make mistakes in discussing influences in political thought than in almost any other comparable field of human reflection. Even so, it is instructive to inquire briefly into the specific sources from which the revolutionary ideology was derived. Who, for instance, were the foreign writers and thinkers most admired and quoted in Chile during the period under review? A few examples will suffice to indicate the extent and range of the Chileans' reading, and the theorists most eminent in their intellectual pantheon. Juan Martínez de Rozas, in his speech to the inaugural session of the 1811 Congress, referred to constitution-making as an art which had formerly employed the attentions of

Solon, Lycurgus, Plato, Aristotle, Cicero, Hobbes, Machiavelli, Bacon, Grotius, Pufendorf, Locke, Moreno, Bodin, Hume, Gordon, Montesquieu, Rousseau, Mably, and other privileged geniuses.[6]

It may be doubted whether Rozas had consulted all of these privileged geniuses, yet he was (in 1811, note) well aware of

---

[1] *Censor de la Revolución*, no. 1, 20 April 1820.
[2] 'Diálogo entre el Dr Juan Loke y el Presidente de la República de Ayti Boyer', n.d. [1820s], F.V., vol. 259, pieza 15. Locke was often misspelled 'Loke' at this time.
[3] *El Liberal*, no. 3, 15 August 1823, p. 21.
[4] *Mercurio Chileno*, no. v, 1 August 1828, p. 242.
[5] I cannot do more than mention one or two examples of this: (1) The scientific explanations of earthquakes by Henríquez in *Aurora de Chile*, tomo 2, no. 4, 28 January 1813, and *Mercurio de Chile*, no. 16, 2 December 1822. (2) Articles from the foreign press in *Colección de Noticias Documentadas*. (3) Articles in *Mercurio Chileno*. (4) Description of the London Stock Exchange in *Mercurio de Valparaíso*, nos. 1239–40, 18–19 December 1839. (5) 'Caminos de fierro en Inglaterra', account of the Liverpool–Manchester Railway, *Mercurio de Valparaíso*, no. 1388, 19 June 1833.   [6] *SCL*, I, 40.

their existence, and it seems likely that some of the more recent members of his gallery of notables had passed through his hands. In 1823, when Rodríguez Aldea[1] published his lengthy political apologia *Satisfacción pública*, he included references to, or quotations from, the following authors: Montesquieu, d'Holbach, Bentham, Cottu, Constant, Daunou, Bernardin de Saint-Pierre, Chateaubriand, Genovesi, Destutt de Tracy, J. B. Say, and Vattel. He also appealed in passing to the authority of St Paul, Joshua, and Moses. The casual mention of great names was, in fact, a familiar device to add weight to a particular argument. Thus in 1822 Dauxion Lavaysse[2] defended the Christian religion against certain attacks, remarking:

Let madmen learn that the greatest geniuses of the last three centuries —Copernicus, Kepler, Galileo, Descartes, Bacon, Leibniz, Newton, Boyle, Samuel Clarke, Malebranche, Torricelli, Huyghens, the Bernouillis, Bossuet, Locke, Pascal, Addison, Harvey, Montesquieu... —all believe in the Divine revelation of Christianity.[3]

Now that there were no longer any restrictions on the type of books that could be read, Chileans enthusiastically availed themselves of all the literature they could lay their hands on. An English traveller reported in the 1820s that in Chile and Peru 'shiploads of French deistical books are now freely imported, and bought up with great avidity'.[4] Even before the end of O'Higgins' time it could be claimed that 'the book trade in Chile, as in America at large, is one of the most productive'.[5] There are many clues to the kind of books which were nourishing the import trade so well. In 1833, for instance, *El Mercurio de Valparaíso* listed some of the works which could be purchased at its offices. Those in

[1] José Antonio Rodríguez Aldea (1779–1841). Adviser to the royalist army in Chile 1814–17; Minister of Finance 1820–3; Senator 1829 and 1831–4; after 1823, an ardent O'Higginist; member of the Congress of Plenipotentiaries 1830.
[2] Juan José Dauxion Lavaysse (*ca.* 1770–1830). His connection with Chile began in 1816 when he met José Miguel Carrera in the U.S.A. and accompanied him to Argentina; arrived in Chile 1822; his polemical activity aroused hostility in Santiago. See Diego Barros Arana, *Don Claudio Gay, su vida i sus obras* (1876), pp. 17–18.
[3] *Observador Chileno*, tomo I, no. 2, September 1822.
[4] Mathison, p. 355. Cf. the 'very extensive importations of French books' in Buenos Aires referred to by Brackenridge, I, 235.
[5] *Mercurio de Chile*, no. 1 [1822], *CAPC*, IX, 206.

Spanish included Fénelon's *Télémaque*, Montesquieu's *Spirit of the Laws*, and *Persian Letters*, and books by Benjamin Constant and Jeremy Bentham. In French, Smith's *Wealth of Nations*, J. B. Say's *Economie Politique*, Raynal's *Histoire Philosophique*, and the works of Filangieri were amongst the books on sale.[1] The general interest in authors like these was satirized in *El Hambriento* in a false 'Movements of Shipping' column which affected to announce the arrival of an Argentine vessel carrying

a trunk containing the following works: Parliamentary Tactics, Compilation of Laws, The *Tauromaquía*, Buchan, and The Art of Cooking. Passengers include Messrs Rousseau, Hobbes, Vossius, Cottu, Bentham, Constant, Montesquieu, Machiavelli, Voltaire, Say, Pufendorf, Grotius, Sully and Genovesi, with their wives and a couple of nieces.[2]

A final illustration will, I think, suffice to confirm what will by now have become apparent. The newspaper press of the 1820s, the period when political philosophizing flourished most richly, quoted an impressive range of thinkers. It would be nearly impossible to list them all, but the ten most popular authors—to judge from the number of times their names were invoked or their works quoted—were Montesquieu, Bentham, Constant, Rousseau, Voltaire, Filangieri, Mably, Paine, De Pradt, and Destutt de Tracy. Montesquieu was the most often quoted, followed by Bentham. Other writers whose names appeared with quite considerable frequency were de Lolme, Smith, Sismondi, Diderot, Cottu, Vattel, Locke, Raynal, and J. B. Say.[3] This list is by no means exhaustive. The Chileans appealed to many other authorities when it suited them to do so, and in particular religious authorities. But by and large, these were their favourite political

---

[1] No. 1317, 22 March 1833.   [2] 'Marítima', no. 8, 20 February 1828, p. 30.
[3] This list is based on a survey of the political articles in a majority of the newspapers published between 1823 and 1829. Time did not permit me to make a complete and detailed list of every foreign source mentioned in every Chilean newspaper printed between 1812 and, say, 1835. Such a list would, I think, throw more light on this problem, but, for the 1820s at least, I believe my list to be substantially accurate. Other writers who were also quoted less often were Helvétius, Kant, Bacon, Bodin, Leibniz, Newton, Schilling, Massillon, d'Alembert, d'Holbach, Hume, Condillac, Blackstone and Volney.

authors. It would plainly be unwise to read too much into any list of this sort. Certain qualifications have to be made. Some writers, obviously, were used to support arguments on specified issues. The works of the Abbé de Pradt, for instance, were indispensable in articles on the relations between America and Europe. Likewise Smith and Say were called into action on economic matters, and Vattel when the law of nations was under discussion.

The commanding position of Montesquieu can hardly be disputed, but it involves something of an enigma. Standing slightly apart from the main stream of eighteenth-century liberal political thought—though profoundly liberal in his own way—he provided no confirmation of the Chileans' reverence for natural rights or popular sovereignty. Yet his admiration for the British Constitution, his exposition of the balance of powers, and his fervent hatred of despotic government, allied to the conservative streak in his nature, endeared him to the creole intelligentsia. Their use of Montesquieu was typical of their use of all political thinkers: they took from him what they wanted and ignored the contradictory elements of his theory. The same applied with particular force to Rousseau. The influence of Rousseau was plainly very widespread in Chile at certain periods—notably during Henríquez' intellectual ascendancy. It was Henríquez who wrote in 1823 that the *Social Contract* 'has been the one classic book of the patriots of South America, Spain, Portugal, etc. Its key ideas have become so well rooted in men's minds, and are... provoking such reasonings and meditations that reforms are now inevitable'.[1] This statement was sweeping, at any rate as far as Chile went. The version of the *Social Contract* edited by Mariano Moreno in Buenos Aires, together with several political catechisms loosely based on Rousseau, plainly circulated and had some effect in the '*Patria Vieja*',[2] but the ideology of the revolution, as will have become clear, preferred representative institutions to direct democracy of the small-state variety, and fell back on the formula of majority will in place of Rousseau's more difficult conception of the general will. But, just as the French Revolution

---

[1] *El Nuevo Corresponsal*, no. 1 [1823], p. 3.
[2] See Donoso, *Ideas políticas*, p. 35; Eyzaguirre, *Ideario y ruta*, p. 127.

paid homage to Rousseau while adopting Siéyès' constitutional theory, so did the Chilean revolution. And it should not be forgotten that there was opposition to Rousseau in Chile as well as enthusiasm for him. The most celebrated and violent attack on him came from the pen of Fray Tadeo Silva, a conservative-minded priest who based his argument on largely religious grounds. Henríquez had praised Rousseau, along with Voltaire and Montesquieu, in the pages of his *Mercurio de Chile*.[1] Silva, while reserving his worst comminations for Voltaire, denounced Rousseau as 'an Apostle of tyranny and despotism',[2] and recalled that he had been expelled from Geneva on account of his *Emile*, though Chile suffered the public sale of this and other works without raising an eyebrow.[3] Silva's attack on Rousseau and other eighteenth-century thinkers was largely religious in character, but a later denunciation of Rousseau concentrated more exclusively on the political aspect. Rousseau was condemned as the spiritual ancestor of Argentine federalism, a begetter of chaos; and the *Social Contract* was stigmatized as 'that Koran of Anarchy'.[4] Chile, then, experienced an echo of the European division of opinion about Rousseau.[5]

The work of Thomas Paine, however, was less diffuse than Montesquieu and more immediately comprehensible than Rousseau. The relative simplicity and extreme directness of the basic notions put forward by Paine were admirably suited to the creole intelligentsia. His anti-monarchism, his call for the American continent to 'prepare in time an asylum for mankind', and his championship of the rights of man—all these themes proved congenial to the Chileans. During the '*Patria Vieja*', both Henríquez and Irisarri appear to have had more than a nodding acquaintance with Paine's writings. Henríquez quoted *Common Sense* in his famous *Aurora* editorial urging independence.[6] Irisarri, it has been suggested, knew Paine through García de Sena's translation and

---

[1] No. 23, 13 March 1823.   [2] *Los apóstoles del Diablo*, p. 13.
[3] *Ibid.* p. 20.
[4] 'Observaciones sobre los serviles anarquistas de Córdova de la Plata', *Década Araucana*, no. 1, 12 July 1825, p. 5.
[5] For this, see Alfred Cobban, *Rousseau and the Modern State* (London, 1964), pp. 22–31.
[6] Tomo 1, no. 17, 4 June 1812.

condensation,[1] which may have been circulated in Chile by Poinsett.[2] Ricardo Levene has shown that, just before the liberation of Chile in 1817, San Martín ordered copies of García de Sena's book for circulation in the territories to be freed.[3] But, like Rousseau, Paine was not without his critics. Dauxion Lavaysse attacked him in his pamphlet *Del federalismo y de la anarquía*, though this was not the main aim of the work.[4] Paine was also condemned, along with Rousseau, in the newspaper attack already mentioned.[5]

A number of other authors whose work must be regarded as influential at one stage of the revolution or another should be mentioned here. Jean-Louis de Lolme was certainly known, and his account of the English Constitution was used by Henríques during the *'Patria Vieja'*.[6] Henríquez also used the works of the Abbé de Malby, from which he printed extracts in *El Monitor Araucano*.[7] The federalist philosophy of José Miguel Infante was certainly influenced by the favourable opinions of federal government to be found in Montesquieu, Mably, Beccaria, Burlamaqui and Bentham: Infante printed some of these opinions in his own newspaper as an edifying series for the faithful.[8] Infante and Juan Egaña both seem to have had some knowledge of Filangieri. Benjamin Constant, whose writings were quoted a good deal in the 1820s, was also regarded as a suitable background authority; though some of his more distinctive theories were, strictly speaking, irrelevant to the Chilean situation, his emphasis on popular sovereignty and the need for moderate constitutional government was widely accepted and shared.

The ideas of Jeremy Bentham also enjoyed a certain vogue, particularly in the 1820s, but not, I think, in any very profound manner. His notions on the mechanics of parliamentary government were often quoted, but it was the Bentham of the *Constitutional Code* rather than the Bentham of the *Fragment on*

---

[1] *La independencia de la Costa Firme justificada por Tomás Paine treinta años ha* (Philadelphia, 1811).
[2] Eyzaguirre, *Ideario y ruta*, p. 138.   [3] Levene, p. 174.
[4] He also attacked William Godwin, p. 3 n. .   [5] See p.   , n. .
[6] E.g. *Aurora de Chile*, tomo 2, no. 12, 1 April 1813.
[7] Tomo 1, nos. 9 and 10, 7 and 11 January 1814.
[8] *Valdiviano Federal*, nos. 23 and 24, 28 January and 19 February 1829.

Government who interested the creoles.[1] Every Chilean took what he wanted from Bentham. Infante might use a glowing description of the progress of the United States, and then ask under what 'system' this had been achieved.[2] Bentham's opinions on law reform might be printed in extensive excerpts, as they were in 1833, as a contribution to the constitutional discussions of that year.[3] It is also true that Irisarri sent some of Bentham's books from London to form part of the National Library collection in Santiago, and that José Joaquín de Mora had been in personal contact with Bentham in London before arriving in Chile.[4] Yet it cannot be allowed that his ideas played much of a part in the formation of the ideology of the revolution, however much they may have been used later on to confirm specific aspects of the ideology. Bentham's views on the social contract and on natural rights do not seem to have been appreciated in Chile, and would probably have been generally unwelcome even if they had been. As a name to be piously invoked from time to time, Bentham was useful; as an expert on the parliamentary government the Chileans so badly wanted to introduce properly, he was an influence; as a mentor pronouncing on fundamental questions, he was largely ignored. Nevertheless, Bentham's name was highly regarded. Reviewing some of Bentham's translated works in 1822, Henríquez wrote:

Nothing could be more useful than the works of Bentham in a century when the representative system and the reform of the old deliriums and injuries are making prodigious advances in Europe and America.[5]

The Chileans frequently acknowledged the influence of the various writers I have mentioned, and to some extent assimilated their ideas. But, in addition, it must be recognized that many of the more concrete ideas which they incorporated into their new

---

[1] It may be noted that Blackstone, the target of the *Fragment*, was sometimes cited as an authority in Chile (see 'Naturalización', *Observador Chileno*, tomo I, no. 4, 11 October 1822).

[2] *Valdiviano Federal*, no. 24, 19 February 1829.

[3] *Correo Mercantil*, nos. 275–85, 2–20 March 1833.

[4] Levene, pp. 250–1. For Bentham in Latin America as a whole, see Levene, ch. 12, and R. A. Humphreys, *The Study of Latin American History. An Inaugural Lecture* (London, 1948), pp. 3–6.

[5] *Mercurio de Chile*, no. 2, [1822], *CAPC*, IX, 228.

political orthodoxy descended fairly directly from the revolutionary examples of France and North America. That the ideas which justified the French and American revolutions were themselves descended from the liberal strain in the Enlightenment can hardly be denied. The Chileans were unable to conceal their intense admiration for the Anglo-Saxon world, and in particular the British Constitution.[1] The Constitution of the United States, which was in reality a formalized revision and adaptation of what some Enlightened thinkers chose to regard as the British Constitution, was the major influence on Chile when it came to the various *cartas* of the revolution, though here again the codes of revolutionary France and the Spanish Constitution of 1812 all reinforced the main source of 1787.[2] But the European element was supreme. Europe was looked on as the major fountainhead of 'enlightenment', even if many of the most striking applications of enlightened political principles had occurred in the United States. The creole admiration for Europe can even be traced in occasional expressions of interest in enlightened despotism. Even though the reforms of Charles III were no longer openly praised—for reasons that will become clear in chapter 5—other exponents of strong but public-spirited government, and reforms 'from above', could be commended from time to time.[3]

This is not to say that in addition to their newly found enthusiasm for 'modern' and enlightened writers, the Chileans did not appeal to older and more traditional authorities as well. Juan Egaña, in his memorial to Ferdinand VII from Juan Fernández, made use of the Laws of the Indies, Suárez, Solórzano and de Soto,[4] and he appears to have known these sources well. It may be doubted, however, whether they were important influences on Egaña. In all likelihood he used them to add respectability to an appeal directed at a government unsympathetic to more modern

[1] See chapter 5, pp.   .

[2] For the influence of the Cadiz Constitution on the Chilean constitution of 1822 see Orrego Vicuña, *Espíritu constitucional*, ch. VII, and on the sources of the 1818 and draft federal constitution of 1826, Shaw, p. 86 and pp. 120–1. The draft federal constitution was greatly influenced by the Mexican document of two years earlier: see Juan Egaña to Mariano Egaña, 1 March 1827, *Cartas de Juan Egaña*, p. 207.

[3] See, for instance, the glowing account of Russian progress since Peter the Great, *Sol de Chile*, no. 14, 9 October 1818, and later issues.   [4] *El Chileno consolado*, II, 5.

ideas. For his part, Camilo Henríquez used an extract from the *Vindiciae contra Tyrannos* to point certain morals about the origins of monarchy and the rights of men,[1] and he also used the Gospels, St Augustine and other religious authorities in the course of his patriotic literary labours.[2] All this was perfectly natural in view of Henríquez' religious background. Despite his intense interest in the Enlightenment and his political commitment, he remained a faithful Catholic to the end. Such a course— the citation of traditional and religious sources—was inevitable in a country where the influence of the Church was one of the strongest in society, where it could be held as a self-evident truth that 'the Catholic Church is the holder of the highest thought',[3] and where an unknown author of 1818 found it necessary to warn that the patriot cause had nothing in common with freemasonry.[4] Popular sovereignty could, of course, be argued as easily from the Spanish sixteenth-century tradition as from the enlightened liberal tradition, and Fray Pedro Arce, for instance, did not hesitate to adopt this approach on one occasion.[5] However, it must not be forgotten that the creole intelligentsia in the earlier years of the revolution had an immense task of propaganda to carry out, and that traditional arguments were extremely useful from this point of view. It cannot be held that the sixteenth-century 'populist' tradition (as it has been called) played any real part in the formulation of the revolutionary ideology, or that its arguments, when used at all, were ever more than complementary to those based on the reasoning of the liberal philosophers of the Enlightenment and the two Revolutions.

Finally, some brief comments may be permitted on the general nature of the revolutionary theory. Its main features can be reduced to a simple set of propositions: There exists an ideal pattern of natural law to which human institutions must ultimately

[1] *Aurora de Chile*, tomo 2, no. 8, 4 March 1813.
[2] See *Catecismo de los patriotas*, pp. 147–8 and 152–3. Cf. sermon of 4 July 1811 (*SCL*, I, 34–8) in which he refuted charges that Catholicism was favourable to despotism.
[3] *El Amigo de la Verdad*, no. 2, 11 April 1823, p. 22.
[4] *Clamor de la Justicia e Idioma de la Verdad* [no. 2], 1817. It is a much disputed point whether the Logia Lautarina can be considered as an orthodox masonic institution.
[5] 'Circular', 6 June 1817, *Gazeta de Santiago de Chile*, 30 August 1817. Arce cited Aquinas, Vitoria and de Soto.

conform. Government is contractually instituted and hence depends on the consent of the governed. Sovereignty, which thus belongs to the whole people, can best be delegated through a representative system of government. The state must be subject to a written constitution which divides the powers equally and separately. Man, despite his contractual involvement in political society, nevertheless possesses certain natural and inalienable rights—liberty, security, property and equality—which it is the first duty of governments to protect. Republican government, to operate effectively, depends on a minimum of public virtue which can best be secured through the enlightenment of the citizens.

Plainly enough, this was a mechanistic explanation of the state, and it depended in the last analysis on the notion of equilibrium. Just as the natural order was harmonious, so was the constitutional order. The propensity to tyranny was discouraged and controlled by a series of checks and balances. The popular tendency towards licence could be counterbalanced by the cultivation of virtue. A man's citizenship in civil society was compensated for by his inalienable rights. In no sense did these theories represent an organic view of the state. Indeed, it was made very clear that the state's sphere of influence was very far from all-inclusive. The natural rights regarded as inalienable were held to be anterior to, and independent of, the social contract.

Some of the political ideas employed by the creoles were already old-fashioned and out of date. Some of their basic premises—the contract, natural rights—had been vigorously attacked long before the Spanish imperial crisis of 1808 which set the revolution in motion. Liberalism was rapidly shifting its ground from the abstract construction of natural law to the solider foundations of Benthamite utilitarianism. But the Chileans can hardly be blamed for having employed the basic concepts they did. What they wanted was a suitable theory to justify the most cataclysmic political change in their history. The old generalized concept of nature, eternal and unchangeable, as the final authority to which they could appeal, was far more useful than any of the theories that had replaced it. The Chileans' instinct in choosing their political ideas was sound.

5

REVOLUTIONARY ATTITUDES

EMOTIONS OF THE REVOLUTION

The political ideas adopted by the Chilean revolution were neither very original nor very profound. But they were by no means the sole element in the revolutionary ideology. Associated with the new body of political doctrine, there was a related complex of other ideas, feelings, vague concepts, strident and aggressive attitudes, and semi-historical theories which went to make up what can properly be styled the mystique of the revolution. Every genuine revolution has its mystique; the Chilean revolution was no exception. And the Chileans' own particular mystique deserves serious attention, for the *tone* of the revolution is in many ways more immediately accessible through the body of emotional attitudes I shall describe in the present chapter than through the relatively stereotyped political philosophy.

The language employed by the leaders of the revolution is of particular interest. Guillermo Feliú Cruz, commenting on the earliest official documents, notes that 'the ideas of liberty...are expressed with a resonant and grandiose lyrical emphasis, with a grandiloquent, oratorical tone, or with a severe and at times truly impressive emotion'.[1] The keynote of revolutionary writing was its enthusiasm. Patriotic enthusiasm was now a virtue, as it naturally had to be in a time of change and revolution, and it expressed itself in many different ways. Enthusiasm was conceived as an element which would operate to the general advantage of the nation. 'May this noble and enchanting enthusiasm flourish as I desire amongst the citizens,' wrote Juan Castellón, 'and we shall be happy, with our virtues.'[2] Enthusiasm, too, created the desire for great and heroic deeds.

[1] *Andréas Bello y la redacción de los documentos oficiales del Gobierno de Chile* (Caracas, 1953), p. 9.
[2] To Diego José Benavente, 4 August 1824, F.V. vol. 821, o. 87.

The Revolutionary Ideology

That fiery September sun which so actively melts the mountain snows and fertilizes the valleys of our beautiful Chile, gives to the sensitive heart a new vigour, and makes it long for ever more famous and ever more glorious deeds.[1]

Enthusiasm caused such heroic deeds as there were to be celebrated with intense joy. It was felt that participation in such events guaranteed a measure of true immortality: 'Our names will be imoortalized in the far reaches of history.'[2]

The exaggeration of feelings was another outcome of this tide of revolutionary enthusiasm. The district governor of Copiapó, for instance, reported the reaction to O'Higgins' first orders and decrees in the following terms:

Without ever losing a moment I authorized their publication, which was carried out by the Deputy Governor Elect of this neighbourhood, which, full of extraordinary Jubilation, expressed itself with *vivas* of joy, proclaiming the triumph of freedom, knowing that the Supreme Arbiter has extended his Omnipotent Hand over the people of Chile.[3]

Three years later the Cabildo of the same township expressed to O'Higgins its feelings on hearing the news of the liberation of Lima: 'The reading...of such precious documents was like an electric fire, which inflamed our hearts to such an extent that we shed tears of the most innocent joy.'[4] The people of Quillota, celebrating the installation of the Junta of 1810 with '*vivas*, acclamations, illuminations, public bonfires and a solemn Mass of thanksgiving',[5] may be regarded as entirely typical. In one way and another, a good deal of perfectly justifiable emotional excitement was generated at frequent intervals throughout the revolution.

Such excitement—quite apart from other elements permanently present in the Spanish American psychology—is the explanation for the exaggerated significance which was often attached to events, and also to institutions. A citizen of La Serena could refer

---

[1] *Gazeta de Santiago de Chile*, 20 September 1817.
[2] 'Viva la Patria Señores' [patriotic speech, Vallenar, 3 March 1817], A.M.I. vol. 38, fo. 219.
[3] Zelada to O'Higgins, 4 March 1817, A.M.I. vol. 38, fo. 33.
[4] Letter of 21 September 1821, A.M.I. vol. 38, fo. 91.
[5] Cabildo of Quillota to the Junta, 29 October 1810, *CHDI*, XVIII, 267.

in 1821 to O'Higgins' Senate as the 'propagator of enlightenment, the crystalline fount of the education and progress of the Republic',[1] even though this was far from being the case. It was not enough merely to report the triumphs of Lord Cochrane. It had to be added that these would assure 'the liberty of a thousand generations'.[2] When the government was valiantly struggling to restore some kind of interprovincial unity to Chile in mid 1825, it was solemnly assured by the Provincial Assembly of Coquimbo that its task was especially noble, for 'the reorganization of a State after its decline is the noblest spectacle of any offered by the history of human affairs'.[3] (The Assembly itself, it is worth noting, was one of the chief hindrances to any such reorganization.) The successes of the Pinto administration were greeted with such unjustifiably sanguine comments as this: 'Chile is today the model for all free countries, a vast precinct of brotherhood and happiness.'[4] Such an assertion could hardly be squared with the mounting partisan bitterness of that moment. The issues at stake in the revolution were believed to be of enormous significance for America and the world in general. As the Coquimbo Provincial Assembly ventured to put it: 'Perhaps the destinies of many Peoples of the world hang on the fulfilment of our own marvellous destinies.'[5] Such ways of expression should always be borne in mind when Chilean writings of the period are discussed.

How did the revolutionaries interpret their own revolution? Occasionally, they saw it as linked to a wider revolutionary process, as part of the 'disordered convulsion suffered by the whole earth'.[6] O'Higgins, for instance, could warn Ferdinand VII that 'the conflagration is universal, the space immense, the fire of the revolution inextinguishable'.[7] Naturally enough, Chile was influenced by the wider world scene. Freire could speak of 'the advantages and institutions which *the spirit of the century*

[1] Lcdo. J. M. Barros, Speech to the Instituto Literario of La Serena, 1 December 1821, *SCL*, v, 492.
[2] *Miscelánea Chilena*, no. 9, 26 March 1821 (*CAPC*, IX, 153).
[3] *Oficio* of 3 July 1825 (copy), F.V. vol. 449.
[4] *El Centinela*, tomo 1, no. 5, 31 December 1828, pp. 17–18.
[5] To the Junta, 9 August 1825, *Registro Oficial de la Suprema Junta*, no. 5, n.d., p. 53.
[6] Manuel de Salas, Representación, 27 July 1811, F.V. vol. 812, pieza 4.
[7] *Manifiesto que hace a las naciones*, 1818, *AR*, I, 33.

demands'.[1] The transformations of Chile were part of a world liberal movement, 'a revolution in the human spirit',[2] 'the near-universal world revolution',[3] and the 'great drama whose outcome is destined, perhaps, to change the political face of the whole world'.[4]

Despite such indications of a wider awareness, it cannot be doubted that the Chileans were primarily interested in their own national revolution, and, to a lesser extent, in the Latin American revolution at large. By some, it was held that what had taken place in America was little more than an inevitable and natural process.

Everything has been organized and is directed by a new order, which it is superfluous to oppose. The nature of things...has worked the change...America has separated from Spain even as a ripe fruit falls from a tree. Who can attach her once more to the branches, when the very course of nature has let her fall?[5]

Such a view was comfortingly infallible, and by and large it is true that most of the revolutionaries held that the revolution was, in the deepest sense, a 'natural' outcome to centuries of oppression. Even so, most people preferred to depict the change as the result of a definite and heroic awakening on the part of the Chilean people. The following description of the events of 18 September 1810, written by a liberal of 1830, may be taken as characteristic of this second and more widespread view.

There dawned the Day of Araucania, the great and famous day. On that day we Chileans awoke from the deep slumber in which we had lain, debased, for three centuries. On that day we courageously broke the bonds that tied us to the metropolis: we shook off the ignominious colonial yoke, and, reading in our hearts the sacred rights imprinted there, cleaving sceptres and trampling down crowns, we appeared before the human race invested with the dignity of free men.[6]

---

[1] Convocation of the 1826 Congress, 15 March 1826, *SCL*, XII, 7. (My italics.)
[2] *La Clave*, no. 66, 5 April 1828, pp. 259–60.
[3] *Monitor Araucano*, tomo 2, no. 13, 21 January 1814.
[4] *El Filantropo*, tomo 1, no. 1, 3 September 1834, p. 1.
[5] *Gaceta Ministerial de Chile*, tomo 2, no. 53, 15 July 1820.
[6] *Defensor de los militares denominados Constitucionales*, no. 17, 22 September 1830.

But the revolution, however heroic, was not conceived of purely as a movement of political separation. A new dignity was involved. A new order had to be created: 'We are already on the way to our new destiny,' it could be written in 1820, 'and we cannot turn back, unless the century in which we live turns back as well.'[1]

What was this 'new destiny'? In the first place, obviously, it was the implantation of the political principles which had now emerged, the creation of a representative government answering to the will of the people. But, in addition, a very noticeable strain of utopianism may be observed. Hopes such as Pedro Trujillo's that Freire would bring Chile the reign of 'enlightenment, peace and philosophy',[2] were common enough, but there also existed a strong feeling that Chile was going to be specially favoured by fortune. 'This privileged country', wrote one commentator in 1823, 'is marked out to cut a great figure amongst civilized nations.'[3] Not even the conservatives of 1830, who were reacting fiercely against many of the attitudes of the revolution, could wholly divest themselves of this belief. *El Popular*, one of their newspapers, assured its readers that the Portales government was going to turn Chile into 'one of the most desirable dwelling-places for mankind'.[4]

This emotional utopianism sprang, almost certainly, from the late-eighteenth-century habit of contrasting Chilean reality with Chilean potential. As we have seen, Manuel de Salas and the little group of economist-precursors were particularly addicted to this habit. On the liberation of the island of Chiloé in 1826, a liberal newspaper told the fortunate *chilotes* that they were now on the point of receiving 'wise institutions worthy of a free land which the world delights in calling the PARADISE OF AMERICA. Oh, Chileans!!!'[5] The possibilities of economic improvement, so dear to the heart of the precursors, continued to exercise a fatal attraction. 'So many agents of prosperity!' once exclaimed

[1] 'Estado actual de la revolución', *Censor de la Revolución*, no. 7, 10 July 1820.
[2] T. D. J. Benavente, 21 July 1824, F.V. vol. 823, fo. 20.
[3] *Observador de Chile*, no. 1, 16 June 1823, p. 4.
[4] No. 7, 8 May 1820, p. 2.
[5] *Patriota Chileno*, no. 8, 3 February 1826, p. 101.

Hipólito Belmont; 'What immense resources for our commerce!'[1]

This by no means unjustifiable faith in the national potential spilled over into lyrical visions of what the future might bring. Material prosperity was the essential feature of all such visions, accompanied by the belief that this prosperity would develop under the influence of wise laws. On the occasion of the declaration of independence in 1818, for instance, the government gazette predicted that

> the land which declines from the Andes to the Pacific will become covered with as many settlements as the beautiful network of streams …can water. Just, beneficent and liberal laws—and honourable, laborious and tolerant men—will renew all the virtues of the cradle of Washington here in the extremities of the South.[2]

That this type of vision was present from the earliest moments of the revolution is shown by a highly lyrical patriotic effusion written fairly soon after the 18 September 1810. Its final picture of a happy and prosperous Chile represents so fully the utopian tendency of some of the more sanguine revolutionaries that it deserves to be quoted at length.

> What a glorious prospect is being prepared for our Chile! Joyous Agriculture will stroll at will, attended by the venerable Plough: the bellowing of cattle will adorn the valleys: the bleating of sheep will resound in the hills. Green landscapes, florid pastures, well-worked harvests, and embellished gardens will rise to North and South, East and West. Abundance with her copious horn will seat herself, smiling, and in pleasing complaisance will possess and govern all these mountains. Then Commerce will come forward, embellished with its splendid form. The rivers and seas will be filled with vessels. The coasts will be covered with cities. The cities will be peopled by inhabitants. The arts will adorn them with elegance. Notwithstanding, Simplicity will appear everywhere, with beautiful variety and well-regulated distribution. Around her the decencies and adornments of life will be poured out in rich abundance. With what joy and pleasure will Industry survey her honest workers, flourishing and secure! Peace will

---

[1] *Minero de Coquimbo*, no. 1, 22 March 1828.
[2] *Gazeta de Santiago de Chile*, 21 February 1818.

wander serenely through these tranquil regions, while Liberty, Virtue and Religion will walk harmoniously embraced, protecting, encouraging and hallowing everything. Happy land! May God permit your happiness to be everlasting![1]

It is particularly noteworthy that the unknown author of this vision should have joined liberty, virtue and religion as the guardian angels of the forthcoming utopia. For, as we have seen, liberty was regarded as inseparable from virtue, and, despite a current of intellectual anticlericalism in the 1820s, few could entirely dismiss religion from their scheme of things.

Such utopianism not only implied a distinctly meliorist view of life, but also an admission of the perfectibility of the human race. This theme particularly attracted the liberals: as Pedro Félix Vicuña[2] put it, they believed that society was drawn by 'the irresistible current of the perfectibility of the human race'.[3] Henríquez maintained that 'the social state is capable of being bettered and perfected'.[4] And at the same time, the doctrine of progress put in its appearance to provide the automatic stimulus which compelled men to seek perfection. The revolution was itself explicable in terms of progress: 'Every bad order engenders a disorder; but this disorder is a transition to a better order.'[5] Progress also involved the frank recognition that many earthly arrangements had to be regarded as temporary and provisional. As Henríquez said in the Preparatory Convention in 1822, 'laws should only last for as long as they remain useful. When experience shows them to be injurious, they should (and will) be revoked...There is no power on earth whose orders are, have been, or ought to be eternal.'[6] This doctrine could be employed in reverse by the conservatives of the Portales period. 'We are of the opinion', wrote Belmont, 'that in civil affairs, the impossible epoch when laws bear the seal of infallibility has still not

---

[1] 'Discurso patriotico dedicado à la memoria del dia 18 de septiembre de 1810' [early 1811], A.B.A. vol. 25-2(3), fo. 791.

[2] Pedro Félix Vicuña Aguirre (1805–74); son of Francisco Ramón Vicuña (President 1829); first editor of *El Mercurio de Valparaíso*; staunch liberal and enemy of Portales; father of Benjamín Vicuña Mackenna. [3] Valencia Avaria, *Memorias íntimas*, p. 98.

[4] *Aurora de Chile*, no. 13, 7 May 1812, p. 55.

[5] *Patriota Chileno*, no. 1, 19 December 1825, p. 6.

[6] Session of 17 August 1822, *SCL*, VI, 77.

arrived.'[1] This was used as an argument to support the demand for
a revision of the 1828 Constitution. But two matters were uni-
versally agreed on during the revolution: first, that the aim of all
law was 'to carry mankind towards perfection',[2] and second, that
this necessarily signified a greater emphasis on the future than on
the past: 'to forget the past, and to think on what is yet to come'.[3]

THE EFFICACY OF LAWS AND CONSTITUTIONS

Progress automatically pushed man in the direction of utopia,
but man could himself aid progress. Good laws, and in particular
a good constitution, were thought to be essential to the task.
'Progress by decree' had more than a few advocates in the period,
and the reverence displayed towards the text of a constitution was
truly remarkable. Chileans regarded their various constitutions as
sacred documents which were, in some mysterious way, efficient
in themselves. 'A good constitution', wrote the author of the
utopian vision quoted earlier, 'is the greatest blessing a society
can enjoy.'[4] This view was shared by almost everybody. O'Higgins
was able to exhort the members of his Preparatory Convention,
telling them that the constitution they produced would be 'the
alliance between Government and People...which assures internal calm, produces abundance, opens up resources and guarantees justice'.[5] A constitution was the necessary basis for concord
and unity in the state. Anticipating the 1828 Constitution, one
liberal newspaper became lyrical and enthusiastic about its effects.
Chile was at last to have

the charter of her liberties and *fueros*, her rights and duties; she will
enjoy the object of her desires; she will rest at the end of her career;
her opinion will be one, for the law which forms her will be one; she
will not be divided into divergent parties; and, united around her
constitution, she will work for her wealth and prosperity.[6]

[1] *Bandera Tricolor*, no. 9, 7 April 1831, p. 33.
[2] *La Clave*, no. 44, 12 February 1828, p. 173.
[3] *Despertador Araucano*, no 1, 3 May 1823, p. 2.
[4] 'Discurso patriotico...', A.B.A. vol. 25-2(3), fo. 789.
[5] *Memorial*, 23 July 1822, SCL, VI, 27.
[6] *Patriota Chileno*, tomo 3, no. 17, 13 January 1827, p. 69.

The view that laws in themselves were the chief agent for building a better society was expressed most radically by José Miguel Infante and the federalists. In an article written soon after the conservative assumption of power in 1830, Infante drew his readers' attention to the fact that the new regime, like all those which had preceded it, promised respect for the laws and philanthropic principles. Infante asked:

And should this at any time deceive the people? No! They should ask: Have we, or have we not, good laws? If we have, then nobody can frustrate the good they must do us. If we have not, then we shall always be the plaything of the errors, caprices and prostitution of Governments.[1]

For Infante, naturally enough, good laws were federal laws, 'laws which would have raised Chile to be the first Republic in America',[2] as he believed to the end of his life. Infante's followers in Valdivia followed their master by asserting that the federal system was efficacious of itself, and that 'its possession will make us happy, its absence unhappy'.[3]

Each constitution produced in the revolutionary period was greeted with renewed expressions of confidence in its staying power and efficiency.

Immortal glory to the Representatives of the People, who have, in the political Constitution of the State, given us a fatherland, the enjoyment of our rights, and the future happiness of the generations still to come![4]

Such was the welcome accorded Egaña's famous document of 1823. The 1828 Constitution received similar applause. It 'contains within itself', said President Pinto, 'the germ of a limitless perfection'.[5] The Vice-Rector of the Instituto Nacional described the *carta* as 'the rainbow which will pour out abundance in all the provinces of the state, and which will work the happiness of a thousand generations'.[6]

The view that laws alone were what was needed to produce the good society may nowadays be thought naïve, yet it was a

[1] *Valdiviano Federal*, no. 32, 19 January 1830, p. 4.
[2] *Ibid.* no. 45, 3 September 1831, p. 2.
[3] 'El Valdiviano Federal' (Valdivia MS version), no. 5, 30 July 1827, Guarda Geywitz, p. 28.
[4] *Redactor Extraordinario del Soberano Congreso*, no. 1, 10 January 1824, pp. 6–7.
[5] 'El Vice-presidente a la Nación', 9 August 1828, *AR*, I, 140.
[6] Blas Reyes, Speech at the *fiesta cívica* of 12 February 1829, *SCL*, XVI, 593.

natural product of the eighteenth-century rationalism which formed so much of the basis of the revolutionary outlook. It rested, perhaps, on the belief that 'everything which happens in the intellectual world happens soon afterwards in the world of reality'.[1] What was necessary, the creole intelligentsia reasoned, was a correct and rational organization of the state; everything else would follow automatically. 'A good constitution', it was thought, 'is nothing more than reason applied to the great interests of society.'[2] As I mentioned in Chapter 4, it was held to be essential that a constitution should observe certain basic rules: practicality, harmony with the customs of the land, and so on. Yet such recommendations did not alter, or even temper, the excessive reverence shown towards the finished product. One or two dissenting voices, it is true, occasionally warned that there was more to governing a state than composing an elegant charter. Irisarri, for instance, complained that 'it is easier to write a constitution than to constitute a state'.[3] Juan Egaña (perhaps somewhat hypocritically in view of his own efforts in the field) came round to the view that constitution-mongering was 'the absurd mania of American countries'.[4] The government newspaper *El Araucano* attacked the idea that a constitution was 'all that was needed to launch us with gigantic strides on the road to prosperity',[5] but curiously enough *El Araucano* was by no means free from the delusion itself, though it suffered it in reverse. In 1830 and 1831 it printed several editorials containing the implicit assumption that the 1828 Constitution—a 'bad' constitution—was responsible for all the evils afflicting the country.[6] On the whole, dissenting voices were rare, and the overwhelming majority of Chileans would have agreed with Freire, in 1826, when he expressed this faith to the Congress: 'A Constitution! This is the universal cry of the Chilean people, the summit of their desires, the foundation on which all my hopes now rest.'[7]

[1] *Amigo de la Verdad*, no. 3, 13 May 1823, p. 25.
[2] *El Constituyente*, no. 1, 3 June 1828, p. 2.
[3] *El Constitucional*, no. 9, 14 August 1833, p. 34.
[4] To Villaurrutia, 17 January 1833, Egaña, 'Cartas, 1832-3', p. 104.
[5] No. 89, 26 May 1832.
[6] No. 12, 4 December 1830; no. 39, 11 June 1831; no. 42, 2 July 1831; no. 66, 17 December 1831.　　[7] 'Mensaje...al Congreso Constituyente', 4 July 1826, *SCL*, xii, 48.

Revolutionary Attitudes

THE EXCUSES FOR FAILURE

The Chilean revolutionaries saw themselves as the leaders of their country as it advanced, aided by progress and good laws, into a new and probably far more agreeable phase of history. It was distressing, therefore, to find that success did not come immediately or with the utopian flourishes they had expected. As time passed, a number of explanations for the difficulties of the revolution became common. In the first place, it was appreciated that the changes initiated by the revolution were of a peculiarly critical nature. The Chileans—as I will show presently—viewed their past with an extraordinary measure of violent hatred, and they looked to their future with excessive optimism. In one sense both their past and their future became ideals, and the transition from one ideal state to the next was, for them, naturally dangerous in the extreme. Chile was experiencing the 'perilous leap from extreme oppression to a freedom of whose limits she is unaware', as Freire put it.[1] It was a theme he echoed in a proclamation of May 1825: 'Everything, everything, is the result of our political infancy. The violent transition from darkness to noonday light—from rigid slavery to absolute liberty—is very critical.'[2] These words express as well as any other the Chileans' concept of their own revolution. The blame for any difficulties could be squarely placed on the authors of the 'rigid slavery'. If Chile were to achieve any progress at all, it was only because she was now 'free from the impediments placed on her by the very bad Spanish administration'.[3] This became a favourite theme. Disorders could be conveniently ascribed to 'common causes, above all the vices of the colonial system',[4] to 'the fatal influence of the old regime which, unfortunately, still survives',[5] and to the persistence of old-fashioned and illiberal superstitions. Chileans, wrote José

---

[1] 'Breve exposición de mi conducta', n.d., F.V. vol. 789, pieza 32.

[2] *El Director Supremo a los Pueblos de la República*, 27 May 1825, SCL, XI, 263.

[3] Echeverría to Higginson, 6 October 1819, Eugenio Pereira Salas, *Las tentativas para la colocación de un empréstito chileno en los Estados Unidos, 1818–1819* (1935), p. 17.

[4] *Registro de Documentos del Gobierno*, no 24, 27 July 1826.

[5] *La Clave*, no. 28, 15 November 1827, p. 110.

Ignacio Izquierdo, were 'very much tied to the darkness'.[1] Those who possessed the additional outlook of anticlericalism lamented the continued influence of the Church. The arrival of the Papal Nuncio in 1824—an occasion of considerable triumph for the Church—provoked Francisco Antonio Pinto to describe the citizens of Santiago as 'idle and foolish', and to comment: 'Before this I had believed—and this confirms it—that Chile was the part of America nearest the rearguard of civilization, but I did not want to believe that we were so stupid, so dishonourable.'[2]

Such views, while answering to the need for an external scapegoat, were hardly very sophisticated. Other Chileans, however, were prepared to look for alternative explanations of the revolution's troubles. It was sometimes appreciated that a revolution could hardly take place like a flash of lightning. 'Politically, as well as physically, the early years are weak.'[3] Martín Orjera, that vocal standardbearer of the more radical variety of liberalism in the 1820s, maintained in 1827 that 'it is not possible to carry out the change from colony to independent nation in the short period of three lustres, not even if the greatest men in the world were doing it'.[4] He later added that, even so, Chile had done more in fifteen years than most European monarchies in as many centuries.[5] But above all, it was held, the revolution needed time, and the people lacked instruction in basic principles. As Freire put it, 'it is necessary to give the people time, so that they can know and understand...their new political existence'.[6] Any political change of importance was bound to entail difficulties and reverses. 'The word *Independence*...' wrote O'Higgins, 'accomplished extraordinary things, but it could not perform miracles.'[7]

Few men, it is fair to say, attempted to work out theories of revolutionary change which fitted the situation. Joaquín Campino went some way towards this, in a highly interesting letter to

[1] To J. M. Benavente, 28 January 1824, F.V. vol. 822, fo. 2.
[2] To D. J. Benavente, 27 March 1824, F.V. vol. 822, fo. 75.
[3] 'Un Chileno', *Contestación al Independiente*, 4 June 1821, *CAPC*, IX, 198.
[4] *Rol de Policia*, no. 1, 28 April 1827, p. 1.
[5] *Ibid.* no. 2, 7 May 1827, p. 5.
[6] To the Junta, 26 July 1825, *Registro Oficial de la Suprema Junta Interior Gubernativa*, no 4, n.d., p. 25.
[7] To an unidentified correspondent, 3 May 1838 [in English], F.V. vol. 645, fo. 18.

Manuel de Salas. At the start of the revolution, believed Campino, very few people in Chile had any real notion of what representative government and the rights of man actually involved. The troubles of the revolution, in fact, were due to the inadequate dissemination of political ideas.

Now I conceive our population to be like those rocks in layers which geologists call *strata*, and the new ideas to be a liquid which penetrates the strata and puts them into ferment. The first layer, which was saturated by the reading of foreign books, began the revolution: but some of them have died, others have become tired and have withdrawn, others have changed their mind, and the spirit has permeated new layers and has put them in ferment in their turn. These explosions, and the difficulty of establishing anything solid, will last until the whole rock is completely saturated.[1]

It is hardly surprising that the prolonged difficulties of the revolution eventually touched off a reaction. Politically, this reaction was embodied in the Portales government. Emotionally, it expressed itself in disillusion and, in some cases, despair. On hearing the news of the changes of 1829–30, José Joaquín Pérez wrote (from the United States) of his compatriots that

now they will be regarded like the other inhabitants of what were formerly the Spanish colonies, that is to say, as contemptible groups of ignorant men, in possession of as many crimes and vices as have dishonoured the human race.[2]

Antonio José de Irisarri, for his part, gave way to a general scepticism. 'I see' he wrote in 1833, 'that the systems established in what was formerly Spanish America have not brought the happiness that was expected; and I have no confidence that these systems are the best for us.'[3] It was easy enough, certainly, to look round and conclude that the civic virtue needed for a successful republican government was entirely lacking in Spanish America. It was easy enough to point out that some patriot governments

[1] To Salas, New York, 28 May 1830, Salas, *Escri os*, III, 260.
[2] To Santiago Pérez, Baltimore, 18 March 1830, F.V. vol. 253, pieza 10. José Joaquín Pérez Mascayano (1800–89) later became President of the Republic, 1861–71.
[3] *El Constitucional*, no. 9, 14 August 1833, p. 34 Irisarri had monarchist sympathies for several years.

had committed acts of 'arbitrariness more terrible than that of the old regime, [and] violations which would not have gone unpunished in those days'.[1] Pinto, in those last tragic months of 1829, believed that there was a 'secret force' dragging Chile towards 'the same calamities as are devouring the other countries'.[2] Yet even at that stage he preserved a hope that Chile would be spared. Hope was indeed a fundamental emotion of the Chilean revolution, and one of the most attractive characteristics of its mystique. In 1823 the newspaper *El Liberal* defined the state of the revolution as: 'In reality, nothing; in hope, a good deal.'[3] It was a simple and yet profound comment.

THE ANTI-SPANISH OUTCRY

I must now turn to a particularly important aspect of the revolutionary mystique: its violently anti-Spanish feeling. Chileans, like other Spanish Americans, were bound to have a definite and highly coloured view of the imperial monarchy against which they had fought. In every way it now became a fixed dogma that any system of government which implied dependence on an overseas metropolis was unnatural. As Henríquez proclaimed, early in 1811, nature itself had given Latin America the resources with which to lead a separate life. Was it not absurd, he asked, 'to go in search of an arbitrary government...on the far side of the seas?' Not only was it absurd; it was 'contrary to fate and the order inspired by nature'.[4] 'There is always a natural clash of interests between a Metropolis and its colonies,' *El Monitor Araucano* told its readers in 1813.[5] The 'incompatibility of a vast Empire and the liberty of the peoples'[6] was noted in many different ways throughout the revolution. More generous intellects noticed sometimes that the imperial relationship was disadvantageous not only to the colonies but also to the imperial

---

[1] *Correo Nacional*, no. 1, 26 September 1833, p. 1.
[2] To Benavente, 15 October 1829, F.V. vol. 822, fo. 91.
[3] No. 1, 28 July 1823, p. 3.
[4] 'Proclama de Quirino Lemachez', Silva Castro, *Escritos políticos*, p. 47.
[5] Tomo 1, no. 64, 4 September 1813.
[6] *Observador Chileno*, no. 1, 20 August 1822 (*CAPC*, x, 116, note D).

power itself. Juan Egaña, affirming that political domination from another continent was 'against the moral and physical order of things', invited the Spaniards to reflect on their own history.

Ministers of Ferdinand! Recall the supreme position which Spain occupied during the reigns of the Catholic Monarchs, of Charles I and Philip II—and the progressive decline which her industry, power and commerce have suffered ever since she gained colonies and implanted an oppressive monopoly and a dark and inquisitorial policy.[1]

It was only one step from such an opinion to the view that the disintegration of the Spanish Empire was a Divine chastisement for the sins of the Spanish monarchy; José Ignacio Cienfuegos[2] believed this.[3]

But, in general, Chileans did not concern themselves with dispassionate critiques of colonial systems. Their attitude towards the Spanish Empire was harsh, total, and dogmatic, as was the Spaniards' attitude towards the colonies. The systematic disparagement and denunciation of the imperial past began at a point before the Conquest. Irisarri condemned Pope Alexander VI's division of the world between Spain and Portugal as unchristian. St Peter, he wrote, would have been scandalized by it.[4] The claim of the Spanish crown to have papal sanction for the conquest of America was strenuously denied. 'The only certain power the Pope has over the world is the spiritual power,' wrote a patriot in 1817.[5] An unknown *cabildante* from Vallenar put the matter more crudely.

From where did Alexander acquire the right to donate lands which were due to God and ourselves alone? From where? From adulation and Monopoly—for I consider the donating Pope to have been quite as monopolistic as the grateful King.[6]

---

[1] 'Apuntes para el manifiesto que debe hacerse en la Declaración de la Independencia de Chile' [1817–18], *Escritos inéditos*, pp. 92–3.

[2] José Ignacio Cienfuegos Astorga (1762–1845). Senator 1814, 1818–22 and 1831–4; Chilean agent in Rome 1822–4; Bishop of Concepción 1832–7; friend of O'Higgins.

[3] Cienfuegos to O'Higgins, 18 January 1822, Vicuña Mackenna, *Vida de O'Higgins*, p. 373.

[4] *Semanario Republicano*, no. 3, 21 August 1813.

[5] *Clamor de la Justicia e Idioma de la Verdad* [no. 1], 1817.

[6] 'Viva la Patria Señores' [patriotic speech, Vallenar, 1817], A.M.I. vol. 37, fo. 217.

The Conquest itself was, of course, a subject fully worthy of brilliantly vituperative treatment. 'Every step which Europe took in the Conquest of America was criminal,' affirmed a righteously indignant patriot in 1813.[1] The unknown citizen of Vallenar whose views on the papal division of the world have already been quoted, dwelt fondly on the savage details of the domination of America.

Let us for a moment speak of the way they enslaved [America]. It was horrible! fearful! With fire and sword, killing and cutting the throats of their natural rulers and all the other Indians (those dear brethren of ours) they found, and who had fallen into their wicked and bloody hands! [They killed them] even though they had surrendered and had grovelled at their foul feet! And even after this awful catastrophe [the Spaniards] took to looting and pillaging their Treasures and Possessions, eventually resorting to the final and wretched excess of delivering them into slavery.[2]

Such pictures of the Conquest could be used, as Henríquez found, as a valuable weapon in the war of ideas. Thus, in an editorial on the extermination of Indians in the sixteenth century, he compared such proceedings with more recent atrocities by the contemporary 'enemies of America'.[3] But quite apart from this, the Conquest occupied a particularly important place in the doctrine of the revolution, for it marked the exact moment when the pristine 'freedom' of America had been overcome, the moment when the natural rights of native Americans had first been trampled down. This view was incorporated into the opening phrases of the Proclamation of Independence.[4] The Spanish Empire was now regarded as little more than 'the monument raised over the ruins of the ancient liberty of America',[5] and this attitude was linked to the idealization of the Indians who had defended that liberty.

Needless to say, special comminations were reserved for the conquerors themselves. Nicolás Pradel dwelt at length on the

---

[1] *Ilustración Araucana*, no. 1, 6 September 1813.
[2] 'Viva la Patria Señores', A.M.I. vol. 38, fo. 218.
[3] *Aurora de Chile*, tomo 2, no. 7, 25 February 1813.   [4] *AR*, I, 13.
[5] 'Sobre la necesidad Justicia y conveniencia...' [early 1811], A.B.A. vol. 25-2(3), fo. 760.

'horrifying scenes of the Almagros, Valdivias and other similar wild beasts who pitilessly devoured the innocent and peaceful Chilean people'.[1] Those who tried to justify the Conquest on doctrinal grounds deserved an even worse treatment. It was argued, for instance, that Juan Ginés de Sepúlveda should be placed alongside Cortés and Pizarro in the catalogue of Spanish monsters, 'and perhaps a little higher' than they, since he publicly approved of their cruelties: 'his *Democrates alter* is enough to make him execrable in the eyes of the friend of humanity and every American'.[2]

Not only was the Conquest a prolonged atrocity in Chilean eyes, but the Empire to which it had given birth was now regarded as the most monstrous and scandalous of all human institutions. It would be tedious in the extreme to repeat the immense number of thunderous denunciations of the colonial era which now poured, in an endless flood, from the pens and printing presses of the newly liberated republic. A few examples, however, will serve to illustrate the depth of Chilean bitterness. Vera y Pintado poetically castigated the 'three centuries of shackles' during which the American had been 'a slave without the rights of man'. Now at last, he continued, Chile was emerging from the shadow of 'that stupendous yoke with which the colonial plan of despotism lowered the continent towards the abyss'.[3] Henríquez, in the prospectus to his *Aurora*, recalled the 'sad and insufferable silence of three centuries...Centuries of infamy and lamentation!'[4] O'Higgins' old friend Casimiro Albano[5] wrote of 'the dark colonial era, when Spanish ignorance and superstition directed the destinies of America'.[6] Such phrases as 'the degradation inseparable from three centuries of slavery'[7] became part and

---

[1] *El Celador*, no. 2, 27 September 1832, p. 2. Innocent the Araucanians may have been, but scarcely peaceful.

[2] 'Bibliografía', *El Telégrafo*, no. 18, 9 July, 1819.

[3] 'Un ciudadano de Chile a la solemne apertura del Congreso' [1811], F.V. vol. 244, pieza 71.

[4] *Prospecto*, p. 1.

[5] Casimiro Albano Pereyra de la Cruz (1783–1849); childhood friend of O'Higgins; his first proper biographer; in exile in Mendoza 1814–17; member of the 1811, 1822, 1824 and 1828 Congresses.

[6] *Colección de Noticias Documentadas*, no. 9, 3 November 1821, p. 3.

[7] *Correo de Arauco*, no. 46, 2 April 1825, p. 205.

parcel of the standard journalistic patois of the time. Only in 1810, it was now believed, had the Chileans realized the true nature of their situation: 'Yes, every Chilean then came to know that slavery was a true death, that to keep silent before despots was a reproach to his exalted character, a gift to oppression, a deafness to the eternal cries of our Mother Nature.'[1]

It will be seen from this that the creole intelligentsia had come to accept an extreme and critical view of the old colonial order; the revolutionaries would have agreed with Francisco de Miranda's description of 'that dark, jealous, and excluding government, which watched over its colonies as an Asiatic tyrant does over his seraglio'.[2] O'Higgins, for instance, could speak of 'the corruption and ignorance engendered during three centuries by the misrule of a corrupt & ignorant Government',[3] even though the outstanding career of his own father hardly supported such an assertion. A long list of grievances was presented on various suitable occasions. In the manifesto which justified Independence, Spain was accused of having monopolized trade, of excluding foreigners, of causing vines and olive-trees to be uprooted, and so on.[4] Juan Egaña, on Juan Fernández, repeated such accusations and expatiated on the small number of viceroys and bishops who had been creoles, on the royal efforts to prevent the spread of enlightenment, and on the eight million Indians supposedly exterminated in the mines of Potosí.[5] Charges made against Spain were sometimes adorned with fanciful touches. Protesting against the economic exploitation of America, Irisarri could write that the Americans 'possessed those metals which, passing to Europe, bore opulence to European families, and which returned as irons and chains to fortify despotism'.[6] Sometimes, too, the shock of the contrast between Chilean conditions and those prevailing in Europe could be explained away by recourse to the darkness of the colonial background. 'Coming to Europe,' wrote

---

[1] *Correo Mercantil-Político-Literario*, no. 62, 16 September 1826.
[2] 'Molina's Account of Chile', *Edinburgh Review*, XIV (1809), p. 335.
[3] To an unidentified correspondent, 3 May 1838 [in English], F.V. vol. 645, fo. 18.
[4] O'Higgins, *Manifiesto que hace a las naciones*, 1818, pp. 19–20.
[5] *El chileno consolado*, II, 14–20.
[6] *Semanario Republicano*, no. 1, 7 August 1813.

Mariano Egaña[1] from Paris, 'one realizes the extent of the evil which weighed down on us under Spanish domination. Slaves to the most brutalized of peoples, we were ignorant of the very existence of the good books that were being published in Europe.'[2]

Mariano Egaña's lament was significant. For if there was one aspect of Spanish colonial policy which particularly appalled the creoles, it was the educational backwardness of the overseas Empire—a backwardness ascribed by the revolutionary generation to a deliberate and calculated policy of repression. Irisarri maintained that the twin bases of Spanish power in the New World had been fear and *ignorance*.[3] Conservatives of 1823 similarly affirmed that 'the Spaniards had a great interest in keeping this vast hemisphere in ignorance, for they knew that this was the only way they could retain it'.[4] The Spaniards, it was widely agreed, had kept America ignorant and its inhabitants backward 'in order to contain them more easily in servitude'.[5] Defects there certainly *had* been in the colonial educational system, as was noted slightly more dispassionately by Henríquez:

> The old institutions were very much against the diffusion of enlightenment...The scholastic method, the plans of study in the schools, the obstacles to the popularization of useful books—all these have been a powerful influence on the backwardness of learning.[6]

The widespread illiteracy of the time was another direct result of the previous system of education; the first concern of any truly liberal government was to eradicate it.[7] But despite the fact that education was limited in scope and backward in its methods, some of the harshness of the Chileans' attitude was due to their changed concept of what education involved and what it ought to do. As we have seen, education was now conceived as a major task for

---

[1] Mariano Egaña Fabres (1788–1846); Secretary to the Junta 1813; exiled to Juan Fernández 1814–17; Minister of the Interior 1823–4; Chilean representative in Europe 1824–8; member of the Constituent Convention 1831–3; one of the chief authors of the Constitution of 1833; a doctrinaire conservative.

[2] To Juan Egaña, 16 February 1828, *Cartas de Mariano Egaña*, p. 302.

[3] *Semanario Republicano*, no. 1, 7 August 1813.

[4] *Amigo de la Verdad*, no. 3, 13 May 1823, p. 28.

[5] *Mercurio de Valparaíso*, tomo 1, no. 27, 12 December 1827, p. 105.

[6] *Aurora de Chile*, tomo 1, no. 13, 7 May 1812, p. 55.

[7] *El Chileno*, no. 1, 22 July 1818.

any government based on the new principles. Education, in short, was a duty. The previous regime, doubtless guilty of some of the charges made against it in this respect, could hardly be blamed for failing to live up to ideals which were alien to its educational philosophy. Bernardo Monteagudo noted: 'The revolution has enlarged our intellectual needs.'[1]

Allied to this dark view of the colonial period there went a general feeling of bitterness towards everything Spanish. Spain, now regarded as 'a cruel and senseless mother who, fearing our growth, did not wish to remove the leading-strings of childhood',[2] became an automatic target for the kind of violent and satirical abuse particularly loved by certain Chilean writers of the period. This anti-Spanish feeling seems to have been widespread amongst the aristocracy and the intelligentsia, but less diffused amongst lower levels of society. Captain Basil Hall, who visited Chile during the O'Higgins regime, left an interesting impression of this. Noting that amongst the 'peasantry' the question of Spain and the Spaniards was treated with calmness, he went on:

We remarked that the upper classes...were filled with animation whenever the subject was mentioned, and never allowed themselves to think of their ancient rulers without expressing the bitterest animosity.[3]

Spain was now the country 'whose pre-eminence in the art of oppression cannot be disputed'.[4] Ferdinand VII was represented as the supreme symbol of tyranny, as (to use the phrase of the decree which abolished his detested head from Chilean coinage) 'usurpation personified'.[5] No longer the 'adorable' sovereign of 1810, Ferdinand was now transformed into 'that monster of perfidy who has never opened his mouth except to vomit forth a crime, who has never taken up a pen except to dip it in blood'.[6] When in 1819 Chileans heard of a particularly vicious caricature of Ferdinand which had appeared in Washington, one patriot

---

[1] *Censor de la Revolución*, no. 7, 10 July 1820.
[2] 'Lo que fuimos', *El Liberal*, no. 1, 28 July 1823.   [3] Hall, I, 20.
[4] *Semanario de Policia*, 5 November 1817.
[5] *Bando* of 9 June 1817, *Viva la Patria, Gaceta del Supremo Gobierno*, 11 June 1817.
[6] *Sol de Chile*, 10 July 1818, p. 5.

newspaper suggested maliciously that copies should be hung over patriotic beds, candles lit beneath, and as much reverence accorded it as would have been accorded genuine portraits of the King during the colonial era.[1]

No element in Spanish political life roused Chilean sympathies, not even Spanish liberalism. Henríquez, it is true, had commented favourably on the activity of the Spanish liberals in 1814,[2] but Juan Egaña fiercely condemned them for doing things in Spain for which they persecuted and murdered Spanish Americans.[3] Others recalled that it had been the liberals who had been the first to take military action against the Americans.

> Who was it who first decreed war by fire and sword?...All that machination of hatred, death and annihilation against the American was the work of those *liberals*, those *constitutionalists*, those *Cortes*, that *Regency*...; *liberality* was something exclusively for Spain. For America, an iron sceptre...[4]

All varieties of Spaniard were to be distrusted, then; and, when in 1820 a new wave of liberalism swept the Spanish Peninsula, Monteagudo's newspaper sourly (and realistically) commented that it was not to be hoped that these latest liberals would be liberal towards America.[5]

If anti-Spanishness was particularly strong in the first ten years of the revolution, the suspicion it created lasted right through the period and beyond. Thus, in 1825, a liberal newspaper objected to the term 'Spanish-American' as unsuitable for Chile. The Chileans' noblest concern, it added, should be to strip themselves of all remaining traces of 'Spanish servitude, and of what is even more degrading, Hispanicism'.[6] Spain, it was believed, still had the recovery of her American dominions as a basic aim: 'Spain has her invisible armies in America, which never sleep and which are always on the alert.'[7] One of the undercurrents in the political

---

[1] 'Caricatura singular', *El Telégrafo*, no. 26, 13 August 1819.
[2] Silva Castro, *Escritos políticos*, p. 160.   [3] *El chileno consolado*, II, 273–5.
[4] *Viva la Patria, Gaceta del Supremo Gobierno*, 7 May 1817.
[5] 'Revolución de España', *Censor de la Revolución*, no. 3, 10 May 1820.
[6] *Década Araucana*, no. 3, 10 August 1825, p. 41.
[7] *Mercurio de Valparaíso*, tomo 3, no. 134, 12 December 1829, p. 269.

warfare of 1822–33 was the rivalry between those who had taken an active part in the revolution and those who had either remained indifferent (like Diego Portales) or who had acted on the royalist side. In September 1824, *El Avisador Chileno* took the step of reprinting the well-known *Acta* of the Santiago Cabildo of 9 February 1817, which had expressed fervent pro-Spanish sentiments on the eve of liberation.[1] This provoked an angry reply from Domingo Eyzaguirre[2] who claimed (not unreasonably) that the *cabildantes* had been forced to subscribe to the *Acta* by the circumstances.[3] It was a small incident, without repercussions, but nevertheless significant. For it was a plain fact that a large section of the creole aristocracy had been able to reconcile itself, at least superficially, with the Spanish crown and its Governor during the reconquest. The suspected existence of a Spanish or pro-Spanish faction was, therefore, a natural theme for the revolutionaries of the 1820s. One liberal newspaper, in 1827, regarded the supporters of the *ancien régime* as one of the three important political groupings in the republic.[4] Another liberal paper, engaged in a similar classification the following year, denounced the existence of a party of 'Spaniards and Hispanicized men, who occupy important positions in the Republic'.[5] Here, then, was the background to the later charges made against Diego Portales, that he had allowed Spanish and pro-Spanish elements to gain too great an influence in Chilean affairs. These charges were concisely expressed by the liberal polemicist Pedro Félix Vicuña, when he claimed that Portales had raised to power a party that had been opposed to independence,[6] or, as he wrote later in his memoirs, 'those we called "goths", who had served Ferdinand VII's cause with fanaticism'.[7] The proposals of the conservative government in the early 1830s to reopen Chilean ports to Spanish shipping,

---

[1] No. 9, 16 September 1824.

[2] Domingo Eyzaguirre Arechavala (1775–1854); brother of Agustín Eyzaguirre; anti-federal member of the 1826 Congress.

[3] *Clamor de la Verdad y del Orden*, p. 2. *El Avisador Chileno* was a constant witch-hunter for suspected royalist elements.

[4] *Patriota Chileno*, tomo 3, no. 15, 5 January 1827, pp. 61–2.

[5] *El Sepulturero*, no. 8, 30 October 1828, p. 58.

[6] *Paz Perpetua á los Chilenos* [no. 6], 28 July 1840.

[7] Valencia Avaria, *Memorias íntimas*, p. 92.

and to send a legation to Spain, aroused considerable (if muted) hostility.[1] In fact, there was probably some substance in the various accusations made against Portales.[2]

THE MIRROR OF THE ANGLO-SAXON WORLD

Anti-Spanishness was paralleled by a curiously strong admiration for Great Britain and the United States. 'What are regarded as the classic lands of liberty?' asked José Miguel Infante towards the end of his life. His answer was, 'England and the United States of the North.'[3] Perhaps this particular feature of the revolutionary mystique is not all that surprising. The importance of the 'classical' English Constitution in the mythology of the Enlightenment made it certain that the Chileans would hold England in high esteem, while the shining anticolonial example of the United States would equally predispose them to look on the Northern republic with favour. In addition, the Chileans were bound to become increasingly aware of Great Britain, whose commercial initiative was converting Valparaíso from a miserable seaside village into a flourishing port where, according to the future Pope Pius IX (who passed through in 1824) one fifth of all the houses belonged to the English colony.[4] The Chilean desire to gain British recognition, as well as the recollection of English services to the patriot cause, was a further factor at work in this. Though Chile failed to secure diplomatic recognition in the 1820s,[5] it remained true that 'the English...by their eminent services to the sacred struggle for our independence, have gained an unanswerable right to the eternal gratitude and esteem of all Americans'.[6]

[1] Mainly in *El Philopólita*, *El Sepulturero* and *El Valdiviano Federal*.

[2] See Sutcliffe, pp. 445–6, for the replacement of Rengifo by Tocornal. Sutcliffe's pamphlet *Foreign Loans, or...information to all connected with the Republic of Chile...from 1822 to 1839* (London, 1840) expounds this viewpoint more fully.

[3] *Valdiviano Federal*, no. 157, 7 May 1840, p. 4.

[4] J. M. Mastai Ferretti, *Diario de viaje a Chile* (1961), p. 261. For the considerable expansion of British trade, see the articles by Domingo Amunátegui Solar and C. W. Centner in *RCHG*, no. 103 (1943); also D. B. Goebel, 'British–American Rivalry in the Chilean Trade, 1817–20', *Journal of Economic History*, II (New York, 1942), p. 190.

[5] See C. W. Centner, 'The Chilean Failure to Obtain British Recognition, 1823–8', *Revista de Historia de América*, no. 15 (Mexico DF, 1942), p. 285.

[6] *El Indicador*, no. 5, 2 March 1827, p. 25.

The Revolutionary Ideology

But whatever the reasons, admiration for Britain as a nation was very frequently expressed. At a banquet in 1827, for instance, Antonio Vergara raised his glass to the hope that 'the existence and prosperity of Great Britain may be as eternal as the Universe'.[1] A liberal newspaper of the same period paid a similarly fulsome compliment: 'England...is the only monarchy in which men have dignity. That country is like the tabernacle where the law of man in society is deposited.'[2] Leaders of English political life were sometimes accorded glowing descriptions. Canning, it was said on one occasion, had proved his liberalism in the way an ancient philosopher might have proved the laws of motion,[3] while Lord Lansdowne was hailed as a 'tireless enemy of all abuses and usurpations'.[4] Regard for Great Britain may be seen with particular clarity in the career of the supreme hero of the revolution, Bernardo O'Higgins. One English traveller found him to be 'particularly attached to everything English'.[5] 'By keeping good relations with ... England', wrote O'Higgins himself, 'we shall establish fundamental principles to our glories.'[6] In exile in Peru, he prepared a grandiose scheme for a maritime alliance between Chile and Britain, believing that this could guarantee both nations a position of absolute supremacy at sea.[7]

The creole intelligentsia in Chile supposed the English Constitution to be supremely efficient: 'To what does England owe that spirit of liberty she breathes, and which is propagated from each Lord down to the humblest seaman? To the excellence of her Constitution.'[8] What particular elements in the constitution appealed to the Chileans? First, there was its supposed balance. Henríquez, for instance, defined England, in terms reminiscent of

---

[1] *Mercurio de Valparaíso*, tomo I, no. 4, 22 September 1827, p. 15.
[2] *Patriota Chileno*, no. 3, 31 December 1825, p. 26.
[3] *Mercurio Chileno*, no. IV, 1 July 1828, pp. 185–6.
[4] *Ibid.* p. 187.   [5] Proctor, p. 108.
[6] To Cochrane, 12 November 1821, Dundonald, I, 292–3.
[7] O'Higgins to Coghlan, Lima, 20 August 1831, with the scheme attached, F.O. 16/16, p. 147. Spanish translations of this project have been printed in Carlos Silva Vildósola, 'Papeles de O'Higgins, un proyecto de Alianza Chileno-Británica', *Revista Chilena*, tomo XVII, no. 68 (1923), p. 209, and in Claudio Véliz, *Historia de la marina mercante de Chile* (1961), p. 364.
[8] *El Autor del Grito*, p. 6.

the eighteenth century, as the perfect example of a mixed government.

The British government is a mean between monarchy, which leads to arbitrariness, democracy, which ends in anarchy, and aristocracy, which is the most immoral of governments and the least compatible with the public welfare. It is, then, a mixed government in which these three systems temper, restrain, and observe one another. Their action and reaction establishes an equilibrium from which freedom is born.[1]

In addition, it was felt, the English system provided for popular pressure and agitation 'without tumults, disorders or insur-rections'.[2] The electoral system was partly responsible for this. 'In England...the use of electoral rights ... has reached the highest degree of perfection.'[3]

The English possessed, in the Chilean view, the one necessary ingredient to make a 'democratic' regime workable: virtue. Violent political upsets were unknown in Britain because of civic virtue; candidates in elections, of whatever party, were 'always disposed to uphold the fundamental laws'.[4] Other specific institutions, such as the jury system, were widely admired.[5] It was believed that in England 'everything combines to favour the man who seeks justice'.[6] Freedom of the press was yet another sign of the perfection of the English mode of life. 'The freedom which every writer in England enjoys of expressing his thoughts', claimed one newspaper, 'is indescribable.'[7] Indeed, Britain owed much of her success to this one freedom; she was 'an incontestable monument to the progress which the cause of principle has made by that means'.[8] According to the commission which drafted the Chilean press laws of 1828, England had gained the control of

[1] *Aurora de Chile*, tomo I, no. 16, 28 May 1812, p. 66.
[2] *El Cosmopólita*, no. 1, 18 July 1822, p. 3.
[3] *Mercurio Chileno*, no. XIII, 1 April 1829, p. 621. But the author of this article, de-scribing electoral practices in England, was guilty of naïvety. Certainly English party committees provided refreshment and transport for the 'poorer electors', but this behaviour was scarcely as disinterested as he implied.
[4] *La Clave*, no. 40, 31 January 1828, p. 157.
[5] *Rol de Policia*, passim.   [6] *Mercurio Chileno*, no. X, 1 January 1829, p. 445.
[7] *El Sepulturero*, no. 19, 25 September 1833, p. 2.
[8] *Vijia Político*, Prospecto, 24 July 1830, p. 1.

authority by public opinion, and the 'slow but certain perfection of her laws' from this cardinal freedom.[1] For his part, José Miguel Infante summed up what he regarded as the strongest foundations of English freedom as follows: 'trial by jury, religious tolerance, and limitless freedom of the press'.[2]

In view of the incompatibility of the colonial background and the new ideals being proclaimed at every turn, it was hardly surprising that Chileans like Infante should dwell on the positive aspects of English life, ignoring the defects. There were, of course, one or two dissenters from this general and (on the whole) rather uncritical admiration. Mariano Egaña, though deeply influenced by his own conservative interpretation of the English constitution, could nevertheless write that the English were motivated by a profound self-interestedness which precluded all ideas of magnanimity,[3] while his father disapprovingly recalled that much of the irreligiousness of the Enlightenment had come from English sources: 'nearly all the objections of the French anti-Christian coryphaeus Mr de Voltaire are taken from the writings of Milord Bolimbroque (*sic*) and other distinguished Englishmen'.[4] An example of deeply rooted personal hostility to the English was provided by the Carreras. But, by and large, criticisms of English life were rare during the revolution, and *El Araucano*'s statement that 'the famous Constitution of England...has served as a text to all statesmen'[5] was far more typical of the general attitude.

As regards the United States, it can be seen that a similar attitude of uncritical admiration operated, together with the additional sentiment of solidarity between countries which had freed themselves from transatlantic colonial rule. The United States now became an 'example and consolation to all peoples',[6] the 'classic land of liberty',[7] the 'regenerative nation of the world',[8] 'that classic country of republicanism',[9] and an ideal

[1] *Informe*, 13 October 1828, SCL, XVI, 357.
[2] *Valdiviano Federal*, no. 146, 1 August 1839, p. 4.
[3] To Juan Egaña, 12 April 1827, *Cartas de Mariano Egaña*, p. 220.
[4] *Memoria sobre libertad de cultos*, p. 22.   [5] No. 41, 25 June 1831, p. 3.
[6] Henríquez, 'Proclama de Quirino Lemachez', Silva Castro, *Escritos políticos*, p. 45.
[7] *La Convención a los habitantes de Chile*, 1822, AR, I, 69.
[8] *Mercurio de Chile*, no. 12, 25 September 1822, CAPC, IX, 356.
[9] *Patriota Chileno*, no. 7, 26 January 1826, p. 91.

state where there existed 'democracy without disorder, aristocracy without privilege, and executive power without tyranny'.[1] Phrases such as these punctuated innumerable newspaper articles. As a good example of the effusive praise showered on the United States, an article written in 1824 may be quoted. Rousseau, Montesquieu and others were attacked for their belief that republics could only function properly in small areas.

If Tacitus had known the admirable artifice of the modern representative system, if, emerging from the temple of immortality in the company of Montesquieu and Rousseau, he could fly on the wings of fame to the City of Washington, he would enthusiastically exclaim: 'This is the Government, this is the political combination, the social guarantee, which my genius discovered in distant perspective and which I believed impossible to realize. Forty-six years of happy experience prove my error. Accustomed as I was to painting the crime and horror of the Imperial government (capable by itself of corrupting any society), I never believed that the human race could reach such perfection, that it could be governed by the principles of reason and philosophy adopted under the auspices of Washington and Franklin...'[2]

But if anything, the North American example, powerful as it was, did not equal that of England. The influence of the 1787 Constitution was supreme, if virtually unacknowledged, yet despite this, the rash of arguments surrounding the federalist controversy in the 1820s sometimes involved the reputation of the United States, and the North American model was brought into question. As will be seen, the success of the United States was adduced as a primary reason for the Chilean adoption of federal institutions,[3] and less emphasis was placed on the United States after the federalist *débâcle* than before it. An anti-federal newspaper of 1827 denounced 'the mania of some people for converting themselves overnight into *Yankees*'.[4] Juan Egaña, attacking all federations, condemned the United States as the 'archetype of republican systems',[5] and even denied that federalism worked

---

[1] *Mercurio de Chile*, no. 5, n.d., *CAPC*, IX, 250.
[2] *Correo de Arauco*, no. 25, 13 August 1824, p. 107.   [3] See chapter 8, pp. 312–3.
[4] *Miscelánea Política y Literaria*, no. 3, 13 August 1827, p. 34.
[5] *Memorias políticas*, p. 16.

very well there. Earlier than this, the desire on the part of some Chileans to imitate the United States had been criticized, both during O'Higgins' government[1] and by Dauxion Lavaysse, who also attacked several aspects of the 'American' way of life such as the fragmentation of religion and the individual yearning for popularity.[2] But by far the most interesting statement on the United States came from Diego Portales in 1822. Hearing of President Monroe's intention to name ministers and representatives to the newly liberated American republics, Portales wrote to his business partner with an extraordinarily acute forecast of the future role of the United States in Latin America. Referring to the fact that the United States had rendered relatively little physical help to the cause of independence, he asked,

Why all this zeal to accredit Ministers and delegates, and to recognize the independence of America...? There's a curious system for you, my friend! I believe that it all follows a previously prepared plan, which is this: to conquer America not by force of arms but by influence in every sphere. This will probably not happen today: but it will tomorrow.[3]

It is clear that, having rejected Spain and the imperial legacy, the leaders of the revolution felt compelled to turn elsewhere for moral support and for an ideal model to follow. The obvious countries to which they should look were Britain and the United States, both of which seemed to present an inspiring spectacle of moderate liberalism in action. The Chilean vision of these countries was an idealized one; the less palatable facts of Anglo-Saxon life were either overlooked or ignored. But the Chilean revolution was not the first, nor will it be the last, to take a foreign model and to hold it up as a mirror in which to measure local progress.

[1] 'El Republicano', *Carta Contextación al autor del Independiente*, Melipilla, 25 May 1821, *CAPC*, IX, 187. Cf. *Contestación al Independiente*, 4 June 1821, *CAPC*, IX, 193.
[2] *Del federalismo y de la anarquía*, pp. 17–18.
[3] To Cea, Lima, March 1822, Cruz and Feliú Cruz, I, 176–7.

Revolutionary Attitudes

The revolutionary rejection of Spain and the Empire was, it is fair to say, closely linked to what may be regarded as the single most important aspect of the new idology: the sense of national identity which was growing up. The revolution undoubtedly extended and enlarged that feeling of regional and provincial pride which can be observed at the end of the colonial period. The events of 1808 and 1810 compelled the creole leaders to act in a distinctively 'national' manner. As Henríquez put it in 1811, 'In the present circumstances [Chile] should be considered as a nation. Everything has combined to isolate her. Everything impels her to seek her security and happiness on her own.'[1] The need to *form* a new nation, and to give it specific national characteristics, was implicit in Juan Egaña's treatise on education, presented to Congress in 1811. Egaña's aim in the treatise was to persuade Congress 'not so much to reform abuses and to correct[2] a People inveterate in its habits, as to create, give existence, politics and opinions to a Nation which has never had them before'. Chile, thought Egaña, was in a good position to undergo this treatment; she was 'free from the influence and violences of corrupt Europe' and 'placed at the extremity of the earth'.[3] Egaña, then, appreciated the inner significance of the events of 1810–11. Later on, after independence, many others shared this appreciation that a new nation was being built. *La Clave* was able to exhort its readers in 1827: 'Let us not lose sight of the epoch in which we live, and the fact that we are the founders of a nation.'[4]

It can be argued, I think, that many attitudes already mentioned point to a new and more concrete sense of nationality. The utopian visions cited earlier were related fairly intimately to peculiarities of Chilean geography. Freire's use of the phrase 'political infancy' implied the belief, plainly, that something had recently been born. The rejection of Spanishness and the total

---

[1] Sermon, 4 July 1811, *SCL*, I, 36.
[2] Written over the deleted word 'regenerate'.
[3] 'Reflexiones sobre el mejor systema de Educacion qe. puede darse a la Juventud de Chile...', F.V. vol. 796, pieza I.   [4] No. 22, 11 October 1827, p. 86.

condemnation of the colonial period reflect the torments of emergence from the chrysalis. All these things are extremely important, but more direct evidence of national feeling should be noted. The word 'patriot' itself is significant. The word *patria* (homeland, fatherland), frequently used at the start of the revolution to denote the whole Spanish Empire, soon began to acquire a much more exclusively local character. An unknown patriot writer of early 1811 considered it essential, for instance, to uphold the 'integrity and good name of the homeland' by opposing the pretensions of the Peruvian Viceroy.[1] During the wars of the '*Patria Vieja*', the cry of '¡ Viva la Patria!' became common, and it was the permanency of the Chilean homeland rather than the imperial community that was being encouraged.

O'Higgins, in a draft proclamation to Chilean soldiers fighting on the royalist side, included an openly nationalistic note in his propaganda: 'How could you forget that you are Chileans, our brethren, from the same homeland and with the same religion, and that you must be free despite the tyrants who are deceiving you?'[2] The fact that Chileans of the lower class could fight on the royalist side (as they did in large numbers) as well as on the patriot side shows that patriotic sentiment had not penetrated very far below a certain level of society. But amongst the creole intelligentsia and the aristocracy it was already a major theme. The concept of *patria* as it developed through the revolution was not a narrow racial one, though it was certainly geographical. European Spaniards and foreigners were welcomed into the community of the homeland provided they supported the cause. Thus Carlos Spano, a *peninsular*, died in battle against the royalists and was suitably honoured by the government, which publicly recalled that his last words had been, 'I die for my Homeland, for the land which adopted me as one of its children!'[3]

When Chile was liberated in 1817 by the Army of the Andes, the same themes of patriotism recurred. Those creoles who returned from a harsh and bitter exile on Juan Fernández could take

[1] 'Sobre la necesidad Justicia y conveniencia...' [early 1811], A.B.A. vol. 25-2(3), fo. 759.
[2] *Proclama*, n.d., *Arch.O'H.*, I 251.
[3] Decree of 11 March 1814, Amunátegui, *Precursores*, III, 559.

renewed delight in the land they had lost, as did Juan Egaña: 'Oh, adorable fatherland! How delightful is your beautiful aspect to one who has suffered! He who had lost you blesses your soil on seeing you once more!'[1] 'Our dear homeland, beautiful Chile,' triumphantly proclaimed Bernardo O'Higgins as his army descended the Cordillera, 'once again occupies the rank of nation!'[2] Up and down the country, Chileans celebrated their return to freedom with tributes of a lyrical kind to their native earth. At Ligua a patriot styling himself 'El Americano del Sud' produced a typical effusion, part of which may be quoted here.

There is no single being whose soul is not cheered merely by pronouncing...*beloved, adorable homeland*...Did the enemies of American freedom perhaps imagine that the sweet word '*homeland*' would once again be proclaimed in Chile, as has been done today?...Those monsters succeeded in silencing it for more than two years, not even permitting the word to be framed on the lips of men. (Oh, enchanting homeland!) But now, freed from her oppressors, she calls on her sons publicly to name her as Mother...Thus the despotic name of *King* will nevermore be revived in our territory, and the enchanting name of MOTHER COUNTRY alone will resound even in the forests.[3]

Chileans had a very clear notion of what constituted their homeland. Definite geographical limits were always borne in mind. Differences of opinion between the provinces of the country did not mean that these provinces had ceased to form part of the homeland. 'There', wrote Carrera in 1812, referring to Concepción, 'are our brothers, the sons of the same mother.'[4] Chile was no exception to the general Latin American pattern in this. Most of the former viceroyalties or captaincies-general had accepted what Giménez Fernández has called the 'provincialist thesis' as far as their boundaries were concerned,[5] though it might just as well be referred to as the 'commonsense' thesis.

---

[1] 'Las Cenas de Marfisa' [verses], *Colección*, IV, 203.
[2] *El General de Vanguardia del Ejército de los Andes a los naturales de Chile*, Arch.O'H. VII, 123.
[3] 'Manuscritos patrióticos que trabajó un amante de la libertad chilena el 26 de febrero de 1817, contra los egoistas y contra los godos', MS 'A', *Arch.O'H.* XVII, 5–6.
[4] To Rozas, Talca, 17 May 1812, *Arch.O'H.* primer apéndice, p. 80.
[5] Giménez Fernández, p. 66.

The Revolutionary Ideology

Bernardo de Vera y Pintado observed as early as 1813 that Spanish America would, on the whole, choose to divide itself along the lines of 'those limits which the provinces have comprehended up to now'.[1] Within these limits, however, Chileans were agreed that a basic political uniformity should prevail. This was shown very clearly in the case of the island of Chiloé. In the 1823 Congress, it was maintained that 'Chiloé, as an integral part of the state, must yield to the majority, and since the majority has freely expressed its will to become constituted, Chiloé must submit'.[2] Some deputies then chose to argue that Chiloé had signed no 'pact' with Chile, but the main arguments expressed amounted to a claim that Chiloé had always 'belonged' to Chile (which, administratively speaking, was untrue) and that if Chiloé were left free to opt out of 'the great family of Chileans', then small townships within the state like Melipilla or Parral could claim the same privilege if they so desired.[3] Such, quite apart from less theoretical considerations, was the argument in favour of liberating Chiloé from Spanish rule.

There can be small doubt that many men experienced a genuine and profound affection for their fatherland during the revolutionary period. Juan Egaña, born a Peruvian but emotionally a Chilean, could write of his 'love for this country, which I regard as my only fatherland'.[4] Nicolás Matorras, after the Figueroa insurrection of April 1811, could proclaim that 'there is no fate, no glory equal to that of being a Citizen of our great Chile'.[5] Supreme Director Freire was able to denounce 'innovations contrary to the *national spirit*'.[6] The Cabildo of Santiago could urge greater efforts in the military struggle against the Spaniards, for 'we shall, in the end, possess a land of our own'.[7]

This national sentiment invested the revolution with its fundamental significance. It was not merely a question of political rights

---

[1] *Monitor Araucano*, 23 November 1813.
[2] Session of 28 August, *Redactor de las Sesiones del Soberano Congreso*, libro 1, no. 4, n.d., p. 35.   [3] Session of 29 August, *ibid.* pp. 37–8.
[4] To Carrera, 17 February 1813, *Escritos inéditos*, p. 126.
[5] 'Proclama patriótica', April 1811, Alvarez Jonte, p. 159.
[6] To the Senate, 5 June 1823, *SCL*, VII, 198. (My italics.)
[7] 'El nuevo Cabildo de la capital a sus habitantes', *Gazeta de Santiago de Chile*, 17 January 1818.

rediscovered; it was the birth of a nation. 'Chile is raised to the rank of nation,' ran a line from a poem recited in the theatre on 12 February 1820.[1] The Proclamation of Independence of February 1818 made this fact known, finally and unequivocally, to 'the great confederation of the human race',[2] of which Chile now became a member. Vera y Pintado incorporated this *motif* into the original (now discarded) version of the Chilean national anthem:

For three centuries they wished to accustom us to live, resigned to our fate, like slaves who, at the sound of their chains, would sooner learn to sing than to groan. But the strong clamour of the FATHERLAND silenced that terrible noise; and the words of Independence penetrated to the heart.[3]

The colonial epoch, then, was not simply an earlier epoch, but different in kind. It was, in Egaña's words, a time 'before there was a fatherland'.[4] In short, the theme of national genesis was a strong one in the revolution, and it may fairly be regarded as the one emotion which carried all the others in its wake. It is irrelevant to claim, as does Encina, that patriotism was restricted in its scope.[5] Nobody would dispute that it was many years before Chilean nationalism spread to all sections of the community, but, if the evidence is considered impartially, it can hardly be doubted that it was a rising force at the time of the revolution. A verse read in 1825 in commemmoration of the Battle of Chacabuco may be allowed to sum the matter up.

Today Chile ceased to be what she was formerly, and began to be what she should have been—independent, free, belonging to herself, just as nature had intended. This was the birth of the peoples, the peoples oppressed by the weight of the centuries.[6]

[1] Vera, 'Introducción a la tragedia de Guillermo Tell', Anrique R., p. 39.
[2] *AR*, I, 14.
[3] 'Canción Nacional de Chile', *Arch.O'H.* XIII, 125.
[4] *Peñalolén y 5 de enero de 1825* [pamphlet] (1825), p. 6.   [5] Encina, *Historia*, X, 71–7.
[6] 'Ramillete', *Boletín de Policia*, no. 2, 1 March 1825, p. 11.

The Revolutionary Ideology

National feeling, having fiercely rejected the legacy of Spain, was compelled to turn elsewhere for an alternative myth. The *conquistadores* had to be condemned as monsters; they could no longer be regarded as the legitimate heroes of the nation. But the Chileans did not have to travel far to find a suitable and acceptable object for their historical reverence. The new national myth was waiting for them on the doorstep, in the form of the Araucanian Indians, 'the proud republicans of Araucania', as Simón Bolívar called them in his Jamaica Letter. Here, the Chileans quickly discovered, was a pantheon of timeless heroes who could hold their own in any company.

What are the Demi-Gods of antiquity alongside our Araucanians? Is not the Greeks' Hercules, in every point of comparison, notably inferior to the Caupolicán or the Tucapel of the Chileans?[1]

As we have seen already, Alonso de Ercilla's epic poem *La Araucana*, with its stirring description of the Araucanian resistance to the Spanish conquest, had played its part in the stimulation of Chilean self-consciousness at the close of the colonial period. The example of Araucanian valour now began to inspire the patriots in their first military campaigns against the royalists. At a celebration in honour of one patriot success, Henríquez toasted 'Araucanian valour, superior to European tactics',[2] and not long afterwards the names of the ancient heroes were invoked to spur on the armies to greater victories.

Oh, patriots...recover your rights, imitating in unity and constancy your Araucanian ancestors, whose ashes repose in the urn of the sacred cause of liberty...May Colo Colo, Caupolicán, and the immortal Lautaro (the American Scipio) be reborn amongst us, so that their patriotism and valour can serve...to frighten the tyrants.[3]

The creoles regarded themselves as the true heirs of the Araucanians. Freire could speak of 'our fathers, the Araucanians',[4] Fran-

---

[1] *La Clave*, no. 22, 11 October 1827, p. 86.
[2] *Monitor Araucano*, tomo I, no. 15, 11 May 1813.
[3] *Ilustración Araucana*, no. 1, 6 September 1813.
[4] Message to Congress, 12 August 1823, *SCL*, XIII, 21.

cisco Calderón[1] could toast the Chileans as 'the sons of Caupolicán, Colocolo and Lautaro',[2] and Henríquez could proclaim, somewhat condescendingly, that 'ancient and meritorious Araucania... looks with pleasure on the youthful and glorious exploits of Colombia, Peru and Buenos Aires'.[3] The adjective 'Araucanian' became a poetic way of saying 'Chilean'.[4] Thus Carrera referred to Chile's struggle as 'the war of Araucanian independence'.[5] Many of the newspaper titles of the period also indicated the identification very clearly.[6]

The realities of Araucanian life, past and present, did not influence the Chilean vision of the ancient Indian as the true precursor of the modern patriot. Juan Egaña saw Araucania as 'the happy region ignorant of the usages of Europe and the vices of the outside world'.[7] The distinctly aggressive and bloodthirsty nature of the Indians at the time of the Conquest was either ignored or presented as 'valour', 'constancy', and so on. A national almanac published in 1824 attempted to revise history accordingly. It contained a list of the 'Araucanian Toquis[8] who, from the Spanish invasion to the peace of 1773, sustained the liberty of the fatherland'.[9] This list preceded the table of Spanish Governors (though it followed the list of Spanish Kings). In a section devoted to celebrated personages from Araucanian history, such figures as Caupolicán, described in a rather European fashion as 'the Toqui Caupolicán I, the Great', were presented in a highly favourable light.

The Chileans found many parallels, however idealized and artificial, between the Araucanian situation in the sixteenth century and their own in the early nineteenth. The Indians had, after all, put up a commendably tough resistance to oppression.

---

[1] General Francisco Calderón Zumelzu (d. 1849); member of the 1823, 1826, 1828 and 1829 Congresses; cashiered 1830; a fervent liberal.
[2] *Gaceta Ministerial de Chile*, tomo 2, no. 13, 9 October 1819.
[3] *Mercurio de Chile*, no. 12, 25 September 1822, *CAPC*, IX, 356.
[4] Encina, *Historia*, X, 55.
[5] Carrera, *Dos cartas del ciudadano José Miguel Carrera a un amigo de Chile*, CHDI, VII, 160.
[6] *El Araucano, Cartas Pehuenches, Correo de Arauco, Década Araucana, Despertador Araucano, Ilustración Araucana, Insurgente Araucano, Monitor Araucano*.
[7] *Cartas Pehuenches*, no. 11 [1819], p. 10.
[8] Paramount chiefs.   [9] *Almanak nacional*, p. 6.

The territories of Concepción and Valdivia will always be classic lands of liberty. Oh! The whole of America had bent the knee, and was kissing the hand of the oppressor, and only the standard of Araucania opposed the banners of the House of Austria![1]

Araucanian government, too, was superior to the government which had attacked it: 'The *Araucanians* governed themselves according to democratic standards which were infinitely more perfect than those of the Republics in Europe at that time.'[2] It is hardly surprising that José Miguel Infante took this a stage further, and discovered that, in fact, the Araucanians had been federalists as well. In a footnote to his own federalist newspaper, Infante claimed that 'the Araucanians were federalists, and, under that form of government, gloriously defended their liberty'.[3] Later on, he asserted that they had demonstrated the superiority of federalism to other systems, for, unlike the 'unitary' Incas or Aztecs, they had successfully resisted the Spaniard.[4]

Given these historical precedents, it became important to establish a sense of solidarity with the remaining Araucanians of the South. Purely political considerations doubtless helped in this process. O'Higgins, for instance, tried to attract Indian support against the royalists by proclaiming to them: 'We know no enemy but the Spaniard;... we are all descended from the same fathers, we inhabit the same clime.'[5] But a rejection of the Spanish Empire and a cultivation of the Indians did not mean that the creoles, descendants of the conquerors, had to vacate the lands formerly occupied by the Indians. If the Spaniards, in their efforts to maintain control of America, claimed the 'right of conquest', then the creoles could retort, with Henríquez, 'If conquest gives rights, then we alone are the owners of these lands. For we can all indisputably claim descent from the *conquistadores*.'[6] The conquest

[1] *Corresponsal del Imparcial*, no. 2, 21 March 1823, p. 10. Cf. *Tizón Republicano*, no. 16, 30 June 1823, p. 184.　　　　[2] *Observador Chileno*, no. 1, 20 August 1822.

[3] *Valdiviano Federal*, no. 43, 8 July 1831, p. 3 n.

[4] *Ibid.* no. 55, 15 March 1832, p. 1. Infante was right to the extent that the Araucanians had often acted as a loose federation of tribes, though they were hardly federalists in his sense. In the second canto of *La Araucana*, the chiefs are made to debate their leadership issue in a manner which might easily be interpreted as broadly 'democratic'.

[5] 'El Director Supremo del Estado a nuestros hermanos los habitantes de la frontera del Sud', *Gaceta Ministerial de Chile*, 13 March 1819.

[6] *Aurora de Chile*, tomo 1, no. 34, 1 October 1812, p. 144.

might be condemned. But it was, after all, an accomplished fact, and after three hundred years the creoles surely had rights of tenure. As Henríquez asked, 'Who can find a region which has always been inhabited [only] by natives?'[1]

This practical consideration did not, and could not, absolve the creole Chileans from trying to form a common community with the Araucanian brethren they now idealized. A most interesting reflection of this optimistic aspiration is to be found in a short dramatic sketch written by Bernardo de Vera y Pintado during the O'Higgins government. The scene is set at the mouth of the River Bío-Bío. The last descendent of the old Araucanian heroes stands meditating alone. A Chilean frigate approaches from the sea. Significantly enough it bears the name *Lautaro*—the 'name of a chief whose eternal fame inspires pride and draws forth tears of tender gratitude to the native'. The frigate draws closer, the crew shouting suitably patriotic slogans. The captain then prophesies utopia in a stirring invocation to the trees of Araucania:

Oh, sturdy *maitenes*, whose trunks were once watered by unmixed blood—the indomitable Araucanian's blood with which he sealed his eternal independence. Today behold beneath thy shade the patriots who are renewing liberty in all the land. A day will come when, associated with the natives of this beautiful forest, we shall form a single family together. Her brilliant ferocity softened, Araucania will then taste the fruits of trade, the arts and the sciences. Agrarian laws will regulate her fields. Industry, and those connections which bring pleasure and wealth, will replace rusticity and indigence.

Having delivered this oration, the captain of the frigate informs the Indian of the liberation of Chile and of O'Higgins' martial prowess. The Indian fetches his wife to join in the celebrations. She is somewhat diffident at first, but the captain reassures her: 'We are not enemies; we are your compatriots.' The two Araucanians finally go aboard the frigate, where everybody sings an appropriate paean of praise to O'Higgins.[2] Much of the mystique of the revolution is present in these lines of Vera's: the utopian

[1] *Aurora de Chile*, tomo I, no. 19, 18 June 1812, p. 77.
[2] 'Introducción a la tragedia El triunfo de la Naturaleza' [performed 20 August 1819], Anrique R., pp. 113–21. Vera's authorship is shown in *El Telégrafo*, no. 55, 14 December 1819 (*CAPC*, VIII, 205 n.).

optimism, the identification of the modern patriot cause with the cause of ancient Araucania, and the belief that all Chileans, whether white or Indian, could live together in a reformed and ideal state.

When it came to practical approaches to the Araucanians, ironically enough, relatively little was achieved by successive Santiago governments. In fact the revolutionaries experienced one set of troubles after another in their dealings with the Indians, who remained stubbornly unappreciative of the advantages of the new liberal order. The patriots' failure to propagandize effectively along the Southern 'Frontier' was exacerbated by the vigorous activity of the royalists. The Peruvian task-forces of 1813–14 were able to mobilize the Indians on their side, and the Church was active in promoting the royalist cause. After the liberation in 1817, Indians were more often than not involved in pro-royalist guerrilla activities under Benavides and later the Pincheiras. Their recalcitrant attitude proved a recurrent problem for the army in the South.[1] There is a good deal of truth in Amunátegui's assertion that 'the influence of the Araucanians in the revolution was only a moral influence, but it was immense'.[2]

In view of the rosy attitude of the revolutionaries towards the glorious Araucanian past, it was unfortunate that the Indians did not take a more positive stance in relation to the revolution. Nevertheless, this did not prevent a few moves in the direction of greater justice for the Indian, even though the question remained largely academic as long as the vast majority of Indians lived beyond the influence of the central government. The first Congress provided for the admission of Indians on equal terms into the Colegio Carolino and other schools, hoping that this would end 'the shocking discrimination that maintains them in their depressed condition'.[3] In 1813 the Junta decreed certain economic aid measures which, it believed, would destroy 'the caste difference' in what by rights should be 'a nation of brothers'.[4] In O'Higgins' time the principle of equal rights was used to estab-

---

[1] This is a résumé of the comprehensive study of Tomás Guevara, 'Los Araucanos en la revolución de la independencia', *AUC*, cxxvii (1910), 219.
[2] *Precursores*, ii, 512.
[3] *Acta*, 5 October 1811, *SCL*, i, 119.
[4] *Reglamento a favor de los indios*, n.d., *SCL*, i, 285–6.

lish that the Indians were eligible for military service,[1] perhaps a somewhat unhappy way of indicating their equality. Amongst the instructions which O'Higgins' Senate tried to force on San Martín before he set off to liberate Peru (where the Indian issue had a far greater practical importance than in Chile) was an article insisting that the Indians there should be granted the same civil rights as everybody else.[2] Later governments were more interested in crushing the last remnants of royalist resistance in the South and the endemic lawlessness which followed, an aim finally achieved by Prieto. Despite this, there were some signs that earlier attitudes were being maintained. In the 1828 Congress, some deputies urged that the Araucanians should be regarded as an integral part of the nation, even if in the past they had been treated separately.[3] In 1829 Nicolás Pradel recommended the appointment of a Consul for Araucania, a measure designed to bring creoles and Indians closer together.[4] A scheme of wider and more utopian proportions, embracing the whole Amerindian race, was sponsored by O'Higgins in exile.[5] It illustrated with some force the philanthropic motives so prominent in the revolutionary attitude towards the 'noble savage'.

AMERICANISM

Emphasis on the nationalist elements in the Chilean revolution should not be allowed to obscure the parallel Americanism which existed at the same time. Chileans were very strongly aware that their own cause was linked to a more general movement. The progress of the patriot cause in northern South America was continually reported in the newspapers, while the ties between Chile and Argentina—and Chile and Peru, of course—exercised a profound influence on the course of the revolution. Plainly enough, there were many automatic reasons why the different countries of Spanish America should be interested in one another.

The cause of America is and ought to be one and the same. The same background, the same language, the same religion, the same tyrants

[1] Senate, *Acta* of 26 February 1819, *SCL*, II, 303.
[2] *Instrucciones*, art. 21, *SCL*, IV, 233.
[3] Speeches by Marín, Recabarren, Navarro and Vicuña, session of 9 June 1828, *SCL*, XVI, 74–5.   [4] *El Penquisto*, no. 4, 22 April 1829, p. 15.   [5] Appendix 2.

and the same love of freedom, the same grievances, and the same interest in separating ourselves from the monarchy—everything, everything obliges us to come closer together, to help and protect each other reciprocally, like individuals of a great family scattered over a vast continent.[1]

The Spanish American Empire had broken up. The structure of political unity had given way, and separate nations had emerged from the general wreck. But the very fact that the provinces of America had previously been united suggested the notion of a new structure of unity. The most obvious way to secure this— given that the provinces *had* become separate nations—was to create an international federation. O'Higgins, for instance, told the United States agent W. G. D. Worthington that 'so soon as Peru is emancipated, we hope that Buenos Ayres and Chile with Peru will form one great confederation similar to that of the United States'.[2] That O'Higgins had mooted this idea earlier is indicated by a letter he received from his friend Fray Pedro Arce in October 1817. 'Let us not deviate by so much as a jot from what we have so often talked about,' urged Arce. 'The legislative power must be continental, the executive independent in each state and by necessity military. In this way the union of America will be indivisible.'[3]

But Chilean proposals for a federal structure for Spanish America did not confine themselves to generalities such as these. The more definite schemes that can be mentioned divide them-selves into roughly two types: those which involved Chile and Argentina alone, and those which embraced all of the newly independent republics. It is to Chile that the credit must go for having opened the first overt negotiations with Buenos Aires on the subject of a federation, but the first Chilean Junta's call for a 'plan, or general conference, to establish general defence' in November 1810[4] was turned down by Buenos Aires.[5] This was

[1] *Argos de Chile*, no. 4, 18 June 1818.
[2] Worthington to Adams, 26 January 1819, Manning, doc. 467, II, 1029–30.
[3] Arce to O'Higgins, 28 October 1817, *Arch.O'H.* VIII, 363.
[4] To the Buenos Aires Junta, 26 November 1810, Archivo de la Nación Argentina, *Documentes referentes a la Guerra de la Independencia*, I, 49.
[5] Buenos Aires Junta to Chilean Junta, 30 December 1810, *ibid.* I, 56. Mariano Moreno's well-known article against schemes of federation appeared in the *Gaceta de Buenos Aires* on 6 December.

in some ways surprising, since the Buenos Aires Junta's instructions to Alvarez Jonte, its first commissioner in Chile, contained a provision that he should further the idea of a 'well-calculated federation between the kingdom of Chile and the provinces of the River Plate'.[1] That Argentina remained interested in a federal scheme embracing Chile—doubtless with a view to extending Argentine leadership—is shown by Pueyrredón's secret instructions to San Martín in December 1816. San Martín was to try to persuade Chile to send deputies to the Congress of the United Provinces in order to form one nation.[2] Chile, not unnaturally, was unwilling to be drawn into any such arrangement. For the great purpose of liberating Peru, Chile would naturally aid Argentina in 'an even stronger league than the one between the Achaeans and oppressed Athens',[3] but a closer political union was never desired. As Irisarri informed the United States diplomatic agent: 'Chile and Buenos Aires are two different States, although the same interests unite us, and we defend the same Cause.'[4] When O'Higgins spoke of imitating the United States, and when his friend Luis de la Cruz hoped they would 'soon become one great American family',[5] they were plainly thinking of wider varieties of federation, and it is by no means fanciful to read into this attitude the antipathy between Chileans and Argentines which had made itself felt during the interim Supreme Directorship of Hilarión de la Quintana (an Argentine officer) in 1817. While a patriot newspaper, in 1818, might try to forget 'those differences between Chileans and *porteños*', and to urge both to act as 'compatriots',[6] such a sentiment, admirable as it was, ran counter to public taste.

It is fruitless to try to determine with any degree of precision when schemes of wider federation originated, and even harder to decide which schemes belonged to an imperial conception and which to a separatist one. Juan Egaña's *Plan de Gobierno* of August

---

[1] 'Instrucciones...' 19 September 1810, Alvarez Jonte, p. 47.
[2] Pueyrredón, *Campaña de los Andes*, facsimile 13.
[3] *Viva la Patria, Gaceta del Supremo Gobierno*, 21 May 1817.
[4] Letter of 22 May 1818 (copy), A.M.I. vol. 46, fo. 10.
[5] Prevost to Adams, 13 February 1818, Manning, doc. 446, II, 914.
[6] *Argos de Chile*, no. 4, 18 June 1818.

1810, which suggested a general congress of American provinces to discuss defence problems, seems to have been the first Chilean proposal.[1] From that time onwards Egaña prepared several relatively detailed schemes of this sort. In October or November 1810 he suggested a 'general gathering of the Spanish colonies' with the aim of a 'mutual defence', though this notion was for little more than a close defensive alliance.[2] At much the same time he drew up a more detailed scheme in thirty-three articles, by which Chile, Peru and Buenos Aires would form a super-state with its external affairs to be decided by a federal authority.[3] This was the basic principle of Egaña's more famous *Declaración de los derechos del Pueblo de Chile*, which I mentioned in chapter 3.[4]

Egaña's activity in favour of confederal schemes in the '*Patria Vieja*' can now be seen to have been fertile, though in utopian ideas rather than in practical results.[5] After the liberation in 1817, the notion of confederation returned. Instructions issued by O'Higgins' Senate to a Chilean emissary in Colombia contained the provision that he should urge the nations of Spanish America to debate their future form of government 'by means of a confederation'.[6] This idea coincided to some extent with Simón Bolívar's, and the Liberator's plenipotentiary, Joaquín Mosquera, encouraged the proposal during negotiations on the treaty between Chile and Colombia in November 1822. Mosquera proposed a 'Congress of Plenipotentiaries' through which the new nations could form a united league or 'society of sister nations'.[7] The treaty which resulted, signed on 20 November 1822, contained provisions for such an assembly, and these were also written into a treaty between Chile and Peru the following month.[8] When in 1823 the Senate expressed the wish to postpone ratification of the

---

[1] *CHDI*, XIX, 108.

[2] 'Proyecto de una reunión general de las colonias españolas para su defensa y seguridad...', *Escritos inéditos*, pp. 43–51.

[3] 'Dieta Soberana de Sud-América', *ibid.* pp. 52–9.   [4] See p. 119.

[5] See Silva Castro, *Egaña en la Patria Vieja*, ch. 5, and Alejandro Alvarez, *La diplomacia de Chile durante la emancipación* (Madrid, n.d.), pp. 255–70.

[6] 'Instrucciones', art. 7, *Acta* of 22 June 1821, *SCL*, V, 209.

[7] Mosquera to Echeverría and Rodríguez Aldea, 5 October 1822, *SCL*, V, 328.

[8] Chile–Colombia, art. 14 (*SCL*, VI, 421); Chile–Peru, art. 13 (*SCL*, VI, 429).

Colombian treaty, Freire put a definite and concise case for the congress idea.

In the eyes of statesmen, the present time is the precise moment when America should open negotiations with Spain, and talk to Europe with a single, united voice. Such is the aim of the American Congress which is stipulated [in the treaty], a measure of the highest importance ...which the Supreme Director...regards as the means by which the independence of this vast hemisphere may be recognized.[1]

In the same year, Manuel de Salas put forward a project for a Congress of Plenipotentiaries, for the purpose of readjusting relations with Europe.[2] It was turned down by the Foreign Affairs Committee of the 1823 Congress as unnecessary.[3] After this, Chilean interest in confederal schemes was considerably diminished. Partly as a reflection of the country's own internal difficulties, and partly because of a distinct undercurrent of hostility to Bolívar, Chile's attitude towards the Congress of Panama was one of relative indifference.[4] Juan Egaña chose the moment, however, to produce a loose scheme for a huge international confederation embracing Latin America, the United States, Spain, Portugal, Greece and Haiti,[5] and also a more limited project finally printed in volume VI of his collected works.

Few voices in the Chile of the revolutionary period were raised against such proposals as these. A writer in *La Aurora de Chile* in 1812 compared the idea of a federation to one of the fantasies of Mercier's *Histoire de l'An 2440*. 'America is too vast', he claimed, 'and our characters too different for us to be able to receive laws from a single legislative body...Such an Assembly...will not

[1] To the Senate, 19 April 1823, *SCL*, VII, 64–5. The Senate dropped the Congress scheme (*Acta* of 23 April).
[2] *SCL*, VIII, 314–15.   [3] *Informe*, n.d., *SCL*, VIII, 364.
[4] Barros Arana, XV, 92–3. Cf. Encina, *Historia*, X, 61–5. Encina's view that Americanism was stronger than patriotism ignores the fact that 'itinerant Americans' (Monteagudo, García del Río, Padilla, Irisarri, Bello, etc.) were never more than a small minority. He is also mistaken, in my view, in ascribing anti-Chilean motives to O'Higgins at the time of the 1836–9 war. O'Higgins' sole concern was to prevent conflict between two American republics: see O'Higgins to Santa Cruz, 10 November 1838, Cruz, *Epistolario*, II, 241.
'Proyecto de una Acta de Confederación y mútua garantía de la independencia de los Estados que en él se mencionan', n.d. *Escritos inéditos*, p. 59.

pass beyond the bounds of fantasy.'[1] This prophecy was absolutely correct. Many reasons have been advanced to explain the Spanish Americans' failure to unite after independence: their geographical isolation, the personalism of some of their leaders, the strong regionalist tradition in Spanish political life, and so forth. These reasons must be regarded as important, but, in addition, it can be seen that after the early 1820s there was relatively little point in establishing a united political structure in Spanish America. All the earlier schemes, without exception, had envisaged setting up a super-state or loose league for some definite purpose: to consolidate military triumph, or to secure reasonable terms in negotiating with European powers. The moment these needs disappeared, the idea of confederation lost force. As far as Chile was concerned, the changes of 1830 onwards brought with them a new and more definitely nationalist policy as far as foreign relations were concerned. Diego Portales based his view of the world which lay beyond the frontiers of Chile on the notions of Chilean self-sufficiency and a Latin American balance of power. His reasons for setting out to destroy the Peru–Bolivian Confederation bear adequate witness to this.[2] With the War of 1836–9, Chile and Spanish America alike passed from an era of mutual aid into an era of active national rivalries, and, in this dubious alteration, it was Chile that led the way.

[1] Tomo I, no. 28, 20 August 1812, p. 118.
[2] See his letter to Blanco Encalada, 10 September 1836, Cruz and Feliú Cruz, III, 452. For Portales' policies and the struggle between Chile and the Confederation see Luis Carcovich, *Portales y la política internacional hispanoamericana* (1937), and Robert N. Burr, *By Reason or Force: Chile and the Balancing of Power in South America, 1830–1905* (Berkeley and Los Angeles, 1965), ch. 3.

PART III

EXPERIMENTS IN GOVERNMENT

6

BERNARDO O'HIGGINS
1817–1823

The patriot defeat at Rancagua in October 1814 was symptomatic of the worsening situation for the revolutionary forces all over South America. But, although the royalists succeeded in re-imposing the old pattern of government in all the South American provinces except those of the River Plate, their position was a good deal less secure than they imagined. The stern policy of repression which the Spanish forces found it necessary to adopt created a strong current of creole resentment and gained a multitude of new adherents to the cause of independence. Added to this, the more determined patriot leaders were absolutely determined to continue the struggle to the bitter end. 1816 was their year of decision. In northern South America, Simón Bolívar resumed his career as Liberator. In the South, José de San Martín prepared to put his grand strategy into effect. From mid 1816 until the meeting of Bolívar and San Martín at Guayaquil in July 1822, the history of South America was very largely the history of the double move-ment of emancipation. It was the Southern movement that in-volved Chile. San Martín's grand strategy aimed at dispossessing the Spaniards of the Viceroyalty of Peru by means of securing a strong base in Chile and then mounting a seaborne expedition to complete the work. Events in Chile from 1817 to 1823 were the outcome of San Martín's decision to pursue this programme to its planned conclusion.

The experiences of the 'Patria Vieja' in Chile had been mixed. Their sequel, between October 1814 and February 1817, was doubly unhappy. The reasonably moderate government of the victorious General Osorio gave way in 1815 to the savage repres-sion practised by Osorio's successor as Governor of Chile, Francisco Casimiro Marcó del Pont. Marcó del Pont's basic policy can best be summed up in his own dictum that he would not even leave the Chileans tears with which to weep.[1] This attitude was speedily answered by brilliant guerrilla resistance led by such legendary figures as Manuel Rodríguez and the *huaso* Miguel Neira. On the far side of the Cordillera of the Andes, San Martín and O'Higgins, who had become intimate friends, planned a more permanent form of vengeance. After the appointment of Juan Martín de Pueyrredón as Supreme Director of the United Provinces of the River Plate in May 1816, their plans were given full backing by the Argentine administration. A number of important political decisions were taken. The suggestion that O'Higgins should be entrusted with the government of Chile after the liberation seems to have emanated from San Martín, whose eyes were fixed on Lima, but Pueyrredón enthuiastically approved it.[2] In July 1816, the Congress of Tucumán finally decreed the independence of Argentina, giving San Martín the moral authority he wanted for his campaign against the royalists. At the beginning of 1817 the Army of the Andes left its base in Mendoza, crossed the Cordillera, descended into Chile, and defeated the royalists at the Battle of Chacabuco (12 February 1817). San Martín and O'Higgins rode into Santiago, where an assembly of notables offered San Martín the government of Chile. As arranged, he stepped down in favour of O'Higgins, who was accepted without demur.[3]

The next six years of Chilean history were dominated by one man, Bernardo O'Higgins, now regarded as the supreme hero of the revolution and father of the Chilean fatherland.[4] O'Higgins' government was personal, though not in the worst sense, and his

[1] Juan Egaña, *El chileno consolado*, I, 198.
[2] See Pueyrredón to San Martín, 2 and 18 January 1817, Pueyrredón, *Campaña de los Andes*, facsimiles 87 and 92.
[3] See Feliú Cruz, 'La elección de O'Higgins'.
[4] There are many biographies of Bernardo O'Higgins Riquelme (1778–1842). In some ways Vicuña Mackenna's *Vida de O'Higgins* is still unsurpassed, while Eyzaguirre, *O'Higgins*, remains the best modern work. O'Higgins' correspondence is printed in Cruz, *Epistolario*, though a fuller collection is gradually being published in *Arch.O'H.* Accounts of the 1817–23 regime from differing viewpoints may be found in Amunátegui and Vicuña Mackenna, *Dictadura de O'Higgins*, and Orrego Vicuña, *Espíritu constitucional*. For a complete bibliography of works on and relating to O'Higgins up to 1945 see José Zamudio Z., *Fuentes bibliográficas para el estudio de la vida y de la época de Bernardo O'Higgins* (1946).

influence (at any rate for the first half of his administration) was probably even greater and more pervasive than that of Diego Portales between 1830 and 1837. O'Higgins' achievement was considerable. Not only did he consolidate the independence of Chile and immensely further the independence of Peru; he also provided the revolution with its longest single period of political stability. There is good reason, therefore, to indicate the main features of his often misunderstood character.

First and foremost, Bernardo O'Higgins was a soldier, and an excellent soldier, but, unlike other great commanders of the Spanish American revolution, he was rarely tempted to set down his political motives and ideas on paper. He never came anywhere near to using those flights of superb rhetoric with which Simón Bolívar, for instance, justified his every action. O'Higgins was in some ways more fitted for the battlefield than for the palace. As his friend Zañartu[1] commented later, there was a 'brilliant and magnificent barrier' between the military and political sides of his nature.[2] Perhaps as a result of this, there were times when O'Higgins came to detest the 'unbearable weight of the administration',[3] though this did not mean that he was indifferent to the allure of power; he himself was later to claim that, at the moment of his abdication, one of his dominant emotions was the love of power.[4] Nor did it mean that he had no political instincts.

O'Higgins modelled himself to some extent on his father, a man from whom he had been totally isolated in childhood—they apparently saw each other only once—but for whom he felt a warm if distant admiration. In his exile, he and his Irish secretary tried to collect as much information about Don Ambrosio as possible, with a view, it seems certain, to composing a biography, a work of filial piety never properly begun.[5] From his father, O'Higgins inherited a number of distinct traits: his practicality, for example. The Viceroy was 'said to have been the most useful

---

[1] Miguel José de Zañartu Santa María (1771–1851); close friend and collaborator of O'Higgins; one of the likely authors of the Proclamation of Independence.
[2] *Corresponsal del Imparcial*, no. 1, 14 March 1823, p. 4.
[3] O'Higgins to J. J. Bustos (*borrador*), 12 August 1822, A.V.M. vol. 98, fo. 24.
[4] To Miguel de la Barra, 5 June 1839, Barros Borgoño, p. 28.
[5] A.B.A. particularly vol. 25-2(9): numerous scattered memoranda and notes as well as a half-drafted preface (fo. 519).

man Chile ever possessed'.[1] The bias towards specific, practical projects was visible at every stage of O'Higgins' career. His final political testament, dictated just before his death,[2] contained a list of practical recommendations rather than political generalities. These facts, however, should not be permitted to obscure an occasionally utopian side to his mentality.[3]

O'Higgins was evidently a very attractive character, with a 'pleasing and cheerful countenance'.[4] His private character was said to be 'truly amiable. He was kind and condescending; apparently more at home in his evening *tertulias* than under the canopy of the Supreme Directorship.'[5] A general preference for simplicity marked him off from some of the other Latin American leaders of the time. The Swiss traveller Schmidtmeyer relates that he lived 'in a plain unexpensive style, apparently from taste as much from any other cause'.[6] This simplicity extended to O'Higgins' political utterances. General José María de la Cruz[7] recalled that his style of expression 'was neither florid nor sophisticated', and that he had a special talent for 'summarizing his ideas within a small framework'. 'In this', Cruz wryly added, 'one saw that he was of the English school.'[8] Lord Cochrane, too, believed that O'Higgins' mind had something of 'an English tone'.[9] At all events, O'Higgins seems to have possessed an uprightness and a straightforwardness that endeared him to his many friends and associates.

Yet the very extent of this 'honest, kind hearted, straightforward, unsuspecting' character, as General William Miller defined it,[10] was something of a disadvantage in public affairs. Maria Graham, an English traveller who came to know the Supreme Director very well, summarized him as 'that good though weak man'.[11] Cochrane believed that O'Higgins' amiable disposition

---

[1] Haigh, p. 165 n.
[2] Luis Valencia Avaria, 'El testamento político de O'Higgins', *BACH*, no. 25 (1943), p. 5.
[3] See chapter 5, 217, and appendix 2.
[4] Schmidtmeyer, p. 308.   [5] Stevenson, III, 276–7.   [6] Schmidtmeyer, p. 308.
[7] José María de la Cruz Prieto (1801–75), son of the patriot general Luis de la Cruz (1768–1828); fought as a Captain at Chacabuco and Maipó; Minister of War, 1830–1; General 1833; leader of the liberal revolt of 1851.
[8] J. M. Cruz, *Recuerdos*, pp. 62–3.   [9] Dundonald, I, 291.
[10] Quoted in R. A. Humphreys, *Liberation in South America, 1806–1827: The Career of James Paroissien* (London, 1952), p. 137.   [11] Graham, p. 358.

was 'too easy to contend with the machinations of those around him'.[1] It was natural that, in dealing with men like San Martín, O'Higgins should have been at a disadvantage, for, as Maria Graham put it, 'he was too apt to rely on the honestness of others from the very uprightness of his intentions'.[2] It was not, however, merely a case of political innocence being defeated by the greater experience of contemporaries. O'Higgins was also remarkably susceptible to personal influences; he was unduly swayed by the judgements of those with whom he had formed close friendships. He tended, too, to credit other people with the same outlook as himself, and, if Cochrane's secretary is to be believed, was slightly diffident about his own abilities, 'always willing to take advice from anyone, but always inclined to consider the last as the best'.[3]

So it is, perhaps, fairly easy to trace the cause of some of the mistakes committed by O'Higgins' government. Not only was the Supreme Director a 'good-hearted man and well-intentioned, but weak and unable to carry right measures into effect',[4] but he was, it can be claimed, excessively dependent on those nearest to him. It was their fault if he

was led to believe that a crooked policy was a necessary evil of Government; and as such a policy was adverse to his own nature, he was the more easily induced to surrender its administration to others who were free from his conscientious principles.[5]

The truth of the matter does seem to lie somewhere here. If the undeniable honesty of O'Higgins made him the greatest Chilean leader of the revolution, it also made him unable to manage some of the political elements with which he was out of harmony; and allowing his ministers too great a degree of confidence was plainly a cause of his final undoing.

How can one reconcile these two complementary facets of O'Higgins' nature and present a model by which to understand him? To one side stands his inflexible sense of honour, shining

[1] Dundonald, I, 69. [2] Graham, pp. 42–3; cf. Dundonald, I, 71.
[3] Stevenson, III, 275–6. [4] Mathison, p. 204.
[5] Dundonald, I, 71.

forth with an integrity which made one North American observer describe him as 'a patriot of the Roman school'.[1] Yet alongside this there was the kind of weakness already mentioned, and the tendency to rely too much on other men's opinions. An unknown Chilean once told William Bennet Stevenson: 'There is too much wax, and too little steel in his composition; however, there are few better, and many worse men than Don Bernardo.'[2] The English traveller Robert Proctor, who met O'Higgins in Valparaíso soon after his abdication, wrote of him that 'his character seems too open and undesigning for times of intrigue and revolution'. Proctor was reminded, when he met O'Higgins, of pictures of Oliver Cromwell,[3] and there is nothing fanciful in a comparison of the two men. Both were great revolutionary generals of austere personal character. Both failed to base their political authority on the bedrock of permanent institutions. Both were obliged to leave the private lives which they preferred,[4] to become outstanding men of action. In the case of the Supreme Director, as with the Lord Protector, 'his errors of judgement are forgotten in the recollection of the goodness of his heart'.[5] It is against this personal background that the nature of O'Higgins' ideas and government must be measured.

O'Higgins' first months in office as Supreme Director of Chile (the unusual title was derived from the Argentine example) were spent on active service against the royalists in the South. While his lieutenants extended patriot rule further and further into the wild area of the Araucanian 'Frontier', O'Higgins himself pinned the bulk of the royalist army into Talcahuano, though his repeated attacks on that 'Gibraltar of America', as he called it, were a failure. The expectation of another expedition from the Viceroyalty of Peru—the Viceroy was far from reconciled to the loss of Chile—caused O'Higgins to withdraw towards the North. At the same time, he ratified the half-accomplished fact of national

---

[1] Worthington to Adams, 8 April 1818, Manning, doc. 452, II, 919.

[2] Stevenson, III, 277.   [3] Proctor, p. 108.

[4] O'Higgins told Juan Mackenna in 1811 that his character best fitted him to be a farmer: Cruz *Epistolario* I, 30.

[5] John Miller (ed.), *Memoirs of General [William] Miller* (2 vols. London, 1828), II, 314.

freedom by issuing the Proclamation of Independence from Talca in February 1818. The action had an element of defiance, for Chile was once again as seriously menaced by the royalists as she had been in 1814, and the first stages of the campaign seemed to be a repeat performance of the patriot disasters of the previous occasion. The royalists were commanded, as before, by General Mariano Osorio, who advanced up-country towards Santiago just as he had done three and a half years earlier. San Martín, badly defeated at the Battle of Cancha Rayada (near Talca) on 19 March 1818, managed to rally the patriot army, but only just in time. On 5 April, he inflicted a decisive reverse on the royalists on the plains of Maipó, at the gates of Santiago. It was an action which, in San Martín's own words, 'decided the fate of South America'.[1] Though the war in the South of Chile was to continue for several years, the heart-land was never again threatened.

O'Higgins and San Martín now turned their attention to the promised expedition to Peru. A compact and efficient naval squadron was speedily built up, so that Chile could gain command of the sea before attempting to dispatch any expedition. Alvarez Condarco, the Chilean agent in London, secured the services of Lord Cochrane, one of the most brilliant British sailors of the age, who agreed to aid the cause of independence by assuming charge of the Chilean navy. Cochrane arrived at the end of 1818, armed to the teeth with liberal sentiments, but with a stubborn consciousness of his status as a Scottish nobleman. Though he soon struck up a cordial and even intimate relationship with O'Higgins, his dealings with San Martín and with O'Higgins' Minister of War, Zenteno,[2] were a good deal less happy, and eventually became stormy in the extreme. Nevertheless, Cochrane's name added lustre to the patriot cause, and his daring exploits in the Pacific, culminating in his astonishing capture of royalist-held Valdivia (3 and 4 February 1820) served as a colourful and fitting prelude to the liberation of Peru.

Command of the sea, brilliantly established by Lord Cochrane

---

[1] San Martín to Castlereagh, 11 April 1818, Webster, 1, 558.
[2] José Ignacio Zenteno del Pozo y Silva (1786–1847); Minister of War 1817–20; Governor of Valparaíso 1821–5; largely responsible for the creation of the Chilean navy; after 1823, a staunch *o'higginista*.

and the infant Chilean navy,[1] was an essential element in patriot strategy, and the mounting of an expedition to Peru was now a practical possibility. To further the great project, Chile and Argentina concluded a solemn treaty of alliance in January 1819, but the increasingly chaotic political situation in the River Plate forced the Chilean government to assume almost complete responsibility for the creation of the expeditionary force. In June 1819 the sympathetic Pueyrredón was obliged to step down from the Supreme Directorship of Argentina, and his successor, José Rondeau, showed himself chiefly concerned to compel San Martín to place his army at the disposal of the menaced central government. This San Martín refused to do. He persuaded the Argentine officers stationed in Chile to continue under his command, and in March 1820 formally proclaimed his 'disobedience'. The promised expedition, largely organized and financed by the Chilean government, was now ready for action. It consisted of some 4,500 men, transported in twenty-three ships (seven warships and sixteen merchantmen), and set sail from Valparaíso on 20 August 1820, O'Higgins' forty-second birthday. A year later found San Martín the Protector of an independent (though only partially liberated) Peru, but a further year brought his career into collision, at Guayaquil, with Simón Bolívar's. The interview between the two great liberators seemed to preclude any possibility of collaboration, and San Martín chose to retire into private life, leaving Bolívar the glory of the final liberation of Peru.

The departure of the Peruvian Expedition in August 1820 marked the zenith of O'Higgins' fortunes. It was his moment of supreme achievement. Thereafter he was mainly concerned with domestic issues, although these had never been wholly absent from his mind. In 1818, partly in response to the demands of a Cabildo Abierto in Santiago, a Constitution had been drawn up to give sanction to the O'Higgins regime. The Supreme Director was given more or less absolute powers, though a small advisory Senate was set up to aid him in the tasks of government. The

---

[1] For the creation of the Chilean navy and its winning command of the sea under Cochrane, see Donald E. Worcester, *Sea Power and Chilean Independence* (Gainesville, Fla. 1962), pp. 17–56.

Senate performed its duties well, but after 1820 it tended to disagree with the Supreme Director on several issues, mostly financial, and these discords accompanied the rising note of public discontent with the regime.

Nevertheless, the O'Higgins government attempted an ambitious programme of reforms, a programme reminiscent in some ways of an eighteenth-century enlightened despotism. Towns were founded; the country was well policed; Santiago was beautified; an agent of the Lancasterian Society of London was brought from Buenos Aires to foster the educational system; Valparaíso grew at an amazing rate, along with foreign trade; the arts began to revive; a theatre was built; the Instituto Nacional, first opened during the '*Patria Vieja*', was re-established; Manuel de Salas collected over eight thousand books for a National Library. In his diplomatic ventures, O'Higgins was rather less successful, though the United States recognized the independence of Chile in 1822. Antonio José de Irisarri was sent on a mission to Europe, with headquarters in London. Though he failed to secure British recognition, he did manage to raise a £1,000,000 loan in the City. José Ignacio Cienfuegos was sent to Rome to settle outstanding ecclesiastical matters, but his mission had no outcome in O'Higgins' time. Some tentative steps were taken towards encouraging immigration.

Despite the exemplary vigour of his government, O'Higgins committed, or at any rate permitted, a number of unfortunate mistakes. His persecution of the Carrera family and its partisans was probably justified; they were passionately opposed to the regime and wanted to destroy it. But his action in sending a bill for legal costs to Ignacio de Carrera after the shooting of his sons Luis and Juan José in 1818 was unnecessarily cold-blooded.[1] The murder of the popular guerrilla leader Manuel Rodríguez was another error. Even though O'Higgins may not have ordered the deed, his impassive reception of the news allowed his enemies to think as much.[2] In the early stages of his administration, too, there was a persistent suspicion that the Supreme Director was controlled

[1] Amunátegui and Vicuña Mackenna, *Dictadura de O'Higgins*, p. 192.
[2] *Ibid.* pp. 215–16.

by sinister influences through the notorious Logia Lautarina, of which he was a member. Excessive weight in his counsels was attributed to Argentines, and José Miguel Carrera's malicious propaganda from Montevideo—to the effect that Chile was on the point of becoming a colony of Buenos Aires—seemed to contain elements of plausibility. But O'Higgins' most fateful error, certainly, was his appointment of José Antonio Rodríguez Aldea as Finance Minister in 1820. Rodríguez Aldea was competent (perhaps too competent) but highly unpopular, and he attracted a good deal of ill-feeling towards the regime, much as Bernardo Monteagudo did for San Martín in Lima. Many reasons have been given for the eventual downfall of the O'Higgins government. Probably the most convincing of these can be found in his refusal to attune his policies to the aims and interests of the landowning aristocracy of Chile, which demanded that any government should protect its livelihood and rely on its constant consultation. Some of O'Higgins' moves in relation to the Church—the prohibition of burial in churches, the grant of permission for a Protestant cemetery, the brusque treatment of ecclesiastical dignitaries, and so forth—seem to have created public anxiety, together with O'Higgins' handful of anti-aristocratic measures. By the start of 1822, an English traveller could note that the 'administration appeared generally unpopular among the thinking parts of the community'.[1]

Matters were brought to a head by O'Higgins' decision to reform his somewhat provisional political system. He ordered the election of a special Preparatory Convention, but chose to intervene personally in the individual elections. The Convention thus chosen met from July to October 1822, and produced a new Constitution which was in many ways moderate and wise. But O'Higgins badly miscalculated by making the assumption that he himself should remain as Supreme Director for the first period established by the Constitution, and since this first period (of six years) could be extended (to ten years) if need be, the public could hardly be blamed for seeing, in the new *carta*, a device to promote the Supreme Director's personal ambition beyond the

[1] Mathison, p. 203.

limits of equity. Meanwhile, the economic situation in the South
—ravaged by almost continual warfare since the liberation—had
become acutely embarrassing. The Intendant of Concepción,
O'Higgins' trusted friend and lieutenant, General Ramón Freire,[1]
finally decided to head a revolutionary movement against the
capital. Soon after receiving news of the Constitution of 1822,
Freire called a provincial assembly, and the whole area came out
in open revolt against O'Higgins. The northern province of
Coquimbo followed suit. A civil war seemed imminent.

San Martín, who had returned to Chile after his resignation
from the Protectorship of Peru, had been lying ill at his estate,
but was well enough to leave Chile in December 1822. Neither
he nor Cochrane showed any willingness to become implicated
in the internal dissensions now rising to their height. Cochrane,
incensed by what he considered his unjust treatment (and, no
doubt, by his failure to have San Martín arrested), shook Chilean
dust from off his feet and, on 18 January 1823, sailed off to further
brief glories in Brazil. Two of the three members of the great
liberating partnership had now departed. The third did not have
to wait long for a similar fate. The revolt of the provinces
prompted the leading citizens of the capital to conspire against the
Supreme Director. On 28 January 1823, in a scene of considerable
drama, O'Higgins finally agreed to abdicate. He transferred power
to a national Junta, and made plans to leave the country. Six
months later, he was finally permitted to take ship for Peru, and a
British sloop, H.M.S. *Fly*, carried him into an exile from which he
never returned. In 1824 he observed part of the last patriot campaign in the Peruvian highlands at first hand, riding alongside
Bolívar. Two years later he lent his tentative support to a military
insurrection in Chiloé. With the arrival of the conservative
regime in 1830, O'Higgins had high hopes of being invited to
return to Chile by his old friend Joaquín Prieto, but they came to

[1] Ramón Freire Serrano (1787–1851); served in the campaigns of the '*Patria Vieja*', in
Admiral Brown's corsair squadron, and in the South of Chile 1817–22; Supreme
Director of Chile 1823–6; President of the Republic 1827; leader of the liberal army in
1830; exiled to Peru 1830, and, after a further revolutionary attempt, to Australia;
permitted to return to Chile 1842. Freire still awaits a proper biographer. The last
period of his life is very obscure.

nothing. His final years were spent either on his estate in the Cañete Valley or in Lima, where he died, in relative poverty, in 1842.

INDEPENDENCE

During the disturbed years of the *'Patria Vieja'*, a large part of Chilean thought on political matters had been devoted to the urgent issue of the relationship with Spain. This issue was now decided, irrevocably, in favour of total independence, which had been defined by Pueyrredón as the main aim of the campaign of liberation in 1817.[1] On receiving the news of the victory at Chacabuco, Antonio José de Irisarri wrote to O'Higgins: 'Remove the mask completely; declare independence without delay; actively solicit recognition from the European powers.'[2] O'Higgins, who had believed in absolute independence for much longer than Irisarri, had little need of advice on this topic. In February 1818, as we have seen, he finally set his pen to the formal proclamation of Chilean independence.

What chiefly compelled independence now was the recent memory of the Spanish reconquest. Rather more than two years of stern repression had left an indelible mark. For O'Higgins, firmly committed to a separatist policy from the start, the reconquest represented little more than the 'parenthesis of our glories',[3] but, to the undecided or wavering, Chile's sudden and compulsory return to a state of 'enforced infancy, without trade, navigation or industry,'[4] as a distinguished foreign visitor described it, was profoundly shocking. Spanish outrages, too, were bound to have a drastic effect on the Chilean temper. As Juan Egaña put it,

This tumult of horrifying circumstances was upsetting in the extreme in America, and particularly in Chile, where men die within the circle where they were born, where the days of man have always been the same, calm and slothful, where no aristocrat has ever been seen on the scaffold, and where there has never been evidence of outstanding virtue or wickedness.[5]

[1] Pueyrredón, *Campaña de los Andes*, facsimile 1.
[2] Letter of 27 May 1817, *Arch.O'H.* IV, 229–30.
[3] O'Higgins, *Manifiesto del Capitan General*, p. 2.
[4] Chamisso, p. 266.   [5] *El chileno consolado*, I, 153.

It is hardly surprising, then, that the horrors (real or exaggerated) of the reconquest should become a favourite theme when the need for independence was celebrated. In the weeks and months following the liberation, a lyrical bemoaning of the 'Neronic ferocity'[1] of the reconquest became common, in the provinces as well as in Santiago. Patriotic speeches contained fulsome references to the 'whirlwind of proscriptions' which had characterized the 'two years of profound and terrible silence', during which the 'Peninsular tyrants and their followers' had remorselessly pursued 'the bloody plan of their usurpation and plunder'.[2] There were, of course, more measured statements of the same theme. Irisarri, for instance, in a little-known book printed in London in 1820, noted that the experience of 1814–17 had been the decisive factor in bringing about independence.

The gallows, the beheadings, the dungeons, the banishments did not achieve anything, except to make the desire to shake off the yoke more general. Our rage suggested a declaration of independence...as the only means of ridding ourselves of tyranny.[3]

Other reasons, however, could be advanced to justify the newly gained independence of Chile. O'Higgins, for instance, seems to have felt that the fundamental reason was essentially 'natural'. The New World, he maintained, no longer *needed* Peninsular leadership, and was obliged to press its rights as a mature and independent entity.

We are demanding the right of a servant who quits his master when ill treated; the right of somebody who, emancipated by his age, finds that he is capable of managing his own affairs;...the right of somebody ceasing to be a pupil (and we are generous enough not to demand a reckoning from the tutor).[4]

This was also Irisarri's view. The whole previous relationship between Spain and her colonies had been wrong, not so much for

---

[1] 'El Americano del Sud', MS 'B', Ligua, 28 February 1817, *Arch.O'H.* XVII, 8.
[2] 'Viva la Patria Señores', Vallenar, 3 March 1817, A.M.I. vol. 38, fo. 217.
[3] *Memoria sobre el estado presente de Chile*, p. 6. Cf. 'Come, Diocletians, Neros and Robespierres! Learn of cruelties which were never within your own tyrannical reach!' in *Memoria sobre los principales sucesos de la revolución de Chile desde 1810 hasta 1814*, n.d. CHDI, II, 210. The atrocities in Chile, however, were not comparable to those in tropical America.   [4] *Manifiesto que hace a las naciones*, 1818, p. 17.

reasons of tyranny or misgovernment (though these had certainly existed) but because of the sheer nature of the two parties concerned.

Have not the Spanish dominions in America, when compared to the poor Peninsula, been much the same as the great body of an elephant compared to its tail? Was it not greater nonsense to pretend that Spain should govern the whole of the New World than to pretend that an elephant's tail should carry out the functions of a head? Is it not certain that any of the Kingdoms of America, even a small one, possesses better means than Spain to become a rich and powerful country?[1]

Some of O'Higgins' other supporters provided other justifications for the separation. One writer claimed that Spanish Americans possessed the same rights as Englishmen, Spaniards, Frenchmen and Germans; all these peoples had once formed part of the Roman Empire, but had since achieved their independence; hence there was no reason why the Americans should not free themselves from the Spanish Empire.[2] Another writer based his argument on the now familiar notion of the breakdown of the social pact. The previous 'contract' between monarch and people had been dissolved; and it could now be seen that this was due to the faults of one of the contracting parties.

Homage rendered to Kings can only last while the social pact remains unaltered...If any infraction of the pact is noted—in order to keep men in a state of degrading servitude—then there is no need to allow this servitude to prevail.[3]

An unknown *cabildante* of Vallenar went further than this. He denied that the social pact between Chile and Spain had ever been valid in the first place. The fictitious oath of loyalty to the Spanish Crown had been taken under the pressure of conquest: 'In order for the oath to be valid and legitimate, it must be taken freely and willingly...before a Competent Judge. The Kings of Spain and their representatives have never been, are not, and

---

[1] *Carta al Observador en Londres*, pp. 36–7.
[2] *La Justicia en Defensa de la Verdad*, 1817, *CAPC*, III, 332.
[3] *Semanario de Policia*, 26 November 1817.

never will be our legitimate overlords.'[1] The Proclamation of Independence itself, perhaps disappointingly, contained few such reasons. Doctrinally, it was of interest only inasmuch as it affirmed Chile's recovery of natural rights previously usurped by the Spaniards. But, though long overdue, the Proclamation set the seal on an affirmative solution to a delicate problem which had occupied Chilean minds since 1810. February 1818 signalized the final removal of the 'mask of Ferdinand VII'.

O'HIGGINS' IDEAS AND PROGRAMME

Bernardo O'Higgins brought to the task of governing this newly independent state a considerable degree of public-spirited unselfishness. John Miers, in later years no friend to Chile, wrote of him that 'he may be said to have been the only man in power who had the good of his country at heart; the only disinterested man who possessed authority: his only ambition was to promote the good of his country'.[2] O'Higgins certainly seems to have kept before him a vision of the future progress of his nation: 'Only the future destiny of Chile has been able to sustain my heart and spirit.'[3] This feeling did not desert him in exile, when he wrote that 'it...only remains for me to devote the remainder of my life in promoting those measures for the welfare and happiness of Chile & Peru which shall best testify the love I bear the former and the gratitude I owe the latter'.[4] Fine words like these are often suspect, but less so than usual, I believe, in the case of Bernardo O'Higgins.

What were his political ideals? In the first place, he accepted the general view as to the significance of the revolution. His vision was no less fervent, no less utopian, than the visions of his contemporaries. In 1824, while he was watching the final stages of the

[1] 'Viva la Patria Señores', A.M.I. vol. 38, fo. 219.
[2] Miers, II, 36. Thanks largely to business disappointments, Miers became, by 1825, 'the most furious detractor of Chile' (Mariano Egaña to Juan Egaña, 21 December 1825, *Cartas de Mariano Egaña*, p. 129) but his information is often accurate and valuable.
[3] *Manifiesto del Capitan General* (1820), p. 5.
[4] To Zañartu, [1832–4] (*borrador*) [in English], A.V.M. vol. 98, fo. 87. O'Higgins sometimes used English in letters to Spanish-speaking friends, as a primitive security device. A good deal of his correspondence in later years was in English.

liberation of Peru, he wrote a long letter to Fray Camilo Henrí-quez, in the course of which he expressed his revolutionary faith in unmistakable terms:

It is evident that the Republics of the New World bear the vanguard of the freedom of the whole world, and that destiny is leading them on to break the chains of the human race; for in the example of America may be found the most encouraging hopes of the philosopher and the patriot. The centuries of oppression have passed; the human spirit yearns for its freedom; and now there shines the dawn of a complete re-ordering of civil society through the irresistible progress of opinion and enlightenment.[1]

But O'Higgins' strong practical bias led him to revise his early views on the possibility of fully representative government in Chile. By the time he came to assume supreme power in 1817, he believed in the necessity for a strong, energetic government to carry the country through dangerous times and to implant a programme of radical reforms. Public agitation could not be tolerated. This was a theme on which he insisted from the moment the Army of the Andes entered Chile in February 1817: 'Order will be established along with liberty.' The words are from his first proclamation.[2] 'In the present circumstances', de-clared a newspaper of 1819, 'what we most need is a *strong and vigorous Executive Power*.'[3] O'Higgins saw it as his duty to supply just this. As one deputy to the 1822 Preparatory Convention put it, 'It was necessary to destroy the monster of anarchy which al-ways raises its venomous head in any country passing from servitude to freedom.'[4]

O'Higgins was very well aware of the need to crush 'anarchy'. Instructions sent to the provinces from the central government throughout his period contained numerous references to the importance of dealing with 'anarchists' and 'enemies of the system',[5] and O'Higgins himself had little patience with those inclined to be disorderly. The discontents of Santiago roused

[1] Letter of 1 October 1824 (*borrador*), Cruz, *Epistolario*, II, 43.
[2] *El General de Vanguardia del Ejército de los Andes a los naturales de Chile*, Arch.O'H. VII, 123.
[3] *El Telégrafo*, no 12, 15 June 1819.
[4] *Mercurio de Chile*, no. 7, n.d., *CAPC*, IX, 279.   [5] A.M.I. vol. 46, *passim*.

him on one occasion to tell San Martín: 'Those people need a big stick; they are very revolutionary; but nobody will joke when the whip cracks.'[1] Dangers at home and abroad, O'Higgins believed, forced him to assume dictatorial privileges, in the manner of ancient Rome.

From the beginning I was charged with the Supreme Directorship, without limitation of powers. In the same way, the free state of Rome, in moments of greatest crisis, used to hide the tables of the law beneath a veil and entrust absolute power to a Dictator.[2]

This notion accorded well with the political ideas elaborated by Camilo Henríquez during his exile in Buenos Aires after 1814. Departing from his earlier ardent liberalism (to which he reverted later), Henríquez insisted on the need for strong, untrammelled government. 'It is indispensable', he wrote, 'that the supreme authority should reside in some very exalted person, if possible someone of august birth... It is indispensable to invest him with the power and force to make himself obeyed and feared.'[3] It was this type of feeling—so alien to Henríquez' earlier *exaltado* liberalism—that caused many Americans to contemplate monarchy as a solution to the problem of firm government.

But however strong the government was, it could not transgress the limits of principle. It had duties as well as powers. As the official gazette expressed it,

Those with whom authority has been deposited know well that they have been placed at the head of the nation in order to give direction to the political mass on behalf of the community, in order to oblige society to follow their own example and fulfil the conditions of the social pact; consequently, they believe themselves to be answerable for the use they make of the resources and powers entrusted to them, and pay the homage due to public opinion.[4]

[1] Letter of 27 July 1817, Cruz, *Epistolario*, I, 104.
[2] *Manifiesto del Capitan General*, 1820, p. 5.
[3] 'Ensayo acerca de las causas de los sucesos desastrosos de Chile' [1815–16], Silva Castro, *Escritos políticos*, pp. 186–7. Henríquez' temporary deviation from liberalism was emphasized by his translation (Buenos Aires, 1816) of part of Robert Bisset's *Sketch of Democracy* (London, 1796), a work which condemned democracy as 'subversive of social order and destructive of happiness' (p. 341) and recommended strong traditionalist forms of government.
[4] *Gaceta Ministerial de Chile*, tomo 2, no. 10, 18 September 1819.

This was a faithful reflection of O'Higgins' own view of the matter. He never forgot that authoritarian government could easily degenerate into despotism, and, indeed, from the moment he became Supreme Director, he strove to find ways of basing his power on the consent of the general will. In the '*Patria Vieja*', he had once described the government of the day as 'a truly paternal government...which issues from the unanimous choice of a free people',[1] and these words perfectly define his own philosophy. In other words, he was to have supreme power, but supreme power responsible to the people. He had to have a definite mandate. And it is significant that he chose to interpret his own elevation to the Supreme Directorship in such terms.

The people of this capital, freely using their inalienable right to give themselves the form of government most suited to their needs, and by the *interpretative will* of the other provinces (which...could not be provided in a more solemn manner), decided unanimously, in Cabildo Abierto, to confer on me the honourable and difficult position of Supreme Director.[2]

It will be seen from this that O'Higgins took it on himself to interpret the will of those provinces which (in February 1817) were still either under royalist rule or in process of liberation. Only in this way could he claim that his elevation to supreme power represented the unanimous wish of the nation. But, whatever the anomalies, O'Higgins evidently believed that some degree of popular consent had been achieved. In addition, he believed firmly that an element of trust between government and governed was essential; he demanded 'that reciprocal trust without which a government becomes impotent, or is forced to degenerate into despotism'.[3]

There is some small evidence to indicate that O'Higgins wanted to institute a fully representative system of government as soon as the first military crisis was over, but was prevented from doing so by his advisers.[4] Whatever the truth of this, it is plain that he

[1] *Proclama*, 28 January 1814, *Arch.O'H.* II, 36.
[2] *Bando solemne*, 17 February 1817, *Arch.O'H.* VII, 170–1.
[3] *Proclama*, 17 February 1817, *Arch.O'H.* VII, 169.
[4] See Miers, II, 94; also the extraordinary notes for a constitution, in O'Higgins' handwriting, providing for a bicameral legislature with frequent elections [1818], A.B.A. vol. 25–4(25), fo. 361.

soon came round to the view that the full introduction of parliamentary rule would have to be postponed to some future date. The unhappy experience of the Congress of 1811 tended to deter Chileans from attempting the experiment again, at any rate too hastily. The 1811 Congress was now remembered as 'that body...with the name of Congress, [which] served only to introduce discord'.[1] O'Higgins himself analysed its failure in his speech to the opening session of the Preparatory Convention of 1822: 'the value of good order had not been experienced', he said, 'and the passion of some men was superior to reason'.[2] Yet the need for some sort of representative element was a crucial part of O'Higgins' political outlook; he could not let it slip away unnoticed. 'My wish', he said in 1822, 'has always been—and I upheld it in the 1811 Congress—that Chile should adopt a representative government, whatever its title.'[3] This did not mean that O'Higgins advocated an indiscriminate suffrage, any more than his contemporaries. General José María de la Cruz,[4] in his recollections of O'Higgins, summarized the hero's views in the following way:

His political principles were republican and democratic, but had nothing to do with that democracy that pretends to submit the exercise of the public administration to the common people. These democratic views notwithstanding, he believed that the exercise of this power belonged solely to the sensible and independent section of the people.[5]

Although he felt that it would be difficult to establish a representative system of government in the immediate future, O'Higgins had little doubt that this was an end he must always keep in view: 'only an energetic and vigorous government could...prepare public opinion to receive suitable institutions in the course of time'.[6] Perhaps O'Higgins' judicious words to the 1822 Convention, quoted overleaf, can be allowed to summarize this aspect of his political philosophy.

---

[1] *Gazeta Ministerial de Chile*, 23 May 1818.   [2] *Acta*, 23 July 1822, SCL, VI, 26.
[3] *Ibid.* SCL, VI, 28.
[4] José María de la Cruz Prieto (1801–75); son of the patriot general Luis de la Cruz (1768–1828); fought as a captain at Chacabuco and Maipó; Minister of War 1830–1; General 1833; leader of the liberal revolt of 1851.
[5] Cruz, *Recuerdos de O'Higgins*, p. 73.   [6] O'Higgins and Irisarri, p. 62.

I an well aware that this honourable Convention is not invested with
the fully representative character that can be found in other constituted countries and which we too *will enjoy later on*; nevertheless, as
it is a respectable public gathering, and the only gathering that could
legally be held at the present time, I direct my words to it as if the whole
Chilean people—whose interests I have watched over like a father—
were congregated in this hall.[1]

Obviously, the representative element was important in any
'liberal system consonant with the enlightenment of this century',[2] and it is of particular interest to note that even in the
earliest months of his regime O'Higgins went to some pains to
consult the general will. The system of *subscripción*, which he used
to gain public assent both for the Proclamation of Independence
and for the 1818 Constitution was, in essence, just such a consultation. Publishing the draft of the 1818 Constitution, O'Higgins
accompanied it with some pertinent comments justifying this
particular method.

My object in preparing this plan for a draft constitution has not been
to present it to the people as a constitutional law but rather as a project,
which must be approved or rejected by the general will...It will never
be said of Chile that, in forming the basis of her government, she went
beyond the rightful limits of equity.[3]

The machinery of the *subscripción* method was simple enough. It
consisted of the opening of two books or registers, in each subdivision of the state, for affirmative and negative signatures.
O'Higgins believed that this plebiscitary mechanism gave him a
suitable sanction for his first measures, and that there were proper
historical precedents.

As the summoning of a Congress was impracticable, Independence and
the Constitution were sworn in an equivalent but more popular manner. In the same way France swore to the Constitution of 24th
Frimaire, Year VIII, and the Consulate of Bonaparte on 18th May
1802; and, to take a worthier example, it was in this manner that God
willed the approval, in the desert, of the Divine Law and the Constitution of the Republic of Israel.[4]

---

[1] *SCL*, VI, 27. (My italics.)
[2] O'Higgins to the King of Holland, 1 April 1817, *Arch.O'H.* VII, 175.
[3] *AR*, I, 52.   [4] *Manifiesto del Capitan General*, p. 6.

In addition to these attempts to base his rule on popular consent, O'Higgins also tried to share his authority in a more constitutional manner. The 1818 Constitution was frankly provisional in character, and contained no proposals for any popularly elected assembly. Its chief feature was the nomination of an advisory Senate to help the Supreme Director govern. It was expressly admitted that this Senate was a substitute for a proper, elected Congress.[1] The Supreme Director was to name the five members of the Senate himself (together with their five *suplentes* or official substitutes), but there was to be no limit to their term of office. Decisions by this Senate could override Directorial opposition after three submissions,[2] and, although it might seem that O'Higgins' power of nomination might render the senators harmless, clashes did sometimes occur. As Alcibiades Roldán noted, in his extensive study of the subject, 'the Supreme Director had a constant fault-finder in the form of the Senate; and...on numerous occasions the power of the one was restrained, directed and even annulled by the power of the other'.[3] This could probably not have happened under a less scrupulous Executive.

The Constitution of 1822 was a far more complex document in every respect, and was, in fact, the first full-scale constitution in Chilean history.[4] A normal bicameral legislature was provided for, the lower house to be elected by the public. During parliamentary recesses a Court of Representatives was to carry out the functions of the legislature *vis-à-vis* the Supreme Director. The Constitution also set up some proper electoral machinery,[5] though this never went into operation. 'Behind all this apparatus and show', concludes a North American commentator, 'stood the simple fact that the Supreme Director was still an all-powerful dictator.'[6] But this statement does little justice to O'Higgins' genuine intention (perverted, as it seems, by bad advice) to bring about a state of affairs where his wide powers would be placed

[1] 1818 Constitution, tít. III, cap. I, art. único. The 1818 *carta* is printed in *AR*, I, 52.
[2] Tít. III, cap. III, art 6.
[3] Roldán, 'Los desacuerdos', p. 178.
[4] The 1822 *carta* is printed in *AR*, I, 69. For general criticism of the 1818 and 1822 *cartas* see Shaw, ch. 4, and Vivanco Cabezón.
[5] Art. 38.   [6] Shaw, p. 94.

more directly under ultimate civilian control. O'Higgins ruled as a dictator, it is true, but his democratic instincts were constantly hinting at the limits of authority.

I must now turn from the nature of O'Higgins' general political outlook to the policies pursued by his government. Obviously, his first aim was to clear Chile of Spanish troops. 'National Liberty must precede Civil Liberty,' roundly affirmed the government gazette a month after liberation.[1] Yet the establishment of civil liberty was one of O'Higgins' aims from the start. After the victory of Maipó, he proclaimed that he was now solely pre-occupied with 'preparing those measures which will assure the Chileans their freedom, without introducing licence, into which other nascent states have fallen'.[2] But O'Higgins' conception of the role of government went very much further than this. The Supreme Director intended to follow a programme of vigorous reforms. A verse hung from the side of the Consulado building during the *fiestas patrias* of 1819 provides a succinct illustration of his hopes in this direction: 'Wretched inertia, persecuted by firm constancy, will flee away.'[3] The backwardness of colonial times, then, was to be replaced with energy and determination, and the desire for real progress. 'Wipe out forever', O'Higgins told the 1822 Convention, 'institutions founded on a colonial plan.'[4] And in his manifesto of August 1820 he pleaded for public co-operation in order 'to uproot the inveterate vices of three centuries; to reform our ideas, customs and institutions through virtue and probity'.[5] Chile had to be *improved*. This was the underlying aim of O'Higgins' government, and John Miers has left an interesting and amusing anecdote which illustrates the theme superbly well:

I have at times spoken to him of the probably distant period, when effectual ameliorations could take place, and he would then expatiate

[1] *Viva la Patria, Gazeta del Supremo Gobierno*, 19 March 1817.
[2] Decree of 18 May 1818, *CAPC*, v, 33.   [3] *El Telégrafo*, no. 39, 8 October 1819.
[4] *SCL*, VI, 28.   [5] *Manifiesto del Capitan General*, p. 8.

on the hope of introducing arts and civilization among the people, and of improving the condition of the poorer classes. On one occasion, in a burst of enthusiasm, he said, 'If they will not become happy by their own efforts, they shall be made happy by force, by God they *shall* be happy.'[1]

We should note, at this point, a strong egalitarian trend in O'Higgins' thought. It seems probable that he went further in his views on equality than the general mass of Chilean revolutionaries. 'By nature I detest aristocracy,' he had written in a now famous letter during the *'Patria Vieja'*, 'and adorable equality is my idol.'[2] The Supreme Directorship gave him a chance to expand on these sentiments which, on their own, might be considered as little more than an angry outburst. His anti-aristocratic views were supported by a small circle of friends. Juan Pablo Fretes, his old revolutionary companion, urged him in March 1817 to 'stifle that aristocracy which is already beginning to raise its head'.[3] O'Higgins' failure to do so cost him his power, but in any case the task was probably beyond him. For, as Pueyrredón had warned San Martín, 'feudalism' still prevailed in Chile 'in all its strength'.[4] But it is clear that O'Higgins went to no very great pains to conciliate the landed aristocracy, and indeed a handful of his measures seem to have been directly aimed at the aristocracy. O'Higgins' most serious attack was the attempted abolition of the *mayorazgos* in June 1818. Rightly or wrongly, the aristocracy believed that the *mayorazgo* was essential to the preservation of its supreme economic and social position—though it is worth noting that the final abolition of the institution, by President Montt in the 1850s, had virtually no effect on the power of the landed oligarchy in Chile. O'Higgins, however, shared the aristocracy's view of the importance of *mayorazgos*, which he regarded as 'one of the abuses established by the feudal government', and, moreover, as one of the abuses 'which most combat the liberal system'.[5] O'Higgins' decree abolishing the *mayorazgos* had no

[1]
[3] Miers, II, 36–7.　　[2] To Juan Florencio Terrada, 20 February 1812, *Arch.O'H.* I, 208.
[4] Fretes to O'Higgins, 9 March 1817, *Arch.O'H.* VII, 199.
Pueyrredón, *Campaña de los Andes*, facsimile 10.
[5] Decree of 5 June 1818, *CHDI*, xxv, 438.

effect at all. But, despite this failure, there were other measures which could prove highly irritating to the aristocracy.

One of the Supreme Director's first acts after assuming power was to decree the immediate removal of noble insignia from public doorways. He announced this measure in uncompromising terms:

In any society an individual ought to distinguish himself solely by his virtue and merit; in a Republic, the use of those hieroglyphics which proclaim the nobility of ancestors is intolerable; [since it is] often a nobility conferred as a reward for services which degrade the human race.[1]

The government gazette strongly supported O'Higgins' move: 'In the end', it asked, 'is all that shameful and scandalous necromancy capable of changing the condition of man?' Nature demanded equality, and O'Higgins' decree was a step towards it.[2]

Six months later, in September 1817, O'Higgins decreed the abolition of all hereditary titles, which he described as 'miserable relics of the feudal system which has ruled in Chile' and as the 'effect of a blind routine'. Under the decree, 'Counts, Marquises, Noblemen or Knights of such-and-such an order' could no longer be given titles, 'nor will they be able to accept them, . . . and will be considered simply as citizens'.[3] Though this measure hardly touched the economic power of the oligarchy, its significance should not be regarded as trifling. The Chilean aristocracy's affection for its titles was profound. An incident recounted in the memoirs of José Zapiola illustrates this point fairly clearly. While disembarking at Valparaíso in 1817, the noble exiles returning from Juan Fernández unpacked their plaques and decorations of nobility, and carried them ashore, much to the surprise of the Argentine soldiers on hand.[4]

O'Higgins' efforts to weaken the influence of the aristocracy failed. But there were other issues to which he could devote his attention with greater chances of success, and two of these—education and immigration—may be taken as representative. His improved society could only be brought about by increased

---

[1] *Bando* of 22 March 1817, *Viva la Patria*, *Gazeta del Supremo Gobierno*, 26 March 1817.
[2] Editorial, *ibid*.
[3] Decree of 15 September 1817, *SCL*, III, 16.   [4] Zapiola, p. 271.

education, and this was a field in which much remained to be done: 'a republic as nascent as ours', wrote one patriot, 'is not populated by sages'.[1] There was a persistence of the old feeling of shame and dishonour at the state of the educational system. The official gazette expressed it like this:

Three quarters of the famous Code of Lycurgus were devoted to education; after so many centuries, and living in the most enlightened century of all, shall we allow our youth to be less civilized than the Spartans?[2]

O'Higgins shared this attitude. The 1818 Constitution gave the Senate special responsibilities towards education,[3] which it ful-filled as well as was possible under the circumstances. O'Higgins himself placed an intensely practical emphasis on education. His words to the Convention of 1822 provide the best indication of his chief preoccupations in this sphere.

The current state of civilization and learning discloses the need to stimulate, or rather to plan, our education and learning in an effective and sufficient manner. We need to shape statesmen, legislators, economists, judges, businessmen, engineers, architects, seamen, hydraulic experts, mechanics, chemists, artists, farmers, merchants...[4]

Education, then, had an essential role in the re-ordering of civil society and in the economic improvement of the country. It was not to be confined to the aristocracy; it is significant that O'Higgins' decree promoting the Lancasterian System in Chile spoke of the need to expand 'the instruction of all classes but especially the poor'.[5]

Education was one way in which Chile could be improved; immigration, believed O'Higgins, was another. In 1819 Juan Egaña gave the government some gratuitous advice on how immigration could be developed. He urged that an open invitation should be extended to families who were leaving Europe because

---

[1] *Sol de Chile*, 10 July 1818, p. 8.
[2] *Viva la Patria, Gaceta del Supremo Gobierno*, 19 March 1817.
[3] Tít. III, cap. III, art. 8.   [4] *SCL*, VI, 28.
[5] Browning, p. 78. The standard work on the attempt to introduce the Lancasterian System is Domingo Amunátegui Solar, *El sistema de Lancaster en Chile i en otros paises sudamericanos* (1895).

of poverty or persecution, with an offer of land, cheap labour, and special privileges.[1] O'Higgins did not carry out this programme to the letter, but he did, through O'Brien, attempt to attract artisans from Britain,[2] and remained sympathetic to schemes of settlement. When Schmidtmeyer proposed that colonies of Swiss emigrants should be established, O'Higgins reported to his Senate that the idea should be considered very seriously, 'in view of the present underpopulated state of Chile'. Swiss emigrants, he added, possessed 'industry, laboriousness, ideas of freedom, a reasonable education, and, above all, the same religion as this country'.[3] Definite incentives would, of course, have to be provided, as he told the 1822 Convention: 'Attracting foreign farmers, workmen, and capitalists is impossible without offering them considerable guarantees, and all the freedom they enjoy in other nations.'[4] O'Higgins remained interested in schemes of emigration long after his abdication from the Supreme Directorship. Not long after the start of his exile in Peru, he opened a correspondence with Sir John Doyle on the subject of Irish emigration to Chile,[5] and in 1831 he told a Royal Navy captain that 'Chile presents the most inviting field in the world for Irish Colonization'.[6]

But by whatever means, Chile had to be developed. This was the fundamental element in O'Higgins' philosophy of government. Trade—'civilization's most executive instrument', as he called it[7]—had to be fomented. Vices had to be eradicated, the country policed, Santiago replanned, colonial society transformed. The various measures taken by O'Higgins—many of them vain—are a part of Chilean history in general, and need not be enlarged on here. The important point is that the regime was a progressive one, within the limitations of the period, and more so than most of the other Latin American regimes of the day. 'As time goes on, as civilization grows, as communication with other

[1] *Cartas Pehuenches*, no. 10, p. 5.   [2] Barros Arana, XIII, 591–2.
[3] To the Senate, 31 January 1821, *SCL*, v, 31. Schmidtmeyer does not mention this scheme in his *Travels into Chile*.
[4] *SCL*, VI, 28.
[5] O'Higgins to Doyle, 13 September 1823, A.B.A. vol. 25-4(13), fo. 660.
[6] To Coghlan, 20 August 1831, F.O. 16/16, p. 149.
[7] To Henríquez, 1 October 1824, Cruz, *Epistolario*, II, 44.

nations increases, we shall discover and understand what is better for us.' The words are Henríquez', from the 1822 Convention,[1] yet they could easily serve as the motto for the O'Higgins government.

MONARCHY OR REPUBLIC?

There was one particular political debate, largely hidden in the shadows, which was carried on for most of the six years O'Higgins ruled Chile: the issue of monarchy. It is a question which quite naturally has aroused a good deal of discussion, and there is little need to rehearse all the evidence in full.[2] But some estimate of O'Higgins' attitude to the various monarchic proposals which circulated seems indicated here.

In the first place, it has to be admitted that for the whole of the six years in question, there existed a very considerable official doubt as to the final form of government an independent Chile would adopt. To the magnates who assembled in Santiago to offer supreme power to San Martín, the choice seemed clear enough: either it was to be 'dictatorship, which...is the most suitable at the present time, or...the absolute republic'.[3] Nevertheless, the issue remained clouded by indecision for several years. It was not until 1823 that the word Republic was used in a Chilean constitution. The Proclamation of Independence, for instance, quite definitely gave the country 'full ability to adopt the form of Government which best suits its interests',[4] thus clearly indicating that a final choice had still to be made. O'Higgins showed no unseemly haste in settling the matter. Irisarri (whose ideas seem to have become monarchist by this stage) urged O'Higgins to make up his mind. European recognition of Chilean independence was difficult, he wrote, 'for nobody knows what it is that has to be recognized, whether it is a democratic republic, an aristocracy, or a monarchy, or a government without principle'.[5] At much the same period, Irisarri wrote in a book he had published in London that 'we cannot for now indicate the form of government which

[1] *Acta*, 17 August 1822, *SCL*, VI, 77.
[2] The fullest account is Domenico Rodríguez.
[3] Ruiz Tagle to San Martín, 15 February 1817, *Arch.O'H.* VII, 160.   [4] *AR*, I, 14.
[5] To O'Higgins, 25 November 1820, *Arch.O'H.* IV, 283.

will be established in Chile'.[1] O'Higgins was not, however, forced into taking a decision by Irisarri's blandishments, and it is entirely possible that he may have been delaying matters because of his flexible approach to the idea of a Spanish American federation. The Senate, instructing a Chilean emissary to Colombia in 1821, ordered him to ascertain the state of public feeling there on the question. Chile's position was

that nothing has been resolved or agreed, that it is hoped that the opinion of South America will become uniform, and, by means of a confederation, will agree what is most in conformity with the public interest...of the federated governments.[2]

O'Higgins confirmed this position in a letter to Irisarri the following March. Peru, Mexico, Colombia and Argentina, he wrote, had not yet decided on their final form of government. Chile should wait for their decision, in order to adopt the same form of government as the other American states.[3] Thus the way was left open for a monarchy in Chile if need be.

That there existed a certain warmth towards monarchist projects is not open to question. It sprang from the general disillusionment of seeing how the earliest experiments in self-government had fared. It was this type of feeling that had caused Camilo Henríquez, otherwise an ardent liberal, to imagine an impartial observer telling the Chileans, 'Republican forms are in contradiction with your education, religion, customs and habits.'[4] Whatever force this sentiment had in Chile on its own merits, the issue was kept alive by the secret activities of San Martín. There is no need to recapitulate here the sorry history of Argentine monarchist schemes both utopian and practical; San Martín and the Lautaro Lodge were in the thick of such plans, but only after the liberation of Chile did there seem to be a chance of fulfilling them. San Martín told an English observer in Buenos Aires in mid May 1817 that the Chileans were better suited to live under a monarchy than under a republic,[5] and to his friend the Earl of

[1] *Memoria sobre el estado presente de Chile*, p. 28.
[2] *Acta*, 22 June 1821, *SCL*, v, 209.
[3] O'Higgins to Irisarri, 16 March 1822, *Arch.O'H.* IV, 321.
[4] Silva Castro, *Escritos políticos*, p. 186.
[5] Staples to Hamilton, 25 May 1817, Webster, doc. 288*a*, I, 553.

Fife he claimed that 'democratical notions' had 'lost ninety per cent' in Chile, just as they had in the Argentine provinces.[1] In a now famous conversation with Commodore William Bowles, at Valparaíso in February 1818, San Martín 'threw out the idea of dividing South America amongst the principal European powers, and forming such a number of kingdoms as might provide for a prince of each royal house'.[2]

The first effect of San Martín's advocacy of such ideas was felt in Chile the following spring. On 29 October 1818, San Martín returned to Santiago from the Argentine, and made it known that the United Provinces were intending to negotiate European recognition on the basis of a monarchic scheme. At the same moment, a set of diplomatic instructions was drawn up for Irisarri, who was on the point of leaving for England as Chilean representative.[3] These instructions, drafted by Joaquín Echeverría and probably Irisarri himself, may or may not have been approved by O'Higgins at this stage; at all events, he withheld his signature. Irisarri, according to the set of instructions, was to give the impression in Europe that Chile

would not be far from adopting a moderate or constitutional monarchy —the form of government which, more than any other, most coincides with...the legislation, the customs, the preoccupations, the hierarchies...and even the topography of the Chilean State.[4]

At the same time Irisarri was to select a suitable candidate for the Chilean throne, preferably from the house of Orange, Brunswick or Braganza. But, while he was on his way through Argentina, Irisarri was told by Bernardo Monteagudo that the instructions were valueless without O'Higgins' signature. Irisarri accordingly returned the text to O'Higgins, asking him to sign it and forward it to London. O'Higgins, it is recorded, summoned the members of the Senate to his presence, and solemnly burned the instructions.[5] Such was the abrupt fate of the only direct Chilean move to

---

[1] To the 4th Earl of Fife, 9 December 1817, *ibid.* doc. 288*c*, I, 557.
[2] Bowles to Croker, 14 February 1818, Graham and Humphreys, p. 226. Cf. Oyarzún and Fernández Valdés, which contains translated extracts from this letter.
[3] San Martín is said to have played a big part in securing Irisarri's nomination: see Yrarrázaval Larraín, 'San Martín y los proyectos monárquicos', p. 5.
[4] Art. 10 of the Instructions, Donoso, *Irisarri*, p. 81.   [5] *Ibid.* p. 86.

import a monarchy. It had probably, in essence, represented little more than a result of 'San Martín's manoeuvrings'.[1]

San Martín's invasion of Peru and the setting up of the Protectoral regime there in 1821 brought the orbit of his monarchism to its apogee.[2] The widespread suspicion that he intended to found a Pacific Empire, with himself as Emperor, was not confined to Peruvians and Chileans.[3] Moreover, he attempted to negotiate with the royalist general Canterac on the basis of a monarchic settlement of the war.[4] Finally, and most significantly of all, he entrusted Juan García del Río and James Paroissien with a secret mission to Europe, with the aim of inviting a European prince to accept the Peruvian throne.[5] San Martín evidently believed that he could associate the Chilean government with the venture. 'I believe you are convinced', he wrote to O'Higgins, 'of the impossibility of making these countries republics.'[6]

What was O'Higgins' attitude to the question of monarchy? It may be true, as the Peruvian historian Paz Soldán suggested, that he had been involved in some kind of tacit agreement with San Martín and Pueyrredón before the liberation of Chile.[7] San Martín, as we have just seen, clearly believed that O'Higgins shared his own views on the desirability of monarchy for Spanish America. But, despite these possibilities, there can be small doubt that O'Higgins rejected monarchy as the solution to the problem of firm government. His behaviour when the 1818 instructions were returned to him, whatever his original part in the drafting had been,[8] is only one of the many pieces of evidence pointing to this. His reaction to the García del Río and Paroissien mission, when it passed through Santiago, was by no means a downright condemnation of monarchy, it is true, but neither did he show any real warmth towards San Martín's scheme. García del Río and Paroissien reported back to Lima that H. E. indicated that he did

---

[1] Yrarrázaval Larraín, 'San Martín y los proyectos monárquicos', p. 11.
[2] See Mitre, III, 236–40.   [3] Miers, II, 31.
[4] César Pacheco Vélez, 'Sobre el monarquismo de San Martín', *Anuario de Estudios Americanos*, IX (Seville, 1952), p. 457.
[5] Paz Soldán, pp. 272–3.
[6] Letter of 30 November 1821, *Arch.O'H.* VIII, 204.   [7] Paz Soldán, p. 268.
[8] Donoso considers it to have been a moment of weakness on his part (*Irisarri*, p. 79); Orrego Vicuña suggests a senatorial conspiracy behind his back (*O'Higgins*, pp. 233–4).

not doubt that our plan was advantageous and adaptable in Peru; but that in Chile, where there was no fixed opinion about forms of government,...the best thing was to let matters continue as at present'.[1]

Here, at any rate, O'Higgins gave the impression that he was playing for time, perhaps in the hope that the scheme would die a natural death—as indeed it did.

But there are several other strong indications of O'Higgins' real attitude towards the issue of monarchy. The United States agent in Chile, W. G. D. Worthington, came straight to the point in one of his conversations with the Supreme Director.

I asked him pointedly...Do you intend to have any kind of Monarchy? He unhesitatingly replied—That they intended to have a confederated Republican form of government.[2]

Another North American agent, Judge Prevost, who had himself been heard to recommend limited monarchy for Chile,[3] received a letter from O'Higgins in 1820 which refuted certain suggestions that he had been planning to introduce monarchy. 'You are convinced', wrote O'Higgins, 'of my republican sentiments, and I can assure you that I would rather die, than to stain my name with such a Dereliction of my Duty and of my principles.'[4] Prevost, apparently enthusiastic about this assurance, forwarded the letter to his government, and later wrote to the Secretary of State with a final verdict on O'Higgins' attitude: 'He is truly a republican Patriot and in heart opposed to everything in the shape of Monarchy and will resist its adoption.'[5]

O'Higgins did not, however, confine his expressions of republicanism to North Americans. At a banquet in honour of the Colombian plenipotentiary Joaquín Mosquera, during which there were several references (in toasts) to monarchic schemes,[6] O'Higgins was reported to have pronounced a resounding

---

[1] Paz Soldán, pp. 273–4.
[2] Worthington to Adams, 26 January 1819, Manning, II, 1029.
[3] Robinson, 'Diario personal', p. 115.
[4] O'Higgins to Prevost, 21 April 1820, Manning, II, 1945.
[5] To Adams, 6 January 1821, *ibid.* II, 1047. Cf. Poinsett's opinion, cited in chapter 3 (see p. 124). [6] *Mercurio de Chile*, no. 12, 25 September 1822, *CAPC*, IX, 356–7.

denunciation of 'the pretension to introduce the decaying system of crowned heads into America'.¹ Two letters written by O'Higgins, both in October 1821, equally attest that this was no passing phase as far as he was concerned. To his friend Gaspar Marín, O'Higgins represented the idea of introducing monarchy as a betrayal of the Chilean revolution: 'It is necessary that we should shun those cold calculators who long for monarchy,' he wrote. He also urged Marín to write a book on politics in order 'to prevent European monarchism' from spreading.² O'Higgins was similarly emphatic to a Peruvian monarchist, José Rivadeneira y Texada. What, he asked, would the reaction of the enlightened nations of the world be when they saw that the outcome of the revolution had been nothing more than 'a nominal change of dynasty?'³ O'Higgins had evidently promised his friend José Ignacio Cienfuegos⁴ that he would sooner be broken into fragments than have to enter into a monarchic agreement.⁵ A good case, therefore, can be made out for O'Higgins as a firm republican resisting the ill-advised pretensions of such monarchists as San Martín. But this is far from suggesting that he never temporized with the monarchists, particularly when San Martín's influence in Chile was at its height. O'Higgins' position, in fact, was a more creditable one than many people realize today. He was undoubtedly under a certain amount of pressure to involve Chile in the various Argentine and Peruvian schemes to establish monarchies, and, at the same time, he could hardly have foreseen that all these schemes were to end in failure.

THE O'HIGGINS REGIME: A VERDICT

Is it possible to give a verdict on the six years of the O'Higgins regime? It is true, as Alberto Edwards has written, that 'the forces... which sustained him were scattered to the four winds on

¹ J. M. Cruz, *Recuerdos de O'Higgins*, p. 75.
² Letter of 18 October 1821, Cruz, *Epistolario*, I, 280–1.
³ Letter of 24 October 1821, Cruz, *Epistolario*, I, 282.
⁴ José Ignacio Cienfuegos Astorga (1762–1845); Senator 1814; Senator 1818–22 and 1831–4; Chilean agent in Rome 1822–4; Bishop of Concepción 1832–7.
⁵ Cienfuegos to O'Higgins, 18 January 1822, Vicuña Mackenna, *Vida de O'Higgins*, p. 262.

his downfall'.[1] In a political sense, at least, O'Higgins' attempt to create the Chilean republic was a failure. And yet it would, as a great modern Chilean historian has put it, 'be an unpardonable error not to proclaim him as the most determined of the reformers, resolved to implant in Chile a regime of tolerance and social justice which would open the way to a system with truly democratic roots'.[2] To O'Higgins fell two principal tasks: first, the organization of military victory in Chile and Peru, and second, the building of a new and transformed Chile. In the first of these objects, discussion of which falls outside the scope of the present study, he was brilliantly successful. In Vicuña Mackenna's vivid phrase, Chile 'was enslaved and became free; free, she freed others'.[3] But, in his domestic policies, O'Higgins never managed to consolidate his rule, and mounting opposition, together with several bad miscalculations on his own part, eventually toppled him from power. But whatever else he may have been, whatever mistakes he may have made, O'Higgins certainly did not merit Bolívar's description of him as 'a stupid despot, hated generally for his bad administration',[4] a view which Bolívar maintained, in the teeth of San Martín's loyal objections, at the Guayaquil interview. O'Higgins was neither stupid nor a despot, and though the Chilean opinion of his administration grew less favourable after 1820, he remained personally popular to the end.

O'Higgins' chief difficulty lay in reconciling his obviously liberal and progressive ideas with the omnipotent 'empire of circumstances'. It was the familiar Latin American dilemma of the times. It was the circumstances, rather than O'Higgins' own reluctance, which prevented the introduction of a fully 'democratic' political system into Chile. 'The experience of eleven years', wrote José María de Rozas in 1821, 'should have taught everybody the infallible *dogma* that freedom is a good juice, but difficult to digest, and that very sound stomachs are needed to

[1] *Organización política*, p. 57.   [2] Donoso, *Ideas políticas*, p. 63.
[3] *Vida de O'Higgins*, p. 262.
[4] Bolívar to Santander, 14 February 1823, Vicente Lecuna (ed.), *Cartas del Libertador* (10 vols. Caracas, 1929–30), III, 146. Yet Bolívar had flattered O'Higgins to his face in a letter written in January 1823 (Vicuña Mackenna, *Vida de O'Higgins*, p. 501 n.) and their later relations were reasonably cordial.

carry it.'¹ The solution, as O'Higgins saw it, was to establish what Julio Heise González has styled a 'legal authoritarianism'.² That the O'Higgins regime was authoritarian is obvious; that it was as legal as possible should by now be similarly clear. For O'Higgins rarely overstepped the mark of the law; and he tried hard to ground his authority in popular consent through vague consultative mechanisms.

The basic element in O'Higgins' attempt to reform Chile was, however, a strong executive power. Feliú Cruz is right, in this sense, to regard O'Higgins as the real precursor of Diego Portales, who also believed in a 'strong and creative government',³ and a more direct link between the two regimes may be seen in O'Higgins' own admission in 1831 that he had once secretly designated Joaquín Prieto, Portales' submissive President, as his political heir.⁴ Yet one should clearly differentiate between the relatively negative (though highly successful) government of law and order devised by Portales and the progressive dictatorship of O'Higgins. Portales lacked O'Higgins' innate optimism and his belief that society *could* be altered. Indeed, he explicitly relied on the inertia of Chilean society to perpetuate his type of government.⁵

O'Higgins may also be said to have been linked to the past as well as to the future. His emphasis on practical projects was in many respects reminiscent of the kind of enlightened rule practised by his own father in Chile and Peru some twenty years earlier. Flattering parallels could be drawn between the two men, with more than a little justification. As Rodríguez Aldea wrote, in 1823, 'The first, by abolishing the *encomiendas*, did away with the last remnants of feudal slavery; the second, sword in hand, transforming the Colony into a Republic, liberated us from political slavery.'⁶ And yet, as I have tried to make clear, Bernardo O'Higgins was more than a liberator. He was a reformer as well. Captain Basil Hall, that indefatigable English travel-diarist, left an eloquent impression of Chile as it was towards the end of O'Higgins' Supreme Directorship:

¹ To San Martín, 6 September 1821, *Arch.O'H.* IX, 134.   ² *150 años*, p. 22.
³ *Pensamiento político*, p. 62.
⁴ Vicuña Mackenna, *Vida de O'Higgins*, p. 583.
⁵ See chapter 9, p. 359.   ⁶ *Satisfacción pública*, pp. 130–1.

Bernardo O'Higgins

A spirit of inquiry and intelligence animated the whole society; schools were multiplied in every town; libraries established; and every encouragement was given to literature and the arts;...in the gait of every man might be traced the air of *conscious freedom* and independence.[1]

This was no mean achievement. Personal integrity, progressive principles, and a practical approach—these qualities set Bernardo O'Higgins apart from many of his fellow liberators. His was an honest failure, indeed a brilliant one.

[1] Hall, I, 78.

7

JUAN EGAÑA
1823-1824

Up to 1822 at least, the course of Chilean history had been intertwined with the epic struggle for the emancipation of the old Viceroyalty of Peru. With the dissolution of the great liberating partnership of O'Higgins, San Martín and Cochrane, Chile moved away from her involvement in the major current of South American history and abandoned her supporting role to the rising states of the North, precariously united in the federation of Grancolombia. For the rest of the 1820s Chile was preoccupied purely and simply with her own problems, unaffected by the march of events elsewhere. Not until the era of Diego Portales and the rise of the Peru–Bolivian Confederation was this political isolation rescinded. The controversy and the turmoil of the decade between the fall of O'Higgins and the close of the period covered in this book were therefore of real interest only to Chileans. The political decisions taken in Santiago no longer had the same importance for patriot strategy and the continental balance of power as they had had during the 'Patria Vieja' and the O'Higgins government.

The abdication of Bernardo O'Higgins on 28 January 1823 had wrenched the three provinces of Chile asunder. The first task of any successor government was to reunite them. The national Junta chosen in Santiago on O'Higgins' downfall soon accepted General Ramón Freire as head of state (21 February 1823), and a meeting of plenipotentiaries from the three provinces sat in the capital to provide a new and more acceptable framework for national unity. On 30 March they signed an 'Act of Union' which brought the provinces together again and prepared the ground for a new Constituent Congress. On the following day, Freire was appointed provisional Supreme Director.

Clerical influence may have played a part in the subsequent elections to the new Congress,[1] but at all events, a largely conservative body was chosen. It opened its sittings on 12 August, and one of its first acts was to confirm Freire as Supreme Director. He was given a three-year term of office. The main task of the Congress, however, was to draw up a new Constitution to replace O'Higgins' ill-fated proposals of the year before. A constitutional committee, in which the influence of Juan Egaña was very marked, soon produced an initial draft, which Congress discussed during November and December. The small liberal element in Congress violently opposed many of the proposals, and presented a counter-draft on 16 December. This was ignored. Egaña's ascendancy was now sufficiently complete to ensure an easy passage for the Constitution. It was promulgated with particular solemnity and enthusiasm on 29 December 1823.

The enactment of the Constitution of 1823 represented a major triumph for Juan Egaña, its chief author. Juan Egaña, it can fairly be claimed, occupied a unique position in the Chilean revolution. With certain notable exceptions, he accepted the fundamental tenets of the revolutionary philosophy, and yet the whole cast of his thought is so different from that of his contemporaries in Chile that it demands the separate treatment it receives in the present chapter. Egaña's career has been described by others,[2] but it is perhaps important to stress its essentially academic nature. Egaña was a born intellectual, a natural speculator in ideas. From the first years of the century, when he was active as secretary to the Junta General de Minería and a luminary at the cultivated *tertulias* of Governor Muñoz de Guzmán, Egaña seems to have spent most of his time writing. He poured out an apparently endless stream of memoranda, reports, draft laws, constitutional projects, philosophical reflections, personal memoirs, bad poems, and private letters full of public thoughts. The scale of Egaña's published output is disconcerting to the student,[3] but many of his

---

[1] See the letters from the liberals Santiago Muñoz Bezanilla and Martín Orjera to the Senate, July 1823, *SCL*, VII, 275, 280.

[2] Cid Celis; Silva Castro, *Egaña en la Patria Vieja*; Amunátegui Solar, *Pipiolos y pelucones*, pp. 17–125.

[3] See Silva Castro, *Bibliografía de Egaña*.

more interesting notes remain unprinted, and still others have been irretrievably lost. The range of his imagination was wide. Amongst his more 'practical' schemes was a design for a primitive typewriter,[1] and he also drafted the basis for an international system of writing[2] and a type of musical language,[3] both for the purposes of universal communication. He foresaw the day when science would become enormously important to life in general, and he could ask the question, 'And what portentous help will electricity render us, the day we know how to understand and control it?'[4]

But it was to politics that Juan Egaña devoted most of his time and energy. In 1811 he drafted a lengthy constitution for Chile which, though never accepted, was printed in 1813 with certain alterations. The 1813 draft was little read. It was not well regarded by those revolutionaries who had time to study it. The Upper Peruvian lawyer Jaime Zudáñez (who had lived in Chile during the '*Patria Vieja*') once described it as 'a miscellany of constitutions put together without meditation'.[5] But in 1823, with the departure of O'Higgins and the election of a largely conservative Congress, Egaña was given his long-awaited chance to become the Lycurgus of Chile, the primordial Lawgiver who, standing at the opening of his country's history, would dictate fundamental precepts to be remembered with gratitude till the end of time. Egaña played out this self-cast role in the Congress of 1823. Although he did not manipulate the constitutional committee as if it were a puppet show,[6] his influence was nevertheless supreme, and the resulting Constitution bore the imprint of his personality in every article. It was conservative, moralistic, and outwardly illiberal, and for all these reasons was doomed to instant failure in the Chile of the 1820s.

The day after the promulgation of the Egaña Constitution, General Freire set off on an expedition to liberate the island of Chiloé, the last remaining section of what Chileans now con-

---

[1] Juan Egaña, *Colección*, IV, 89–96.
[3] *Ibid.* 96–104.   [3] *Ibid.* 81.   [4] *Ibid.*
[5] To O'Higgins, 3 April 1817, *Arch.O'H.* VIII, 257. But even so, Zudáñez asked O'Higgins to send him a copy.
[6] Cid Celis, p. 118.

sidered as national soil to remain in royalist hands. If Freire had doubts about the Constitution, he refrained from making them public. For the time being, at any rate, he had more pressing preoccupations. The royalists in Chiloé were well entrenched, and brilliantly commanded by Antonio de Quintanilla. Freire was compelled to withdraw without success, and he returned to Santiago in June 1824. By now he was well aware that most of his more liberal friends had taken up an uncompromisingly hostile attitude towards the Constitution. Freire, too, had already come to the conclusion that the document had to be modified. During the whole period of his absence in the South, a tussle between liberals and conservatives had been taking place in the capital, the liberals trying hard to undermine the Constitution, the conservatives upholding it and insisting that its complex provisions should be put into practice. The Constitution's chief defender was Juan Egaña's son Mariano, who, as Minister of the Interior, was working vigorously to implement it. At the end of April, however, the Senate named Mariano Egaña as Chilean Minister to Europe, and with his departure it became clear that the days of Juan Egaña's political creation were numbered.

The *dénouement* came swiftly. On 14 July 1824 Freire presented his resignation to the Senate. On being asked to reconsider his position, he claimed that he could no longer govern under the 1823 Constitution. On 17 July, the Senate agreed that constitutional reforms were necessary. Two days later, there were public demonstrations against the Constitution in the streets of Santiago. The Senate immediately conferred wide powers on Freire, and sections of the Constitution were suspended. A new Congress was summoned. It met on 22 November, and, in just over a month, it reached what now seemed an inevitable conclusion. The 1823 Constitution was condemned as wholly unsuitable for Chile, and was declared null and void on 29 December 1824, exactly a year after its initial promulgation. Juan Egaña himself ascribed the downfall of his masterpiece to the personal hostility of some of the leading liberals, notably Francisco Antonio Pinto and Diego José Benavente. He remained bitter about the fate of the 1823 Constitution to the end of his life.

MORALITY, VIRTUE AND CUSTOM

Juan Egaña accepted the common notions of the revolution. Thus, at the beginning of the draft constitution of 1813, he stated quite simply and concisely that

all men are born equal, free, and independent;...to live in society they sacrifice part of their wild and natural independence, but they preserve, and society protects, their security and property, and civil liberty and equality.[1]

Article 29 of the same document reads: 'The sovereignty of the Republic resides fully and fundamentally in the whole body of citizens.'[2] Elsewhere Egaña wrote: 'It is certain that the people is the legitimate master of its own sovereignty; and that the people cannot be deprived of these rights except for its own good.'[3] Egaña's basic acceptance of the doctrines of the contract and of popular sovereignty cannot, therefore, be called in question. At the same time, it is quite clear that he refused to draw the same conclusions from these doctrines as his contemporaries. One example will suffice at this stage. In the view of most Chilean patriots, popular sovereignty implied a system of elections and elected assemblies. But Egaña, both in 1813 and in 1823, provided for a non-elected, temporary legislative body whose members were drawn from a 'pool' of well-qualified citizens residing in the capital city. Popular sovereignty expressed itself only in the election and supervision of government functionaries and employees. Egaña was by no means unable to reconcile himself to the doctrine of popular sovereignty—as Galdames suggests[4]—but he refused to believe that it automatically led to popular control over the processes of government. He criticized the majority of 'modern' constitutions on the ground that they permitted the citizens to exercise too much sovereignty in this respect.[5]

Egaña's political thought was essentially conservative in character, and his models are particularly instructive. He was greatly influenced by the examples afforded by classical antiquity. Sparta

[1] *SCL*, I, 212.   [2] *Ibid.* 214.   [3] *Breves notas*, p. 246.
[4] *Evolución constitucional*, p. 620.   [5] *Examen instructivo*, p. 29.

and Rome commanded his special interest, and so did the empires of the Incas and the Chinese. In 1819, he wrote that

> we should seek as models those nations which have some similarity to our own, and which have maintained the strength and happiness they received from their first institutions over many centuries. Such was the very ancient and famous empire of China, and, above all, the gentle, provident and paternal empire of the Incas.[1]

Elsewhere he wrote of the 'astonishing obedience and adoration of the Peruvians towards their Incas'.[2] When, in 1824, Mariano Egaña was trying to implement the provisions of his father's constitution, he used the example of the Inca state to justify the minute administrative subdivisions envisaged in the *carta*.[3] Juan Egaña's regard for these dead empires had a simple cause. He saw in them a confirmation of his own prescriptions.

> The Abyssinians, the Incas, the Chinese: these are or were the most despotic sovereigns in the world, but their People were the least vexed and oppressed:...for, in the first two Empires, the influence of Religion has been great, and the influence of Customs considerable: and in China customs go to make up the Constitution and all the vital acts.[4]

Egaña's interest in China—a thoroughly 'enlightened' interest—is of particular importance. In the course of some 'imaginary conversations' he wrote in the 1820s, he sketched what for him were the truly noteworthy features of that empire. The passage is worth quoting at some length.

> Let us turn our eyes to the most ancient and flourishing Empire on earth: China. You will know that her internal trade (and perhaps her external trade too) surpasses that of the whole of Europe, and that the treasures of the world are gathered together there. Even so, there is domestic and public order, and an extreme submissiveness and respect towards the Government and Magistrates; for their guarantees and liberties are very different from our own.
>
> There all the laws have been transformed into customs, and all customs are directed to public decency and the respect and

---

[1] *Cartas Pehuenches*, no. 11, pp. 4–5.   [2] *Colección*, v, vi.
[3] To the *Delegado* of San Fernando, 31 March 1824, A.M.I. vol. 46, fo. 453.
[4] To Melchor José Ramos, 31 March 1828, F.V. vol. 802, pieza 14.

consideration due to Fathers, as domestic chiefs, and the Magistrates, as public chiefs.

There, without the guarantees of ministerial responsibility, and the rights of man, the Government is restrained, partly because opinion and custom have made it patriarchal, but especially because of the Sovereign's obligation to choose as functionaries only those men whose education and learning show them to be the most honest and instructed. This Aristocracy of wisdom and probity...is preferable to all democratic elections.[1]

Such a description may well have idealized the Chinese Empire, but it was certainly a superb reflection of the main themes of Egaña's own private ideology, as I must now show.

Egaña's fundamental concern in political thinking was the question of morality, opinion, and the formation of virtuous national customs. 'Morality...' he wrote, 'is the basis of all guarantees; without virtues, there are no customs, and without customs, no liberty.'[2] The ideal state, in Egaña's view, could only emerge when all its inhabitants had acquired permanently virtuous customs. The only guarantee of a long-lasting society was to transform written laws into unwritten ones, into customs observed spontaneously.

Everything that was good in the admirable government of the Incas, everything that contributed to the prolonged permanence of Sparta and China, was due to this great principle of transforming laws into customs.[3]

These words might be taken as the *leitmotiv* of all Egaña's political theory. Elsewhere, he noted that good customs had formed the basis for the endurance of other societies: he mentioned Rome, Persia, and the Arabs and Jews.[4] Implicit in all such statements was the view that 'success' on the national scale was bound up with surviving the test of history. A society which lasted for millennia, or at any rate centuries, was a 'good' society.

---

[1] 'Democracia. Dialogo entre Oliberio Cromwel Protector de Inglaterra y el Cardenal Richeleuil, primer ministro de Luis 13', F.V. vol. 259, pieza 15. Richelieu is lecturing Cromwell.

[2] Exposición de la Comisión de Constitución, 24 November 1823, *SCL*, VIII, 462-3.

[3] *Examen instructivo*, p. 18.

[4] To M. J. Ramos, 31 March 1828, A.M.I. vol. 46, fo. 453.

For Egaña, then, a state had little chance of achieving success unless its inhabitants shared a common system of morality. He criticized the 'modern' constitutions of his day for failing to appreciate this important fact. No 'modern' constitution, he suggested, tried to make men better or to 'give them morality'.[1] As he said in 1811, 'a People can only be happy with a certain amount of education and a general morality', and he referred, on the same occasion, to 'Plato's great principle—that a good code of laws is a treatise on morality'.[2] The chief function of morality and good customs, Egaña believed, was that they brought into existence the reign of opinion, which provided a dynamic force in the life of any nation: 'Opinion is the mainspring of our actions; it is stronger than laws: it is the Monarch's sceptre and the executioner's sword.'[3] It was essential, therefore, that men should be brought to recognize the supremacy of opinion.

All the philosophy of political legislation consists in placing men under the rule of opinion, and in obliging them to remain under it and to be directed by that main element of morality...; those who today are eunuchs and singers in Italy were the rulers of the world when they lived by glory and opinion.[4]

It may be noted here that Egaña's estimate of the Chilean ability to reach such a level was not markedly optimistic. He wrote on one occasion that Spanish America could attain the same heights as Europe only 'within several centuries',[5] and in 1833 he told Joaquín Campino: 'I have never doubted that the Spanish colonies need something like two centuries of moulding, under a Government they fear and respect, in order to create customs.'[6] Against this gloomy forecast, Egaña once expressed the view that the implanting of good national customs in Chile would not be excessively difficult, since Chile was in her infancy as a nation, and children were notoriously easy to control.[7]

---

[1] *Examen instructivo*, p. 22.
[2] 'Reflexiones sobre el mejor systema de Educacion, qe. puede darse a la Juventud de Chile, escritas pr. superior Orden del Congreso legislativo del Reyno, Año de 1811', F.V. vol. 796, pieza 1 (no pagination).　　　　　　[3] *Ibid.*
[4] Exposición de la Comisión de Constitución, 24 November 1823, *SCL*, VIII, 463.
[5] 'Dialogo entre Juan Adams Presidte. de los Estados Unidos y el Barón de Humboldt naturalista y consejero del Rey de Prusia', F.V. vol. 259, pieza 15.
[6] Egaña, 'Cartas, 1832–3', p. 108.　　　　　[7] *Examen instructivo*, p. 29.

THE INCULCATION OF MORALITY

So far it might be supposed that Egaña was merely restating and emphasizing an element which was present in the common revolutionary philosophy: the need for virtue. But Egaña differed from his fellows in allowing this special concern to colour his entire political outlook. While his contemporaries meditated on the division of the powers, on popular sovereignty, or on the natural rights of man, Egaña devoted enormous energy to devising and prescribing the rules by which morality might best be inculcated. The outcome of his studious application to the problem was a coherent, if eccentric, system of specific recommendations.

Punishments, to take a first example, had a cautionary rather than a corrective effect in Egaña's political philosophy. Their whole purpose should be complementary to the workings of opinion, 'which is stronger than laws, guns or scaffolds'.[1]

When you want to characterize the political economy and legislation of a people, examine (1) whether the laws punish vices or prevent them, and (2) whether morality is cared for and directed, or whether crimes are punished only when they become contentious.[2]

Egaña firmly believed in the deterrent effect of sentences, as a means of inspiring respect for national morality. In his *Código Moral*, for instance, he stipulated that the worst crimes should be punished by garrotting, accompanied by awesome and lugubrious ceremonies.[3] Egaña left little doubt as to which he considered the worst crimes. Offences of honour, such as the breaking of contracts, should have special penalties, he believed;[4] and other dangerous vices included gambling, drunkenness, duelling, atheism, and satire against the established order of society.[5] It is worth noting in passing that Egaña did not share some of his contemporaries' approval of the jury system: 'Habit is necessary in order to judge in cold blood.'[6]

---

[1] *Cartas Pehuenches*, no. 12, pp. 7–8.   [2] *Ibid.*
[3] Art. 449, *Colección*, v, 203.   [4] *Breves notas*, p. 251.
[5] *Código Moral* (*Colección*, v), arts. 336–61; cf. *Breves notas*, p. 251.
[6] *Breves notas*, p. 254.

Juan Egaña

But the reign of opinion had to be encouraged by rewards as well as deterrents. Here Egaña was particularly inspired by the example of the ancient world. 'In our own times...' he sadly wrote, 'there are no triumphs, Olympic games, civic crowns,... and...we do not live under the sway of opinion and enthusiasm for national glory.'[1] This was the basic reason for the elaborate system of rewards and public festivals included both in the 1813 draft constitution and in the *Código Moral*. The 1813 draft constitution contained recommendations for the recognition of civic merit. Two grades were established, both of them to be conferred on well-deserving citizens.[2] The 1823 Constitution included much the same system, and also ordered noteworthy examples of patriotic action to be recorded at intervals in a special *Mercurio Cívico*.[3] In the *Código Moral*, intended by Egaña as an official appendage to the 1823 Constitution, several special grades of civic merit were laid down,[4] and an ultimate arbiter of rewards and prizes, to be known as the Grand Magistrate of the National Morality, was envisaged.[5]

It was in fact the *Código Moral* (consisting of 625 articles, eventually printed in a volume of 268 pages) which represented Juan Egaña's maturest thought on the whole question of rewards, prizes and public festivals. Egaña regarded the *Código Moral* with considerable affection. He considered it to be 'the fruit of my whole life's meditations', claiming that it 'resolved and regulated all the great questions that currently preoccupy the legislative bodies of America'.[6] Not altogether surprisingly, therefore, some of Egaña's more picturesque fantasies attained their meridian in the pages of the Code. This was particularly true of the section devoted to public festivals. The draft Constitution of 1813 went some way towards laying down rules for the observance of suitably moralizing festivals;[7] the *Código Moral*, it is fair to say, completed the exercise. Needless to say, the four main national festivals envisaged in the Code were designed to inculcate specific points of morality. The first, to be held annually on 12 February

---

[1] *Colección*, v, v. [2] Arts. 69–77, *SCL*, I, 218–19.
[3] Arts. 250–4 and 259. [4] Títs. VI–VII. [5] Art. 237.
[6] To Ramón Rengifo [1830–6], F.V. vol. 420, pieza 8. [7] Art. 251.

(the anniversary of Chacabuco), was to be styled the 'Festival of Public Beneficence', and the second, to be held on 5 April (the anniversary of Maipó), the 'Festival of Justice and Public Morality.' This second festival would be the occasion for the display of symbolic statues: Abraham and Isaac, depicting filial piety; Leonidas in the Pass of Thermopylae, denoting respect for the magistrates; and finally Aristides marching into exile and Socrates drinking hemlock, to represent submissiveness to the laws. A third festival, the 'Festival of National Agriculture and Industry', was to be observed every 18 September, and a fourth, to be celebrated with special dances and rituals, was planned as an annual commemoration of the great blessing of the Constitution of 1823.[1]

Naturally enough, religion was also to play a predetermined part in the establishment of virtuous customs. Religion, Egaña believed, was fundamental to any society. 'Religion', he wrote, 'is the axis, the motor, not only of the morality of a people, but of its national character, its customs, and its adherence to and respect for civil institutions.'[2] It followed logically enough from this that religion should be uniform within the state. 'Without a uniform religion', wrote Egaña, with a disapproving side-glance at England, 'one can create a nation of traders, but not of citizens.'[3] The absence of religion was fatal to any society. A republic of atheists, Egaña claimed, would need 'an Inquisition a thousand times more horrible and persecuting than the Spanish',[4] an assertion which does not wholly conflict with the experience of the twentieth century. But atheism was only one degree worse than religious diversity, which was almost equally fatal. Egaña summarized his conclusions on this point in a short book he wrote to justify restraints on religious liberty in Chile.

1. The multitude of religions in a single state leads to irreligion; and this is the tendency of our century.

2. Two religions in a state lead to a struggle which must terminate either in the destruction of the state or of one of the two religious parties.

3. Religious uniformity is the most effective means of consolidating the tranquillity of the great mass of the nation.[5]

---

[1] Tít. x, 'Fiestas Cívicas'.   [2] *Colección*, IV, 59.
[3] *Breves notas*, p. 250.   [4] *Memoria sobre libertad de cultos*, p. 4.   [5] *Ibid.* p. 16.

Though Egaña's private religious faith need not be doubted,[1] it is clear that he saw religion as an instrument of the state, as the third conclusion quoted above indicates very strongly. It would, he wrote, be intolerable not to have 'a National God to Whom to pray in times of misfortune'.[2]

This viewpoint imposed an important limitation on freedom of expression. Egaña thought that it was 'a political error to confuse liberty of thought with liberty to propagate corrupt or incendiary thoughts throughout the human race'.[3] Thought and expression were not the same thing, and the division between them was implicit in the terms of the social contract.

It is true that a man does not sacrifice the domain of his thoughts to the social pact; but he *has* sacrificed the domain of his external actions, for these can influence order and public morality, and society has the right to make them conform to the state's system of political organization.[4]

Speech and writing had to be regarded as external actions. 'With respect to society', Egaña wrote, 'only thought is absolutely free; speech and writing belong to political jurisdiction, since they can so influence the domestic and social order.'[5] The most obvious application of this view was in the sphere of the freedom of the press. Egaña was not slow to appreciate the role of the press in inculcating morality. In his *Plan de Gobierno*, presented to the Governor in August 1810, he recommended the immediate acquisition of a printing press in order 'to make public opinion conform to the principles of the Government'.[6] In the Constitution of 1823 he laid down that the press would be free, and indeed 'rewarded inasmuch as it contributes towards creating morality and good customs'. The press would also be permitted to conduct a 'useful examination' of a wide range of human activities.[7] But at the same time, it was firmly prohibited from meddling with the 'mysteries, dogmas, religious discipline, and the morality generally approved by the Catholic Church'.[8] A complex system of censorship was established.[9]

[1] See *Colección*, IV, 1–55. [2] *Memoria sobre libertad de cultos*, p. 31.
[3] *Examen instructivo*, p. 22. [4] *Memoria sobre libertad de cultos*, p. 18.
[5] *Colección*, IV, 64. [6] *CHDI*, XIX, 106. [7] Art. 262, *AR*, I, 135.
[8] Art. 263. ii, *ibid.* [9] Arts. 264–8, *ibid.*

The Church itself was by no means exempt from a place in Egaña's 'system'. He advocated a thoroughgoing Erastianism, and the 1813 draft constitution actually contained one section regulating church affairs.[1] The *Código Moral* also concerned itself with these matters, introducing a special hymn 'of homage to the Supreme Being' into all celebrations of Mass,[2] and insisting on the subordination of the ecclesiastical to the secular arm. 'The clergy', stated the Code, 'does not have political opinions; it obeys the *de facto* government; it carries out its spiritual functions.'[3] To compensate for these minor limitations, the Church was to enjoy a religious monopoly. Egaña did not wish to penalize the followers of other religions, but he doubted the wisdom of allowing them the right to worship in their own way. 'Let us not condemn to death men who do not believe as we do,' he advised; 'but do not let us form a family together with them.'[4]

Nothing could be left to chance when the inculcation of morality was concerned. The arts had to be supervised, as well as religion. Thus the *Código Moral* laid down rules for artistic events. 'No dramatic spectacle will be permitted which does not foment virtues.'[5] Of the various arts, Egaña seems to have taken most interest in music. His views on the subject were loosely Platonic. It was wrong, he felt, to regard music as 'an art of pure pleasure'.[6] It should become a definite science.

Tell me, then: What is Moral Philosophy? Nothing more than the science of ruling the passions. And what is Music? The art of moving, exciting, or calming them. Therefore music should be the medium by which the passions are directed to the most useful ends.[7]

The Chinese Empire was once again called in to support Egaña's argument.

The nation which has best preserved its existence and customs (China) holds the rite of music to be so inviolable that, even though the power of the Emperor is limitless, all the efforts of Kam-hi did not secure the

---

[1] Tít. XII, explained in *Breves notas*, p. 248.   [2] Art. 12, *Colección*, v, 20.
[3] Art. 35, *ibid.* 29.   [4] *Breves notas*, p. 250.
[5] Art. 176, *Colección*, v, 81.
[6] 'Reflexiones sobre el mejor systema de Educacion....1811', F.V. vol. 796, pieza I.
[7] *Ibid.*

admission of European music...For that wise people believed the use of music to be closely linked to the conversation and the uprightness of customs.[1]

Elsewhere Egaña contrasted Chinese sense with Chilean stupidity. Chinese music, he claimed, had never been 'meaningless...They fail to understand our own aimless and undignified music.'[2] Music, then, was to be harnessed to the great national purpose. 'Let us apply ourselves', urged Egaña in 1811, 'to form moral or physical ideas from music, just as the Chinese do.'[3] Perhaps it was this idea which later became the starting-point for his scheme (already mentioned) of creating a universal 'musical' language for international communication. But, at all events, he never attempted to lay down a specific code for composers, even though the *Código Moral* recommended that music for national occasions should be 'majestic, simple and pathetic' in character.[4]

It was, of course, inevitable that Egaña should devote a considerable amount of time to examining the most obvious way of inculcating morality. In 1813 he wrote that,

in government, it is indispensable to regard the education of children as the most significant matter—to rear them in the spirit of love towards the constitution, in the simplicity of the ancients, and, in one word, in all the principles which ought always to govern their opinions, sentiments and habits.[5]

Certain kinds of education were, however, better avoided: 'an excess of culture, particularly of religious and political knowledge, produces restlessness, pride, and a spirit of innovation',[6] none of which things Egaña regarded with much sympathy. But these reservations apart, he was an enthusiastic believer in the possibilities of education, even if he gave it an emphasis that was unusual. From the start of his political career in 1810, with the *Plan de Gobierno*, until within a few years of his demise, with the

---

[1] 'Reflexiones sobre el mejor sistema de Education...1811', F.V. vol. 796, pieza 1.
[2] *Examen instructivo*, p. 34.
[3] 'Reflexiones sobre el mejor sistema de Educacion...1811', F.V. vol. 796, pieza 1.
[4] Art. 179, *Colección*, v, 84.
[5] *Breves notas*, p. 252.
[6] *Colección*, IV, 66.

last of his various memoranda on the subject,[1] he was active as a promoter of educational schemes, and perhaps his only rival in this respect was the zealous Manuel de Salas. In the *Plan de Gobierno* of August 1810 his basic preoccupations were already clearly discernible. Chile, he wrote, should attempt to set up 'a great college of the arts and sciences; above all, a civil and moral education capable of giving us character and customs'.[2] In 1811, in a lengthy memorandum to Congress—the one unprinted work of Juan Egaña's which surely demands publication for its own sake— he advocated the establishment of an 'Instituto Nacional', open to all classes and age-groups, and he himself played a notable part in the creation of the school which bore that name in 1813.[3]

Egaña's memorandum on education, presented to Congress on 24 October 1811,[4] represents one of his fullest, and most interesting statements on the subject. At the beginning of his 'Reflections', Egaña announced that his purpose was more than the examination of the specific needs of schools. What was wanted, he wrote, was to establish the basis of an education suitable for a new and infant nation. He recalled that Rome and Athens had risen to greatness from unpromising beginnings; Chile could do the same. He proceeded into a panegyric of ancient educational methods: 'In all good faith, we must admit that the ancients were superior to us in military strategy, Politics, Rhetoric, History, Poetry and in all fields to which they dedicated themselves.' It was necessary to take what was good from ancient education, and above all to notice that its cornerstone was 'the free and spontaneous range which that education gave to the imagination'. Ancient learning had been based on a union of scientific, physical, and moral disciplines. In 'modern' Europe, Egaña contended, there were too many purely scientific academies.

One need hardly ask which subject was to receive preferential treatment in Egaña's ideal educational system.

---

[1] 'Memoria sobre el mejor systema de aprender y enseñar las ciencias y formar la moralidad de los jovenes' (1832), *Colección*, VI, 1–67.

[2] *CHDI*, XIX, 103.

[3] Silva Castro, *Egaña en la Patria Vieja*, ch. 8.

[4] 'Reflexiones sobre el mejor systema de Educacion...1811', F.V. vol. 796, pieza 1. For the date of submission, see Roldán, *Primeras asambleas*, p. 197.

Juan Egaña

The study of moral Philosophy has flourished in all those great nations which have recognized the force of patriotic love, the union of the citizen with his government, the permanence of customs, and respect towards religion and the laws, viz.: the Persians, the Greeks, the Romans, the Chinese.

Egaña went on to make certain recommendations regarding the study of moral philosophy. Music should be employed, and national history should occupy a specially important place in the curriculum. But the main object, Egaña believed, was to unite all the different branches of education into one general scheme. There was an intimate connection between a good education and the designs and purposes of government, and the ultimate aim of all education, of course, should be 'to form customs and national character'. It was essential that 'education should be made public, general, and sustained, and that the laws should lay down the Citizen's duties from infancy to manhood'.

It will by now have become clear that Egaña's view of the ideal government for Chile implied a fairly rigorous control over every significant aspect of national life. Virtue was to be encouraged by an elaborate system of deterrents and rewards, to be stimulated by national festivals, and positively inculcated through the arts, religion, and education. Egaña's desire to control in order to inculcate, and his fundamental preoccupations, were most clearly defined in Article 249 of the Constitution of 1823, which ordained the preparation of a

moral code that will detail the duties of the citizen in all the periods of his life and in all states of society, creating his habits, activities, duties, public instructions, rituals and pleasures, all of which transform laws into customs and customs into civic and moral virtues.[1]

Egaña did not, unfortunately, express himself at any great length as to the type of society he wished to see emerge from these complex arrangements, though here and there he left clues. In his *Ocios filosóficos*, for instance, he seems to have regarded the ideal country as largely composed of 'small agricultural settlements' most of whose families would own their own land, the remainder

[1] *AR*, I, 133.

of the population being occupied in 'manufacturing, avoiding the arts of luxury and superfluity'.[1] Egaña was distrustful of great concentrations of wealth. His ideal society would be free of both large cities and excessive inequality of incomes.

I believe that extreme poverty is as prejudicial to the social order as proud opulence... Mexico is the cradle of money, and London receives all the precious metals of the earth and is the home of prodigious wealth: even so, beggars form more than a quarter of the population of both Mexico and London.[2]

An agricultural nation like Chile, thought Egaña, should not tempt Providence by indulging in overseas commerce. This was one of his more frequently repeated warnings. 'A merchant marine', he wrote, 'excites the inclination towards luxury, ambition and conquest...Without navigation, the industrious Chinese live in tranquillity, and are served by the whole world.'[3]

Private morals, too, were subjected to Egaña's earnest consideration. The *Código Moral* established strict principles of paternal authority in the individual household. Wives, for instance, were to be obliged to obey their husbands, while sons were to remain under absolute paternal jurisdiction until the age of twenty-four.[4] The significance of such provisions as these can best be appreciated in the light of Egaña's view that the state in some way reflected the type of arrangement which prevailed within the family. 'A state', he once wrote, 'is a family writ large.'[5]

In the illustrative notes which accompanied the 1813 draft constitution, Egaña tried to foresee what kind of future Chile would experience. 'Her tranquil and moderate character', he wrote, 'will preserve her from the strong and fickle passions inspired by revolution, or the spirit of domination and aggression.'[6] Chile, he observed, was neighbour to two potentially troublesome states. Argentina would always aspire to glory, while Peru would remain feverish and volatile. One day, Egaña supposed, the two

---

[1] *Colección*, IV, 56.   [2] *Ibid.* 57.
[3] *Breves notas*, p. 248; cf. *Examen instructivo*, pp. 37–8, and *Colección*, IV, 60–1.
[4] Arts. 53 and 61–6.   [5] *Colección*, IV, 63.
[6] *Breves notas*, p. 247.

countries would come to look on each other as rivals. Chile 'must be the Switzerland of America, and never take part in their dissensions'.[1] It is ironical that Chile's eventual role in the international relations of the Latin American states in the nineteenth century was by no means Swiss in character.

CONSTITUTIONAL PRESCRIPTIONS

I must now turn to Egaña's constitutional ideas.[2] For Chile he recommended 'the republican government, combining aristocracy and democracy, which, as Aristotle says, is the most perfect'.[3] Pure democracy (in the Aristotelian sense) would, he thought, always remain a bad and unworkable form of government.[4] The best government would invariably show some sort of bias towards aristocracy. Writing in 1828, Egaña noted 'that in Rome, England, and other states where Aristocracy is mixed with democracy, the men who are distinguished by their civic virtue always come from the nobility'.[5] Egaña admitted that the worst possible alternative was absolute monarchy, but despite this he continued to regard democracy in any form with the deepest suspicion: 'There is nothing easier than to establish despotism and tyranny by means of the People.'[6] Popular direct legislation, he believed (along with the majority of other political theorists of the age), could only work effectively in small areas. Democracy in this sense was practicable in a small city state, but certainly not in a vast province of the Spanish American Empire.[7] Elected congresses were of debatable value, for they endangered public stability by giving undue opportunities to partisan demagogues. Parliamentary government might work, Egaña conceded, in a country like England, where virtuous national customs had already been established,[8] but in a country like Chile there was little justification for the experiment. In 1828, when he was trying

---

[1] *Breves notas*, p. 247.
[2] For discussions of the Constitution of 1823, see Galdames, *Evolución constitucional*, pt. 2, ch. 2; Shaw, pp. 99–106; Santa María, *Memoria histórica*, pp. 293–302.
[3] *Breves notas*, p. 246.   [4] *Colección*, IV, 68.
[5] To M. J. Ramos, 31 March 1828, F.V. vol. 802, pieza 14.
[6] *Ibid.*   [7] *Memorias políticas*, pp. 56–7.
[8] *Ibid.* pp. 60–4.

to influence the drafting of the Constitution of that year, Egaña advised one deputy that the government should always take a hand in popular elections 'without depriving the People of the illusion of their elections',[1] but always ensuring 'that there should not be elections in small districts or territories, for these are and always will be a prolific source of disorder'.[2] Only in his last constitutional project, the brief 'interim' *Carta Constitucional* of the later 1820s,[3] did Egaña admit the idea of an elected national assembly. His earlier schemes disregarded the notion altogether.

Egaña was convinced that although a government should have considerable powers, it needed some kind of moral check. This he believed could best be provided by a body of patricians, which in the 1813 draft he styled the *Tribunal de la Censura* (Tribunal of Censure), and in the 1823 Constitution the *Senado Conservador y Legislador* (the Conservative and Legislative Senate). Such a body would have the power of veto over all laws coming from the government,[4] but, in the event of this veto being used, the law concerned would merely be suspended until the occasional legislative body known as the *Cámara Nacional* (National Chamber)— composed of specially qualified citizens resident in the capital— had time to meet to consider the matter. The Senate or Tribunal of Censure also had the more positive duty of watching over the customs of the country, directing education, and implanting a general morality. In the 1813 draft constitution this body was defined as

the tutelary magistracy, to which is entrusted the observance of the laws and the strength of customs;... it directs public morality and education...Its power is neither executive, legislative or judicial, but of simple guardianship.[5]

Egaña believed that any institution of this sort should necessarily last for a long time, and that it was backed by historical precedents, for it was noticeable that 'in Rome, Venice and England,

---

[1] To M. J. Ramos, 31 March 1828, F.V. vol. 802, pieza 14.   [2] *Ibid.*
[3] Printed in *Colección*, II, 89.
[4] 1823 Constitution, art. 38; 1813 draft, art. 44.   [5] Art. 42, *SCL*, I, 215.

the nobility has always been established for life, and has been independent of popular elections; the natural tendency of those corporations is to resist the government and protect the people'.[1] In the 1813 draft, therefore, it is hardly surprising that Egaña gave his Censors a ten-year term of office,[2] while the Senators of the 1823 Constitution received a six-year term with the chance of indefinite re-election.[3] The general similarity of Egaña's proposals for a 'Guardian Senate' to the suggestions which Bolívar made for a Moral or Fourth Power[4] will doubtless not go unnoticed. Egaña's idea antedated Bolívar's by several years. Egaña, it should be mentioned in passing, believed that he had some influence on the framing of the Bolivian Constitution,[5] but there is no direct evidence that this was the case.

It will be seen that these arrangements for a body of patrician guardians and for a non-elected National Chamber set Egaña's constitution quite apart from its fellows. The National Chamber bore no relation whatsoever to the elected Congresses of other Latin American constitutions. Its members were chosen by lot from a 'pool' of highly qualified citizens resident in the capital, and were styled *consultores* (counsellors). They constituted a 'temporary assembly' whenever the legislative process made this necessary. There was thus no element of popular representation in the National Chamber, nor were the provinces allowed to participate in its discussions. Egaña rejected the theory of the balance of powers. He denied that it existed in England: 'today in England the executive power formally partakes of the powers of the legislative'.[6] But whether it existed in England or not, Egaña still regarded it as a dangerous principle. If the balance was perfect, he argued, then this was bound to reduce the powers to impotence; and an imperfect balance would lead to conflict between the powers.[7]

---

[1] *Memorias políticas*, p. 73.   [2] Art. 91.   [3] Art. 36.
[4] See Bolívar's remarks in his Angostura address, in Vicente Lecuna (ed.), *Proclamas y discursos del Libertador* (Caracas, 1939), pp. 228–9, and his address to the Constituent Congress of Bolivia, 25 May 1826, *ibid.* pp. 325–6.
[5] Juan Egaña to Mariano Egaña, 16 August 1826, *Cartas de Juan Egaña*, p. 186. Cf. his Letter to a Deputy [1826–7], F.V. vol. 789, pieza 35.
[6] *Breves notas*, p. 244.
[7] Exposición de la Comisión de Constitución, 24 November 1823, *SCL*, VIII, 461.

Other aspects of Egaña's constitutional theory may be noted briefly. Popular sovereignty was by no means excluded from Egaña's vision, but it was to be embodied in public control of local functionaries rather than in a national elected assembly. Thus the 1823 Constitution provided for electoral assemblies in each subdivision of the republic,[1] whose main function was to be the election of these functionaries and their reappointment by process of review every two years.[2] Egaña conceived this method as the best way of permitting popular sovereignty a legitimate expression. Local government also received scrupulous attention at Egaña's hands. The republic was to be divided and subdivided in a symmetrical and logical fashion, and the smallest administrative unit was to consist of ten households. A unit of one hundred households was to become the 'political base for customs, virtues, police and statistics'.[3] Egaña evidently believed that officials to staff these various subdivisions could easily be found, even the overseers for the ten-household units. Mariano Egaña, replying to criticisms and protests from a district governor on this point, insisted that

a peon, a wretched peasant, could very well carry out this job. You surely cannot suppose that the inhabitants of our countryside are grosser and more miserable than the native Peruvians, or even our own Chileans in the age of the Incas. And *they* had the same division down to the *decurias*: that is to say, men who watched over the conduct and good order of ten families.[4]

Mariano Egaña also claimed that the new subdivisions of the state were as nearly 'natural' as it was possible for them to be.

One or two minor items from the 1823 Constitution should also be mentioned. A 'Directorate of the National Economy' was set up,[5] which Egaña described as the gathering together of previously disunited institutions.[6] The Constitution also provided for a special emergency committee to come into existence in the

---

[1] Arts. 75–81; cf. 1813 draft, tít. i, sec. 4.   [2] Arts. 97–8; cf. 1813 draft, tít. ix.
[3] Art. 196.
[4] To the *Delegado* of San Fernando, 31 March 1824, A.M.I. vol. 46, fo. 453.
[5] Tít. xvii, arts. 180–9.
[6] Exposición de la Comisión de Constitución..., *SCL*, viii, 463.

event of civil war, to consist of three men who would attempt to mediate between the rival bands.[1] Both these provisions separate Egaña's document even further from the other Latin American constitutions of the time.

THE FAILURE OF EGAÑA'S UTOPIA

'The present Code is the permanent Constitution of the State,' announced Article 276 of the 1823 Constitution. Its promulgation was attended with the most extravagant festivities.[2] Egaña himself claimed that it was received with 'truly extraordinary applause from the people'.[3] Yet it never went into operation. It was suspended in July 1824, and formally abrogated by a new Congress in December of the same year. The breakdown of Egaña's utopian order was not, however, wholly unexpected or unanticipated. The first criticisms of the 1823 Constitution were pronounced even before the document had been approved by Congress. The small liberal opposition in the 1823 Congress opposed the *carta* before it was finally drafted. Pedro Trujillo wrote of the 'thousand political blasphemies'[4] of Egaña's proposals, while, as soon as these were known in full, the newspaper of the liberal group attacked what it described as 'dreams of a delirious imagination'.[5] The newspaper agreed that the new constitution was 'truly original', but turned this into an argument against it, for it then asserted that it was unwise to 'experiment at the expense of the welfare, prosperity and tranquillity of nations'.[6] In the congressional sittings of 24 and 25 November 1823, Trujillo and Fray Pedro Arce mounted their grand attack. The constitution, they affirmed, provided for too many new jobs at a time 'when we should shun that mania for public offices for which the Spaniards are so harshly criticized';[7] there was too little popular representation; the word 'Congress' did not feature

---

[1] Arts. 269–74.   [2] Barros Arana, XIV, 189–90.

[3] 'Memoria para la historia de la Constitución', in Vicuña Mackenna, *Historia jeneral*, IV, 370.

[4] To Benavente, 18 October 1823, F.V. vol. 823, núm. 216, p. 3.

[5] *El Liberal*, no. 17, 21 November 1823, p. 138.   [6] *Ibid.*

[7] *Redactor de las Sesiones del Congreso*, libro 1, núm. 17, 18 December 1823, p. 160.

in the draft;[1] and so on. Trujillo maintained that the central characteristics of the *carta* were its tyranny and fanaticism.[5] He, Arce, and Isidro Pineda presently submitted their own rival draft, rejected by Congress. Its essence, according to Diego Barros Arana, was 'a moderate and reasonable liberalism'.[3]

In an atmosphere of growing liberalism, the 1823 Constitution was plainly an unacceptable and disappointing document. Pedro Trujillo explained,

Just when we most needed to reanimate public spirit, to inflame people's hearts, to impose truth and principle, to replenish the public treasury and create land and sea forces..., along came a new political apocalypse to confuse and impoverish us.[4]

Egaña himself ascribed the downfall of his masterpiece to the hostility of the liberals Benavente[5] and Pinto,[6] and in this, it seems, he was largely correct. Freire, too, had a hand. In February 1824 he wrote to Benavente, telling him that 'the Constitution must soon be reformed; this has been my view ever since I realized that it was in no way adaptable to our present circumstances'.[7] The task of undermining the 1823 Constitution was made considerably easier by the departure from Chile of Mariano Egaña, who, as Minister of the Interior, had been making strenuous efforts to implement the new political organization in the provinces.[8]

In general, however, there was little theoretical criticism of the Constitution, and even less sympathetic understanding of its basic premises. 'I consider it void, vicious, inept,' said Infante during the abrogation debates in December 1824.[9] It had overthrown popular rights, claimed Casimiro Albano.[10] Its failure to set up a proper

---

[1] *Redactor de las Sessiones del Congreso*, libro I, núm. 17, 18 December 1823, pp. 160–1.
[2] *Ibid.* I, núm. 18, 20 December 1823, p. 184.
[3] Barros Arana, XIV, 179. Barros Arana noted that this draft was amongst his papers, but I was unable to trace it there.
[4] To Benavente, 16 February 1824, F.V. vol. 823, núm. 217, p. 4.
[5] Diego José Benavente Bustamante (1789–1869); ardent *carrerino*; Minister of Finance 1825; first a supporter, later an opponent, of Portales.
[6] 'Memoria para la historia de la Constitución', *loc. cit.* IV, 371–4.
[7] To Benavente, 17 February 1824, F.V. vol. 821, núm. 77, p. 102.
[8] Ministerial letters, January–March 1824, A.M.I. vol. 46.
[9] Session of 15 December 1824, *SCL*, X, 146. [10] *Ibid.* X, 148.

elected legislature was plainly its least attractive feature to the liberals. Others suspected that the complicated provisions of the *carta* were, quite simply, impossible to operate. Its 'fatal impediments', as Zenteno put it,[1] its 'complex mechanisms,... its excessively exact and regulating spirit', as Freire said two years later,[2] were dubious aspects. It was felt that the number of new public functionaries required under the Constitution was unobtainable in Chilean conditions. Pinto, in a famous attack, claimed that at the moment of the suspension of the Constitution in July 1824, some twenty thousand officials still had to be found.[3] Local governors, he affirmed, had objected to implementing a document many of them scarcely understood.[4]

A more serious criticism, perhaps, was that to legislate for the rest of time, as Egaña wished to do, was both foolish and pretentious. As Freire said, at the opening of the Congress of 1824, 'Inexperience and thoughtlessness inspire the desire to give permanent constitutions to nations which are still in the process of change.'[5] Pinto viciously mocked the 1823 Congress, asking, 'Had the necessary knowledge been sufficiently popularized in Chile for that Congress to legislate in a permanent manner?'[6] He commented on the fact that this 'permanent' Constitution had been discussed and then sanctioned in fifteen days flat.[7]

It soon became fashionable to deride the 1823 Constitution as (to use the words of Pedro Félix Vicuña) a

heterogeneous mixture of bizarre theories, modern institutions, and Greek and Roman institutions which ruled over nations very different from our own...That farrago of political utopias perished as soon as it was born, on account of its confusion and becauset he people could not even understand it.[8]

---

[1] To Benavente, 29 July 1824, F.V. vol. 823, p. 99.
[2] Message to the Constituent Congress, 4 July 1826, *SCL*, XII, 44.
[3] *Memoria del Ministro del Interior*, p. 6.
[4] 'Piezas justificativas', *ibid.* p. 17.
[5] 22 November 1824, *SCL*, X, 32.
[6] *Memoria del Ministro del Interior*, p. 8.
[7] *Ibid.* p. 9.
[8] Valencia Avaria, *Memorias íntimas*, pp. 31-2. Vicuña's more famous son, Benjamín Vicuña Mackenna, was later to describe the Constitution as more fitted for the moon than the earth: *Diego Portales*, I, 128.

A newspaper of 1827 condemned the Egaña constitution as more obscure than St John's Apocalypse.[1] But such criticisms as these were both superficial and unfair. The Constitution was far from incomprehensible, even if its form was ponderous and long-winded. Its basic principles are clear enough; but it is possible, of course, that Egaña's contemporaries were unable to take into account the whole background of his previous and subsequent writings. The breakdown of the Constitution must in the last resort be ascribed to its 'own ideal perfection', as Freire generously put it, 'which could not be adapted to the customs of the inhabitants or to received ideas'.[2] Here is the one indisputable reason for the failure: a complex and moralistic constitution tinged with prescriptive conservatism was purely and simply the opposite of the 'received ideas' of the time and of what the liberals in Chile wanted.

Egaña himself considered the rejection of his utopia a huge and terrible injustice. He was flattered by the interest in it taken by Europeans,[3] and later claimed that more had been written about the 1823 Constitution abroad than about any other Latin American constitution.[4] This was a small crumb of comfort after a devastating political defeat.

Egaña's own peculiar emphasis in political theory was, on the whole, alien to the common revolutionary philosophy. Though he accepted the basic notions of the contract and of popular sovereignty, it can hardly be argued that they played much of a part in his own theory. The entire cast of Egaña's mind was conservative rather than liberal, and at times he seems to write as if he were a cross between an enlightened despot and a German Romantic. He could affirm, for instance, that 'that saying of Bonaparte's—"everything *for* the people, nothing *by* the people" —is to a certain extent infallible,' and he could claim that of the two extremes of liberty and slavery, the latter was, in the last resort, to be preferred.[5] Yet, at the same time, Egaña found him-

---

[1] *El Independiente*, tomo I, no. I, 28 September 1827, p. I.
[2] Message to the Constituent Congress, 4 July 1826, SCL, XII, 44.
[3] Cid Celis, p. 164.
[4] 'Carta de un Ciudadano á un Diputado al Congreso Nacional de Chile en 826', F.V. vol. 120A, pieza 12.   [5] To M. J. Ramos, 31 March 1828, F.V. vol. 802, pieza 14.

self able to share some of the common anti-despotic poses of the revolution,[1] and he was as much a child of the Enlightenment as his more liberal contemporaries. He was profoundly affected by the Enlightenment's admiration for the ancient world and for the Chinese Empire. His scheme for a guardian senate of Censors stemmed directly from his readings in classical antiquity, but also, perhaps, through Filangieri.[2] The whole atmosphere of his work is imbued with the moralistic spirit of Fénelon, whom he also read and admired.

The distinctive qualities of Juan Egaña's political outlook made him the great 'original' of the Chilean revolution, and one of the more interesting Latin American theorists of the period of independence. If his ideas seem unattractive, as they did to the liberals of 1824, this is doubtless because of the unmistakable element of regimentation which they appear to embody. Yet it should not be forgotten that Egaña's utopian prescriptions were intended to help bring about a state of affairs where freedom could rest securely on the solid foundations of virtue and custom. Egaña, in short, wished to create the kind of stratum of traditional practices and liberties which Edmund Burke so eloquently defended in the case of England.[3] Egaña's complex regulations would, in the end, disappear. They would be replaced by the spontaneous observance of public and private conventions based on a common morality. Egaña would perhaps ultimately have agreed with Confucius that the best state is the one with fewest laws, and the perfect state one with no laws at all. The 1823 Constitution was the instrument which would set Chile on the long road to that utopia. But it was based in the realms of

[1] In his newspaper *La Abeja Chilena*, no. 3, 24 June 1825, p. 23, he printed the farewell hymn of the Four Sergeants of La Rochelle.

[2] See Filangieri, *La Scienza della Legislazione*, lib. I, cap. viii. Egaña's apologetic writings on behalf of his two constitutional projects were well documented. In the *Breves notas* of 1813 he either cited or mentioned Lacroix, Lloyd, Raynal, Rousseau, Aristotle, Montesquieu, Filangieri, Hume, Genovesi, Smith, Price, Cicero, Voltaire, Plato, Thomas More, Xenophon and the *Espíritu de los mejores diarios*. In his *Examen instructivo* a decade later he used much the same sources, adding Vattel and Bentham, and quoting statistical information on England derived from J. E. T. de Montvéran, *Histoire critique et raisonné de l'Angleterre, au 1er Janvier 1816* (8 vols. Paris, 1819–22). Egaña was one of the two or three best read men in Chile at this period.

[3] It would be pleasant to suppose that Egaña had read Burke; but I can find no evidence that he had.

Platonic fantasy. Its underlying conservatism was out of harmony with the revolution. Its details were too complicated. When President Prieto accused the liberals, in 1833, of having succumbed to 'theories as fascinating as they were impracticable',[1] he might with justice have included Juan Egaña in his strictures. For Egaña's conservatism was far more utopian than the liberalism which tore down the impressive fabric of his Constitution.

[1] *El Presidente de la República a los Pueblos*, 25 May 1833, *AR*, I, 160.

8

FEDERALISM AND LIBERALISM
1824–1829

The Congress which assembled in November 1824 to destroy the Egaña Constitution soon presented the country with a depressing picture of totally negative achievement. Egaña's defunct political utopia was formally interred, but the new deputies were unable to discover a suitable formula to put in its place. The Congress moved into 1825 dominated by bitter private wrangles and tortuous procedural discussions which had little relevance to the national situation. The new British consul, C. R. Nugent, reported home in February 1825 that Congress had wasted its time 'upon mere formalities'.[1] General Freire, the Supreme Director, described its character as 'turbulent and boisterous'.[2] The growing disorder and moral bankruptcy of the Congress soon had a disastrous effect on the nation as a whole. On 20 April 1825 the Province of Concepción recalled its deputies and established its own Provincial Assembly. Freire quickly dissolved Congress, and five days later (22 May) the Province of Coquimbo, under the leadership of Francisco Antonio Pinto, followed Concepción's example and set up an assembly of its own. On 15 June Freire met the most prominent citizens of Santiago in a public assembly and agreed to govern with the advice of a new Junta. At the same time he tried hard to heal the dissensions between the provinces. In July he ordered the convocation of another national Congress, but Santiago was the only province which elected deputies, and when the Congress met in September it was unable to act nationally. This did not prevent the deputies from conducting a bitter quarrel with Freire over the issue of the projected second

---

[1] Nugent to Canning, 23 February 1825, F.O. 16/2, p. 177.
[2] To Benavente, 16 April 1825, F.V. vol. 821, p. 105. For examples of the low debating standards in this Congress, see Vicuña Mackenna, *Historia jeneral*, IV, 394–400.

expedition to Chiloé. On 7 October, Congress suspended Freire from the Supreme Directorship. Freire countered immediately, and dissolved the truncated Congress by force.

At the beginning of November 1825, Freire set up a Directorial Council to govern Chile during his planned absence in the South. The Council was headed by José Miguel Infante, who had by this time adopted fanatically pro-federalist views. Though the roots of Chilean federalism may doubtless be sought in the dissensions between the capital and the provinces, the influence of ideologues such as Infante gave the movement an enormous impetus. In January 1826, the Directory divided Chile into eight new provinces, in order to prepare for a fully federal regime. Freire, meanwhile, was meeting with success in Chiloé, where the royalist troops under the obdurate Quintanilla finally surrendered on 19 January, bringing the military phase of the Chilean revolution to an end. Freire arrived back in Santiago on 6 March, and almost immediately summoned a new Congress. The elections took place in mid May, and the Congress itself met in July, on the high tide of federalist sentiment. Freire chose this moment to resign as head of state. He was succeeded by Manuel Blanco Encalada,[1] who became, in point of strict fact, the first President of the Republic, the title of Supreme Director having been abolished. Neither Blanco Encalada's presidency (July to September) nor that of Agustín Eyzaguirre (September 1826 to January 1827) was much of a success, since the political initiative was now firmly in the hands of the Congress. Several important federal reforms were enacted, a draft constitution was produced, and Chile seemed on the verge of becoming a fully federal republic. The situation was largely dominated by one man: José Miguel Infante, the acknowledged coryphaeus of federalism.

The need to suppress a military insurrection in January 1827 brought Freire back to the helm, but he did not stay long. The atmosphere was growing steadily more hostile to federalism, and, on 5 May 1827, Freire's vice-president, Francisco Antonio Pinto,

---

[1] Manuel Blanco Encalada (1790–1876); with O'Higgins and Zenteno, chiefly responsible for the creation of the Chilean navy and its commander before and after Lord Cochrane; commander of the Chilean expeditionary force in Peru 1837, but replaced by Bulnes after the treaty of Paucarpata.

took over as head of state. By this time Chile was beginning to suffer from all the effects of prolonged political uncertainty. Confusion and lawlessness were on the increase, and many people were expressing deep anxiety. Already in 1825 Zenteno, the Governor of Valparaíso, had written to the exiled O'Higgins, telling him that 'disorder and anarchy reign...I am terrified to think about the future.'[1] Rodríquez Aldea told his old chief much the same tale: 'It is impossible to give you a true idea of this unfortunate country. Its aspect alters every day; it advances towards debasement and ruin.'[2] By 1826 the growing community of British traders was beginning to feel the same way.[3] Mutinies amongst the soldiery, and provincial disorders on a local scale, helped to aggravate such worries. The Aconcagua area, for instance, was in an almost continuous state of effervescent turmoil during this period. The rate of ordinary crime seems to have been unusually high as well. President Prieto claimed in 1841 that during his term of office (1831–41) the *annual* total of offences had been much the same as the *weekly* total during the liberal period.[4] Chile now presented a sorry appearance to those beyond her shores. 'Chile has reached the final degree of national humiliation...,' wrote O'Higgins to San Martín in January 1827; 'the country is null and void in all her parts.'[5] And this sad situation had its effects, too, on the social life of Mariano Egaña in London. For, as he wrote, 'such is the sorry state of Chile in the opinion of Europe that I am ashamed for anyone to see and recognize me in the street'.[6]

There can be little doubt that on many occasions during this period the central government failed to exert itself. 'The government's orders are regarded here with the greatest disdain,' wrote Pedro Trujillo from Valparaíso in 1825.[7] General Freire himself was a tolerant and generous man, but lacked 'the sort of talent calculated to make a wise and politic governor of a young state'.[8]

---

[1] To O'Higgins, 25 February 1825, *CHDI*, xxxvii, 151.
[2] To O'Higgins, 28 April 1825, *CHDI*, xxxvii, 341.
[3] British merchants at Valparaíso to C. R. Nugent, 28 May 1826, F.O. 16/5, p. 122.
[4] *Exposición*, p. 320.   [5] Letter of 12 January 1827, *Arch.O'H.* IX, 5–6.
[6] Mariano Egaña to Juan Egaña, 16 November 1825, *Cartas de Mariano Egaña*, p. 119.
[7] To Benavente, 24 February 1825, F.V. vol. 823, fo. 43.
[8] Proctor, p. 100.

Although he was probably by no means 'destitute of political courage', as Colonel Tupper believed,[1] he tended to allow matters to work themselves out without attempting to impose a specific government policy or to give a convincing lead himself. Yet Freire, for all his sins of omission, was very much the sort of Supreme Director the liberals of the 1820s wanted. As he himself wrote, 'Under my direction, Chile has seen political novelties; but she has not seen scaffolds, breaches of faith, persecutions, spoliations, taxation, or oppression of the freedom to speak and express one's thoughts.'[2] In this sense the Freire regime—and, indeed, the whole period from 1824 to 1829—was, as Isidoro Errázuriz later put it, 'a luminous interruption, an oasis of humanity and frankness between the dark proscriptions of the first Dictatorship and the greater proscriptions and condemnations of the epoch that followed'.[3] The failure of the governments of the 1820s can, in part at least, be ascribed to the circumstances. For these were 'times of political effervescence and faction'.[4] It was, perhaps ironically, José Miguel Infante who best summed this up. 'To govern in revolutions is difficult,' he said in 1824. 'Men have a proud spirit, incapable of being subjected to the law.'[5]

The atmosphere of the mid 1820s was certainly one of quite considerable frustration. There was a strong and noticeable undercurrent of disillusionment and anxiety even among the politicians who dominated the period. It is clear that the republic suffered from prolonged moments of disorganization, and these generated a sentiment of despair. 'The country is travelling to its ruin,' gloomily announced the newspaper *El Cometa* in 1827.[6] And yet there were compensating factors as well. Political discussion was conducted by a wider range of people than ever before, and the mid-1820s witnessed the development of a strongly political newspaper press. Many of these new newspapers were short-lived: 'they die almost as soon as they are born', wrote Pedro

[1] Sutcliffe, p. 255.
[2] 'Breve exposición de mi conducta', n.d., F.V. vol. 789, pieza 32; cf. Zapiola, p. 111.
[3] I. Errázuriz, p. 42.
[4] Concepción Provincial Assembly to Supreme Director, 29 October 1825, *SCL*, XII, 249.
[5] Session of 4 December 1824, *SCL*, X, 86.   [6] No. 1, 16 February 1827, p. 4.

Trujillo.[1] Their multiplication had begun immediately after the abdication of O'Higgins. 'The day after, the Republic was covered with newspapers,' it was recalled in 1831; 'a deluge of leaflets, libels and journals inundated every township.'[2] The provincial press, however, fared less well than that of the capital. *El Minero de Coquimbo* complained in 1828 that out of a possible readership of ninety thousand in its province, only some fifty to sixty subscriptions had been forthcoming.[3] Though some of the newspapers of the period exercised the peculiarly Chilean talent for satire to an excessive extent, there can be small doubt that on the whole freedom of the press produced good results. As Mora's journal, *El Mercurio Chileno*, commented in 1828:

many of these [newspapers], passing beyond the limits of moderation and decency, have done real damage to the cause which they affected to defend. But, in general, nobody will deny them the merit of having created a public tribunal to which the supreme power has frequently had to submit.[4]

By the time Francisco Antonio Pinto became acting President in May 1827, the wave of federalism in Chile was slowly receding. Opinion in Congress had become divided where previously it had been almost unanimous. Discussions on the draft federal constitution did not proceed beyond the first few articles. A vigorous opposition to federalism was mounted by Juan Egaña in the Provincial Assembly of Santiago. Pinto's first months in office were far from tranquil. He had to contend not merely with the political turmoil of the moment, but with natural disaster—there was extensive flooding in June 1827—and with disorders in the provinces. Congress, however, finally dissolved itself in June, and a National Commission was set up to supervise the country's emergence from federalism. The Commission was given the task of ascertaining provincial opinions on the future form of government for Chile, and was instructed to draft a new Constitution (which it left to the next Congress). In August 1827 some of the

---

[1] To Benavente, 23 July 1824, F.V. vol. 823, p. 21.
[2] *Bandera Tricolor*, no. 21, 9 September 1831, p. 95.   [3] No. 13, 14 June 1828, p. 47.
[4] 'Prospecto', no. 1, 1 April 1828, p. 1. Between O'Higgins' abdication and the end of 1829 there appeared some 101 newspapers; of these 58 produced less than ten issues. For a list, see Silva Castro, *Prensa y periodismo*, pp. 73–103.

federal laws were suspended, and by December a new Constituent Congress was in the making.

The Congress, the fifth since the fall of O'Higgins, met partly in Santiago and partly in Valparaíso. The committee which drafted the new constitution enjoyed the advice and help of José Joaquín de Mora, the distinguished Spanish man of letters and itinerant liberal. Mora's influence was almost as decisive in 1828 as Juan Egaña's had been in 1823. The Constitution, signed by President Pinto on 8 August 1828, was a good, perhaps even an outstanding document. It struck a sane balance between federalism and centralism, though its explicit abolition of *mayorazgos* was bound to create conservative discontent. The outlook for Chile was now encouraging. The Pinto government was (and was known to be) well intentioned and conciliatory. Pinto himself was widely admired, even by political opponents, and the British consul could write, reasonably realistically, of the 'generally improved state of Chile since his government'.[1]

The moderate liberalism which informed all the actions of the Pinto administration expressed itself most notably in an emphasis on freedom of the press, which was now guarded by an exemplary law,[2] and in a vigorous and positive attitude towards education. Pinto himself disposed that one pupil from the Instituto Nacional should lunch each day at the presidential palace,[3] and José Joaquín de Mora's new school, the Liceo de Chile, was encouraged by the grant of a former army barracks as premises and by a scheme for forty-two government scholarships. A liberal newspaper claimed in 1829 that education was receiving an 'immense impulse' from the government,[4] and, while this was doubtless an exaggeration, it seems clear that Pinto's intentions in the field were both ambitious and progressive.

A guarantee of public stability seemed to be implicit in Pinto's appointment of Francisco Ruiz Tagle[5] as Finance Minister

[1] John White to Lord Aberdeen, 25 September 1829, F.O. 16/9, p. 178.
[2] Printed in *SCL*, XVI, 395.   [3] Barros Arana, XV, 302.
[4] *El Fanal*, no. 5, 14 May 1829, p. 18.
[5] Francisco Ruiz Tagle Portales (d. 1860); leading conservative politician; member of the 1811, 1822 and 1828 Congresses; Senator 1812; Minister of Finance 1828–9; President of the Republic February to March 1830.

(23 July 1828) and of General Joaquín Prieto[1] as commander of the
army in the South (22 December 1828). Both men were to some
extent unsympathetic to the liberal trend of the 1820s. Ruiz
Tagle was a *pelucón* conservative, Prieto vaguely O'Higginist.
But their willingness to work with Pinto helped to foster a
climate of national unity. Towards the end of 1828, José Ignacio
Zenteno wrote to O'Higgins with a detailed analysis of the
political situation in Chile. He noted the continued antipathy
between liberals and conservatives, but added: 'Even so, Pinto,
Prieto and Tagle are the men who enjoy the greatest popularity,
and, if they continue in the positions they respectively occupy
today, order will certainly be guaranteed.' Zenteno, himself anti-
liberal, nevertheless paid tribute to a number of administrative
and financial reforms carried out by the government, and was
confident that peace and stability could be assured.[2] But at the
same time, nobody in Chile could fail to be aware of the gradual
crescendo of partisan bitterness which marked the political life of
the country at the end of 1828 and the beginning of 1829. Hostility
to the Pinto administration was stimulated and directed by a
relatively new political faction, known to the public as the
estanqueros, whose moving spirit was a hitherto non-political
businessman called Diego Portales. If Pinto stayed on as acting
President, it was widely agreed, little need be feared. But would
he? Pinto's enthusiasm for the Presidency declined as the bitterness in public life became more acute.

In the first half of 1829 the full machinery of the 1828 Constitution went into operation for the first time. Elections were held
for the *cabildos*, the Provincial Assemblies, the Chamber of
Deputies, and the electors responsible for voting for the offices of
President and Vice-President. The elections were conducted amidst
scenes of considerable disorder, and the liberals gained a substantial victory. On 14 July, however, Pinto asked the Permanent
Commission (which was in session during the congressional

[1] Joaquín Prieto Vial (1786–1854); distinguished patriot commander and friend of
O'Higgins; member of the 1823 and 1828 Congresses; commander of the army in the
South 1828–31; led the 1829 revolt against the liberal regime; President of the Republic
1831–41.
[2] Zenteno to O'Higgins, 23 December 1828, *CHDI*, xxxvii, 153.

recess) to excuse him from the government on the grounds of ill-health. The chairman of the Commission, Francisco Ramón Vicuña, took the oath as provisional President during Pinto's absence.

Congress reopened at Valparaíso on 13 September 1829. Its first task was to scrutinize the votes cast for President and Vice-President by the college of electors. Under the rules laid down by the Constitution, nobody was able to fill either office unless he had an absolute majority of votes. Pinto, the candidate of the liberals, fulfilled this condition and was elected President of the Republic. But the issue of the Vice-Presidency proved more difficult to settle. None of the candidates, it transpired, had secured an absolute majority. Congress itself was now required to proceed to a second election. An absolute majority was once again stipulated. The result of the congressional vote was as follows: Joaquín Vicuña (liberal), 29; Francisco Ruis Tagle (conservative), 24; Joaquín Prieto (O'Higginist), 2; blank voting papers, 3. Despite the fact that Joaquín Vicuña had failed to obtain the required absolute majority, the liberal-dominated Congress decided to proclaim him as Vice-President. There were obvious logical grounds for this decision, but it was politically tactless in the extreme. The conservative forces in the country seized on the 'illegality' of the vice-presidential election and made it their excuse to come out in open revolt against the government. President Pinto, whose only wish by this stage was to resign from the presidency altogether, proposed new congressional elections as a means of restoring national unity. Congress rejected this plan out of hand, and, at the beginning of November, Pinto finally transferred his authority to the president of the Senate, Francisco Ramón Vicuña. By now, however, events were far beyond the control of either President or Congress. The period of political experiment was over.

Such, in outline, were the most important events in Chile between December 1824 and November 1829. But before proceeding to a description of the main trends of political opinion in this period, I must make some reference to the question of political parties. The departure of O'Higgins in 1823 cleared the ground for a wider diversity of political factions and groupings than had existed previously. It is true that political parties in the modern sense did not really appear in Chile before the 1850s, with the foundation of the Liberal and Conservative Parties, but even so there *did* exist rough-and-ready alliances of like-minded politicians in the 1820s. Some historians—notably Encina[1]—have attempted to schematize these alliances, but in reality hard and fast categories will not apply. In the first place, the boundaries between one group and another were often rather vague. Alleances could shift frequently and easily. Thus Diego José Benavente, who began the period as an ardent liberal and as a minister in the Freire government, ended up as an *estanquero* and supporter of Portales. José Miguel Infante, the leader of the federalists, found no difficulty in attaching his name to the famous liberal proclamation of January 1828, even though he was soon to become a bitter opponent of the Pinto government. Personal rivalry, too, played its part. As one newspaper commented in 1827, 'disputes between parties become private feuds'.[2]

Only if these qualifications are borne in mind can any reasonable indication of the political 'parties' of the 1820s be given. Two main political tendencies can be discerned without difficulty: liberalism and conservatism. Neither tendency expressed itself in the form of a coherent, organized, and disciplined group. There were no whips in the various Congresses of the time. Nevertheless, political opinion did tend to divide itself roughly along liberal and conversative lines. The conservative camp consisted of roughly three recognizable elements towards the end of the decade. The most sizable of these was the *pelucón* ('big-wig') element, which consisted of the more traditional land-owning aristocrats in the state. The *pelucones* became progressively more disturbed as the 1820s advanced. Though more or less neutral until 1829, they eventually came to flirt with any political group which promised them 'honours and positions', and 'a future surrounded by nobility, titles and homage'.[3] The *pelucón* conservatives were complemented (and, in the end, controlled) by a less

[1] *Historia*, x, 17–18. Encina's definition of 'aristocratic liberals' as something distinct from *pipiolos* is misleading; all moderate liberals were nicknamed *pipiolos*.
[2] *Verdadero Liberal*, no. 4, 16 January 1827, p. 14.
[3] *La Ley y la Justicia*, no. 2 [November–December 1829].

doctrinaire but more inflexible faction known as the *estanqueros* or more simply as 'the *Estanco*'.[1] The *estanqueros* believed in tough, centralized government and an end to political debate. Some eminent liberals—most notably Diego José Benavente and Manuel José Gandarillas—were attracted by this philosophy, but the movement was directed, inspired and led by Diego Portales. In addition to the *pelucones* and *estanqueros*, there was also a small but apparently united group of O'Higginists, whose sole aim was the restoration of 'the veteran of republican ideas,...the representative of our glory, and the director of our first steps on the path of emancipation'.[2] The O'Higginists, largely inspired by the faithful Rodríquez Aldea, viewed the various liberal regimes of 1824–9 with disfavour. In practical terms, none of these three broadly conservative elements enjoyed power between 1824 and 1829, though individual conservatives sometimes collaborated with the liberal governments. It was a coalition of conservative forces, spurred on by Portales, which was able to carry out the conservative revolt of 1829–30.

The liberal camp was similarly divided. The main stream of the liberalism of the 1820s was moderate and conciliatory, and was graced by such outstanding personalities as Freire and Pinto. The liberals were known by various names. During the period of the Pinto administration, they styled themselves 'constitutionalists' or 'ministerialists', but were generally referred to by their opponents as *pipiolos* ('novices'). (As with 'whig' and 'tory' in England, terms like *pelucón* and *pipiolo*, originally used in a rather derogatory way, were adopted by those to whom they were applied.) Federalism was an offshoot of liberalism. Many liberals were federalists during the time of Infante's ascendancy (1825–7), and many changed back again afterwards. There was also a third, less weighty (though vocal) section of liberals sometimes referred to as *populares*. Broadly speaking, these popular-liberals represented the extreme left wing of the Chilean revolution.[3]

---

[1] The administration of the state *Estanco* (tobacco monopoly) was entrusted to Diego Portales and his business partner José Manuel Cea in August 1824. The federalist-dominated Congress of 1826 decided (21 September 1826) that it should be returned to the Treasury. This decision had the effect of plunging Portales into politics.
[2] *El O'Higginista*, no. 3, 12 February 1831.   [3] See Appendix 1.

Such divisions as these, as I have already suggested, must be considered as loose in the extreme. Chileans themselves were not always aware of them. A popular-liberal newspaper of 1828, for instance, could claim that Chile was divided into two parties only: the *estanqueros*, and those who opposed the *estanqueros*.[1] A newspaper of 1831 gave a similarly general definition of the rise and fall of political parties:

From 1818 to 1823 the party of O'Higgins triumphed, and then the party of D. Ramón Freire, which divided into the factions of *pelucones* and liberals, who later on called themselves *estanqueros* and 'ministerialists' or *pipiolos*. The *estanqueros* succumbed in 1827, and the *pipiolos*, triumphing with the election of D. Francisco Antonio Pinto, believed themselves indestructible.[2]

In its following issue, the same paper added the federalists to this scheme of things.

Bearing these factors in mind, however, it is still possible to give a brief account of the events of 1823–9 in terms of the interplay of political parties. The 1823 Congress, as we saw in chapter 7, was largely dominated by undifferentiated conservative elements. The period immediately following the downfall of the Egaña Constitution saw the rise to power of the liberals, headed by Freire, Pinto, Benavente, and Joaquín Campino, whose *tertulia*, according to Juan Egaña, was 'the focus of the government's deliberations' at that time.[3] In 1825, however, moderate liberalism was supplanted by the strong current of federalism headed by Infante. Federalism swept the Congress of 1826, but began to recede the following year. The liberals returned to power under Pinto, somewhat weakened. The number of desertions from the federalist movement was high, constituting for Infante a 'true political apostasy'.[4] But the possibilities of liberal coherence had been shattered by the federalist experience. Neither the federalists nor the popular-liberals could reconcile themselves to the Pinto

[1] *El Sepulturero*, no. 8, 30 October 1828, p. 58.
[2] *Antorcha de los Pueblos*, no. 3, 21 January 1831, p. 4.
[3] To Mariano Egaña, 25 October 1824, *Cartas de Juan Egaña*, p. 77.
[4] *Valdiviano Federal*, no. 23, 28 January 1829, p. 1.

regime, and ended up by giving their tacit support to the conservative reaction.

It was during the Pinto regime that the conservatives, who
had been out of office since the time of Egaña's ascendancy, under-
went their striking renewal at the hands of Portales. The rise of
the *estanqueros* as a powerful political group was quickly appreciated by the liberals as a very serious development. It seemed
obvious to them that the *estanqueros* were prepared to stimulate
political controversy for as long as it suited them to do so. 'On
the specious pretext of general utility', claimed a liberal newspaper
in May 1829, 'they are undermining the foundations of our
social pact.'[1] 'The *Estanco*', wrote the fervent liberal politician
and publicist Santiago Muñoz Bezanilla, 'is the germ of all the
ills which surround us.'[2] As will be seen in chapter 9, the *estanqueros* under Portales were successful in their self-appointed
mission of destroying liberalism and remoulding the republic
according to their own austere prescriptions.[3]

THE ATMOSPHERE OF LIBERALISM

Liberalism in one form or another dominated the period of
experiments between 1824 and 1829, and the mentality of the
movement demands some explanation. The liberals (*pipiolos*,
federalists and *populares* alike) accepted the common political
doctrine of the revolution. Thus 'the necessary foundations for a
people to be truly free' were defined by a liberal newspaper in
1827 as follows:

Popular election of representatives.—Their periodical renewal.—
Division of the powers.—Freedom to think and to publish one's
thoughts.—Abolition of privileges and titles which place some citizens
on a different level from others.—Trial by juries.—...Absolute
equality before the law.[4]

[1] *Verdadero Liberal*, no. 69, 29 May 1829. Cf. no. 68, 22 May.
[2] *El Centinela*, no. 21, 27 June 1829, p. 81.
[3] I have accepted here the general lines presented by Alberto Edwards in Edwards and
Frei, pp. 22–5. Encina's account (*Historia*, x, 18–21) seems to complicate the issues unnecessarily.
[4] *Miscelánea Política y Literaria*, no. 1, 31 July 1827, p. 7.

Some special emphases may be discerned in such a definition: the insistence on equality before the law, for instance, and on the abolition of titles. Yet there is nothing very far removed from the common body of beliefs of the revolution. What, therefore, marked the liberals off from other tendencies? For it is clear that there *were* differences between the *liberal* political philosophy of the revolution and the outlook of 'the liberals' of the 1820s.

In the first place, the liberals were conscious that the process of emancipation consisted of something more than a mere transfer of political power from the Spaniards to themselves. There were, in fact, two revolutions involved, not one. 'By the first, we became free men; by the second we must become *happy*. For the first, virtue was enough; for the second we need virtue joined with education. The second revolution is more difficult, since we must gain the victory over ourselves.'[1] The second'' revolution still had to be undertaken. In the well-known liberal proclamation which preceded the elections of 1828, the leaders of the movement issued a stirring clarion-call to action: 'LIBERALS, COMRADES, from today let our motto be: ORDER, AND WORK TO ESTABLISH THE REPUBLIC ON THE RUINS OF THE COLONY!'[2] It was a striking phrase. What did it mean? It implied something more than the end of the 'colony' in a literal sense, for that had already taken place under O'Higgins. Yet in 1827 *El Monitor Imparcial* could still claim: 'We must revolutionize the Colony in order to build the Republic on its ruins.'[3] The 'Colony', then, was principally a symbol for aspects of colonial life which particularly distressed the liberals, most notably the autocratic tradition and the excessive influence of the aristocracy.

Individual liberty was a basic strand of liberal thought, and the liberals of the 1820s supposed that it could not be reconciled to the existence of an autocratic executive power. The destruction of autocracy implied the establishment of a responsible self-

[1] *Despertador Araucano*, no. 1, 3 May 1823, p. 1.
[2] 'Proclama. Los Liberales de Santiago a los de todos los pueblos de la República', in *Mercurio de Valparaíso*, tomo I, no. 39, 23 January 1828, p. 153. Among those who signed this manifesto were Infante, the popular-liberal Carlos Rodríguez, and the future conservative president Joaquín Prieto, as well as such orthodox leaders as Pinto. This once again indicates the looseness of 'party' lines in the 1820s.
[3] 'Opiniones sobre formas de gobierno', no. 2, 23 August 1827.

governing community: 'Those imperious words "command" and "obey", irreconcilable with equality,...have been wiped out. We shall obey ourselves alone.'[1] But the sovereignty of the community had its limits. Like most other political thinkers of the revolution, liberals wanted 'a Constitution which, while proscribing aristocracy in any form, will neither abandon us to a savage democracy'.[2] They were confident that Chile could be steered between the Scylla of despotism and the Charybdis of anarchy. Despotism was allied to aristocracy, and aristocracy could best be tempered and weakened by a firm insistence on equality before the law. The considerable liberal emphasis on this point lent itself to satire. Juan Egaña, for instance, gave vent to his exasperation in the following depiction of the liberal attitude: 'Let every citizen be equal. Make it a grave crime for anyone to be taller or shorter, wiser or more ignorant...'[3]

The tendency particularly noticeable among liberals of all descriptions was the desire to limit the powers of the executive. A strong executive, they felt, automatically led to despotism. The 'ingredients of the force and vitality of executive action', as the committee which drafted the abortive federal constitution put it, were 'very prejudicial and ominous' to free institutions. A republic did not run nearly so great a risk by reducing and narrowing such 'ingredients'.[4] The really important thing, believed Francisco Ramón Vicuña, was to provide Chile with 'a law before which the tyrants must tremble'.[5] The people had to be made aware that 'their solid welfare consisted of...establishing guaranteeing institutions which, under the rule of law, would defend them from arbitrary power'.[6] This theme appeared in one form or another in liberal writings throughout the period under discussion. The great danger, in the liberal view, was that the

[1] *Minero de Coquimbo*, no. 24, 15 November 1828, p. 86.
[2] *Monitor Imparcial*, no. 5, 13 September 1827.
[3] 'Décimas que publicó un buen patriota, cuando, derogada la constitución del año 1823, se proponían muchos proyectos extravagantes, y que manifiestan el desorden de aquella época', in Egaña, *Colección*, VI, 207.
[4] Informe de la Comisión de Constitución, 25 June 1826, printed in *Patriota Chileno*, tomo 2, no. 48, 26 August 1826, p. 200.   [5] Session of 6 July 1826, *SCL*, XII, 55.
[6] The Junta of Santiago to the Santiago Provincial Assembly, 29 March 1823, *SCL*, VII, 26.

executive authority might be permitted to become too powerful: 'What is important', asserted the constitutional committee of 1828, 'is that all power should have its limits'.[1] President Pinto, on the occasion of the promulgation of the Constitution of 1828, rejoiced publicly that it set up 'the most formidable guarantees against the abuses of any kind of authority, of any excess of power', though at the same time he warned against 'parliamentary omnipotence' as well.[2] *El Mercurio de Valparaíso* joyfully proclaimed that Chile 'today swears to a charter which opposes a thousand firm and secure walls against oppression'.[3]

It is scarcely surprising that this deeply held liberal conviction should have expressed itself, more often than not, in a general disinclination on the part of the various congresses to collaborate with the executive power. When President Blanco Encalada submitted his resignation in 1826, he made no secret of the fact that this had been the cause of his decision.[4] Even the normally permissive Freire was driven to protest on one occasion: 'It is a very dismal error to believe that the man who administers the Executive Power is the nation's greatest enemy; this absurd concept could well plunge the country into the horrors of disorder.'[5] Far from accepting Freire's mild condemnation, the advisory Junta then helping him govern Chile replied: 'It is not a dismal error, as you put it...It is a political dogma, a truth.'[6] Though Freire enjoyed the confidence of liberals and federalists alike, the mere fact that he was Supreme Director indicated that he was a potential despot. As one deputy put it, in the Congress of 1824–5, 'No individual's liberty ever suffered detriment at his hands; but even so, we must forearm ourselves for the future.'[7]

As might be expected, this conviction of the potential evil of the executive power reached its most extreme (and indeed picturesque) expression in Infante and the federalists. 'All govern-

[1] *SCL*, xvi, 17.
[2] *El Vice-presidente de la República a la Nación*, 9 August 1828, *AR*, I, 139.
[3] 'Himno a la jura de la Constitución Chilena en Valparaíso', tomo 2, no. 10, 27 September 1828, p. 39.
[4] Blanco Encalada to Congress, 7 September 1826, *SCL*, xiii, 44.
[5] To the Junta, 26 July 1825, *Registro Oficial de la Suprema Junta*, no. 3, n.d., p. 24.
[6] Junta to Supreme Director, n.d., *ibid.* p. 29.
[7] Session of 13 December 1824, *SCL*, x, 136.

ments tend to despotism,' said Infante in 1828,[1] and he himself incarnated pure and undefiled suspicion towards all regimes and heads of state. 'We must not deceive ourselves,' he wrote in 1829. 'The sole safeguard of the people must be the law; it should never depend on the good will of the ruler.'[2] To Infante's way of looking at things, any good that statesmen did was little more than an accidental by-product. 'Washington did so much good for mankind because the LAWS OF THE NORTH AMERICAN FEDERATION placed him in the happy position of being unable to do bad.'[3]

This view led Infante to produce, in the Congress of 1826, an astonishing proposal to regulate the procedure for the occasions the head of state visited the Chamber. There were, thought Infante, far too many ostentatious distinctions and marks of deference accorded the Executive on these occasions.

Everyone knows that the Legislative Power is the one which represents the majesty of the nation, and that the man entrusted with the Executive Power is nothing more than an official of the nation... These distinctions, so improper and insulting to the people, must vanish from amongst us.[4]

Infante's plan to 'reduce the Executive to his proper limits' consisted of the following points: first, no deputy was to leave the Chamber to receive the President; second, nobody was to stand up as the President entered; third, his seat was to be placed in the main body of the hall, on the same level as the seats of the deputies; and, fourth,

The Executive will make his statement, preserving due decorum and respect towards the Chamber and to each one of its Representatives. If this is lacking, the president [of the Chamber]—and, in the [president's] failure to do so, *any deputy present*—will call him to order.[5]

Infante, of course, represented an extreme, and his extraordinary proposal could be scorned by Juan Egaña[6] with some degree of

---

[1] Session of 11 March 1828, *SCL*, xv, 306.
[2] *Valdiviano Federal*, no. 31, 21 December 1829. An article written, ironically enough, in support of Prieto's revolt.
[3] *Ibid.* no. 3, 19 December 1827, p. 4.
[4] *Proposición*, 22 August 1826, *SCL*, xii, 397–8.
[5] *Ibid.* xii, 398.   [6] To Mariano Egaña, 29 August 1826, *Cartas de Juan Egaña*, p. 188.

justification. But the tendency which could produce such a motion was deeply rooted in Chilean liberalism in the 1820s.

Francisco Antonio Encina has tried to explain this tendency in terms of the political mentality of the Basque race, which he regards as fundamental to an understanding of Chilean history. 'The Basque mentality', he writes, 'conceives liberty purely as the negation of government.'[1] But, after all, such a conception has never been the exclusive property of the Basques, and its appearance in Chile in the mid 1820s can best be seen as an expression of the desire of the liberal aristocracy to retain its hold on political power and to prevent any return to the kind of situation which had existed under O'Higgins. In this respect, some significance can be attached to the general reaction against O'Higgins which now occurred. His government was condemned as little more than 'the stupid liberticide's tyranny',[2] and such feelings were kept alive by O'Higgins' tentative support for the brief military insurrection in Chiloé in 1826, when further execrations of the hero appeared in the newspapers; he was described, for instance, as

the tyrant O'Higgins, that man of blood, that monster who knows no limits to his vengeance, who dominated Chile so despotically for more than six years, who, as the Nero of our century, was not satisfied with shedding the innocent blood of our best fellow citizens, excusing his murders by the pretext of "public order"...[3]

At the same time a minor cult of the Carrera brothers and the *guerrillero* Manuel Rodríguez began to find favour.[4] The Carreras and Rodríguez could be regarded (though somewhat inaccurately) as vaguely 'libertarian' in contrast to the 'despotic' O'Higgins—a tradition which has survived into some areas of modern Chilean historiography.[5]

By no means unconnected with this liberal rejection of the legend and reputation of O'Higgins was an undercurrent of

[1] *Portales*, I, 78.   [2] *El Liberal*, no. 2, 6 August 1823, p. 9.
[3] *Registro Público*, tomo I, no. 7, 9 June 1826, p. 89.
[4] Good examples of this are the long poems 'Al esclarecido y memorable General D. José Miguel Carrera y a sus ilustres hermanos' and 'Al inmortal Coronel D. Manuel Rodríguez' in *Correo de Arauco*, no. 32, 9 October 1824, p. 139.
[5] Alemparte, *Carrera y Freire*, for instance.

hostility towards Simón Bolívar. Bolívar's intentions towards Chile were extremely suspect—perhaps not altogether unjustifiably—and this, as well as the liberals' distaste for strong executive power and 'great men' in general, was responsible for diminishing the Liberator's stature in Chilean eyes. The newspaper *El Cometa* suggested in 1827 that if Bolívar's monarchist schemes succeeded in Grancolombia, he would soon find 'a pretext to round off his empire and inoculate Chile against her constitutional *virus*'.[1] There were occasional attacks on Bolívar in other liberal newspapers throughout the period,[2] and indeed beyond, for his death in December 1830 was reported in the government daily unaccompanied by the lyrical and effusive commentaries which might have been expected.[3]

The essence of the distinctive liberal thought of the 1820s in Chile was its rejection of strong government and its emphases on individual liberty and equality before the law. These features were a forceful development, though by no means a radical extension, of the common doctrine of the revolution. The liberals' aspiration towards 'a spontaneous, democratic and very liberal government', as O'Higgins' cousin Tomás put it,[4] was in many ways one of the most attractive aspects of the entire revolution, yet it failed to take into account some of the basic realities of Chilean life, and by identifying its chief enemy as the Executive power, reduced to the status of 'a monkey with its hands tied up', as Mariano Egaña scornfully wrote,[5] the liberal group deprived itself of the one instrument which could have set about 'destroying the Colony' in an effective manner. In 1829 the Intendant of Santiago told his Provincial Assembly: 'With the law in your hand, you are going out to work in a virgin terrain, to prepare a happy future for the generations who will come after us.'[6] He expressed an impeccable hope, but in one chief respect his

---

[1] *La Cola del Cometa*, no. 4, 8 March 1827, p. 12.
[2] See *Correo de Arauco*, no. 36, 9 November 1824; 'Orden del día', El Centinela, no. 10, 5 February 1829; 'Correspondencia—importante', *Mercurio de Valparaíso*, tomo 2, no. 96, 2 June 1829.
[3] *El Araucano*, no. 29, 2 April 1831, p. 1.
[4] Tomás O'Higgins to Bernardo O'Higgins, 9 July 1823, A.B.A. vol. 25-4(20), fo. 234.
[5] To Juan Egaña, 21 July 1827, *Cartas de Mariano Egaña*, p. 264.
[6] [Pérez Cotapos], *Mensaje del Intendente de la Provincia* (1829).

hope was misplaced. For Chile in 1829 was not a virgin territory on which the ideal liberal state could be constructed with ease. This, perhaps, was the liberals' most serious error.

THE ORIGINS OF FEDERALISM

Federalism, which swept through Chile for two brief years, may best be considered as an extension of the liberal desire to achieve individual freedom and self-government, and as a deepened hatred of the executive power. Yet in one form or another, federal sentiment had been a part of the revolution from its earliest moments. 'Those ideas of federation are not recent in Chile,' said a deputy to Congress in 1825.[1] Joaquín Campino tried, during the same debate, to put the federalist agitation of the moment into its historical perspective.

If we go back to the beginning of our revolution, we will recall that the strongest stimulus that made us start it, the archetype and example which suggested itself to everyone, was the federal government of the North Americans. Such was the language which was uniformly spoken in every part of Spanish America.[2]

The federalist movement of the mid 1820s was, in fact, a development stemming from the persistent assertion of local and provincial rights which had occurred throughout the revolution. It is to this particular trend that I must first turn, therefore. The first instances of federal or semi-federal feeling must be sought in the 'Patria Vieja'.

The first strong assertion of local rights against what was conceived to be excessive influence on the part of the capital occurred in 1811. On 8 January of that year, the Cabildo of Santiago demanded that the number of deputies representing the capital in the forthcoming national Congress should be raised from six to twelve. The Junta agreed to this request.[3] Before Congress assembled, the small group of *exaltado* deputies, headed by Juan Martínez de Rozas, protested that this disposition contradicted

---

[1] Session of 28/29 April 1825, *SCL*, XI, 213.   [2] *SCL*, XI, 211.
[3] Roldán, *Primeras asambleas*, p. 33.

the 'general will of the kingdom'.[1] The withdrawal of the *exaltados* from Congress was justified by this argument.[2] Manuel de Salas submitted a long memorandum on the whole question. He cited the examples of the United States and the Netherlands, and suggested that it was a basic principle that equal rights should be accorded equal areas. Santiago, he maintained, was depriving the province of Concepción of its just rights under the 'contract of association'. Salas urged deputies to remember 'the fate of the men of Segovia, Zamora and Burgos in the middle of the sixteenth century'. Following the North American example, Salas proposed that the provinces should be equally represented in a Senate.[3] A more common proposal, rejected by Salas in his memorandum, was for some degree of provincial control over the Executive. This view—that each province should contribute one member to the national Junta—now achieved some currency.

The need to heal the breach between Santiago which developed in the final months of 1811 kept the idea of a 'federal' Junta very much alive. It was an explicit aim of the revolution which brought José Miguel Carrera to power,[4] and became one of the bases of the treaty signed between O'Higgins and Vásquez de Novoa on behalf of the two provinces on 12 January 1812. Article 4 of the treaty embodied the principle of one member from each province in the national Junta. Article 8 gave the Junta the task of deciding whether or not to create a Senate based on the principle of two members from each of the provinces. And Article 18 contained a general statement that no province had the right to exact submission from another.[5] Though the treaty was never ratified by Carrera and hence never went into operation, it was an interesting and important indication of the prevailing view on provincial rights.

In April 1812, when the hostile armies of Santiago and Concepción confronted each other across the River Maule, Carrera and hsi great rival Rozas finally met, and, although their brief encounter was fruitless, they left an important exchange of notes

<hr />

[1] Protest dated 24 June 1811, *Arch.O'H.* I, 113.
[2] *Exposición* of the radical deputies, 12 August 1811, *ibid.* I, 115.
[3] *Representación*, 27 July 1811, F.V. vol. 812, pieza 4.
[4] *Acta* of Cabildo Abierto, 15 November 1811, *SCL,* I, 187.
[5] *Arch.O'H.* I, 181–6.

behind.[1] Carrera conceded that the provincial government established by Rozas at Concepción had the right to enjoy 'all the
authority, jurisdiction and faculties granted to the Intendants...
before the change in the old system of government',[2] while
Rozas, for his part, maintained that any system of national
government in Chile 'is and ought to be representative, so that
the equality of rights of all the peoples may be maintained and so
that some do not become colonies of others'.[3] Leaving aside the
grave personal and political differences which caused Rozas to
make his stand against Carrera, it is clear that a germ of federal
feeling was to be found in the Concepción camp, and that the
abortive treaty of January 1812 was the beginning of an approach
to federalism.[4]

In the middle of 1812 Joel Roberts Poinsett, the North American diplomatic agent in Chile, submitted to Carrera a draft
'Constitutional Code of the United Provinces of Chile',[5] which,
simplifying some of the features of the United States constitution,
incorporated the principle of provincial participation in the
executive and legislative powers.[6] But Carrera's own pitiful
attempt at a constitution in October 1812 contained no such
provisions.[7] In the course of time, this led to a reaction from the
provinces. In December 1813 the citizens of Concepción once
again proposed that the 'superior government' should be composed of representatives from the provinces as well as from the
capital.[8] But a far weightier protest against the Carrera 'constitution' came from the newly created province of Coquimbo. The
Cabildo of La Serena agreed to accept the 'constitution' of 1812
only if significant modifications were introduced. The Kingdom
of Chile, observed the Cabildo, was divided into 'three equal
parts' by population. These were the three provinces. It was the

---

[1] *Arch.O'H.*, *Primer Apéndice*, pp. 69–82.
[2] Carrera to Rozas, Talca, 14 May 1812, *ibid.* p. 73.
[3] Rozas to Carrera, Linares, 17 May 1812, *ibid.* p. 76.
[4] Bartolomé Mitre, in relating these events, accused Rozas of 'an inorganic federalism',
and described the January 1812 treaty as 'in form and in essence a pact of federation'
(Mitre, I, 333–4). As an Argentine, Mitre may well have had a greater instinctive knowledge of what constituted federalism than any Chilean historian.
[5] Printed in Collier and Feliú Cruz, pp. 71–86.
[6] Cap. 2, art. 1, and cap. 9, art. 1. [7] *SCL*, I, 259–61.
[8] Varas Velásquez, p. 134.

obligation of the capital to 'equalize with the other peoples with regard to the number of its representatives' in the Junta. The Americans had refused to send deputies to the Spanish Cortes because equal representation had been denied them. Concepción and Coquimbo should have the same right to elect members of the national Junta as Santiago, for 'being ruled by one's own laws and constituting one's own governments, is the foundation of civil liberty and the keystone of a popular system'.[1]

The issue of provincial rights in the '*Patria Vieja*' was in many ways unimportant when compared to the urgent questions of independence and the relationship with Spain. Nevertheless, Chilean federalism probably took its origins from that period. A more doctrinaire approach was reflected in the propaganda work of Camilo Henríquez, who showed his approval of federal government in an article in *El Semanario Republicano*,[2] but this was of smaller importance than the precedents already mentioned. While such precedents certainly stemmed from the powerful Spanish tradition of 'cantonalism' in politics, it cannot be concluded that theoretical federalism was not in operation as well. Henríquez claimed in 1815 that many of the advocates of provincial rights during the '*Patria Vieja*' had been protagonists of federal doctrine.[3]

During the government of Bernardo O'Higgins, ideas such as these had little chance of expression, and O'Higgins himself suppressed such vaguely and incoherently federalist movements as that of the Prieto brothers. But the hostility of Concepción and Coquimbo towards Santiago was an important element in O'Higgins' overthrow. Infante was later to claim that O'Higgins' 'spirit of capitalism' was a major reason for the revolt against him,[4] while Concepción leaders of the time accused Santiago of having taken over 'all the rights of old Spain'.[5] At all events, it

[1] *Acta* of the Cabildo of La Serena, 1 May 1813, Varas Velásquez, pp. 137–8.
[2] 'Idea de gobiernos federativos', *Continuación del Semanario Republicano*, no. 12, 15 January 1814.
[3] 'Ensayo acerca de las causas de los sucesos desastrosos de Chile', in Silva Castro, *Escritos políticos*, p. 189. See also Roldán, *Primeras asambleas*, p. 105.
[4] Session of 14 September 1825, *SCL*, XI, 369.
[5] 'Paizanos: Despertemos de nuestro adormecimto' [January 1823], A.B.A. vol. 25-3(2), fo. 207.

became clear after January 1823 that the relationships between the provinces were going to form a complex and delicate issue. The Concepción Provincial Assembly announced that it would only agree to restore its links with the other two provinces when it was certain that the 'system of equality' assured that Santiago would not 'attempt, against justice, to carry off a preponderance of dominion and representation'.[1] It was no coincidence that Camilo Henríquez should choose this moment to advocate a federal system for Chile,[2] for he was by no means alone in regarding this as the logical solution to the prickly problem of provincial rights.[3] This type of proposal seems to have frightened the Junta of Santiago, which commissioned an anti-federal pamphlet.[4] The 'Act of Union of the Provinces' signed on 30 March 1823 incorporated the idea of equal provincial representation in a Senate, and recommended the redivision of Chile into six provinces.[5] A redivision into eight provinces, urged by the Senate in June 1823,[6] seems to have had as its main aim the reduction of the influence of Santiago by distributing parts of its territory to other authorities.[7]

Throughout the brief period of Juan Egaña's ascendancy in Chilean politics, federalism was temporarily damped down again, though the small liberal opposition in the 1823 Congress produced a draft constitution which contained, yet again, the scheme whereby the Senate should be composed of two members from each province.[8] Opinion was divided on the question of the effect of Egaña's Constitution on provincial rights. A liberal newspaper of the time attacked the Constitution on the ground that it ended 'provincialism',[9] though two years later it was claimed that Egaña 'laid the foundations for federalism when he established departmental councils in his defunct constitution'.[10]

---

[1] To the Cabildo of Talca, 7 March 1823, *CAPC*, x, 366.
[2] *Mercurio de Chile*, no. 23, 13 March 1823, *CAPC*, IX, 459–62.
[3] See *Corresponsal del Imparcial*, nos. 1 and 2, March 1823.
[4] Dauxion Lavaysse, *Del federalismo y de la anarquía*. See Levene, p. 177 n.
[5] *AR*, I, 97.
[6] *Acta* of 11 June 1823, *SCL*, VII, 190.
[7] Senate to Supreme Director, 13 June 1823, *SCL*, VII, 197.
[8] Barros Arana, XIV, 178–9.
[9] *Redactor de las Sesiones del Congreso*, no. 17, 18 December 1823, p. 161.
[10] 'Apuntes y observaciones sobre las causas del movimiento revolucionario del 8 del presente mes', *Década Araucana*, no. 9, 28 October 1825, pp. 42–3.

THE FEDERAL UTOPIA AND ITS ENEMIES

It can be seen from this that when the provinces of Chile burst apart from one another as a result of the bankruptcy of the 1824–5 Congress, they possessed all the precedents they could have possibly required. Federalism had been a possibility throughout the revolution. The immediate cause of its sudden growth in 1825 seems to have been the mounting tension between the two outlying provinces and Santiago, coupled with a basic distrust and dissatisfaction with the Congress: 'the province of Concepción', said the deputy for Quirihue, 'detests the Congress more than the fiercest tyrant, and has more than enough reason for so doing'.[1] Infante noted, in the Santiago Provincial Assembly later in 1825, that 'the provinces have always complained that there exists a spirit of capitalism in Santiago'.[2] The Provincial Assembly of Coquimbo expressed this feeling more violently: 'We would prefer any state of political existence to the ignominious degradaation of seeing ourselves slaves to the insane caprices...of the capital.'[3] Whatever the cause, there was now quite definitely a desire on the part of the provinces, 'an embryonic and perhaps not very clearly conceived desire,' as Joaquín Campino put it, 'to have a local or municipal authority'.[4]

It should be noted here that the aims of Concepción and Coquimbo appear to have differed during the federalist phase of the 1820s. Concepción, by suggesting a scheme for a nine-man Senate (three from each province) to Freire,[5] tried to secure recognition of provincial equality in a more or less traditional way. Such was the tenor of an *acuerdo* taken by the Concepción Provincial Assembly in 1826. The main task of provincial assemblies was conceived to be the suggestion of local measures to the national Congress, while Congress, for its part, was urged to adopt a practical and lasting constitution which, without openly clashing with the opinions of the People or the tendency of the Provinces as made

---

[1] J. B. Cáceres, Session of 20/21 February 1825, *SCL*, x, 427.
[2] Session of 14 September 1825, *SCL*, xi, 369.
[3] To Freire, 10 July 1825, *SCL*, xi, 320.
[4] Session of 28/29 April 1825, *SCL*, xi, 211.
[5] To Freire, 30 May 1825, *SCL*, xi, 267.

manifest since the beginning of the revolution, should form a centre of unity and establish a fairly vigorous Government.[1]

Coquimbo, on the other hand, represented a more uncompromising trend of opinion. Its hostility to the capital seems to have been more intense than Concepción's, and its Provincial Assembly assumed, in the words of the British vice-consul, 'the Power of framing and establishing their own local and provincial laws, distinct from, and independent of any Control from the General Government of St Jago'.[2] The 'Fundamental Law of Coquimbo' enacted by the Provincial Assembly asserted: 'The Assembly reserves to itself the faculty of reviewing the political Constitution of the Nation and those laws which have a fundamental character, in order to ratify them or not.'[3]

It would be an exaggeration to say that the theory of the Chilean federalists reached any marked degree of sophistication or systematization, even at the hands of Infante, the wordy coryphaeus of the movement. Such arguments as were adduced can be mentioned fairly briefly. In the first place, the federalists held that their 'system' was the only legitimate way of securing provincial rights. As Infante said, in September 1825,

When the provinces say to us, 'We want federation,' they are saying, 'We wish to name our own governors, we wish to have our own assemblies so that they can administer the internal affairs of the province.' Could there be a juster ambition?[4]

The claim was just, believed the federalists, because of the geographical distances which separated the provinces from the capital: 'the more distant the extremities are from the centre, the more they need a local government'.[5] There was, too, a distinct feeling that local interests could only be adequately safeguarded by local people. Cienfuegos put this idea forward during the great debates on federalism in July 1826. 'Governors should be natives or citizens of the district that elects them,' he said. 'Otherwise,

---

[1] *Acuerdo* of 12 May 1826, F.V. vol. 445 (no pagination).
[2] Carter to Nugent, 22 May 1825, F.O. 16/2, p. 282.
[3] Ley Fundamental de Coquimbo, 2 July 1825, *SCL*, XI, 256.
[4] Session of 14 September 1825, *SCL*, XI, 369.
[5] *Patriota Chileno*, tomo 2, no. 48, 26 August 1826, p. 201.

they will not have the necessary resolve to stimulate the prosperity of their areas.'[1]

But federalism represented something more than the final settlement of the claims of the provinces. It expressed in a deepened and intensified form the liberal antipathy to strong executive power. As the Provincial Assembly of Coquimbo put it: 'There is no other means of depriving the government of that amplitude of power which unity confers.'[2] Infante rapidly converted this view into a dogma. 'Unity', he said in 1828, 'tends to the oppression of the peoples, federation to their liberty.'[3] Federalism was the best way of extending the freedom of the individual into every corner of the republic. 'Everything must be free among the peoples,' said Cienfuegos, 'so that all parts of Chile breathe freedom; but' he added, significantly, 'a prudent and moderate freedom.'[4] From this point of view, it was thought, a federal structure offered positive advantages by giving individuals everywhere a real opportunity to acquire virtuous democratic habits. 'The great advantage of this form of government', Henríquez had written in 1823, 'is that it provides a practical way of forming the moral education of the people.'[5] Even the most primitive countries, claimed one newspaper, had their 'periodical assemblies, in which they ventilate and settle their common affairs'.[6] There could be no case against federalism on the ground that Chilean customs were against it. Customs, argued Infante, could be changed. In 1810, for instance, the Chileans had been unaccustomed to exrecising popular sovereignty, but they had begun to learn.[7]

A weightier argument for federalism, as far as Infante and his followers were concerned, was the example of the United States. Many seemed to have believed that the exclusive reason for the success of the United States was its federal form of government. 'That country is happy,' proclaimed the Coquimbo Provincial

[1] Session of 6 July 1826, *SCL*, XII, 54.   [2] Manifesto, 6 October 1826, *SCL*, XII, 31.
[3] Session of 11 March 1828, *SCL*, XV, 317.
[4] Session of 6 July 1826, *SCL*, XII, 55.
[5] *Mercurio de Chile*, no. 23, 13 March 1823, *CAPC*, IX, 462.
[6] *Patriota Chileno*, tomo 2, no. 48, 26 August 1826, p. 199.
[7] *Valdiviano Federal*, no. 55, 15 March 1832, p. 2.

Assembly; it was Chile's clear duty to imitate it.[1] Henríquez had claimed that the marvels of the United States and England were the result of their institutions *alone*.[2] Infante was to state this theme more baldly some time later, in his federalist newspaper *El Valdiviano Federal*: 'To what do the twenty-four states that make up the North American Union owe their equal advance to prosperity? To their federal institutions.'[3] Once this simple idea was grasped, it was repeated time and time again. It was now more than enough that 'the immortal Washington, the incomparable Jefferson, and the memorable Adams all believed that federal government was the most useful and beneficient type'.[4] Many Chileans also took some of the more sanguine pronouncements of the Mexican government at face value, and assumed that Mexican 'progress' was due to the 1824 federal Constitution. Chile, it was felt, should look to

the recent example of Mexico, whose rapid and extraordinary progress is due to the adoption of this system, which should serve to undeceive those who persuade themselves that a certain degree of education is necessary before the system can produce the salutary effects it has produced in North America.[5]

Though in general it can hardly be inferred from the evidence that other Latin American federal movements had much of an influence on Chilean thinking, speeches by Francisco Ramón Vicuña during the debates of July 1826 show that there was at least some consciousness of the federal 'wave' then affecting different parts of the continent.[6]

Believing as he did that the federal institutions were efficacious of themselves, it was logical for Infante to claim that under such a system the economic advancement of the provinces would be automatically assured,[7] and to predict that federation would increase Chilean stature more rapidly and effectively than twenty new regiments.[8]

---

[1] *Circular a los partidos*, 23 May 1825, *SCL*, XI, 257.
[2] *Mercurio de Chile*, no. 23, 13 March 1823, *CAPC*, IX, 462.
[3] No. 55, 15 March 1832, p. 2.   [4] F. R. Vicuña, Session of 10 July 1826, *SCL*, XII, 92.
[5] *Patriota Chileno*, no. 14, tomo 2, 13 May 1826, p. 62. Cf. Fariñas' remarks, Session of 10 July 1826, *SCL*, XII, 90.   [6] *SCL*, XII, 55 and 91–2.
[7] Session of 10 July 1826, *SCL*, XII, 91.   [7] Session of 6 July 1826, *SCL*, XII, 58.

But even though the Chilean federalists failed, in the last analysis, to make out a particularly convincing case, the character of their movement remains interesting in itself. What Infante envisaged by 'an absolute federal government' as he called it,[1] can best be appreciated in the laws enacted by the Congress of 1826,[2] in the draft federal Constitution,[3] in the 'Project for a Constituent Act of the Chilean Federation' published in September 1826,[4] in the 'Provisional Regulation for the Regime of the Provinces' drawn up by Infante in 1828,[5] and in the pages of *El Valdiviano Federal* and other newspapers friendly to the federalist cause. From documents such as these, there emerges a beautifully organized plan of government, the chief feature of which is the duplication of power relationships at all levels of the state: national, provincial, and municipal. Thus the President of the Republic bears the same relationship to the federal legislature as the Governor-Intendant bears to his Provincial Assembly; and this is roughly reproduced at municipal level. As the constitutional committee of 1826 put it,

These municipalities and mayors, in their sphere, are what the assemblies and the governors are in theirs; and these, in their turn, resemble the great powers of the nation.[6]

What was suitable for the nation as a whole, argued Infante, was obviously suitable for each fraction of the nation.

If the general authority of the Republic is to be nominated by everybody...then the municipal authorities, which preside over and interest a fraction, should be nominated by that same fraction.[7]

In his 'Provisional Regulation' of 1828, Infante went so far as to suggest provincial Senates as well as Assemblies.[8] At all levels, the executive power was to be elected popularly and directly. The law of 29 July 1826 even provided for the election of priests

---

[1] *SCL*, xv, 310.   [2] Collected in *AR*, i, 210-14.
[3] *SCL*, xiv, 75-85.
[4] *Correo-Mercantil-Político-Literario*, nos. 57-8, 5-7 September 1826.
[5] *Valdiviano Federal*, no. 12, 26 April 1828.
[6] Informe de la Comisión de Constitución, 25 June 1826, in *Patriota Chileno*, tomo 2, no. 48, 26 August 1826, p. 203.   [7] *Registro Oficial de la Suprema Junta*, no. 1, p. 7.
[8] It is perhaps surprising, in view of the use made of the U.S. example by Chilean federalists, that this was not suggested more often, and this may point to a strain of realism not usually associated with the movement.

in parishes which were, or were about to become vacant, subject to later approval by the ecclesiastical authorities.

Such provisions represented a genuine attempt to allow the popular will its truest and most spontaneous expression. It was the doctrine of popular sovereignty carried to its furthest extreme. If some federalists seemed to want separate governments for 'each district, each township, and even each family',[1] this ought not to be considered surprising; for federalism was widely regarded as 'that *maximum* of perfection in a representative system'.[2] Infante was fully convinced that Chile was ready for federal institutions and that these were completely necessary. He believed that the people only needed awakening for them to achieve political advances of a spectacular kind. 'In Chile', he wrote, 'there is already a mass of enlightenment which only needs to be stimulated by probity and a true public genius, to draw the Republic out of its abjection.'[3] Only a savage clique of centralists stood between Chile and this bright and happy future, and, with the decline of federalism as an active force, Infante's conviction on this point hardened into dogmatism. 'The centralists are, with respect to the provinces, what the Spaniards were to America in another era,' he wrote in 1829.[4] Infante's biographer was probably wrong to describe this sort of attitude as an 'inexcusable caprice',[5] for capriciousness formed no part of Infante's earnest nature; but it can hardly be denied that in his later years he was inclined to regard any nominally 'federalist' movement as automatically authentic. He remained enthusiastically disposed towards the Argentine federalists of the period.[6]

---

[1] *Monitor Imparcial*, no. 2, 23 August 1827. It cannot be doubted that Chilean federalism *was* extremely decentralist. In 1831 a conservative newspaper claimed that during the federal period in the provinces 'some demagogues came to form the insane plan of making themselves independent' (*Bandera Tricolor*, no. 28, 17 November 1831, p. 111). The federal law of 13 July 1826 provided that, in the event of a violent dissolution of Congress, the provinces would 'reassume' their sovereignty (*AR*, I, 211).

[2] *Registro Oficial de la Suprema Junta*, no. 2, n.d., p. 22.

[3] *Valdiviano Federal*, no. 28, 30 July 1829, p. 4.

[4] *Ibid.* no. 25, 21 April 1829. Cf. his absurd comparison of Pinto with Marcó del Pont (no. 31, 21 December 1829).

[5] Santa María, *Vida de Infante*, p. 112.

[6] See, for instance, his eloquent tributes on the death of Facundo Quiroga (*Valdiviano Federal*, no. 93, 15 March, and no. 94, 24 April 1835).

In January 1826, Juan Egaña warned Joaquín Campino against allowing the direction of Chilean affairs to degenerate into 'a brotherhood of charity rather than a republican government'.[1] Federalism, by attempting to extend representative government as far as was humanly possible, laid itself open to such accusations, for in many ways its attitude was astonishingly libertarian. But it was never completely so. A federalist could insist on the sacredness of the right of property as well as the next man. In 1831, for instance, Infante attacked a regulation issued in the Rancagua district which stipulated that no *inquilino* could be dismissed without good reasons, which were to be noted and filed away by the local magistrate. This, wrote Infante indignantly, was an affront to landowners.[2]

The opponents of federalism, reduced in numbers though they were to start with, generally managed to marshal more impressive and reasonable arguments than the federalists themselves. They concentrated on the obvious weaknesses of the federal position. The notion that progress could be achieved merely by implanting a particular set of institutions was harshly attacked. General Luis de la Cruz, for instance, regarded federalism as a red herring. For, as he put it during the debates of July 1826, 'the liberty of the peoples depends...on democracy; this can either be unitary or federative'. In the Chilean case, he argued, federalism was both unnecessary—since Chile had always been a unitary state—and perilous.

Federalism produces the same effects in a nation as division does in a household. It breaks down the building...and establishes a division where none existed formerly. If a family becomes divided, will its various members, who previously had the use of their goods in common, do better on their own?[3]

This was the fundamental objection raised by Infante's opponents. It was not enough to attack, as did Casimiro Albano in 1828, those 'writers among us who suppose that all that is necessary is

[1] Egaña, 'Cartas...a Campino', p. 45.
[2] *Valdiviano Federal*, no. 51, 13 December 1831, p. 3. Cf. his remark quoted in chapter 4 (see p.   , n.   ).
[3] Session of 10 July 1826, *SCL*, XII, 91.

to reprint the constitution of the North Americans'.[1] It was too simple and easy to make the point that the success of federalism in the case of the United States did not necessarily imply its success when applied to Chile.[2] The opponents of federalism could supply the reason why these attitudes were wrong-headed. The Thirteen Colonies had, to all intents and purposes, been separate political units before their independence. A federal structure, therefore, had been fully justifiable as a means of bringing together previously disunited states.

In North America, where they tried to constitute States which had been separate and independent from their foundation, *federation* had to produce, and did produce *union*; but in Chile, which has always been called and has in fact been *one* kingdom, captaincy-general or presidency, federation must produce the division of the former union.[3]

The United States, by adopting a federal system, had merely provided a suitable framework for existing political institutions, and it was impossible to ignore the sharp difference between 'the perfection which they gave to the form already established' and 'the leap which we wish to make from the Spanish regime to the federal system'.[4] As Dauxion Lavaysse had put it in 1823, the 'United States gave themselves the only System of Government which could and should have been given'.[5] In the case of Chile, the creation of a federal system would, as Irisarri suggested some years later, be like 'marriage contracted by an individual with himself',[6] plainly a ludicrous concept.

Other criticisms of the federalist position were more concerned with the practical impossibilities of establishing the system in Chile. It was argued (falsely) that federalism, like the steam-powered printing press, demanded a perfect balance of components: 'if the cylinders present the slightest inequality, if there is the slightest delay in the movement of each part, then instead of

---

[1] Session of 11 March 1828, *SCL*, xv, 316.
[2] Martín Orjera, Session of 11 March 1828, *SCL*, xv, 315.
[3] 'Todavía una palabra sobre federación', *El Cometa*, no. 8, 18 April 1827, p. 39.
[4] 'Oficio del Diputado de Illapel a la Asamblea Provincial de Coquimbo', Santiago, 14 September 1826, F.V. vol. 812, pieza 13.
[5] *Del federalismo y de la anarquía*, p. 20.
[6] *El Constitucional*, no. 9, 14 August 1833, p. 35.

a correct impression ugly blots will appear'.[1] Chile, it was thought, lacked the necessary balance. Domingo Eyzaguirre argued, realistically enough, that federalism would involve the country in a completely unnecessary, not to say expensive, multiplication of parallel institutions in each of the provinces. If Santiago still only had one hospital, if payments to the army were still in arrears, he asked, how could Chile possibly embark on such a programme at all?[2] As the Concepción Provincial Assembly noted, towards the end of 1826, many of the provinces might have to oppose the federalization of Chile because of their general lack of resources.[3] This lack was striking in some areas. Chiloé suffered from a deficiency of men competent enough to make up the provincial assembly.[4] The Valdivia assembly claimed in 1829 that it could not afford to pay for the services of either a cleaner or a secretary.[5]

It was easy, too, to blame the growing disorders of the republic on federalism. Direct popular election of governors and priests caused considerable scandal,[6] and in some of the provincial assemblies parties were clashing violently, and no internal discipline existed. The more *exaltado* groups were revealing 'a tendency towards provincial sovereignty which will end in the total dissolution of the state'.[7] There was no real need for 'those little sovereign republics (*republiquetas*) without men and without resources', as Juan Egaña called them.[8] It is hardly surprising that the federalists were satirized mercilessly for their lack of understanding of the country's real needs. 'Although our beloved country is in mortal danger', ran one satirical verse, 'and although the whole nation is in a state of rebellion—*it matters little, if we have federation.*'[9] Two years later the same liberal newspaper printed

[1] *Miscelánea Política y Literaria*, no. 2, 6 August 1827, pp. 19–20.
[2] Session of 11 July 1826, *SCL*, XII, 104.
[3] To Congress, 3 December 1826, *SCL*, XIII, 353.
[4] *Patriota Chileno*, tomo 3, no. 18, 17 January 1827, p. 75.
[5] To the Governor-Intendant, 23 June 1829, A.V.M. vol. 15, pieza 9.
[6] See the speeches during the Session of 15 May 1827, *SCL*, XIV, 386.
[7] *El Cometa*, no. 8, 18 April 1827, p. 37.
[8] 'Carta de un Ciudadano á un Diputado al Congreso Nacional de Chile en 1826', F.V. vol. 120 A, pieza 12.
[9] 'Federación o muerte', *Verdadero Liberal*, no. 20, 20 March 1827, p. 99.

an extremely funny satirical prophecy of what Chile would be like in 1830, were the federalists to regain their influence.

The republic enjoys perfect calm.—The Province of Coquimbo is undergoing a revolution—Aconcagua has risen en masse—...In Colchagua the federal authorities have been hanged—In the Maule the Government has been declared an outlaw...In Valdivia they have decided to march on the Capital (though they will have to build the road first)...[1]

It is significant that this satire should have been printed in a liberal newspaper. For, as soon as the practical consequences of federalism were noticed, liberals and conservatives alike—not to mention a good few federalists as well—realized that, as far as Chile was concerned, the federal system was 'only suitable for... the Golden Age, or the century of the patriarchs'.[2] The people of Santiago, who had cheered the enactment of the motion constituting Chile a federal state in July 1826,[3] gave vent to laughter when the cry of 'Viva Infante!' was raised in the Plaza de Armas two years later.[4]

THE PINTO ADMINISTRATION

Of the regime of Francisco Antonio Pinto from 1827 to 1829, little need be said here. It attempted to give the main current of liberalism in Chile its most solid and dignified political expression, and it seemed for a time as if this would succeed. The new atmosphere of confidence which gradually emerged was a strong contrast to the general disillusionment which had prevailed at the time of the breakdown of the federal experiment. Pinto himself was a tolerant and generous man, and his aims were high. 'Pinto...' wrote the French scholar Claude Gay, 'wished to adapt to Chile the maxims of Rivadavia.'[5] His basic object was to keep Chilean politics within a framework of legality, and to prevent party conflicts from growing too violent. 'Sr Pinto, then, proposes to create a constitutional spirit,' observed one liberal

[1] 'Marzo 4 de 1830', *Verdadero Liberal*, no. 66, 9 May 1829.
[2] *El Hambriento*, no. 2, 27 December 1827, p. 6.   [3] *SCL*, xii, 106.
[4] *Clave de Chile*, tomo 2, no. 3, 24 July 1828, p. 9.
[5] 'Sur l'histoire du Chili et la révolution' [Notes], Archivo Gay-Morla, vol. 52, fo. 396.

editorialist. 'He is working for it, and is achieving it; and he places himself at the head of those who are disposed to obey the laws...'[1] He was aided in this aim by his own personal talents: 'he possessed the art of contenting everybody', admitted a conservative newspaper after the downfall of the liberal regime.[2]

This particular approach was undoubtedly responsible for the creation of a new spirit of confidence. Thus Pinto's own supporters were able, as early as mid 1827, to hail the work of his government as 'the end of misfortune and the start of a new regeneration',[3] while Gandarillas and Benavente, future supporters of Portales, expressed this same optimism at greater length:

Chile advances naturally towards prosperity even in the midst of all the setbacks she has suffered...Trade, agriculture, industry and education have all made great progress. The rights of the citizen are respected, and freedom exercises a limitless sway.[4]

One liberal newspaper admiringly exclaimed: 'This government has the ability to work, to administer!'[5] Though much remained potential rather than realized, public confidence in the government continued throughout 1828. At the end of the year, *El Mercurio de Valparaíso*, in an effusive editorial, praised Pinto in lyrical tones and foretold greater progress.

Hail, fortunate Chile! after a long series of vicissitudes you have raised, in this year of 1828, a monument as marvellous as the soaring Andes! Hail, dwelling-place of free men, the fatherland of smiling Amalthea, abode of sincerity and hospitality! You have been reborn![6]

Though the clouds of impending crisis shadowed 1829, it was still generally agreed that Pinto, and Pinto alone, could give Chile the internal tranquillity she needed. The British Consul reported home in July 1829 that

the zealous and anxious labours of the Vice-President[7] for the Honor and prosperity of the State have been fully manifested throughout his

---

[1] *El Fanal*, no. 2, 14 May 1829, p. 18.
[2] *Bandera Tricolor*, no. 22, 17 September 1831, p. 98.
[3] *La Clave*, no. 1, 21 June 1827, p. 4.   [4] *La Aurora*, no. 1, 16 June 1827, p. 2.
[5] *Verdadero Liberal*, no. 51, 28 June 1827.
[6] Tomo 2, no. 37, 31 December 1828.
[7] Pinto had been Freire's Vice-President and retained the title throughout his administration.

Government, and though the Party called the Estanqueros has in the most hostile and foul manner thrown every obstacle in the way of it, in order to induce his resignation, I firmly believe, should he resume it, that his energy and firmness will…secure to the Country a still better management of its resources and a more just and systematic administration of its affairs in general.[1]

In short, there was some justification for the belief, expressed by *El Mercurio de Valparaíso* on the occasion of Pinto's final withdrawal from the political scene, that 'Sr Pinto has regenerated this happy people, summoning it to greatness'.[2]

The breakdown of the alliance between Pinto and Ruiz Tagle, and the decision by Prieto to support the conservatives in a final showdown with the liberals, made the end of the liberal government inevitable. Yet the Constitution of 1828, the regime's finest achievement, might well have caused trouble on its own account, even if events had not forced the issue. The Constituent Congress of 1828 had set high standards of debate and was a contrast to the acrimonious and futile congresses of the recent past,[3] and the Constitution itself was drawn up with the help of José Joaquín de Mora,[4] whom even Juan Egaña was forced to admire,[5] though Manuel de Salas found him 'somewhat ideological'.[6] 'The popular principle is the one which dominates in this constitution,' explained a long article in Mora's review *El Mercurio Chileno*: '…everything emanates from the people and is directed to its welfare'.[7] The constitution, believed the liberals, 'contains all the precautions which the most ardent friends of liberty long for to calm the fears which the exercise of power might inspire in them'.[8] Yet the provisions of the constitution, impeccably liberal as they were, were too much influenced by immediate circumstances. Federal principles still had enough power in Chile to ensure that

[1] White to Aberdeen, 18 July 1829, F.O. 16/9, p. 31.
[2] 'Interior', tomo 3, no. 68, 25 September 1829, p. 135.
[3] See *Clave de Chile*, tomo 2, no. 78, 3 February 1829, p. 310.
[4] Suggestions that his influence was not as great as has traditionally been held have been refuted by Ricardo Donoso in 'José Joaquín de Mora y la constitución chilena de 1828', *Cuadernos Americanos*, vol. C, no. 100, año XVII (1958), p. 400.
[5] T. M. J. Ramos, 31 March 1828, F.V. vol. 802, pieza 14.
[6] To Campino, 15 August 1828, Salas, *Escritos*, III, 84.
[7] No. VI, 1 September 1828, p. 280.   [8] *Ibid.* p. 279.

the constitution provided for provincial assemblies,[1] yet these failed to satisfy the federalists, who regarded the attributions of the assemblies as 'very limited and almost insignificant',[2] while the conservatives, for their part, considered the constitution as 'federal in every sense'.[3] Colonel Tupper, a supporter of the liberal regime, for which he gave his life, thought that the popular elections were too frequent,[4] and certainly two years seems to have been too short an interval from the viewpoint of good government and the maintenance of public order.

But it would be wholly unfair to blame Mora's skilfully drafted constitution for the downfall of the liberal regime in Chile. Pintos' administration had, as Francisco Ramón Vicuña put it, been 'conciliatory and sensible,... a point of light in the midst of the anxieties that agitate the other republics of America'.[5] But deeper influences were at work. The administration's base of political support had never been as comprehensive as liberals liked to claim. Portales and his friend, sickened by recurrent public disorder, were eager to impose a new and very different political order. And Pinto himself withdrew from the tasks of government. The disputed vice-presidential election of September 1829 gave the conservative forces their long-awaited chance to bring down the curtain on the Chilean revolution.

[1] See Roldán, 'El centralismo', pp. 411–12.
[2] *Valdiviano Federal*, no. 33, 11 February 1830, p. 1.
[3] Rodríguez Aldea to O'Higgins, 12 February 1831, *CHDI*, XXXVII, 91.
[4] Quoted in Sutcliffe, p. 268.
[5] *Mensaje al Congreso Nacional*, 13 September 1829, *SCL*, XVIII, 61.

9

THE CONSERVATIVE REACTION
1829–1833

The decade which followed the final establishment of independence in Spanish America saw a difficult readjustment to the new conditions of republican government and national freedom. Loosely speaking, the history of Spanish America in the mid 1820s was moulded by a reaction against the strong (usually military) authorities which had secured independence. Thus Mexico and Central America alike, in the Constitutions of 1824–5, rid themselves of the legacy of Iturbide. The insurrection of 1826–7 in Venezuela was, in part at least, a local protest against the centralizing tendencies of the government of Grancolombia. With the departure of Bolívar from Peru, federalist sentiment swept the country and was not without its effects on the decentralizing constitution of 1828. The peculiar circumstances of the River Plate continued to foster a drastic struggle between the central government and provincial *caudillos*. Chile, as we have seen, experienced a wave of liberalism and federalism after the removal of O'Higgins and the largely irrelevant episode of the Egaña Constitution. Towards the end of the 1820s, however, it became apparent that the political utopia which the creoles joyously anticipated had failed to instal itself. The widespread disorder and turmoil of the period created a strong current of disillusionment, the most famous expression of which was the final, despairing verdict of Simón Bolívar that to serve a revolution was to plough the sea. The new republics soon discovered that there were two ways to proceed politically: either they could allow chaos to continue indefinitely, extinguished only by brief interludes of tyranny, or alternatively they could accept the establishment of personal dictatorship over long periods at a time. In practice, Peru, Bolivia and Colombia adopted the first

21-2

situation; Paraguay, Argentina, and Venezuela adopted the second. Only one Spanish American republic succeeded in breaking away from this pattern altogether. During the early 1830s, Chile managed to put a stop to disorder without accepting a personal tyranny. By creating a strong but impersonal authority, the Chileans were able to pave the way for later constitutional government and the establishment of a genuinely democratic tradition. This was largely the work of one man, Diego Portales, and it began with the breakdown of liberal government in the spring of 1829.

The dissident elements in Chilean politics proved too strong for the relatively fragile machinery of liberal constitutionalism. Pinto's administration had been tolerant and unprovocative, and yet it had failed to build up the consensus which Pinto himself desired. The *pelucón* conservatives, representatives of the traditional land-owning aristocracy, could only view with displeasure the abolition of their time-honoured *mayorazgos*, an explicit provision of the 1828 Constitution, and their deeply religious instincts were offended by Pinto's anticlericalism. The *estanqueros*, for their part, had grown increasingly dissatisfied with the government's inability or unwillingness to deal harshly with disorderly elements. During 1829, through such organs as the newspaper *El Sufragante*, the *estanquero* programme had been made clear: Chile needed a strong, centralized and businesslike government which would suppress rebelliousness and establish a powerful aura of authority. The O'Higginists, relying on General Prieto in the South, were prepared to join forces with *pelucones* and *estanqueros* alike to bring about the restoration of their hero, whom they believed the only man capable of giving stability and progress to the country.

News of the disputed vice-presidential election of September 1829 reached Concepción, Prieto's headquarters, at the end of the month. On 4 October the Provincial Assembly withdrew its recognition from the Congress, the President, and the Vice-President, and named Prieto as its new Intendant. Eight days later the Provincial Assembly of the Maule came out in support of the Concepción move, and it became plain that a full-scale revolution was in the offing. The conservatives' excuse was that the Constitution had been violated; it was necessary to 'restore' the rule of law. By the end of October, troops were moving northwards towards the Capital, under the command of Manuel Bulnes.

The national Congress, its decision hastened by a conveniently timed earth tremor, now returned from Valparaíso to Santiago, where it reopened on 14 October. But its deliberations were no longer of any importance to anybody. On 7 November a public assembly of some thousand people approved a motion from the *estanquero* Manuel José de Gandarillas to set up a national Junta to take over from the Congress. The provisional President of the Republic, Francisco Ramón Vicuña, refused to have anything to do with the new Junta. 'I have sworn to uphold the constitution of the State,' he wrote. 'I cannot betray that high trust.'[1] His words were vain. On 12 November he was compelled to leave the city, and just over a month later he gave himself up to the provincial authorities in Coquimbo, which had meanwhile declared for Prieto.

By now Bulnes and the army of the conservative revolution were within twenty-five miles of Santiago. There they were joined by Diego Portales, Rodríguez Aldea, Manuel Rengifo[2] and other anti-liberal leaders. Portales brought money to replenish the army's limited funds. But serious hostilities with the liberal troops in Santiago, which had passed under the command of General Francisco de la Lastra, were avoided until 14 December, when Prieto, who had by this time joined the conservative forces, faced Lastra at Ochagavía. The battle was indecisive, but prompted a short-lived peace settlement, by which both armies came under the supreme command of the much respected General Freire, who had returned to public life as a member of the Junta set up on 7 November. Freire arranged for the election of a new national Junta—largely conservative in composition, thanks to liberal abstentions—but was unable to tolerate Prieto, who was steadily moving his army into the capital. On 18 January 1830 Freire broke with Prieto and took the remnants of the liberal

[1] Vicuña to the Junta, 11 November, quoted in Barros Arana, xv, 429.
[2] Manuel Rengifo Cárdenas (1793–1845); Portales' Finance Minister 1830–5; Senator 1834–7; brother of Ramón Rengifo (c. 1795–1861), one of the wittiest conservative writers of the time.

army to Valparaíso in order to make a stand against the conservatives.

Freire's departure from Santiago lost him the civil war. The conservatives were now in control of the capital and of much of the rest of the country, and their grip tightened quickly. On 12 February 1820 a specially summoned Congress of Plenipotentiaries assembled, and abrogated all the acts of the 1829 Congress. Francisco Ruiz Tagle, the *pelucón* who had served in Pinto's government, was appointed President of the Republic. The influence of the Plenipotentiaries was decisive in moving Chile away from liberalism and towards the new conservative order: 'all the laws and measures agreed on by that body...were the moulds into which the Conservative Republic later settled'.[1] But it was the energy and singlemindedness of one man, Diego Portales, which drove the revolution inexorably forward. In March he was instrumental in forcing the resignation of Ruiz Tagle from the presidency and in securing the appointment of the more compliant José Tomás Ovalle.[2] On 6 April, Portales became Minister, taking on the portfolios of the Interior, the Exterior, War and Marine. He thus became the most powerful man in Chile.

The personality of Diego Portales[3] has never ceased to exercise a deep fascination for historians. It was a strange blend of private hedonism and public austerity. Portales' capacity for womanizing and guitar-playing contrasted sharply with his considerable astuteness as a businessman and his utter ruthlessness as a statesman. On the one hand was the man whose life was rich in friendships, a gay and amiable figure; on the other the austere servant of the state

---

[1] Olga Retamal Ide, 'Congreso de Plenipotenciarios de 1829 a 1830' (unpublished *Memoria de prueba*, Santiago, 1955), p. 118.

[2] José Tomás Ovalle Bezanilla (1791–1831); member of the 1823, 1824 and 1826 Congresses; President of the Republic 1830–1. The town of Ovalle in the Province of Coquimbo was named after him.

[3] For Diego José Víctor Portales Palazuelos (1793–1837) see, in order of importance, Vicuña Mackenna, *Diego Portales*, perhaps his best historical work; Ramón Sotomayor Valdes, *El Ministro Portales* (1954); Encina, *Portales*. Hugo Guerra Baeza, *Portales y Rosas* (1958) provides an interesting if not very illuminating comparison with the Argentine tyrant. Portales' letters are printed in Cruz and Feliú Cruz. A useful anthology of his writings—mainly epistolary—is Raúl Silva Castro, *Ideas y confesiones de Portales* (1954).

who, on his own famous admission, would have shot his own father if this were necessary for public order. Rodríguez Aldea, who pinned his vain O'Higginist hopes on Portales' success, wrote that he possessed 'a lively and enterprising character and an incredible energy; but, at the same time, he was false, inconsistent, wilful, a man of implacable hatreds'.[1] Pedro Félix Vicuña, the impassioned liberal who opposed Portales and all his works, later wrote that his genius would have done honour to a better cause,[2] and believed that at heart he had held liberal principles.[3] Portales' superb skill as an administrator is not open to question. His businesslike efficiency was marked in the extreme, and his governorship of Valparaíso, for instance, a model.[4] But his modern disciples and admirers—most notably Alberto Edwards and Francisco Antonio Encina—have done him a disservice in submitting him to virtual deification. Portales' political 'impersonality', much stressed by his followers, has often been exaggerated; indeed, many of his actions seem to have been motivated by personal rancour as well as patriotic spirit. But, despite the excesses of his admirers, Portales' place in history is secure. Without his firmness the transformation of Chile between 1830 and 1833 would never have taken place at all.

While the conservative regime was installing itself in the capital, Freire was desperately trying to mount a counter-attack. In January and February 1830 he took his troops by sea to Coquimbo and temporarily reasserted liberalism in the province. At the start of February, liberal forces in the South recaptured Concepción, but their triumph was ephemeral. Doubling back down the coast from Coquimbo, Freire landed at Constitución on 7 March and prepared to confront the punitive expedition which the conservatives were sending south under Prieto. In 15 April Freire moved across the River Maule and occupied Talca, but his army of around seventeen hundred men was now outnumbered, and two days later he was finally checkmated by Prieto at the Battle of Lircay. The liberal cause was in ruins. The Province of

[1] 'Sucinta idea de lo que ha ocurrido en Chile', 1831, *CHDI*, xxxvii, 77.
[2] *Paz Perpetua á los Chilenos*, no. 6, 28 July 1840, p. 1.   [3] *Ibid.* p. 6.
[4] See A.M.I. vol. 66, *passim*, and Vicuña Mackenna, *Diego Portales*, I, 201–18.

Concepción submitted to the conservative regime at the start of May, and at the end of the month Freire himself was arrested and immediately banished to Peru.

Nobody now dared dispute the conservatives' mastery of Chile. Slowly but surely Portales consolidated his hold. Both before and after the Battle of Lircay, prominent liberal officers who showed an understandable lack of enthusiasm for the new order were cashiered, Lastra and Pinto among them. Subversion in any form was ruthlessly countered. Liberals who expressed their distaste for the new regime through the newspaper *El Defensor de los Militares Denominados Constitucionales* (expressly founded to vindicate the cashiered liberal officers) and its equally forthright successor *El Trompeta* were arrested and exiled. One of them was José Joaquín de Mora, who had his revenge in the form of a venomously witty (and accurate) set of verses pointing out the contrast between the active Portales, the real power in the land, and his puppet President, José Tomás Ovalle, 'who just signs things'.[1] Mora's poem has endeared itself to later generations of Chileans, to whom satire is a natural form of self-expression.

But the President 'who just signs things' was in poor health, and in March 1831 he resigned his office, to die within a fortnight. The Commission of Plenipotentiaries chose General Prieto to fill the vacant presidency, but, until his formal assumption of power in September 1831, Fernando Errázuriz,[2] who had once been nicknamed 'Ferdinand VIII' for his extreme conservatism,[3] acted as provisional head of state. During the first half of 1831, the small Chilean electorate—the liberals generally abstaining—chose a new Congress, ratified Prieto's appointment as President, and made Portales Vice-President (a post he unwillingly held until its abolition under the 1833 Constitution). The new Congress met on 1 June. One of its first tasks was to decide whether or not to reform the 1828 Constitution. This had been publicly urged with increasing frequency from the beginning of the year, even though

---

[1] *El Trompeta*, no. 14, 25 February 1831 (its last issue).
[2] Fernando Errázuriz Aldunate (1777–1841); member of the 1811, 1822 and 1823 Congresses; member of the Junta 1823; member of the Congress of Plenipotentiaries 1830–1.
[3] Vicuña Mackenna, *Vida de O'Higgins*, p. 441 n.

one of the express aims of the 1829 revolt had been to 'restore' the Constitution following its violation by the liberals. On 21 June the Senate enacted its famous resolution that 'the Constitution...needs to be altered and modified'.[1] A Grand Constituent Convention was set up to carry out the task. It consisted of sixteen deputies, six leading public servants, four men of letters, four landowners, two ecclesiastics, two prominent merchants, and two mining proprietors. They began their labours in October.

Portales stepped down from power on 13 August 1831, though retaining the portfolio of War for a further eleven months. Throughout the revolution he had consistently refused to become head of state, remaining true to his own famous dictum that he 'would not exchange the Presidency for a *zamacueca*'.[2] When Prieto formally took charge of the state in September 1831, Portales refused to take the oath as Vice-President (though he retained the title) for fear that he might have to take up the succession in the event of Prieto's death. Thereafter he took no official part in the work of the government, living most of the time in Valparaíso (whose Governor he became) or on a small estate he bought in the Ligua Valley, until a new turn of events brought him back for his second and final term as Minister (from September 1835 to his murder in June 1837).

But whether in or out of the government, Portales was the inspiration of the conservative regime, its mentor and director. From the start, he made it utterly clear that the government was not disposed to tolerate subversive activity or administrative inefficiency from anybody. Nor would Portales allow his central purpose—the establishment of an unchallengeable authority—to be deflected by political intrigue from his own supporters. His dealings with the O'Higginists illustrate this point exactly. As we have seen, Rodríguez Aldea and the O'Higginists supported the 1829 revolt in the hope that Prieto, an old friend of O'Higgins, would assist them in restoring him to power in Chile. Portales gave Rodríguez Aldea the impression that he was by no means

[1] Barros Arana, XVI, 64.
[2] Vicuña Mackenna, *Diego Portales*, I, 56. *Zamacueca*: popular Chilean dance nowadays more usually known simply as the *cueca*.

opposed to O'Higgins,[1] and in the first months of 1830 there was evidently some speculation in Santiago as to whether Prieto might not bring back the hero.[2] From 1830 to 1832 the O'Higginists put out a veritable barrage of propaganda,[3] but, as time passed, they began to suspect that Portales and Prieto had concluded a firm agreement to prevent O'Higgins from returning.[4] Thereafter the O'Higginists made several half-hearted attempts to prise Prieto and Portales apart,[5] and speculated about the possibility of a break between the two men.[6] This was by no means wishful thinking on their part; rumours of disagreement between the President and his nominal Vice-President were not uncommon. But the O'Higginists' hopes were, in fact, unfounded. Portales had made sure of Prieto's personal allegiance early on in the revolution. By November 1830 Prieto was writing to him: 'Our friendship is indissoluble, and in absolutely no way do I prefer the friendship I have with General O'Higgins.'[7] Though Prieto openly admitted on one occasion that he would prefer the return of O'Higgins to a liberal *revanche* with Freire at its head,[8] it is plain that he became increasingly irritated by the O'Higginist propaganda,[9] and that his elevation to the presidency tempered his natural desire to allow his old friend to revisit Chile. Portales, for his part, was uncompromisingly opposed to any such possibility, which he felt might threaten the stability of his own political creation. When his Minister of War, General José María de la Cruz, showed open signs of O'Higginism, Portales forced him to resign (17 January 1831).[10] When, in June 1832, Gaspar Marín proposed in the Chamber of Deputies that O'Higgins should be given back his title of Captain General, Portales in-

---

[1] 'Sucinta idea de lo que ha ocurrido...', 1831, *CHDI*, xxxvii, 85.

[2] White to Aberdeen, 28 May 1830, F.O. 16/12B, p. 91.

[3] See *El O'Higginista*, and various manifestos reprinted in *CHDI*, xxxvii, 49–55.

[4] Vicente Claro to O'Higgins, 26 January 1832, C. Vicuña Mackenna, *Papeles de Claro*, II, 87.

[5] Prieto, *Cartas a Portales*, pp. 46–7 n.; untitled poem of 10 stanzas with the refrain 'Prieto no es estanquero', n.d., A.V.M. vol. 101, fo. 189.

[6] Claro to Rodríguez Aldea, 15 and 19 September 1832, C. Vicuña Mackenna, *Papeles de Claro*, II, 171, 174.

[7] Prieto, 'Cartas a Portales', p. 25.

[8] *Ibid.* p. 45.   [9] *Ibid.* pp. 24–5, 46–52.

[10] See Portales to Garfías, 5 January 1832, Cruz and Feliú Cruz, I, 376–7.

sisted that this should be stopped, and thus helped effectively to bar the return of the liberator to his native land.[1]

Other, less political, influences were helping to transform Chile along with Diego Portales. The intelligent policies of Manuel Rengifo soon restored the country's finances to a healthy condition. The growth of foreign trade, notably British trade, continued. British commercial interest in Chile had been reflected in the 1820s by the establishment of consular missions at Valparaíso, Coquimbo and Concepción, while the presence of a British naval force in the Pacific demonstrated, to use the delicate expression of a sea-captain of the period, 'that we could command a proper adherence to the Law of Nations'.[2] The Chilean economy was also enormously stimulated by the discovery in May 1832 of a rich deposit of silver at Chañarcillo near Copiapó. The guerrilla activity which the Pincheira brothers had headed intermittently from the Cordillera near Chillán was finally defeated by General Bulnes early in 1832, thus ending a long history of crimes and depredations in the area. And no narrative of the period, however brief, could fail to mention the arrival in Chile, in June 1829, of Andrés Bello, soon to become famous as one of the foremost humanists, jurists and educationalists of the Spanish-speaking world. Bello was born a Venezuelan, but died a Chilean. He collaborated with the conservative regime from the start, by contributing to the government newspaper *El Araucano*; he took charge of its foreign affairs section and sometimes even proof-read.[3] As a senior civil servant, he created a distinctive administrative style for Chilean public documents, and it seems probable that he was responsible for all the presidential Messages between 1832 and 1860.[4] Bello's later effect on the intellectual life of Chile was, of course, incalculable.

The Grand Constituent Convention set up in September 1831 had speedily adjourned in order to allow a subcommittee to consider the constitutional question in detail. By the middle of

---

[1] Barros Arana, XVI, 232-5.
[2] Capt. T. J. Maling to Rear-Admiral Sir George Eyre, 5 October 1825, F.O. 16/5, p. 331.
[3] Pedro Grases, *Tres empresas periodísticas de Andrés Bello* (Caracas, 1955), p. 14.
[4] Guillermo Feliú Cruz, *Andrés Bello y la redacción de los documentos oficiales del Gobierno de Chile* (Caracas, 1951), pp. 14, 45.

1832 it became obvious that a completely new constitution, rather than a partial amendment of the old, was in the process of creation. The Convention reassembled in October 1832, and immediately set about the task of reviewing various draft proposals and preparing the final version. Portales himself was not a member of the Convention, and had little to do with its deliberations. The man chiefly influential in devising the new constitution was Mariano Egaña, a doctrinaire conservative whose affection for Britain and considerable physical girth won him the amusing nickname of 'Lord Callampa'.[1] Egaña's extreme conservatism was to some extent countered by Manuel José de Gandarillas, whose approach was somewhat more liberal. It also seems likely that Andrés Bello was consulted in private about the draft of the constitution,[2] and that he may even have had a hand in the final editing.[3] Considerable and detailed work was done by the Convention, and it took seven months before the draft was presented to the public. The new Constitution was strongly authoritarian in character, its chief feature being an emphasis on presidential power. It was promulgated by President Prieto on 25 May 1833.

'Chile will long remain the Theatre of a dreadful Anarchy,' reported the British consul in 1831.[4] Impartial observers were slow to appreciate that the Portales regime was likely to last any longer than its predecessors. But Portales built well. By the time the 1833 Constitution institutionalized the new order, Chile was well on the way to the stability for which she was envied by other Latin American republics in the remainder of the nineteenth century—a stability which even in the present century has only been interrupted at rare intervals. The state constructed by the work of Diego Portales did not merely survive; it outlasted its creator. When the businessman-dictator was murdered in June 1837, the structure of his Conservative Republic remained firm. This was a unique achievement.

[1] Amunátegui Solar, *Pipiolos y pelucones*, p. 120 n.
[2] Pedro Lira Urquieta, 'Don Andrés Bello y la Constitución de 1833', *BACH*, año XVII, no. 43 (1950), pp. 56–7.
[3] *AR*, I, 215.   [4] White to Aberdeen, 3 April 1831, F.O. 16/13, p. 104.

The Conservative Reaction

The leaders of the conservative revolution of 1829–33 grounded their political doctrine in a distinctive and significant view of the recent events through which their country had been passing. Much of the conservatives' behaviour after 1830 is inexplicable unless this background is taken into account. One of the best and most concise expressions of the distinctive conservative interpretation of the liberal period was given by President Joaquín Prieto at the end of his term of office in 1841. He referred to the years between 1823 and 1829 in the following terms:

Sufficient precautions had not been taken against the perils of an infant state, which everywhere have brought insecurity, disorder, disunity, immorality, and all the vices of a long and sometimes incurable anarchy. We found ourselves in the midst of a crisis that had to determine the future destiny of our country.[1]

This attitude had grown up, throughout the period in question, as a natural conservative reaction to the disorganization which accompanied the liberal and federal experiments. Juan Egaña, for instance, was constantly complaining in one form or another of the 'disorderliness, childishness and giddiness of the Ministers',[2] and he could claim, somewhat exaggeratedly, that this was the result of allowing 'the ordinary people' of Chile to vote in elections: 'in the name of liberalism, no disruptive or seditious principle is omitted'.[3] When Manuel José de Gandarillas described the 1824–5 Congress as 'that gathering of animals and knaves',[4] he was at least partly justified by the behaviour of the deputies. For, as Rodríguez Aldea reported to O'Higgins, 'The Congress is doing nothing, nor is it capable of doing anything. It is dominated by hatred and a true Jacobinism.'[5] José Ignacio Zentena came to much the same conclusion at much the same

---

[1] Prieto, *Exposición*, p. 319. For a lengthy expression of the same view, written at the time of the resolution of the crisis, see '¿Cuál es el orígen de la instabilidad de las instituciones en Chile, y cómo podrá afianzarse la establidad?' in *Bandera Tricolor*, nos. 20–4, 25 August to 10 October 1831.
[2] To M. Egaña, 20 January 1825, *Cartas de Juan Egaña*, p. 93.
[3] To M. Egaña, 2 January 1825, *ibid.* p. 83.
[4] To Benavente, 22 January 1825, F.V. vol. 821, num. 104, p. 134.
[5] Letter of 28 April 1825, *CHDI*, xxxvi, 341.

time: 'The people...insult the *soi-disant* sovereign authority. Factions become impassioned, yet none of them has a leader. Public opinion does not exist, for each man has his own opinion...'[1] These reactions were typically conservative, and they played their part in producing the crisis of 1829.

The war of words which continued in the newspaper press throughout the liberal–federal period was an important factor in exciting reactions such as these. The *estanquero* newspaper *El Sufragante* condemned what it called 'the disastrous policy of inventing words with which to hypnotize the common people, dividing them into parties which do not exist and provoking them to disorder'.[2] In 1824 the former royalist Meneses protested against 'the free exercise of calumny with notable abuse of the liberty of the press' which he affected to find in the country.[3] Under Pinto's government, *El Sufragante* later commented, 'Insolence was enthroned'.[4] It is true that some of the biting satires published in the later 1820s were personally offensive and insulting—as well as extremely witty—and that such writings could, as Gandarillas and Benavente solemnly warned, produce 'anarchic effects'.[5] But it can certainly be argued that, on the whole, the Chilean press was by no means as irresponsible as was later claimed, even if it was intensely vigorous, and that the conservatives themselves generally dealt harder blows than those they received.[6]

It is clear that Diego Portales shared such doubts about liberalism from the mid 1820s onwards. In February 1826, while a member of the Consultative Council then advising the government, he objected to the federalist scheme for the popular election of district governors on the ground that the 'circumstances' were not right, and helped to prevent that particular measure from being immediately enacted.[7] In the same year, he was reported as having expressed the hope that 'education and enlight-

---

[1] To O'Higgins, 25 February 1825, *CHDI*, xxxvii, 151.
[2] No. 1, 31 May 1829, p. 1.   [3] J. F. Meneses, *A los pueblos de Chile* (1824).
[4] No. 6, 22 September 1829.   [5] *La Aurora*, no. 23, 22 December 1827, p. 3.
[6] As the case of *El Hambriento* shows. For the vigorous newspaper battles of 1826–8 see Donoso, *Sátira*, pp. 16–23, and Silva Castro, *Prensa y periodismo*, pp. 84–95.
[7] *Diario de Documentos del Gobierno*, no. 66, 10 February 1826.

enment rather than a horrible tyranny should dampen down the fire of passion that is going—I mean, that *could*—plunge us into ruin'.[1] The slip of the tongue was significant, for it showed clearly that Portales believed that Chile was running grave risks under a federal regime. He was irritated, too, by the constant newspaper polemics of the time. When his friend Benavente signalized his intention to enter the lists on one occasion, Portales wearily wrote:

How sorry I am that you are going to do battle with *El Insurgente*. Don't you see that the forces are so unequal? It has already said that you are a thief; tomorrow it will say that it saw you commit a treacherous murder. You will reply that this is false. And who will have won?[2]

Portales' involvement in practical politics with the revolt of 1829 must be seen, I believe, as the direct result of his impatience with the liberal wordiness of the journalism of the day, and his distaste for the recurrent disorders which seemed to be the inevitable accompaniment of liberalism. The liberal contention that Portales' 'motive was nothing more than vengeance against those who had deprived him of the *Estanco*'[3] cannot be completely accepted, even though Portales gravely resented the curtailment of the *Estanco* contract which he and his business partner Cea had held.

While the conservatives in Chile grew more and more infuriated, Mariano Egaña meditated on the same problems in the relative isolation of London, his interpretation of Chilean events doubtless distorted by the one-sided accounts he received from his father. In 1827, when Juan Egaña sent his son a draft of his *Carta Constitucional*, an 'interim constitution' which embodied a few concessions to liberal principle, Mariano replied with an enraged attack on liberalism in general:

This democracy, father, is the greatest enemy of America; it will cause her many disasters more, and eventually bring her down to

---

[1] *Patriota Chileno*, tomo 2, no. 55, 30 September 1826, p. 230.
[2] To Benavente, 21 March 1827, Cruz and Feliú Cruz, I, 253. *El Insurgente Araucano* was a violent popular-liberal newspaper. Its later issues attacked Benavente's record in relation to the *Estanco*.
[3] Valencia Avaria, *Memorias íntimas*, p. 46.

total ruin. Federations, insurrections, conspiracies, continual anxieties which discourage trade, industry and the diffusion of useful knowledge; in fact, as many crimes and nonsenses as have been committed from Texas to Chiloé—all of them are the effects of this democratic fury which is the greatest scourge of nations without experience, without correct political notions.[1]

Mariano Egaña had expressed much the same view, though in less vivid language, on an earlier occasion in the same year (1827). He had added an important comment: 'The remedies must be radical; and for the ills which Chile suffers the only remedy I can think of is the one suggested by the two greatest statesmen of their age, Talleyrand and Metternich: restore legitimacy...'[2] Like Simón Bolívar at the Ocaña Convention, Mariano Egaña called for 'inexorable laws' to contain disorder and to set up a supreme and unquestionable executive authority. The disorganization of Chile, he felt, had produced the destruction of public morale, the degeneration of patriotic spirit, an apathetic character and a marked degree of indifference.

The legislators, then, must be inexorable and must never permit the constitutional establishment of anarchy in the shadow or in the name of popular power, liberality of principles, republican government, or other pieces of jargon incomprehensible to the heedless or perhaps malignant multitude which longs only for disorder.[3]

Having said this, Mariano Egaña rejected the liberal innovations which he detected in his father's *Carta Constitucional*. Certainly, he agreed, the utopian Constitution of 1823 needed revision, 'but not in a democratic direction'.[4] The conservative reaction had found its intellectual champion.

CONSERVATIVE DOCTRINE

There was a small but tough core of doctrine underlying the political transformations which took place in Chile after the revolt of 1829, and its starting-point was the experience of the 1820s.

---

[1] To Juan Egaña, 21 July 1827, *Cartas de Mariano Egaña*, p. 263.
[2] To Juan Egaña, 12 April 1827, *ibid.* p. 230.
[3] To Juan Egaña, 21 July 1827, *ibid.* pp. 263–4.   [4] *Ibid.* p. 271.

The conservatives felt, generally speaking, that the liberal and federal governments had erred gravely in two essential respects. First, they had tried to set up regimes which were out of harmony with the fundamental realities of Chilean life. Secondly, they had been dangerously and foolishly lenient towards offenders against the State.

That the laws should reflect the conditions and customs of the country was a basic theme with the conservative rebels. President Errázuriz was told by his Senate in 1831 that 'the best institutions are vain if they do not rest on custom'.[1] The main vice of the 1828 Constitution, according to this theory, was that the institutions it established lacked any genuine 'consideration...of the nation's circumstances'.[2] Any fundamental law should take into account the general level of education and public morality of the nation concerned. This point was well put by Pedro Urriondo in 1831:

General ideas are always related to the education of the masses, just as they are its product. And although it is permissible to desire perfection of civilization, neither time nor the means employed up till now have been sufficient for us to leave the limitations of what the recentness of our emancipation permits. Thus, in order to give ourselves a constitution we must follow the scale of our knowledge; and the further we have become removed from that scale, the further have we fallen back.[3]

The 1828 Constitution, then, had been guilty of an excess of ideology. As Vicente Bustillos put it, in 1832, 'like the sinister tree which Virgil places at the mouth of Hell, it seems to contain all the social evils'.[4] 'To insist on making a constitution a priori is nonsense', he added,[5] for 'a constitution should not be the product of genius or the consequence of trials and experiments, but the result of what is necessary to society'. In short, it should be 'supported by customs'.[6]

At the same time, the conservatives believed, a government

---

[1] *Oficio* of 6 June 1831, *SCL*, XIX, 87.
[2] M. Egaña, J. M. Irarrázaval, and A. Vial, *Informe*, 13 June 1831, *SCL*, XIX, 96.
[3] To the Comisión Permanente, 17 February 1831, *SCL*, XIX, 28.
[4] 'Memoria sobre la reforma de la Constitución', presented to the Grand Constituent Convention on 6 November 1832, *SCL*, XXI, 179.
[5] *Ibid.*   [6] *Ibid.* 177.

had to ensure that its laws were *observed*. This view, fully emphasized now, was in part a reaction to those extreme liberals who had
maintained, a year or two earlier, that in the absence of a constitution nobody could be tried for committing crimes, since
'law' did not exist.[1] It was now laid down that 'observance of the
laws is the very foundation of the social order',[2] an unexceptionable statement but one which would have sounded slightly unusual from a liberal of the 1820s, and which almost echoed
O'Higgins' emphasis on order.[3] 'Let us all help to uphold the
laws,' urged the conservative paper *El Popular* in 1830.[4] Again this
was an unexceptionable exhortation, but it represented a new
emphasis. The new rulers of Chile saw it as their task to 'restore'
the rule of law. As Ruiz Tagle put it, on taking the oath as
President of the Republic: 'Let us work together on the difficult
task of restoring the rule of the laws, and dampen the sinister
discord which menaces our infant liberty.'[5] The new, firm approach was well to the fore in the proclamation with which
President Prieto introduced the 1833 Constitution. 'It is not my
duty', he said, 'to analyse this reform [of the constitution]; my
obligation is to guard it and to make it guard.' Concluding, he
issued a solemn warning: 'As the guardian of your rights, I must
solemnly declare that I shall fulfil the dispositions of the constitution,...making use of all the means it confers on me, however rigorous these may seem.'[6] A comparison of Prieto's stern
dicta with the introductory proclamation issued by President
Pinto with the Constitution of 1828 is commentary enough on
the difference between the two regimes.[7] The tone of the two
documents is completely dissimilar. Chile had moved from one
world into another.

The previous governments, then, had ignored the two basic

[1] *El Insurgente Araucano* had claimed, in defence of some mutineers, that 'where there is no law there is no crime': no. 1, 10 February 1827, p. 3. The mutiny, it added, 'has not infringed any laws, for these did not exist, and this exonerates all crime' (*ibid.* p. 6.)
[2] Junta of Santiago to Congress of Plenipotentiaries, 12 February 1830, *SCL*, XVIII, 216.
[3] Cf. *La Convención a los habitantes de Chile*, 1822, *AR*, I, 70: 'The general welfare is founded on observance of the laws.'
[4] No. 20, 16 August 1830, p. 4.   [5] 18 February 1830, *SCL*, XVIII, 232.
[6] *El Presidente de la República a los Pueblos*, 25 May 1833, *AR*, I, 160.
[7] *AR*, I, 138.

principles I have mentioned. It was perhaps natural that something approaching a *leyenda negra* should grow up when conservatives contemplated the experience of the recent past. Thus *El Popular*, a strident supporter of the new order, analysed Freire's conduct in scathing terms. His career in the 1820s was undervalued; he was criticized for having destroyed 'the best Constitution we ever saw' (the 1823 *carta*!), and by implication chided for having over-thrown O'Higgins.[1] The same newspaper painted Pinto's brief moment of power as chaotic and absurd in the extreme. Pinto's conduct had been 'artful, weak, biased, hypocritical and cruel'.[2] General Prieto, too, joined in such denigrations, describing the Novoa brothers,[3] for instance, as 'those monsters of anarchy'.[4]

The principal remedy for such a state of affairs, and indeed the main political concept of the Chilean conservatives, was strong government. The most famous, perhaps even the classic, definition of this theme had been given by Diego Portales himself some ten years earlier, in a letter to his business partner. Well known as these words are, they deserve to be quoted in full, for they display the essence of Portales' thinking on politics.

Democracy, which self-deceived men proclaim so much, is an absurdity in countries like those of America, which are full of vices, and whose citizens completely lack the virtue necessary for a true *Republic*. Nor is *Monarchy* the American ideal: if we come out of one terrible monarchy merely to go into another, what do we gain? The *Republic* is the system we must adopt; but do you know how I conceive it for these countries?—a strong, centralizing Government, whose members are genuine examples of virtue and patriotism, and thus set the citizens on the straight path of order and the virtues. When they have attained a degree of morality, then we can have the completely liberal sort of Government, free and full of ideals, in which all the citizens can take part.[5]

[1] No. 5, 27 April 1830.
[2] No. 10, 29 May 1830, p. 1; cf. no. 8, 13 May.
[3] Manuel Fernando Vásquez de Novoa López de Artigas, and his brother Félix Antonio, were prominent Concepción liberals. Manuel had been a member of the Senate of 1824 and the Congresses of 1828 and 1829.
[4] To Portales, 7 August 1830, Prieto, *Cartas a Portales*, p.   .
[5] To Cea, Lima, March 1822, Cruz and Feliú Cruz, i, 771. This letter, it seems probable, was prompted by rumours of San Martín's monarchist schemes.

This letter is interesting not only because it shows how early Portales was thinking in these terms, but also because it indicates an underlying trend towards liberalism. This liberalism, however, was for the future, perhaps even the far future. The first thing was to make a start. For the present, Portales distrusted any government which temporized unduly with popular opinion. Measuring his own views against those of British politicians of the day, he once referred to George Canning as 'too liberal, in my opinion', and professed a deep admiration for the Duke of Wellington, who, he thought, 'will not look for excuses to persecute anybody, but will not lose any opportunities which come his way for correcting the rebellious and making an example of bad men by punishing them; and, in short, will never compromise with the enemies of order, truth, honesty and decency'.[1] The strength and firmness of the conservative regime would be its first most noticeable feature. Government would be strong, and institutions unshakable.

It is interesting in this context to note that Mariano Egaña was also thinking along these lines—doubtless influenced by his father—before he left Chile for Europe in 1824. In the draft of a farewell letter to Freire, he gave his prescriptions for social stability:

I recommend to you the Fatherland, this suffering Fatherland...It is sufficient for its welfare that you should carry on as you have up till now, and that those enemies of order who perturb our citizens by promoting worries and discontents should feel the weight of your indignation with a holy strength. In the name of the Fatherland, I recommend stability in public institutions. I am certain that nothing would discredit us more than constant alterations in our Laws...[2]

It was Mariano Egaña who, from London, best defined the importance of strong government. Woefully painting the disorders of his native land, he observed that these 'threaten us with eternal unhappiness if there is not energy in the government, and if the government is not given the means to retore us, and to go on affirming that restoration afterwards'.[3] What was needed, in the

---

[1] To Antonio Garfías, 17 April 1832, Cruz and Feliú Cruz, I, 173-4.
[2] [April 1824?] (*borrador*) F.V. vol. 801, pieza 22.
[3] To Juan Egaña, 21 July 1827, *Cartas de Mariano Egaña*, p. 264.

conservative view, was 'activity, frankness and decision' in governments,[1] and in May 1829 the *estanquero* newspaper *El Sufragante* had demanded much the same thing, though somewhat more explicitly: 'The country is crying out for a man who has the capacity to direct it, and whose energy...can destroy the ambitious men who have degraded the government, and can raise the government to the dignity it deserves. Enough of contemplation!'[2] Such a government would have to be firm; that went without saying. But more than this, it would also have to retain its hold on public awe and respect: 'the ruler who shows a lack of strength...publicizes the depth of his own incapacity, and provokes contempt'.[3] A President, it was now argued, should acquire a certain remote majesty. He should be immmune from satirical criticisms. He needed

sufficient authority to give an impulse to the administration, to suppress the aspirations of revolutionaries, and to punish the insolence of certain incendiary writers who involve the national prestige in their calumnies...If authority fails in its duties, it ought to be attacked with positive documents, in a direct way, and not by poetic jokes which take away its quality of majesty. A government without majesty will collect nothing but scorn.[4]

It need hardly be stressed that this view of the executive signified a lessening of interest in the legislative branch of government. Legislative omnipotence was a feature of the 1828 Constitution singled out for attack: 'since this exaggerated democracy makes the legislator omnipotent, it humbles the Executive Power and cuts across its attributions in such a way as to establish a totally insignificant authority'.[5] This rejection of parliamentary power may be seen most clearly in the 1833 Constitution.

But if the conservative government was to be strong, it was not to be completely irresponsible. Its leading role in society was not to be questioned; yet it had to observe certain conditions. Opposition, for instance, was to be permitted provided it

---

[1] *La Opinión*, no. 1, 3 May 1830, p. 1. [2] No. 3, 17 June 1829, p. 4.
[3] *Ibid*, no. 4, 26 June 1829, p. 2.
[4] *Bandera Tricolor*, no. 28, 17 November 1831, p. 123. But it would be as difficult to abolish satire in Chile as it would football.
[5] Vial, Elizalde and Gandarillas, *Informe*, 24 October 1831, *SCL*, XXI, 11.

conducted itself with decency and dignity. Indeed, the formation of a 'moderate' opposition was a key point in Portales' own programme, such as it was. His aim here was for a 'decent, moderate opposition', and he wrote that 'we wish to approximate ourselves as closely as possible to the English method of conducting opposition'.[1] The press had a part to play in this, believed Portales. 'I do not want the press to remain silent and to lose its power,' he wrote, 'but I would like it...to publish the truth without acrimony.'[2] The fate of *El Philopolita* illustrates what happened in practice to a newspaper which attempted to work along these lines; it was hounded out of existence.

Public probity and impersonality, felt Portales, were essential to government. A government should try to place itself beyond criticism by acting honestly and straightforwardly, and thus, as Portales had said in his letter to Cea in 1822, set an example to the citizens of the State. 'If [the government] follows a straight, undeviating path,' he wrote, 'nobody will dare to complain.'[3] When a public functionary asked for his advice, Portales replied: 'The only plan of conduct I can and ought to indicate to you is this—scrupulously fulfil the obligations of your job...In short, do not present any flank on which you can with justice be attacked.'[4]

Did the idea of monarchy ever cross Portales' mind as an answer to the problem of establishing a firm and unchallengeable government? The question must, on the face of it, seem astonishing. In his famous letter to Cea, already quoted, Portales dismissed monarchy outright. Nor can it be said that there had been much of an audience for monarchist proposals during the 1820s. It is true that George Canning apparently believed, at any rate in 1823 and 1824, that the Chileans could be induced to accept a constitutional monarchy,[5] though where he got the idea from remains mysterious. It was not wholly improbable that 'the constitutional monarchic form of government...had its partisans

[1] To Garfías, 16 March 1832, Cruz and Feliú Cruz, I, 472.
[2] To Garfías, 2 January 1833, *ibid.* II, 325.
[3] To Garfías, 30 August 1830, *ibid.* 274.
[4] To Miguel Dávila, 6 February 1833, *ibid.* 350–1.
[5] C. W. Centner, 'The Chilean failure to obtain British recognition, 1823–8', *Revista de Historia de América*, no. 15 (Mexico DF, 1942), pp. 286–7.

amongst us', as one newspaper asserted in 1827,[1] and other
newspapers took it upon themselves to warn republicans against
this threat from time to time.[2] Some individuals may have had a
specific preference for monarchy. Irisarri, for example, indicated
in 1833 that he was by no means unsympathetic to the idea.[3] He
and others had been accused by Infante in the pages of his federalist newspaper,[4] and it was perhaps natural for a man like Infante
to assume that privileged classes and *unitarios* alike had an automatic tendency towards monarchism.[5] Nevertheless, the prevailing Chilean attitude was summarized in the words of one of
Colonel Beauchef's toasts: 'May Kings, those illustrious ingrates,
unknown up till now in South America, remain unknown for
ever!'[6] The monarchist issue, then, departed with Bernardo
O'Higgins. Yet despite this, and despite Portales' own anti-
monarchism, it was nevertheless possible for the British consul,
John White, to report home in June 1830 that

many of the most intelligent, most wealthy and influential people of
the Capital are quite unreserved in saying that the country cannot long
remain undisturbed under a republican government, and that the only
means of securing respect to it both at home and abroad would be by
its assuming a monarchical Government. Señor Portales...has so
expressed himself to Mr Caldcleugh, and even authorized him to
make these sentiments known to His Majesty's Ministers.[7]

Alexander Caldcleugh, a notable member of the British community in Chile, had already left on a visit to England, and was
back in Chile at the start of 1832. Whether he passed on Portales'
'sentiments' cannot be ascertained. But an interesting (if academic)
question is raised. Did Portales ever think in terms of establishing
a monarchy? Plainly it would have been a solution to the problem
of creating a government which had 'majesty'. But there is no
precise evidence, and the idea of monarchy is conspicuously
absent from Portales' correspondence. In any case, the President

[1] *Clamor del Pueblo Chileno*, tomo I, no. 3, 19 December 1827, p. 2.
[2] *El Liberal*, no. 28, 4 September 1824, and No. 33, 14 October 1824.
[3] *El Constitucional*, no. 9, 14 August 1833, p. 34.
[4] *Valdiviano Federal*, no. 71, 1 August 1833, p. 4, and no. 72, same date, p. 4.
[5] *Ibid.* no. 52, 26 December 1831, p. 2.
[6] *Observador de Chile*, no. 1, 16 June 1823, p. 8.
[7] White to Aberdeen, 30 June 1830, Webster, I, 371.

of the Conservative Republic enjoyed powers which made him a king in everything but name.

The conservative regime needed its formal consecration, and this was provided by the celebrated Constitution of 1833, one of the few Latin American constitutions noted for its longevity and considered by Juan Bautista Alberdi to have been as original in its own way as the Constitution of the United States.[1] At first, it seems, the conservative government, which came to power with the express aim of 'restoring' the Constitution of 1828, showed little inclination to tamper with that document. The British consul was able to report in February 1830 that all parties were satisfied with it.[2] Yet, even as early as this, Portales' close friend Antonio Garfías was advocating its abolition, and the summoning of a new constituent congress.[3] Prieto, too, seemed anxious to do away with a document which, as he put it, 'so degrades us and spoils the good we have proposed to do'.[4] This support in high places doubtless strengthened the Santiago Cabildo's famous recommendation in February 1831 that the constitution should be revised, and by June that year a congressional committee had finally condemned the 'disruptive maxims' of 1828,[5] thus setting in motion the machinery for amendment and revision. The Grand Constituent Convention heard what were probably the most detailed and conscientious constitutional proposals Chile had witnessed up to that date,[6] and considered several alternative drafts, the most important of which was Mariano Egaña's. Egaña's project, known usually as the *Voto Particular*, reflected his extreme doctrinaire conservatism, and included a provision for the indefinite re-eligibility of the President,[7] an idea rejected by the Convention in favour of the re-election of the President for a second five-year term. Though Egaña's *Voto* was

---

[1] *Bases i puntos de partida para la organización política de la República Argentina* (2nd edn. Valparaíso, 1852), p. 160.

[2] White to Aberdeen, 7 February 1830, F.O. 16/12A, p. 59.

[3] *Estafeta de Santiago*, no. 1, 9 February 1830, p. 1.

[4] To Portales, 7 August 1830, Prieto, *Cartas a Portales*, p.   .

[5] Egaña, Irarrázaval and Vial, *Informe*, 13 June 1831, SCL, XIX, 96.

[6] They are printed in SCL, XXI, 4–354, and the work of the Convention is narrated in Galdames, *Evolución constitucional*, pp. 863–907, and Barros Arana, XVI, 301–32.

[7] Art. 22. The *Voto* is printed in SCL, XXI, 70, and discussed in Galdames, *Evolución constitucional*, pp. 886–99.

discarded, its influence on the final version of the constitution was by no means inconsiderable. It is clear that the constitution altered its form significantly between the earliest proposals and the finished document. The scheme for hereditary senators—a feature of Egaña's *Voto*—was dropped,[1] and, largely at Gandarillas' insistence, so was the plan for provincial assemblies,[2] though, perhaps surprisingly, not until the very last moment.

Portales, it is worth mentioning here, seems to have been rather uninterested in the constitutional issue.[3] He was deeply sceptical about written laws and their effect, and probably regarded them as of secondary importance. In 1832 he told Joaquín Tocornal: 'I believe we are in the position of having to avoid partial reforms which will complicate the labyrinth of our machine still further, and that to think in terms of a formal, general and radical [political] organization is not a task for our times.'[4] The doctrinaire legalism of Mariano Egaña often irritated Portales, although the two men admired each other deeply. On one occasion, having listened to Egaña's views on the necessity for scrupulous legal proceedings, he relieved his feelings by writing to his friend Garfías: 'One can never understand lawyers: and, *carajo!*[5] what use are constitutions and bits of paper unless to remedy an evil that one knows to exist, or is about to exist...? An accursed law, then, [if it] prevents the government from going ahead freely at the opportune moment.'[6] Despite this, it is clear that the Grand Constituent Convention gave Portales and the conservatives just what they needed in the way of a constitution.

The Constitution of 1833 has naturally enough been the subject of several important critiques,[7] and I do not intend to analyse its provisions in detail here. Even so, some of its features illustrated

---

[1] Session of 12 December 1832, *SCL*, XXI, 238.

[2] Session of 1 May 1833, *SCL*, XXI, 317. For a discussion of this issue, see Roldán, 'El centralismo', pp. 411–16.

[3] See Vicuña Mackenna, *Diego Portales*, I, 142 n.

[4] Letter of 16 July 1832, Cruz and Feliú Cruz, II, 227.

[5] What are politely called 'Chileanisms' are scattered throughout Portales' correspondence.

[6] Letter of 6 December 1834, Cruz and Feliú Cruz, III, 378.

[7] The Constitution is printed in *AR*, I, 161. For discussions of its provisions see Cifuentes, Huneeus Gana; Galdames, *Evolución constitucional*, pp. 909–70; Barros Arana, XVI, 332–6. For a list of commentaries up to 1925 see Galdames, *op. cit.* p. 962 n.

the essential concerns of the Portales regime with considerable clarity. The supreme position of the President was given a special emphasis by being related to a formal oath,[1] a stipulation absent, in general, from previous Chilean *cartas*. The President was permitted to stand for re-election at the end of his first five-year term,[2] a provision which led in practice to the four decennial administrations that followed and which was well suited to maintain what became known as 'the regime of authority'. The President's emergency powers were particularly important. If Congress was in recess—which meant, in practice, most of the time—he could declare a state of siege in any part of the country, and the gravity of this power was summarized in the following terms: 'If any area of the Republic is declared to be in a state of siege, the rule of the Constitution is suspended within the territory comprehended by the declaration.'[3] The supremacy of the Executive over the Legislature was decisive. The President could veto any law, which delayed its enactment for at least a year, and the measure thus vetoed had to be reintroduced within two years or the whole procedure had to start all over again.[4] We should note, however, that Congress was left with the power to approve the Budget, taxation and the armed forces on an annual basis, after the English pattern.[5] Presidential power was firmly cemented in the provinces, where he was to be represented by an Intendant, defined as his 'natural and immediate agent'[6] and appointed by the President alone. Some of the main aims of the conservative reaction thus became embodied in written form. An extremely strong presidential form of government was instituted. The head of state was given all the instruments he could possibly have desired to suppress disorder and to guarantee stability. Provincial 'licence', so strongly frowned on by conservatives during the federal period, was counteracted by the directness of the link between President and Intendant. And last, but by no means least, an ultimate aristocratic check on the Executive was assured by means of an annual parliamentary review of certain vital matters. No conservative could have asked for more than this.

[1] Art. 80.   [2] Art. 61.   [3] Arts. 82, xx, and 161.   [4] Arts. 40–51.
[5] See Heise González, *150 años*, pp. 41–2.   [6] Art. 116.

The Conservative Reaction

'The Constitution of 1833', one of its modern apologists has claimed, 'founded institutions of the strongest authoritarianism along with institutions which were highly favourable to liberty.'[1] The authoritarianism was more apparent at first than the liberty. One cannot doubt Portales' good faith in hoping for an ultimate liberalization of the type of regime which he created, but it seemed a long way off while he himself still ruled in Chile. In the 1820s, Mariano Egaña had laid down the principle that

> a people has all the liberty which is fitting for it through just two fundamental laws: (1) that the laws should be enacted, and the taxes decreed, by a sufficient number of representatives from all classes of society; (2) that judges should enjoy full independence and security in the exercise of their functions. Here, then, is the essence of public liberty.[2]

Observance of these two tenets would, Egaña thought, bring about 'liberty without democracy',[3] and this phrase may be said to represent the basic aim of the fathers of the 1833 Constitution. But, if the above statement of Egaña's is taken as a basis, it can be said that the Chilean people were deprived of their public liberty on both counts under the 1833 regime. Judicial independence was menaced by the President's ability to appoint the Supreme Court,[4] and, under the new electoral laws as eventually framed, there was no guarantee whatsoever that 'all classes of society' would be adequately represented.[5] It will be recognized, of course, that liberty without *democracy* (i.e. representative government with a Congress balancing Executive power) was a contradiction of the main principles of the revolution for independence. But, this apart, it is also clear that the conservatives failed to live up to the ideals which they had imposed in 1830. I must, therefore, consider the political atmosphere of the period a little more closely.

[1] Cifuentes, 'La Constitución de 1833', p. 38.
[2] To Juan Egaña, 21 July 1827, *Cartas de Mariano Egaña*, p. 263.
[3] *Ibid.* p. 270.　　　　　　　　　　　　[4] F. Errázuriz, p. 269.
[5] Amunátegui Solar, *Democracia en Chile*, p. 72.

To the conservatives themselves, of course, the regime accomplished what it set out to accomplish. José Ignacio Zenteno, for instance, told Bernardo O'Higgins' secretary: 'Since Lircay a new and happier epoch has opened...in which elements of order and organization unknown in previous administrations... have been slowly but progressively developing.'[1] By the end of his term of office, plainly, President Prieto could justifiably pride himself on the attainment of internal stability, victory in the war with Peru–Bolivia, and a return to financial solvency. As he put it in his presidential Message of 1841: 'Our social edifice has serenly and majestically displayed its excellence in the midst of the storms which have wrought havoc in every other part of Spanish America.'[2] Even ex-President Pinto eventually came round to this view. By the mid 1840s we find him telling San Martín: 'It seems to me that we shall resolve the problem of how to be republican while still speaking the Spanish language.'[3] Yet there was another side to the picture, and it must be confronted squarely.

There can be no doubt that Portales and the *estanqueros* exercised an extremely tight grip on power from the first moments of the conservative rebellion. A Swedish traveller who had come to know Chile in the 1820s noted one aspect of the complete control now gained by the victorious political faction.

The people have little hope of liberating themselves from this political yoke. The *Estanco* holds all the resources of the country and the means of keeping itself in power; and it is even influencing the younger generation, for it is natural that any young man with the aptitude and the ambition to pursue his career has to try to win the favour of this society if he wishes to succeed.[4]

Pedro Félix Vicuña had foreseen this situation in the closing days of 1829: 'the *Estanco* is our overlord, and there is nothing left to us but humble repentance'.[5] Once Portales had a hold on power

---

[1] To John Thomas, 15 July 1832, *CHDI*, xxxvii, 158.
[2] Prieto, *Exposición*, p. 319.
[3] Letter of 8 December 1845, *Arch.O'H.* ix, 108.
[4] C. E. Bladh, 'La República de Chile', *RCHG*, no. 116 (1950), p. 281.
[5] *Avisador Imparcial*, no. 1, 26 January 1830, p. 3.

he refused to let it go, and some of his conservative allies discovered this to their cost. As the liberal newspaper *El Trompeta*
put it, in the form of an untranslatable pun, 'Nadie quería
Estanco, pero todos quedaron estancados.' ['Nobody wanted the
Estanco, but everyone was cornered.'[1]] 'Portales', the O'Higginist
Ramón Mariano de Aris commented bitterly, 'has cowed...a
million people.'[2]

This tight and ruthless grip on power was something new in
the Chilean experience. The government was asserting its authority so sternly that it attracted the attention of the British consul.
Portales, according to John White, was 'vigilant, active and
firm',[3] and his 'energy, firmness and courage'[4] guaranteed
Chilean stability. In 1833, the consul noted the totality of Portales'
grip more disapprovingly:

every measure of the Government emanates from him, and no department throughout the State, without his approbation, dare execute any
orders, even for its internal Regulation, be they of importance or not...
The Criminal Courts are secretly influenced by him.[5]

Such comments as these are of particular interest. The British
consuls in Chile throughout this period can hardly be said to
have gone far out of their way to glean political intelligence, and
their reports in general did not attain a high level of information.
Judgements of this sort, then, could very well represent a genuine
sense of shock, perhaps even of outrage.

There was plenty on which a sense of outrage could feed. The
new powers conferred on the Executive were, as we have seen,
enormous. 'With us', Pedro Félix Vicuña wrote in 1836, 'a
president's power is the same, with only very small differences, as
a constitutional monarch's.'[6] And while Portales was alive, at
least, the President seemed willing to obey his every dictate. As
Vicente Claro asked,

[1] No. 5, 7 January 1831.
[2] To O'Higgins, 9 December 1832, quoted in Vicuña Mackenna, *Diego Portales*,
I, 121.
[3] To Aberdeen, 16 December 1830, F.O. 16/12B, p. 268.
[4] To Aberdeen, 3 April 1831, F.O.16/14, p. 103.
[5] To Palmerston, 30 January 1833, F.O. 16/20, pp. 49–50.
[6] *Paz Perpetua á los Chilenos*, no. 3, 27 May 1836, p. 3.

Who would have believed that Portales—unknown in the revolution, a royalist without the slightest reputation—could be giving instructions to the President of the Republic, and could so fill the country with terror that nobody dares to speak, let alone write?[1]

Did Prieto fear Portales, as Claro claimed?[2] Despite occasional rumours of a rift between the two men, it can hardly be denied that Prieto was Portales' faithful servant.

To contemporaries, the Portales regime seemed to be badly lacking in many of the proper attributes of representative government. The elections held were mere formalities: 'all the elections have been without opposition, and...scarcely a fifth of the citizens entitled to vote actually did so'.[3] O'Higgins' secretary, John Thomas, has left an interesting illustration of the kind of methods used by the regime to secure electoral allegiance. Thomas had been told of some Civic Guards voting in Valparaíso in 1840.

The *Hall of Election*...was occupied...by an *armed force*—...when the *Civicos* came to vote their *officers* insisted on seeing their *ballot lists*, and if not in support of the *Government* candidates *they tore them*.[4]

Congress could not be said to function properly. The newspaper *El Chileno* affirmed in 1835 that the new Constitution had intended the Senate to represent the propertied classes, and the Chamber of Deputies the remaining elements in the State. But the Deputies had virtually no influence as compared with the Senators. Hence it could be said that 'the proprietary class is represented genuinely, the other only nominally'.[5] The submissiveness of the legislatures after 1833 aroused Pedro Félix Vicuña's particular wrath. He deeply regretted

the sight of those silent halls which, in so short a time, seemed to have put centuries of backwardness between themselves and the beautiful discussions with which other legislatures [in the 1820s] displayed the eternal principles of liberty, and where the citizens who won the independence of their country had a seat as of right.[6]

---

[1] To O'Higgins, 8 March 1832, C. Vicuña Mackenna, *Papeles de Claro*, II, 104.
[2] *Ibid.*
[3] *Paz Perpetua á los Chilenos*, no. 2, 13 April 1836, p. 10.
[4] Thomas to O'Higgins, 26 April 1840, F.V. vol. 645, fo. 28.
[5] *El Chileno*, no. 3, 5 September 1835, p. 10.
[6] *Paz Perpetua á los Chilenso*, no. 2, 13 April 1836, p. 10.

Freedom of the press, that cardinal requirement of the revolutionary philosophy, seemed equally to be endangered under the new conservative order. *El Imparcial* complained as early as March 1830 that although the press laws enacted by Pinto's government still operated in theory, newspapers were being ruthlessly persecuted and no real freedom was tolerated.[1] *El Imparcial* never produced a second issue. In contrast to the exuberant multiplication of newspapers in the 1820s, only three new journals appeared in 1831, and only one of these achieved more than three issues. In 1832 some five new papers came out, in 1833 six, and in 1834 three.[2] This rapid decline could be attributed to immediate and sinister causes. In 1832, when the reform of the Constitution was in progress, *El Mercurio de Valparaíso* suggested that as many newspapers as possible should be founded, so as to express the general will more effectively. But, it added, 'unfortunately the press remains completely silent'.[3] In part this was due to Portales' insistence that all public functionaries should immediately institute libel proceedings when attacked in the press, but the general climate of terror was also responsible for producing the journalistic silence.

Portales himself has been widely praised for having encouraged a decent and serious opposition press, even collaborating in founding an opposition newspaper, *El Hurón*.[4] But *El Hurón* confined itself to recommending even firmer measures against dissident elements and to a few very mildly carping references to government policies. Portales may have been able to claim that such violently hostile anti-conservative papers as *El Defensor de los Militares Denominados Constitucionales* and *El Trompeta* represented threats to stability, yet even when his own friends in the so-called 'Philopolita' group published restrained and impeccably serious critiques of ministerial actions, their newspaper was driven out of existence. *El Philopolita*, in fact, had opened with a tribute to the 1833 Constitution: 'Our political Constitution is the best possible for our circumstances.'[5] Its criticisms were mainly directed against

---

[1] No. 1, 8 March 1830. [2] Silva Castro, *Prensa y periodismo*, pp. 112–18.
[3] Tomo 7, no. 90, 15 June 1832, p. 179.
[4] See his letter to Garfías, 16 March 1832, Cruz and Feliú Cruz, I, 481–2.
[5] No. 1, 3 August 1835, p. 1.

ultra-clerical elements, which had enjoyed a new influence since 1830, and the proposal to send a legation to Spain. 'The Philopolitas', it declared, 'are personal friends of the President and supporters of his administration.'[1] But in its penultimate number the theme had changed to open despair:

We began a decent and serious opposition to certain ministerial dispositions, as we have been explaining in previous numbers; and in answer, we have received insults, injuries, violent comments and absurd threats...[2]

In the fourteenth issue of *El Defensor de los Militares*, José Joaquín de Mora and other friends of the exiled Freire had published a satirical 'press law' supposedly enacted by the 'King of the Congos'. Its main provisions were that the press should be free provided that it produced nothing but praise for the King and, secondly, that no satire was to be employed.[3] To many in the 1830s Portales' attitude towards the press savoured more than a little of this approach. Opposition newspapers were lucky to survive at all in such an atmosphere. More often than not they succumbed.[4]

In general, it can be said that the atmosphere in Chile after 1830 was one of fear and trembling. As *El Trompeta* put it, most people in Chile had wanted 'laws and guarantees; but the laws are mocked and the guarantees destroyed. In Concepción men are persecuted and banished without cause and without reason.'[5] The British consul used harsh words to describe the situation as he found it at the beginning of 1833: 'Personal freedom is insecure;— Humanity, Honor, Justice and Mercy are disowned, though guaranteed by the constitutional law.'[6]

Political passions at this stage seem to have been as inflamed and bitter as at any moment of Chilean history. That there was considerable opposition to the new order is undeniable. At the

---

[1] No. 5, 2 September 1835, p. 4. [2] No. 13, 28 October 1835, p. 2.
[3] No. 14, 15 September 1830.
[4] It is worth mentioning, however, that Infante continued to expound his federalist philosophy in *El Valdiviano Federal* throughout the period. The government almost certainly regarded this as an insignificant threat to stability.
[5] No. 5, 7 January 1831.
[6] White to Palmerston, 30 January 1833, F.O. 16/20, p. 52.

time of the rebellion, *El Mercurio de Valparaíso* defined the conservative revolutionaries as 'a horde of men who believe themselves to be Heaven's delegates, empowered to do what they like with this country...; men who, at the time of Peninsular rule, advised in the work of extermination'.[1] Another newspaper pointed out that although the rebellion was being staged in the name of the 1828 Constitution, the conservatives had started by committing infractions of more than thirty articles of that document.[2] It was natural enough that the defeated liberals should oppose what Freire described as a 'secret club of revolutionaries trying to destroy the Republic',[3] and should work, even from exile, to regain control of 'that nation cruelly frustrated in its most pleasing hopes,...transformed today into the victim and plaything of a hypocritical and fratricidal faction'.[4] But the reaction to Portales seems to have passed beyond the bounds of liberal partisanship; it was wider than this. 'The aversion...to the present Government of Chile', wrote the British consul in May 1830, 'seems almost universal.'[5] A year later he described the regime as 'detested by the People at large.'[6] In April 1833 he was still writing that Portales was 'greatly exclaimed against by the people on account of his arbitrary measures'.[7] There was probably some truth, then, in what an English traveller told José Joaquín de Mora in Lima, that 'from the Bío-Bío to the Atacama Desert there is a cry of execration and a universal preparation for revolt'.[8] It is also worth recalling that Portales himself, often gripped by sudden spasms of pessimism, had the recurrent belief that his government was on the point of falling.[9]

The two main points of the liberal opposition's case against the regime were, first, the repressive measures it used, and second, its manipulation by Portales and his clique. The liberal sense of

---

[1] Tomo 3, no. 122, 27 November 1829, p. 244.
[2] *Amigo de la Constitución*, no. 1, 26 January 1830, p. 1.
[3] To Fernando Errázuriz, 5 April 1830, *SCL*, XVIII, 318.
[4] *El Ciudadano Ramón Freire a sus Conciudadanos, Lima, 10 de Julio de 1830, CHDI*, XXXVII, 41.
[5] White to Aberdeen, 28 May 1830, F.O. 16/12B, p. 93.
[6] To Aberdeen, 3 April 1831, F.O. 16/14, p. 103.
[7] To Palmerston, 9 March 1833, F.O. 16/20, p. 115.
[8] To O'Higgins, 12 February 1834, Amunátegui, *J. J. de Mora*, p. 303.
[9] See, for instance, his letter to Garfías, 30 November 1831, Cruz and Feliú Cruz, I, 343.
   Cf. Encina, *Portales*, I, 142–3.

outrage can best be illustrated in a stanza which appeared in *El Defensor de los Militares* in September 1830:

When the genius of good presided o'er us, when reason alone rewarded our services, Tyranny with sacrilegious voice violated the rights which duty guarded. Banishment, disorder, anarchy now oppress those who formerly breathed freedom. The altar of the law is pulled down. The rights of man are profaned.[1]

There was, in verses such as this, not merely the natural bitterness of a party abruptly removed from office, but an additional sense of shock at the excessively harsh procedures of the triumphant faction. To the *exaltado* Infante, the Portales regime became a perfect example of despotism. In 1841 he wrote that in some ways it would be better to have no laws at all rather than the 1833 Constitution, for 'legalised despotism is doubly more sinister to freedom than is arbitrariness'.[2] The president's emergency powers, used several times before the end of the 1830s, were condemned as unnecessarily wide. Their use, it was felt by liberals, was only justifiable in a true national emergency, such as the invasion of the homeland by a foreign power.[3] Thanks to despotic provisions such as this, Chile had become a country

which for ten years has suffered a policy completely opposed to the foundations of her government; which has witnessed the shattering of a constitution which protected her rights and its replacement by a totally contrary constitution bearing all the horrors of despotism in just one of its laws.[4]

Perhaps the most shocking thing, for liberals, was the disappearance of an untrammelled newspaper press such as they had enjoyed during the 1820s. 'There is no surer sign of a country's slavery than the pride and clamour of one party and the silence of the other... The silence is as lugubrious as the grave.'[5] The more persistent liberals, like Pedro Félix Vicuña, tried to keep

[1] No. 16, 18 September 1830.
[2] *Valdiviano Federal*, no. 169, 5 April 1841, p. 2.
[3] *El Sepulturero*, no. 27, 3 June 1840, p. 5. Vicuña Mackenna later showed that between 1833 and 1863 emergency powers had operated for *one third* of the time. *Diego Portales*, I, 137–8 n.   [4] *Paz Perpetua á los Chilenos*, no. 5, 4 June 1840, p. 1.
[5] *El Defensor de los Militares*, no. 3, 24 July 1830.

their spirits up by supposing that liberalism was on the point of overthrowing the regime.

'Vain fears,' the friends of the government will say; 'an Octavian peace and the silence of all parties promise us an eternity in power.' It is a false calculation, a deceptive appearance. The silence is like the silence which Etna and Vesuvius keep while they are preparing the sinister lava which burns and shakes the earth.[1]

But the volcanoes did not explode, despite Vicuña's hopes and Portales' fears.

The second theme of liberal criticism was directed against the manipulation of the state by 'hidden' elements and also against the removal of a whole generation of liberal politicians who had played a part in the original liberation of Chile. Joaquín Campino, in an interesting letter to Manuel de Salas, protested in 1834:

We have an ostensible and titular government while the real and effective power is invisible and irresponsible. This is a false, degrading and annoying position—as is all falsehood—and, moreover, one which suggests bad faith and trickery.[2]

There was, too, much liberal bad feeling over Portales' removal of a weighty group of national leaders—men like Pinto and Lastra. Portales' most provocative action, in fact, was one of his first: the wholesale cashiering of liberal officers who had opposed the rebellion but who had not participated in the civil war. Many of these officers had enacted heroic roles in the struggle for independence.

How can we ever forget the victors of Chacabuco, the men who bore liberty to the Peruvians, the men who made the Republic whole in the memorable expedition to Chiloé, the defenders of the Constitution, in short, the victims of Lircay?[3]

Finally, there was the deep-rooted suspicion that the *estanqueros*, who dominated the conservative regime from the start, had

---

[1] *Paz Perpetua á los Chilenos*, no. 1.
[2] Letter of 1 July 1834, Salas, *Escritos*, III, 283.
[3] *El Trompeta*, no. 8, 27 January 1831, p. 1.

merely been engaged in an act of financial revenge against the men who had deprived them of the *Estanco*, and that theirs was a government 'where the only thought is filling the pocket'.[1]

There has, in general, been a regrettable tendency among some Chilean historians to ignore these aspects of the Portales regime. Admirers of the businessman-dictator prefer to regard the new conservative regime as 'the most gigantic labour ever performed by anybody in Latin America. Without enacting laws and proclaiming principles, [Portales] created a government worthy of the name.'[2] Plainly it cannot be denied that the 'fruits of general order, prosperity, spiritual culture and public works'[3] which followed the establishment of the conservative regime deserve a sympathetic treatment. The Portales regime and the decennial administrations which came afterwards had many fine achievements to their credit. But at the same time it would be unwise, as well as unjust, to forget or ignore the 'silence, and...dark shadows'[4] which were the most noticeable feature of the early years of the Age of Portales.

THE END OF THE REVOLUTION

The counter-revolution of 1829–30 may be said to have been one of the most fundamentally important moments in the history of Chile. If the ascendancies of O'Higgins, Juan Egaña, Infante and Pinto can now be seen as unsuccessful experiments, only interesting in their own right, the government imposed on Chile by Diego Portales under the presidencies of Ovalle, Errázuriz and, most lengthily, Prieto, was so great a success, historically speaking, that some features of its mould are still with Chile in the 1960s. What, then, was the true nature of the rude shock administered by Portales and his collaborators to the infant body politic of Chile? I am obviously obliged to sketch some sort of answer to this question.

---

[1] *El Defensor de los Militares*, no. 12, 10 September 1830. This phrase, which appeared in a satirical news report describing events in 'Turkey' (i.e. Chile), aroused Portales' particular wrath.
[2] Edwards, *Organización política*, p. 104.   [3] Huneeus Gana, p. 114.
[4] 'Saludo al año treinta y seis', *El Sepulturero*, no. 23, 19 January 1836, p. 177.

During the 1820s, optimistic faith in the power of the written word undoubtedly went too far. The basic doctrines of the revolution were exaggerated. Both Juan Egaña and José Miguel Infante tried to undertake a task which was, in the end, bound to fail: the building of an ideal state on the basis of abstract principles. Egaña's moralistic enthusiasm for ancient and distant ways of life and Infante's passionate admiration for the modern United States were superficially poles apart. In fact they were closely related to one another. Both reflected the love of an ideal pattern which refused to take into account the realities and needs of Chile in the early nineteenth century. With the Pinto regime, the revolution once again found its feet. Utopian ideologizing came to an end, even if a certain brand of dogmatic partisan liberalism persisted. The Pinto administration tried to put the basic and common doctrines of the revolution into operation. Pinto could claim, with some degree of justification, that the 1828 Constitution 'partakes of a religious and moral character well suited to our habits and desires'.[1] The word 'desires' should be noted. The revolution had created *desires*. The liberals envisaged their task not merely as the elaboration of a workable state, but also as a state which answered to their doctrinal prescriptions as well. There were imperfections in the 1828 Constitution, certainly, but it must be argued that the authors of that document were fully aware of this—they provided, after all, for a Constituent Convention to meet in 1836 for the purposes of realistic revision and amendment. It seems more than probable that the 1828 Constitution could have been made to work, if shorn of its less desirable features,[2] and if there had existed a political atmosphere less torn by arrogant egoism and non-cooperation.

But the plain fact is that the liberal republic never had a chance to show its merits. Portales and his friends, by an initial act of illegality and violence in answer to a minor constitutional irregularity, ushered in a new phase of Chilean history. Their counter-revolution resulted in a social order which retained a striking similarity to that of the colonial epoch, a social order in

---

[1] *El Vice-Presidente a la Nación*, 9 August 1828, *AR*, I, 140.
[2] Cf. F. Errázuriz, pp. 35-6.

which 'public safety and the integrity of property'[1] became virtually interchangeable terms. Heise González is overstating the case when he describes the Conservative Republic as 'the last and most beautiful chapter of Spanish colonial history',[2] for the revolt of 1829 must also be seen as a victory for those efficient business elements represented by Portales himself[3] as well as the traditionalist *pelucones*. It was this mercantile element which caused the new regime to adopt a deliberate policy of economic development which in a broad sense can be regarded as by no means unprogressive. Manuel Rengifo, for instance, summarized this aspect when he wrote that his financial policy was aimed at stimulating enterprise 'for industry to prosper, wealth to form, and for the people to gain...an ever growing welfare that will better their social condition'.[4] This, together with the tradition of impersonal government and the keeping of the public peace, represented positive features of the conservative order. It is even possible that Portales himself may have been unaware of some of the more doctrinaire anti-liberal tendencies of men like Mariano Egaña.[5]

Nevertheless the liberal ideology, which lay at the heart of the Chilean revolution, was rejected in practice by the Portales regime, while Mariano Egaña and others led a conscious retreat from liberal doctrine. This constitutes the most serious accusation that can be levelled against Portales. As Joaquín Dampino put it:

The present order of things is the work of violence. It is true that it is supported by the two most respectable classes in any society: property and the clergy, which have always ruled in ordered and peaceful times. But we cannot disguise the fact that we live in a time of revolution, and that numbers are against it.[6]

In other words, the revolution had been cut short. Between 1818 and 1829, Pedro Félix Vicuña believed, there had always existed 'a permanent clash between liberal principles and the old ideas consecrated by three centuries of oppression and tyranny'.[7] Then

---

[1] Municipality of Copiapó to the Visitador de Oficinas Fiscales, 17 June 1834, A.M.I. vol. 59, fo. 47.   [2] *150 años*, p. 45.   [3] See Segall, p. 14.
[4] To O'Higgins, 21 January 1842, A.V.M. vol. 87, fo. 134.
[5] See Vicuña Mackenna, *Diego Portales*, II, 353.
[6] To Manuel de Salas, 1 July 1834, Salas, *Escritos*, III, 283.
[7] *Paz Perpetua á los Chilenos*, no. 6, 28 July 1840, p. 2.

came the revolt of 1829. 'The revolution for independence rapidly began to go backwards, both morally and politically.'[1] Some years later that great political dissenterIsidoro Errázuriz wrote that 'our political legislation changed direction completely in 1833. It left the path of American democracy in order to move closer to the model of Constitutional Europe.'[2] Reading an assessment of this type, one is inevitably reminded of Mariano Egaña's admiration for Talleyrand and Metternich. And the cynical realism of those two statesmen is recalled in one of Portales' own best definitions of the art of government: 'The stick and the cake, justly and opportunely administered, are the specifics with which any nation can be cured, however inveterate its bad habits may be.'[3] In Portales' own time, it has to be admitted that the 'stick' was far more in evidence than the 'cake', even if it might be unfair to blame Portales himself for everything that was committed within his extraordinary shadow.[4] In another graphic and well-known sentence, Portales wrote that 'the social order in Chile is preserved by the weight of the night;...the masses' near-universal tendency to repose is the guarantee of public tranquillity'.[5] Portales, then, saw the traditional inertia of Chilean society not as something to be combated but as a fundamental support for the type of government he proposed to institute. He saw no way of lightening 'the weight of the night', only a regime of law and order. This was something, and nobody should deny it; but it was not what the Chilean revolution wanted, and its innate pessimism contrasted violently with the humane optimism of earlier years.

The political commotions of the 1820s can best be interpreted as fruitful experiments, implicit in the process of revolution. Like other Latin Americans, the Chileans had set out, as one anonymous English writer had put it, 'to establish the best government on the ruins of the worst'.[6] There were certain to be profound difficulties

---

[1] *Paz Perpetua á los Chilenos*, no. 6, 28 July 1840, p. 3.   [2] I. Errázuriz, p. 61.

[3] To F. Urizar Garfías, 1 April 1837, Cruz and Feliú Cruz, III, 486.

[4] See, on this subject, the interesting apologia of J. M. Yrarrázaval Larraín, 'Portales "Tirano" y "Dictador"', *BACH*, año 4, no. 8 (1937), p. 11.

[5] To Tocornal, 16 July 1832, Cruz and Feliú Cruz, II, 228.

[6] *On the Disturbances in South America* (London, 1830), pp. 28–9.

as the creoles emerged from their colonial status: 'They doomed themselves to a considerable period of disturbances. No power, no wisdom, could save them from this result; it was as infallible as destiny.'[1] It would no longer be agreed by historians that the colonial regime was the worst of all possible governments, or that the liberal order which the creoles wanted to create was the best. Nevertheless, the creoles themselves assumed that this was the case, and it was the fundamental element of their revolutionary belief. By October 1829, the Chileans had already gone further than most other Latin Americans in the search for a solution to their problems along the lines inherent in the revolutionary philosophy. If good will had prevailed, the readjustment might have been completed.

Instead, conservative irritation reached breaking point. Reacting violently to a political disorganization which had already begun to recede, and to an instinctive suspicion that Chile was being weakened by the liberal regime,[2] Portales and his allies imposed their own kind of readjustment. In doing so, they destroyed the revolution, and much of what a modern historian has called 'the single effective gain which emancipation gave us: political and cultural consciousness, the desire to overcome the inertia and backwardness of the colonial period'.[3] Chile was saved from the continental tidal wave of anarchy which swept through Spanish America in the nineteenth century—and this was a unique achievement—but she was saved at a cost. There can be no certainty that so extreme a deliverance was at all necessary, however much it may have been made probable by the political and social forces at work. It is for this reason that the establishment of the Conservative Republic must be interpreted as a moment of profound tragedy, as well as the genesis of a new order whose success, in terms of staying power, was so spectacular. For the coming of Diego Portales marked the end of the revolution; and it had been a revolution of high hopes and generous sympathies.

---

[1] *On the Disturbances in South America* (London, 1830), p. 20.
[2] 'Don Manuel de Salas formerly said, "To conquer Chile the only force Bolívar needs to send is a boot with a spur on it." Now [July 1829] he says, "It isn't even necessary for the boot to have a spur"' (Vicente Claro to Miguel Zañartu, July 1829, C. Vicuña Mackenna, *Papeles de Claro*, I, 112).   [3] Jobet, p. 34.

APPENDIX 1. SOCIAL CHANGE AND POPULAR LIBERALISM

THE REVOLUTION AND SOCIAL CHANGE

It is now a gigantic commonplace to say that the Latin American revolutions for independence were mainly political in character; 'their primary effect', C. C. Grifin has written, 'was to throw off the authority of a transatlantic empire rather than to bring about a drastic reconstruction of society'.[1] Certain social changes *did* take place, it is true. Slavery was abolished; legal disabilities applied to racial groups were abandoned; a new and cosmopolitan trading element grew up. But a radical shift in society did not occur, was never intended, and would have been wholly unwelcome to the creoles. This did not make the Latin American revolution of 1808–26 any the less a revolution, though an age conditioned to think in sociological categories may find this hard to accept. To the Latin Americans themselves, their emancipation was not merely a perfunctory transfer of political power from Spain to America, but a revolution of profound significance. But it clearly was not a *social* revolution in the sense that the French and Russian revolutions were.

It cannot be emphasized too frequently that the leadership of the revolution, in Chile as elsewhere, was aristocratic in character. As the French scholar Claude Gay concisely put it, 'the revolution in Chile was carried out by respectable persons; the people took no part in these revolutions'.[2] The Chilean aristocracy, landowning, traditional, religious, contrasted with the mercantile oligarchy of Buenos Aires, and so it is small wonder that the Argentines sometimes complimented themselves on being more progressive than their Chilean partners. Bernardo de Vera y Pintado, for example, was able to write in 1813 that 'the new order of things, which in appearance stifled the old oligarchy, has been a solemn hypocrisy to root [the oligarchy] in the eternal slumber of this immobile People'.[3] But it was not only the Argentinian who appreciated the real nature of the revolutionary

[1] 'Economic and Social Aspects of the Era of Spanish American Independence', *HAHR* XXIX (Durham, N.C.. 1949), 170.
[2] Notes on a conversation with Francisco Meneses, n.d., Archivo Gay-Morla, vol. 52, pieza 14 B, fo. 67.
[3] To the Government of the United Provinces, 7 January 1813, Márquez de la Plata, p. 93.

Appendix I

leadership in Chile. During the Spanish reconquest, the Consulado of Santiago produced an admirable definition:

Some are powerful landowners, others clerics and lawyers of outstanding talent and enlightenment—and all of them with interminable family relationships and ramifications which extend from one end of the kingdom to the other.[1]

It would obviously have run counter to the aims and interests of the great creole families to have introduced any genuine element of social change into their revolutionary ideology. The more acute English travellers noted this. John Miers, for instance, wrote that 'the present order of affairs...is the same as the former under another name: all acts, all new establishments, differ only in title',[2] and he later drew attention to the existence of 'the small, powerful aristocracy which is so inimical to the general interests of the community'.[3] Remarking on the upper-class enthusiasm for politics, and the relative indifference of the lower classes, Captain Basil Hall observed that

with regard to the effects of this Revolution, the upper and lower classes are differently circumstanced. The peasant's station in society has not been materially changed by the subversion of the Spanish authority; while...his landlord...has gained many advantages.[4]

It is probable that Chile, lacking the diversity of races and interest groups that existed in places such as Peru or Mexico, actually had fewer opportunities for social change, a point made by C. C. Griffin.[5] But despite this factor, and despite the natural indifference of the creole elite to social reforms of a drastic character, there nevertheless did exist certain elements which advocated a more profound and radical alteration in society. The most famous social revolutionary of the period, and also the one about whom least is known, was Fray Antonio Orihuela, a Franciscan associated with the artisans of Concepción. Orihuela produced one passionate proclamation (1811) and then disappeared from history. His ideas were peculiarly violent and anti-aristocratic. 'Do not forget', he reminded his followers, 'that differences of class and rank were invented by tyrants...to keep the common people in servitude.' The lower classes, he wrote, were obliged to toil

---

[1] 'Exposición del Consulado de Santiago al Rey', 2 November 1816, *Arch.O'H.* xix, 413.
[2] Miers, ii, 139.   [3] *Ibid.* 363–4.   [4] Hall, i, 20.
[5] 'Economic and Social Aspects...', *HAHR*, xxix, 170.

Appendix I

in all weathers and under the worst of conditions while the titled nobility lived and slept in comfort. His conclusion was stirring:

Awake, then, and reclaim your usurped rights! If it is possible, wipe out from the ranks of the living those wicked men who oppose your happiness; and, over their ruin, raise an eternal monument to equality![1]

Orihuela's advice was not needed, and his proclamation was an isolated document, stemming as much from the evangelical egalitarianism of Franciscan life as from any later tradition.[2]

As we have already seen, Bernardo O'Higgins also tended to look upon the traditional aristocracy as an enemy, and tried somewhat unsuccessfully to reduce its influence, but this, at any rate in part, seems to have come from the philanthropic tradition of the Enlightenment, and was a reflection of the ideas of the economist-precursors such as Manuel de Salas.[3] With the 1820s, however, and with the growth of liberalism as a definite and discernible political grouping, a highly emotional current of social radicalism became apparent. It expressed itself in the form of attacks on the position and scale of values of the landowning aristocracy rather than in practical suggestions for social reform. Such attacks were, indeed, a subsidiary aspect of orthodox moderate-liberal thinking. The famous liberal proclamation of January 1828 criticized what it called 'the old and ominous colonial preoccupations'.[4] In part at least, liberal hostility to the aristocracy sprang from the fact that many of the most vocal leaders of the group were lawyers, 'doctors', soldiers—in other words, urban elements—with different interests.[5] Amongst these liberals, there were many who would have agreed with Pedro Trujillo when he wrote in 1824 that 'up till now we have only varied forms, without altering substances'.[6]

Throughout the 1820s, inside and outside the orthodox liberal grouping, there can be observed a distinctive current of anti-aristocratic propaganda. In 1824 the newspaper *El Advisador Chileno* asked: 'What have we achieved by destroying the material force of the overseas aggressors, if we have implanted in our minds the vulgar notion that this was the principal opposition to the progress of freedom?'[7]

[1] *Proclama*, 1811, *SCL*, I, 359.   [2] Segall, p. 6.
[3] On this question, see Villalobos, 'El bajo pueblo'.
[4] *Mercurio de Valparaíso*, tomo I, no. 39, 23 January 1828, p. 153.
[5] See Guillermo Feliú Cruz, 'Una esquema de la evolución social de Chile en el siglo XIX', in his *Abolición*, p. 293.
[6] To Benavente, 25 February 1824, F.V. vol. 823, núm. 218, fo. 6.
[7] No. 5, 11 August 1824, p. 34.

Appendix I

The same newspaper soon identified the true enemies of freedom as the aristocrats: 'We are resolved', it proclaimed, 'to bury despotism and the pride of those classes, even if only beneath our own ruins.'[1] Those two indefatigable popular-liberals Nicolás Pradel and Manuel Magallanes, attacked the monopoly of power and wealth by a hereditary caste in their newspaper *La Lechuza*. They appealed to Freire and Infante to bring about 'the equality which for eighteen years has been promised without effect',[2] and posed a satirical question: 'Who can doubt that societies were instituted with the laudable aim that everyone should work...while just a few—always the same few or their descendants, even if stupid—enjoy power and preference?'[3] The French polemicist Dauxion Lavaysse, who supported the moderate current of liberalism, combined this with a number of personal attacks on the conservatives which savour a little of social revolution. In 1825 he castigated 'those persons who are still enamoured of the antiquated concepts and habits of Feudalism and the Decrepit Castilian Aristocracy',[4] and 'our over-pious Aristocracy...with its insensate opposition to the opinions of the century'.[5] The harshening of the liberal–conservative rivalry in 1829 brought him back to his theme with a fierce onslaught on the *pelucones:*

Wrapped up in their old ideas, fortified in their feudal memories, accustomed to swell with pride in the midst of a vast and humble retinue of *inquilinos*, majordomos, parasites and sycophants—they are laughing at us, and are congratulating themselves on still not having been caught out.[6]

Despite attacks such as these, no plan for a shift in the Chilean social structure was ever suggested. Aristocrats, along with Kings, might be dismissed as 'Sacred Imposters of the Earth',[7] yet nothing was envisaged to move them from their privileged position. If anything, the liberals of the 1820s were even less interested in the condition of the poorer classes than the late-colonial economist-precursors had been. 'The poor farmer', claimed *El Avisador Chileno*, 'finds himself in a state of confusion between cries of liberty and the insults of despotism, between proclamations of philanthropy and the most fearful poverty and obstruction of resources.'[8] Chile, it went on, badly needed 'a system

---

[1] No. 10, 20 September 1824, p. 84.   [2] No. 2, 29 April 1829, p. 6.
[3] *Ibid.*   [4] *Década Araucana*, no. 2, 22 July 1825, p. 24.   [5] *Ibid.*
[6] *Verdadero Liberal*, no. 67, 13 May 1829.
[7] *Década Araucana*, no. 16, 13 May 1826, p. 215.
[8] No. 4, 24 April 1824, p. 27.

Appendix I

of protection for the poorer classes'.[1] This phrase reminds one of a point made by Camilo Henríquez during the 'Patria Vieja'.

Public assistance is one of society's sacred debts. Society ought to provide means of subsistence to its unfortunate citizens, either by procuring them some kind of work or industry, or by preparing means of existence for those who are in no condition to work.[2]

Another echo of this sentiment is to be found in the 1818 Constitution, where it was laid down that 'the Supreme Director and other functionaries...are essentially obliged to alleviate the poverty of the unfortunate, and to provide them with all the paths to prosperity'.[3] Such statements would, perhaps, be considered surprising if Chile's political liberalism had been accompanied by social and economic liberalism. But this was not the case. The Chilean treatment of social and economic questions was still cast within a neo-mercantilist framework during the revolution, despite a few individual protagonists of liberal ideas.[4] And the responsibility of the state for promoting and regulating specific enterprises was very much a neo-mercantilist responsibility.

POPULAR LIBERALISM

The mention of an anti-aristocratic current within the revolution leads naturally to a discussion of the elements most likely to have been responsible for it. There can be little doubt that there was an extremist wing to the liberal movement of the 1820s. Its composition varied according to the moment, but its essential programme—if it can be called that—remained much the same throughout. What Nicolás Pradel referred to in 1829 as 'the POPULAR cause'[5] had as its main aim the deepening and strengthening of some of the major features of liberalism, particularly equality before the law, the weakening of the aristocracy, and so forth. Popular-liberals wanted the revolution to maintain 'a clear, frank and popular character'[6] without compromising with the aristocracy. At times, the popular-liberals found themselves supporting the orthodox moderates; during the federal period many of them adopted federal clothing; and later, some of them attacked the Pinto regime from, so to speak, the left.[7]

[1] Ibid. p. 28.
[2] Catecismo de los patriotas, p. 149.
[3] Tít. I, cap. 2, art. 13. AR, I, 55.
[4] See Will, pp. 7–13.
[5] El Penquisto, no. 4, 22 April 1829, p. 13.
[6] Década Araucana, no. 9, 28 October 1825, p. 143.
[7] See Espectador Chileno; Tribuno del Pueblo Chileno; El Penquisto.

Appendix I

What were the attitudes of popular-liberalism? The aspiration for some indefinite form of social change has already been noticed. In addition, we may observe an extreme emphasis on freedom of expression. The various popular-liberal newspapers took intense delight in laying bare the dark corners of public life and in defending unpopular causes. They also tended to express a sense of dramatic desperation. One deputy to the 1826–7 Congress, for instance, is said to have proclaimed: 'Liberty will not be attained in Chile except by blood, which will flow in torrents!'[1] This feeling undoubtedly prompted some *populares* to involve themselves in the many tumults which punctuated the final years of liberal rule. Thus Martin Orjera's paper *El Insurgente Araucano* openly justified the mutiny of January 1827 on the familar ground that the people had a natural right to revolt when a government failed to secure their happiness. The Urriola mutiny of June 1828 seems to have enjoyed a similar measure of popular-liberal and federal support.

Throughout the liberal period there was genuine fear in government circles that extremism would grow in strength. José María de Rozas, for instance, spoke in the Santiago Provincial Assembly of 1825 of 'revolutionary democracy which destroys all the principles of good Government'[2] while the liberal-federal Congress of the following year found it expedient to issue a general warning to the public: 'It is necessary... for you to close your ears to the malicious suggestions which the anarchists—who speculate with disorder—are trying to inspire in you.'[3] In 1828 the British consul noted the existence of 'persons who gain more by revolution than by well-regulated Government'.[4] One such person, undoubtedly, was Manuel Aniceto Padilla, an Upper Peruvian professional agitator[5] connected with and supported by both federal and popular-liberal elements. He came to occupy a dominant place in the counsels of Infante—it is said that he sometimes prompted Infante during the latter's performances in Congress[6]—and this may have caused the federal leader to lose a good deal of his public prestige.[7] It can be deduced that by the end of the 1820s men

[1] *Verdadero Liberal*, no. 14, 28 February 1827, p. 67.
[2] Session of 14 September 1825, *SCL*, XI, 366.
[3] *Proclama. El Congreso Nacional a sus comitentes*, n.d. *Registro de Documentos del Gobierno* no. 24, 27 July 1826.
[4] White to Dudley, 30 August 1828, F.O. 16/7, p. 208.
[5] See Barros Arana, XIV, 56 n.; Encina, *Historia*, IX, 249–55; and *Volcán Chileno*, no. 3, 18 May 1826, p. 10.   [6] Zapiola, p. 116.
[7] Vicente Claro to O'Higgins, 6 January 1827. C. Vicuña Mackenna, *Papeles de Claro*, I, 73.

like Padilla had managed to create a certain amount of mob sentiment, especially in Santiago. One reason advanced for holding the first sessions of the 1829 Congress in Valparaíso instead of in the capital was the avoidance of the less responsible popular leaders who abounded in the latter city. These were defined by one writer as 'the permanent chiefs of discontent, the tireless creators of lodges', who controlled 'the proletarian mass of rebelliousness, that herd of automata ever disposed to act wickedly as long as there is someone to direct and pay'.[1]

During the Pinto administration, the *populares* and the more intransigent federalists turned their attention to attacking the regime, thus preventing any possibility of presenting a united front to the gathering forces of the conservative reaction.[2] Unfortunately, they went even further than this, and, like Infante, supported the revolt headed by Prieto, which ushered in the reaction. *El Espectador Chileno*, a popular-liberal paper, hailed Prieto as a great liberator, and quoted him a suitable extract from *Lo Araucana*: 'By you the state has been redeemed!'[3] By this act of treachery, popular-liberals must take a share of the blame for the disaster of 1829–30.

The Conservative Republic after 1830 was as odious to the *populares* as it was to their more moderate brethren. For, even if a solid phalanx of all liberal elements had ever wished to effect some slight modification of the social structure, it was now too late. Government fell completely into the hands of the traditional oligarchy and its mercantile supporters. One of the irritants, which compelled the change as far as the conservatives were concerned, was the abolition of the *mayorazgos*, which was felt to be a direct assault on the power and position of the aristocracy.[4] At all events, the fathers of the 1833 Constitution, to use Luis Galdames' words, 'established the government on the foundation of a traditionally respected aristocracy, bearing its interests in mind above all else; and this aristocracy possessed the sources of the national production'.[5] It is hard to deny the modern verdict that the State in the Conservative Republic became the 'strong instrument of the estate-owning class'.[6] Had the liberals, rather than

[1] *Verdadero Liberal*, no. 79, 14 August 1829.
[2] See *Espectador Chileno*; *Tribuno del Pueblo Chileno*; *El Penquisto*.
[3] No. 13, 28 December 1829. The quotation was from Caupolicán's speech to Lautaro in canto III.
[4] For the long-drawn-out controversy over *mayorazgos* in the 1820s, see Donoso, *Ideas políticas*, pp. 117–45.
[5] *Evolución constitucional*, p. 960.   [6] Jobet, p. 9.

the conservatives, been responsible for the shaping of Chilean destinies after 1830, the government would still have remained basically aristocratic in nature. The interests of property would still have been uppermost in the minds of the delegates to the Constituent Convention, had it met, as was originally intended, in 1836. But public and open discussion of all matters, including the question of social change, would have been allowed to flourish, and the influence of the less oligarchic members of the elite would have made itself felt. Instead, the conservatives had their way. Significantly and symbolically enough, the 1833 Constitution effectively re-established the *mayorazgos*. This was as good a sign as any that the revolution had come to an end.

APPENDIX 2. O'HIGGINS' PLAN FOR AN AMERINDIAN EMPIRE

The following is an extract from a draft letter prepared by Bernardo O'Higgins for his secretary, Mr John Thomas. It was written at Montalván[1] in December 1837 for Thomas to recast and elaborate, and is reproduced here partly because of its value as a curiosity, and partly as an illustration of the philanthropic idealism with which some creole revolutionaries showed towards the Amerindian. The letter opens with some reflections on O'Higgins' medical history and his admiration for Ambrosio O'Higgins. This brings him on to the subject of the Araucanian Indians.

One of the first objects which occupied my father's becoming a public man was the Amelioration of the Condition of the indigeneous Inhabits of the New World, frequently designated 'the Red Race', and the first public school I ever entered was one founded by him for the Education of the Sons of the *Araucanian Caciques*;[2] I need not therefore add how highly he appreciated the chiefs of this invincible people. These Chiefs indeed took pride in saying that the only Spanish Governor who c^d boast of having conquered them was Ambrosio O'Higgins, whose paternal effection for them acquired a Victory, which the Veterans of Charles the 5th, Philip the 2nd, c^d never achieve. —Altho' it was my lot to have governed Chile for a longer period than my father & with more absolute power, yet the fierce & sanguinary struggle for Independence never allowed me a moments respite, much less the sufficient leisure to prosecute the great & philanthropic plans of my father. No sooner therefore had the Victory of Ayacucho sealed the Independence of South America than I retired into private life, and a great portion of the 13 years which have since elapsed I have devoted to the consideration of these plans.—My first playmates were Araucanians, and the history with which I first became acquainted was that of the heroes and sages of that unconquerable people, the race to which such a people belonged therefore excited and have continued to excite in me the deepest interest. I have during the last 13 years reflected with as much intensity & devotion on the prospect

---

[1] O'Higgins' estate in the Cañete Valley, Peru.
[2] The Franciscan college at Chillán.

of being instrumental towards establishing an Empire inhabited solely by the Aborigenes of America, and where with the blessings conferred by Christianity & Civilization that race w^d have an Opportunity of proving that in all respects they are not inferior to any other race which inhabits this Globe.—I have anxiously looked at the Map of the World with that view, & was rejoiced to find that a space existed that most admirably suited to the object, & to the application of which to that purpose no sound or rational objection c^d be raised. The space to which I allude lies between Latitude 32 & 54° N. Latitude & between the Rocky Mountains and the Pacific Ocean,[1] & which territory is now in the actual & undisturbed possession of independent tribes of Indians with the exception of a few thousands under the management of Missionarys in New California. Its dominion over these Missions the Mexican nation would I am convinced resign with pleasure for the important object of acquiring Christian neighbours whose peaceable Conduct w^d be guaranteed by the Governments of the United States and England, (and allow in to add that an alliance for such an object may truly be called a holy alliance), and with confidence on the high ground of humanity, I call upon them to form what may truly be called a 'holy alliance' (? w^d not Russia consider this a Sneer, if so it had better be omitted). I repeat that I appeal with Confidence to those Great Powers because they have already given the most unquestionable proofs of their anxiety to better the Condition of the Human race by abolishing the African Slave Trade, & by great & successful Efforts to better the Conditions of their Subjects in their vast Empires. If my proposal to establish an Aboriginal Empire should meet the approbation of these great Powers, it will in that case be desireable that all Aborigines to the East of the Rocky Mountains should be located to the West of them, and that the United States and Great Britain should pay respectively the Expenses of removing those who reside within the boundaries of the U. States and the Canadas respectively; an Expense which I have no doubt they will pay with pleasure, it being now proved by the experience of the last 300 years that the red & white races cannot increase & prosper in the same territory— & the former must be overwhelmed by the tide of the latter rushing with an irresistible impetuosity from the shores of the Atlantic to the Rocky Mountains, which Mounts can alone present an effectual barrier for the protection & preservation of that Race

[1] The area now occupied by the States of California, Oregon and Washington, part of the Province of British Columbia, and part of Lower California.

Appendix II

who were the Owners of the New World at the time of its Discovery by Columbus. That the remnant which at present exists of this once numerous race is not unworthy of such protection & preservation I trust will be evident from the facts stated in the accompanying document,[1] which are taken from the most respectable authorities, viz.— Humboldt (add as many more as you can)—With respect to the form of Government the Congress will have no difficulty in deciding upon the best, as well as the means of supporting it during its infancy—as the pecuniary assistance necessary for that purpose will be but a trifle to mighty nations who are able & willing to make great much less small sacrifices in the glorious Cause of Humanity. Instead of fleets and armies the new Empire would only require a few hundred Missionaries, whose support w^d be attended with but little Expence.[2]

[1] No trace of this.

[2] A.V.M. vol. 98, fos. 184–5. Spelling and punctuation reproduced as in the original. A final, much-polished version of this letter, in Thomas' writing and dated 29 June 1838, addressed to President Martin Van Buren, may be found in A.B.A. vol. 25-4(20), fo. 437. Vicuña Mackenna does not mention this plan in his biography of O'Higgins, though he quotes the phrase 'my first playmates were Araucanians' (*Vida de O'Higgins*, p. 677 n.). Vicuña Mackenna suggests that some of the more fanciful schemes drawn up by O'Higgins in exile were originally Thomas' (p. 677 n.) but whatever the origin of the idea, it is plain that O'Higgins eagerly adopted it and was ready to put it forward as a practical proposition to world leaders. Though O'Higgins obviously assumed too much in supposing the British and American governments to be ready to sponsor this utopian scheme, it was still geographically and politically feasible in the 1830s.

SOURCES

A. MANUSCRIPT SOURCES

Archivo Nacional de Chile, Santiago de Chile
Archivo Eyzaguirre, vols. 8, 20, 27 and 35.
Archivo Gay-Morla, vol. 52.
Archivo del Ministerio del Interior, vols. 38, 46, 59, 66 and 81.
Archivo de don Benjamín Mackenna, vols. 15, 87, 98, and 101.
Fondo Varios, vols. 120A, 244, 253, 259, 420, 445, 645, 697, 789, 801, 802, 812, 821, 822 and 823.

Biblioteca Nacional de Chile, Santiago de Chile
Archivo de don Diego Barros Arana, vols. 25-2(3), 25-2(4), 25-2(5), 25-2 (9), 25-3(2), 25-4(13), 25-4(20) and 25-4(25).
Colección de copias de manuscritos de don José Toribio Medina, vols. 218, 219 and 224.

Public Record Office, London
F.O. 16 (Chile), vols. 1-20 inclusive.
F.O. 72 (Spain), vols. 152 and 169.

B. CONTEMPORARY NEWSPAPERS AND JOURNALS

Note. The title of each publication is followed by the number of issues, the dates, and the name or names of the editor(s), where these details are known. All newspapers and journals were published in Santiago unless otherwise noted.

La Abeja Chilena. 8. 1825. Juan Egaña.
El Almirez. 2. 1828. Manuel and Ramón Rengifo.
El Amigo de la Constitución. 4. 1830. Bruno Larraín and Joaquín Trucos.
El Amigo de la Verdad. 4. 1823. Juan Francisco Zegers and Bernardino Bilbao.
La Antorcha de los Pueblos. 6. 1830-1. Diego Antonio Elizondo.
El Apagador. 1. 1823. Miguel Zañartu and Gabriel Ocampo.
El Araucano. 1830–
El Argos de Chile. 22, 1818. Francisco Rivas. Reprinted in *CAPC*, VII.
La Aurora. 26. 1827. Manuel José de Gandarillas and Diego José Benavente.
La Aurora de Chile. 112. 1812-13. Camilo Henríquez.

Sources

El *Avisador Chileno*. 17. 1824-5. Francisco Fernández.
El *Avisador Imparcial*. Coquimbo. 2. 1830.
La *Bandera Tricolor*. La Serena. 41. 1831-2. Hipólito Belmont.
Boletín de Policía. 2. 1825. Juan Francisco Zegers.
El *Canalla*. 4. 1828. Santiago Muñoz Bezanilla and Manuel Magallanes.
Cartas Pehuenches. 12. 1819. Juan Egaña.
El *Celador*. 9. 1832. Nicolás Pradel, with help from Vicente Claro.
El *Censor de la Revolución*. 7. 1820. Bernardo Monteagudo.
Reprinted in *CAPC*, IX.
El *Centilela*. 22. 1828-9. Santiago Muñoz Bezanilla.
El *Chileno*. 2. 1818. Manuel José de Verdugo. Reprinted in *CAPC*, VII.
El *Chileno*. 3. 1835. Ladislao Ochoa.
Clamor de la Justicia e Idioma de la Verdad. 2. 1817. Reprinted in *CAPC*, III.
Clamor de la Patria. 7. 1823. Miguel Zañartu.
El *Clamor del Pueblo Chileno*. 6. 1827-8. ladislao Ochoa.
La *Clave, Periódico Político y Noticioso*. 100. 1827-8. Melchor José Ramos and others.
La *Clave de Chile*. 111. 1828-9. A continuation of *La Clave*.
La *Cola del Cometa*. 8. 1827. Melchor José Ramos.
Colección de Noticias Documentadas por diversos papeles públicos que dan una idea del actual estado político de la Europa y America y de la influencia que resulta de los sucesos en favor de la libertad americana. 10. 1821. Casimiro Albano.
El *Cometa*. 14, 1827. Melchor José Ramos.
El *Constitucional*, 14, 1833. Manuel and Ramón Rengifo.
El *Constituyente*. 5, 1828. [Manuel José de Gandarillas and José Joaquín de Mora.
El *Coquimbano*. La Serena, 3. 1830. Juan Fariñas.
El *Correo de Arauco*. 50. 1824-5. Juan José Dauxion Lavaysse.
Correo Mercantil. Diario Comercial y Político. 400, 1832-3.
Correo Mercantil-Político-Literario. 74. 1826. Melchor José Ramos, Bruno Larraín, and others.
Correo Nacional. 1. 1833.
El *Corresponsal del Imparcial*. 3, 1823.
El *Cosmopólita*. 16. 1822. Santiago Blayer.
El *Cosmopólita*. Valparaíso. 22. 1833. Juan Francisco Zegers.
La *Década Araucana*. 19. 1825-6. Juan Francisco Zegers and Juan José Dauxion Lavaysse.

Sources

El Defensor de los Militares Denominados Constitucionales. 20. 1830. Various 'friends of Freire'.

El Despertador Araucano. 2. 1823.

Diario de Documentos del Gobierno. 83. 1825–6. José María Astorga.

Documentos Oficiales. 32. 1830.

El Duende de Santiago. 19. 1818. Antonio José de Irisarri.

El Espectador. 1. 1827. Nicolás Pradel.

El Espectador Chileno. 13. 1829. Nicolás Pradel.

La Estafeta de Santiago. 1. 1830. Antonio Garfías.

El Fanal. 10. 1829. Juan Fariñas and others.

El Filántropo. 2. 1834. José ndelicato.

Gaceta de Chile. 16. 1828–29. Ramón Rengifo.

Gazeta Ministerial de Chile. 1818–23. Ignacio Torres and others. Reprinted in CAPC, v, vi, and Arch. O'H. xi, xii, xiii (further volumes to come).

Gazeta de Santiago de Chile. 37. 1817–18. Bernardo de Vera y Pintado.

El Hambriento. 10. 1827–8. Generally attributed to Portales, Gandarillas, Benavente and the Rengifo brothers.

El Hurón. 12. 1832. Portales' tertulia.

Ilustración Araucana. 2. 1813. Reprinted in CHDL, xxiv.

El Imparcial. 1. 1830. Juan Fariñas.

El Independiente. 1. 1821. August Brandt.

El Independiente. 18. 1827. Juan Fariñas and Francisco Fernández.

El Indicador. 9. 1827. Francisco Fernández.

El Insurgente Araucano. 8. 1827. Martín Orjera.

La Justicia en Defensa de la Verdad. 1. 1817. Reprinted in CAPC, iii.

La Lechuza. 2. 1829. Nicolás Pradel and Manuel Magallanes.

La Ley y la Justicia. 3. 1829. Pedro Félix Vicuña.

El Liberal. 48. 1823–5. Nos. 1–25: Diego José Benavente and Pedro Trujillo; Nos. 26–48: Manuel José de Gandarillas.

Mercurio de Chile. 25. 1822–3. Camilo Henríquez. Reprinted in CAPC, ix.

El Mercurio Chileno. 16, 1828–9. José Joaquín de Mora.

Mercurio de Valparaíso. 1827–0. In progress. Since 1900 the main edition of this distinguished newspaper has been printed in Santiago as El Mercurio.

El Minero de Coquimbo. La Serena. 25. 1828. Hipólito Belmont.

La Miscelánea Chilena. 14. 1821. Joaquín Egaña Fabres. Reprinted in CAPC, ix.

Miscelánea Política y Literaria. 5. 1827. Juan Francisco Zegers.

Sources

El Monitor Araucano. 180. 1814–13. Camilo Henríquez. Reprinted in *CHDI*, xxvi and xxvii.

El Monitor Imparcial. 29. 1827. Nicolás Pradel and Santiago Muñoz Bezanilla.

El Nuevo Corresponsal. 2. 1823. Camilo Henríquez.

El Observador de Chile. 1823.

El Observador Chileno. 7. 1822. Reprinted in *CAPC*, x.

El Observador Imparcial. La Serena, 7. 1830.

El O'Higginista. 3, 1831. Vicente Claro. Reprinted in C. Vicuña Mackenna, *Papeles de Claro*, ii, 243.

La Opinión. 33. 1830. Ramón Rengifo.

El Patriota Chileno. 110. 1825-6. Juan Francisco Zegers.

Paz Perpetua á los Chilenos. 6. 1836–40. Pedro Félix Vicuña.

El Penquisto. 5. 1829. Nicolás Pradel.

El Philopolita. 15. 1835. Diego José Benavente, Manuel José de Gandarillas, and Ramón Rengifo.

El Popular. 20. 1830.

Redactor de las Sesiones del Soberano Congreso. 18. 1823-4.

El Redactor de la Educación. 6. 1825. Ambrosio Lozier.

Registro de Documentos del Gobierno. 84. 1826–7. Bartolomé Mujica.

Registro Oficial de la Suprema Junta Interior Gubernativa. 6. 1825. José María Astorga.

Registro Público. 8. 1826.

Rol de Policía. 12. 1827. Martín Orjera.

Semanario de Policía. 19. 1817. Mateo Arnaldo Hoevel. Reprinted in *CAPC*, iii.

Semanario Republicano. 24. 1813–14. Antonio José de Irisarri; followed by Camilo Henríquez.

El Sepulturero. 27. 1828-40. Nicolás Pradel and Manuel Magallanes.

El Sol de Chile. 31. 1818. Juan García del Río.

El Sufragante. 13. 1829–30. Manuel José de Gandarillas.

El Telégrafo. 75. 1819–20. Juan García del Río. Reprinted in *CAPC*, viii.

Tizón Republicano. 17. 1823. Santiago Muñoz Bezanilla.

El Tribuno del Pueblo Chileno. 2. 1829. Martín Orjera.

El Trompeta. 14. 1830–31. Various 'friends of Freire'.

El Valdiviano Federal. 206. 1827–44. José Miguel Infante.

El Verdadero Liberal. 79. 1827–9. Pedro Chapuis, Pedro Félix Vicuña, Melchor José Ramos, Bruno Larraín, and others.

El Vijía. Valparaíso. 7. 1828.

Sources

El Vijía Político. I, 1830.

Viva la Patria. Gaceta del Supremo Gobierno de Chile. 16. 1817. Bernardo de Vera y Pintado. Reprinted in *CAPC*, III.

Volcán Chileno. 3. 1826. Manuel Magallanes and Tadeo Urrutia.

C. BOOKS, PAMPHLETS, ARTICLES

Note: Unless otherwise stated, all works in the following list were published in Santiago de Chile.

Where the name of the author of a book is definitely known but does not actually appear on the title page, it is given in square brackets.

Abascal y Sousa, José Fernando, *Memoria de Gobierno,* ed. V. Rodríguez Casado and J. A. Calderón Quijano. 2 vols. Seville, 1944.

Alemparte R., Julio. *El cabildo en Chile colonial.* 1940.

Alemparte R., Julio. *Carrera y Freire, fundadores de la República.* 1963.

Alemparte R., Julio. 'Causas y carácteres generales de la independencia hispanoamericana', *BACH,* año 17, no. 43, 1950, p. 25.

Almanak Nacional para el Estado de Chile en el año bisiesto de 1824, [ed. Mariano Egaña?] 1824.

Almeyda Arroyo, Aniceto. 'En busca del autor del Catecismo político cristiano', *RCHG,* no. 125, 1957, p. 216.

Alvarez Jonte, Antonio. República Argentina, Ministerio de Relaciones Exteriores y Culto, *Colección de documentos históricos de su archivo: vol. I. Diplomacia de la Revolución: Chile. I. Misión Alvarez de Jonte.* Buenos Aires, 1958.

'Amor de la Patria, José'. *El Catecismo Político Cristiano dispuesto para la instrucción de la Juventud de los Pueblos Libres de la América Meridional.* 1810. In Ricardo Donoso, *Catecismo político cristiano,* p. 95.

Amunátegui, Miguel Luis. *La alborada poetica en Chile despues del 18 de setiembre de 1810.* 1892.

Amunátegui, Miguel Luis. *La crónica de 1810.* 3 vols. 1876.

Amunátegui, Miguel Luis. *Don José Joaquín de Mora. Apuntes biográficos.* 1888.

Amunátegui, Miguel Luis. *Don Manuel de Salas.* 3 vols. 1895.

Amunátegui, Miguel Luis. *Los precursores de la independencia de Chile.* 3 vols. 1910.

Amunátegui, Miguel Luis and Vicuña Mackenna, Benjamín. *La dictadura de O'Higgins.* Madrid, n.d. Biblioteca Ayacucho.

Amunátegui Solar, Domingo. *La democracia en Chile* and *Teatro Político.* 1946.

Sources

Amunátegui Solar, Domingo. *Historia social de Chile.* 1932.

Amunátegui Solar, Domingo. *Jesuitas, gobernantes, militares y escritores.* 1934.

Amunátegui Solar, Domingo, 'Noticias inéditas sobre Juan Martínez de Rozas', *AUC,* cxxvii [1911], 27.

Amunátegui Solar, Domingo. *Pipiolos y pelucones.* 1939.

Amunátegui Solar, Domingo. 'El principio de la revolución y el progreso de la idea de la emancipación', in *CHDI,* xxx,v.

Amunátegui Solar, Domingo. *Recuerdos biográficos.* 1938.

Amunátegui Solar, Domingo. *La sociedad chilena del siglo XVIII. Mayorazgos y títulos de Castilla.* 3 vols. 1901–4.

Anrique R., Nicolás. *Ensayo de una bibliografía dramatica chilena.* 1899.

Archivo de don Bernardo O'Higgins. In progress, 1946–0.

Archivo de la Nación Argentina. *Documentos referentes a la Guerra de la Independencia y Emancipación política de la República Argentina: Paso de los Andes y Campaña Libertadora de Chile.* 2 vols. Buenos Aires, 1917.

Arcos, José Agustín. 'Tribulaciones de un patriota durante la Patria Vieja', no. 110 (1947), p. 336.

El Autor del Grito del Patriotismo al Liberal. ? 1824–5.

Barros Arana, Diego. *Historia jeneral de Chile.* 16 vols. 1884–1902.

Barros Borgoño, Luis (ed.). 'Carta inédita del Director Supremo Bernardo O'Higgins sobre su abdicación', *RCHG,* no. 101, 1942, p. 22.

Batllori, Miguel. *El Abate Viscardo. Historia y mito de la intervención de los jesuitas en la independencia de Hispanoamérica.* Caracas, 1953.

Belaunde, Víctor Andrés. *Bolívar and the Political Thought of the Spanish American Revolution.* Baltimore, 1938.

Benavente, Diego José. *Memoria que el Ministro de Hacienda presenta al Congreso de la República de Chile.* 1924.

Biblioteca Nacional de Chile. *Semana Retrospectiva de la Prensa Chilena. La prensa chilena desde 1812 hasta 1840.* 1934.

Bladh, Carl E. 'La República de Chile, 1821–28', *RCHG,* no. 115, 1950, p. 349 and no. 116, 1950, p. 238.

Bland, Theodoric. 'The Present State of Chile, 1818' In *Arch.S.M.* XI, 114.

Brackenbridge, Henry M. *A Voyage to South America, performed by order of the American Government, in the years 1817 and 1818, in the frigate Congress.* 2 vols. Baltimore, 1819.

Sources

Browning, Webster E. 'Joseph Lancaster, James Thomson, and the Lancasterian System of Mutual Instruction, with Special Reference to Hispanic America'. *HAHR*, IV (1921), p. 49.

Caldcleugh, Alexander. *Travels in South America, during the years 1819–1820–1821*. 2 vols. London, 1825.

Carrera, José Miguel. *Un aviso a los pueblos de Chile*. Montevideo, 1818.

Carrera, José Miguel. 'Borrador de un manifiesto de don José Miguel Carrera', *RCHG*, tomo XL, no. 44, 1921, p. 245.

'Carta que un Chileno escribió al Excmo. Señor Don José de Gálvez, Secretario de Estado del Despacho Universal de Indias, y se la dirigió por el parte el real sitio del Pardo', *RCHG*, tomo LXXXVIII, no. 96 (1940), p. 219.

Celis Muñoz, Luis. 'El pensamiento político de Manuel de Salas', *AUC*, año CX, nos. 87–8, 1962, p. 5.

Chamisso, Adalberto de. 'Mi visita a Chile en 1816', *RCHG*, tomo LXXXVIII, no. 96, 1940, p. 239.

Cid Celis, Gustavo. *Juan Egana, constitucionalista y prócer americano*. 1941.

Cifuentes, José María. 'La constitucion de 1833', *BACH*, año I, no. 1, 1933, p. 31.

Cifuentes, José María. 'Don Mariano Egaña, su vida y su obra', *BACH*, año 13, no. 34, 1946, p. 5.

Cleveland, Richard J. *A Narrative of Voyages and Commercial Enterprises*. 2 vols. Cambridge, Mass., 1842.

Colección de antiguos periódicos chilenos, ed. Guillermo Feliú Cruz. In progress, 1951- 0. Volume numbers not printed on title-page, but listed on back cover.

Collier, William Miller and Feliú Cruz, Guillermo. *La primera misión de los Estados Unidos de América en Chile*. 1926.

Cruchaga Tocornal, Miguel. *Estudio sobre la organización económica i la hacienda pública de Chile*. 2 vols. 1878–81.

Cruz, Ernesto de la (ed.). *Epistolario de don Bernardo O'Higgins*. 2 vols. 1916-19.

Cruz, Ernesto de la and Feliú Cruz, Guillermo (ed.). *Epistolario de don Diego Portales*. 3 vols. 1936–7.

Cruz, José Maria de la. *Recuerdos de don Bernardo O'Higgins*. 1960.

[Dauxion Lavaysse Juan José.] *Del federalismo y de la anarquía*. 1823.

Documentos del archivo de San Martín. 12 vols. Buenos Aires, 1910–11.

Sources

Domenico Rodríguez, Raúl di. *La gestión monárquica en Chile.* 1962.

Donoso, Ricardo. *Antonio José de Irisarri, escritor y diplomático.* 1934.

Donoso, Ricardo. *El Catecismo político cristiano.* 1943.

Donoso, Ricardo. *Las ideas políticas en Chile.* Mexico DF 1946.

Donoso, Ricardo. *La sátira política en Chile.* 1950.

Dundonald, Thomas Cochrane, 10th Earl of, *Narrative of Services in the Liberation of Chili, Peru and Brazil, from Spanish and Portuguese Domination.* 2 vols. London, 1859.

Edwards, Alberto. *La fronda aristocrática en Chile.* 1928.

Edwards, Alberto. *La organización política de Chile.* 2nd edn. 1955.

Edwards, Alberto and Frei Montalva, Eduardo. *Historia de los partidos políticos chilenos.* 1949.

Egaña. Juan. *Breves notas que ilustran algunos artículos de la Constitución.* 1813. In *SCL*, I, 243.

Egaña, Juan. *Cartas de don Juan Egana a su hijo Mariano, 1824–28.* 1946.

Egaña, Juan. 'Cartas, 1832–33', *RCHG*, no. 116, 1950, p. 93.

Egaña, Juan 'Cartas...de don Juan Egaña dirigidas a don Joaquín Campino', *RCHG*, tomo V, no. 9, 1913, p. 37.

Egaña, Juan. *El chileno consolado en los presidios, ó filosofía de la religión.* 2 vols. London, 1826.

Egaña, Juan. *Colección de algunos escritos políticos, morales, poéticos y filosóficos.* 6 vols. vols. I-II printed together; vol. III never issued. vols. I, II and IV, London, 1826–30; vols. V and VI, Bordeaux, 1836. For the complex printing history of this collection see Silva Castro, *Bibliografía de Egana*, pp. 159–63.

Egaña, Juan. *Escritos inéditos y dispersos*, ed. Raúl Silva Castro. 1949.

Egaña, Juan. *Examen instructivo sobre la constitución política de Chile promulgada en 1823.* 1824. In SCL, IX, 13.

Egaña, Juan. 'Memorias de los servicios públicos del dr. dn. Juan Egaña', *RCHG*, tomo XXVII, no. 31, 1918, p. 5.

Egaña, Juan. *Memoria política sobre si conviene en Chile la libertad de cultos.* Lima, 1827.

Egaña, Juan. *Memorias políticas sobre las federaciones y legislaturas en general y con relación á Chile.* 1825.

Egaña, Mariano. *Cartas de don Mariano Egana a su padre, 1824–29.* 1948.

Egaña, Mariano. 'Diario de don Mariano Egaña 1833–1836', *BACH*, año I, no. I, 1933, p. 57.

Encina, Francisco Antonio. *Historia de Chile desde la prehistoria hasta 1891.* 20 vols. 1942–52.

Sources

Errázuriz, Fernando. *Chile bajo el imperio de la constitución de 1828.* 1861.

Errázuriz, Isidoro. 'Juicio sobre don Diego Portales', in Cruz and Feliú Cruz, II, 31.

Eyzaguirre, Domingo. *Clamor de la Verdad y el Orden.* 1824.

Eyzaguirre, Jaime. *Archivo epistolar de la familia Eyzaguirre 1747–1854.* Buenos Aires, 1960.

Eyzaguirre, Jaime. 'La expulsión de los jesuitas y la independencia de América', *Revista Chilena,* no. 119-20, 1930, p. 172.

Eyzaguirre, Jaime. 'Las gacetas de Procopio', *Revista Chilena,* no. 121-22, 1930, p. 499.

Eyzaguirre, Jaime. *Ideario y ruta de la emancipación chilena.* 1957.

Eyzaguirre, Jaime. 'Las ideas políticas en Chile hasta 1833', *BACH,* año I, no. I, 1933, p. 13.

Eyzaguirre, Jaime. *O'Higgins.* 3rd edn. 1950.

Feliú Cruz, Guillermo. *La abolición de la esclavitud en Chile.* 1942.

Feliú Cruz, Guillermo. 'La elección de O'Higgins para Director Supremo de Chile', *RCHG,* tomo XXIII, no. 27, 1917, p. 337.

Feliú Cruz. *El pensamiento político de O'Higgins.* 1954.

Fuenzalida Grandón, Alejandro. *La evolución social de Chile.* 1906.

Fuenzalida Grandón, Alejandro. *Historia del desarrollo in elec ual en Chile, 1541–1810.* 1903.

Galdames, Luis. 'Los dos primeros años de la Constitución de 1833', *RCHG,* no. 79, 1933.

Galdames, Luis. *Historia de Chile: La evolución constitucional desde 1810 hasta 1833.* 1925.

Gandarillas, Manuel José de. *Don Bernardo O'Higgins. Apuntes históricos sobre la revolución de Chile,* in *CHDI,* XIV. First printed in *El Araucano,* nos. 176–99, 24 January to 4 July 1834.

García Huidobro, Elías. 'Las Cortes de Cádiz y las elecciones de los diputados de Chile', *RCHG,* tomo IV, no. 8, 1912, o. 330.

Gay, Claudio. *Historia física y política de Chile.* 24 vols. *Historia,* 6 vols. Paris, 1844–54.

Gerbi, Antonello. *La disputa del nuovo mondo.* Milan–Naples, 1955.

Giménez Fernández, Manuel. *Las doctrinas populistas en la independencia de Hispanoamerica.* Seville, 1947.

Gómez de Vidaurre, Felipe. *Historia geografica, natural y civil del Reino de Chile,* ed. José Toribio Medina. 2 vols. 1889.

Encina, Francisco Antonio. *Portales. Introducción a la historia de la época de Diego Portales.* 2 vols. 1934.

Sources

Graham, Gerald S. and Humphreys, R. A. (ed.). *The Navy and South America, 1807–1823.* London, 1962. Publications of the Navy Records Society, vol. CIV.

Graham, Maria. *Journal of a Residence in Chile during the year 1822.* London, 1824.

Guarda Geywitz, Fernando. *El 'Valdiviano Federal' y el federalismo en Valdivia.* 1957.

Haigh, Samuel. *Sketches of Buenos Ayres and Chile.* London, 1829.

Hall, Basil. *Extracts from a Journal written on the coasts of Chile, Peru and Mexico in the years 1820, 1821, 1822.* 2 vols. Edinburgh, 1826.

Heise González, Julio. *150 años de evolución institucional.* 1960.

Henríquez, Fray Camilo. *Catecismo de los patriotas.* 1813. In Silva Castro, *Escritos políticos,* p. 147.

Henríquez, Fray Camilo. *Proclama de Quirino Lemachez.* 1811. In Silva Castro, *Escritos políticos,* p. 45.

Humphreys, R. A. and Lynch, John. *The Origins of the Latin American Revolutions, 1808–1826.* New York, 1965.

Huneeus Gana, Antonio. 'La constitución de 1833', *RCHG,* tomo LXXIV, no. 79, 1933, p. 231.

Irisarri, Antonio José de. *Carta al Observador en Londres, ó impugnación a las falsedades que se divulgan contra America.* London, 1819.

Irisarri, Antonio José de. *Memoria sobre el estado presente de Chile.* London, 1820.

Jobet, Julio César. *Ensayo crítico del desarrollo económico-social de Chile.* 1955.

Johnson, John J. 'Early Relations of the United States with Chile', *Pacific Historical Review,* XIII, Berkeley, Calif., 1944, p. 260.

Johnston, Samuel Burr. *Cartas escritas durante una residencia de tres anos en Chile,* trans. José Toribio Medina. 1917.

Konetzke, Richard. 'La condición legal de los criollos y las causas de la independencia', *Estudios Americanos,* II, Seville, 1950, p. 31.

Letelier, Valentín (ed.). *Sesiones de los Cuerpos Lejislativos de la República de Chile, 1811–1845.* 1887–1908.

Levene Ricardo. *El mundo de las ideas y la revolución hispanoamericana de 1810.* 1956.

Malaspina Alejandro. *Viaje político-científico alrededor del mundo por las corbetas Descubierta y Atrevida.* 2nd edn. Madrid, 1885.

Manning William R. (ed.). *Diplomatic Correspondence of the United States concerning the Independence of the Latin American Nations.* 3 vols. New York, 1925.

Sources

Marín Balmaceda, Raúl. 'Conceptos políticos y administrativos de Portales', *BACH*, año 4, no. 8, 1937, p. 208.

Marquez de la Plata, Fernando, [ed.]. *Correspondencia de don Bernardo de Vera y Pintado que se conserva en el Archivo General de la Nación Argentina y Biblioteca Nacional de Buenos Aires.* Buenos Aires, 1941.

Mathison, Gilbert Farqhuar. *Narrative of a Visit to Brazil, Chile, Peru and the Sandwich Islands during the years 1821 and 1822.* London, 1825.

Matta Vial, Enrique. 'El diputado de Chile en las Cortes de Cádiz don Joaquín Fernández de Leiva' *RCHG*, tomo XXXIII, no. 37, 1920, p. 307.

Matta Vial, Enrique. 'La Junta de Gobierno de 1810, y el Consejo de Regencia, y el Virrey del Perú', *RCHG*, tomo XXXVIII, no. 42, 1921, p. 52.

(Matta Vial, Enrique and Feliú Cruz, Guillermo), *Colección de historiadores y de documentos relativos a la indepencia de Chile.* 37 vols. 1900–54.

Medina, José Toribio. *Actas del Cabildo de Santiago, durante el período llamado de la Patria Vieja, 1810–1814.* 1910.

Medina, José Toribio. *Bibliografía de la imprenta en Santiago de Chile desde sus orígenes hasta febrero de 1817.* 1891.

Medina, José Toribio. *Historia de la Real Universidad de San Felipe de Santiago de Chile.* 1928.

Medina, José Toribio. *Historia del Tribunal del Santo Oficio de la Inquisición en Chile.* 2 vols. 1890.

Meneses, Juan Francisco. *A los pueblos de Chile.* 1824.

Meza Villalobos, Néstor. *La actividad política del reino de Chile entre 1806 y 1810.* 1958.

Meza Villalobos, Néstor. *La conciencia política chilena durante la monarquía.* 1958.

Miers, John. *Travels in Chile and La Plata.* 2 vols. London, 1826.

Milet-Mureau, M. L. A. *Voyage de La Pérouse autour du monde.* 4 vols. Paris, 1797.

Mitre, Bartolomé. *Historia de San Martín y de la emancipación sudamericana.* 3 vols. Buenos Aires, 1887–8.

Molina, Juan Ignacio. *The Geographical, Natural and Civil History of Chili.* 2 vols. London, 1809.

Moulton, William. *A concise extract, from the sea journal of William Moulton, written on board of the Onico, in a voyage from the port of New London in Connecticut, to Staten-Land in the South Sea...* Utica, N.Y., 1804.

Nichols, Roy F. *Advance Agents of American Destiny.* Philadelphia, 1956.

Sources

O'Higgins, Bernardo. *Manifiesto que hace a las naciones el Director Supremo de Chile de los motivos que justifican su revolución y la declaración de su Independencia.* 1818. In *AR*, I, 17.

O'Higgins, Bernardo. *Manifiesto del Capitan General de Egercito Dn. Bernardo O'Higgins a los Pueblos que dirige.* 1820.

O'Higgins, Bernardo and Irisarri, Antonio José de. *Manifiesto del Gobierno a los Pueblos que forman el estado de Chile.* 5 May 1818. In *Arch.S.M.* XI, 60.

Orrego Vicuña, Eugenio. *El espíritu constitucional de la administración O'Higgins.* 1924.

Orrego Vicuña, Eugenio. *O'Higgins. Vida y tiempo.* 2nd edn. Buenos Aires, 1957.

Oyarzún, Luis and Fernández Valdés, Juan José. 'Los planes políticos de San Martín en 1818', *BACH*, año 17, no. 43, 1950, p. 71.

Paz Soldán, Mariano Felipe. *Historia del Peru Independiente: Primer Período, 1819–1822.* Lima, 1868.

Pereira Salas, Eugenio. *Buques norteamericanos en Chile a fines de la era colonial.* 1936.

Pereira Salas, Eugenio. 'La influencia norteamericana en las primeras constituciones de Chile', *Boletín del Seminario de Derecho Público*, año 13, 1944, p. 58.

[Pérez de Cotapos, José Antonio]. *Mensaje del Intendente de la Provincia a la Primera Asamblea Constitucional al instalarse.* 1829.

Pinto, Francisco Antonio. 'Apuntes autobiográficos', *BACH*, año 8, no. 17, 1941, p. 69.

Pinto, Francisco Antonio. *Memoria del Ministro del Interior en Contestación al Message del Senado.* 1824.

Prieto, Joaquín. *Cartas de don Joaquín Prieto a don Diego Portales*, ed. J. M. Yrarrázaval Larraín. 1960.

Prieto, Joaquín. *Exposición que el Presidente de la República, Don Joaquín Prieto, dirije a la nacion chilena el dia 18 de setiembre de 1841, último de su administración.* In *SCL*, XXXIX, 318.

Proceso seguido por el Gobierno de Chile en 1810, contra don Juan Antonio Ovalle, don José Antonio de Rojas, y el Doctor Don Bernardo de Vera y Pintado, por el delito de conspiración. In *CHDL*, XXX.

Proctor, Robert. *Narrative of a Journey across the Cordillera of the Andes, and of a Residence in Lima…* London, 1825.

Pueyrredón, Carlos A., ed. *La Campaña de los Andes: Cartas secretas e instrucciones reservadas de Pueyrredón a San Martín.* Buenos Aires, 1942.

Sources

Ramírez Necochea, Hernán. *Antecedentes económicos de la independencia de Chile*. 1959.

Raposo Morales, Aníbal. 'Aspecto intelectual de Chile en los primeros años del singlo XIX', *BACH*, año 3, no. 5, 1935. p. 141.

Robinson, Jeremy. 'Diario personal, Mayo-Junio 1818', *RCHG*, tomo LXXXV, no. 93, 1938, p. 99.

Rodríguez Aldea, José Antonio. *Satisfacción pública del ciudadano J.A.R., ex-ministro de Hacienda y Guerra*. 1823.

Roldán, Alcibiades. 'El centralismo de la constitución de 1833', *RCHG*, tomo LXXIV, no. 79, 1933, p. 410.

Roldán, Alcibiades. 'Los desacuerdos entre O'Higgins y el Senado Conservador', *AUC*, tomo LXXXII (1892–3), pp. 177, 351, and 643.

Roldán, Alcibiades. *Las primeras asambleas nacionales 1890*.

[Salas, Manuel de.] *Diálogo de los porteros*, 1811, in *CHDI*, XIX, 167.

[Salas, Manuel de.] *Escritos de don Manuel de Salas y documentos relativos a el y a su familia*. 3 vols. 1910–14.

Santa María, Domingo. *Memoria histórica sobre los sucesos ocurridos desde la caída de don Bernardo O'Higgins hasta la promulgación de la constitución dictada en el mismo ano*, in Vicuña Mackenna, *Historia jeneral*, IV, 121.

Santa María, Domingo. *Vida de don José Miguel Infante*. 1902. Biblioteca de Autores Chilenos, vol. X.

Schmidtmeyer, Peter. *Travels into Chile over the Andes in the years 1820 and 1821*. London, 1824.

Segall, Marcelo. *Las luchas de clases en las primeras decadas de la República de Chile, 1810–1846*. 1962.

Shaw, P. V. *The Early Constitutions of Chile*. New York, 1930.

[Silva, Fray Tadeo]. *Los apóstoles del diablo*. 1823.

Silva Castro, Raúl. *Bibliografía de don Juan Egaña*. 1949.

Silva Castro, Raúl. *Egaña en la Patria Vieja*. 1959.

Silva Castro, Raúl. *Prensa y periodismo en Chile*. 1958.

Silva Castro, Raúl (ed.). *Escritos políticos de Camilo Henríquez*. 1960.

Stevenson, William Bennet. *A Historical and Descriptive Narrative of Twenty Years' Residence in South America*. 3 vols. London, 1825.

[Sutcliffe, Thomas]. *Sixteen Years in Chile and Peru, by the Retired Governor of Juan Fernändez*. London, 1841.

Talavera, Manuel Antonio. *Revoluciones de Chile. Discurso histórico, diario imparcial, de los sucesos memorables acaecidos en Santiago de Chile por un vecino testigo ocular*, in *CHDI*, XXIX.

Sources

Thomas, John. 'Los proyectos del Virrey O'Higgins', *RCHG*, tomo XI, no. 15, 1914, p. 128.

Tocornal, Manuel Antonio. *Memoria sobre el primer gobierno nacional*, in Vicuña Mackenna, *Historia jeneral*, I, 103.

[Torres, Ignacio], *Advertencias precautorias a los habitantes de Chile*. 1808. In *CHDI*, VIII, 33.

[Torres, Ignacio]. *Informe a la Junta Central de Aranjuez sobre varios sucesos ocurridos en Santiago de Chile en los años de 1808–1809*. 1809. In *CHDI*, VIII, I.

Valencia Avaria, Luis. 'La declaración de la independencia de Chile', *BACH*, año 9, no. 23, 1942, p. 37.

Valencia Avaria, Luis. ed. *Anales de la República. Textos constitucionales de Chile y registros de los ciudadanos que han integrado los poderes ejecutivo y legislativo desde 1810*. 2 vols. 1951.

Vancouver, George. *A Voyage of Discovery to the North Pacific Ocean and Round the World*. 3 vols. London, 1798.

Varas Velázquez, Miguel. 'El reglamento constitucional de 1812: Nuevos documentos', *RCHG*, tomo XIV, no. 18, 1915, p. 107.

Vicuña Mackenna, Benjamín. *El Coronel don Tomás de Figueroa*. 1884.

Vicuña Mackenna, Benjamín. *Introducción a la historia de los diez años de la administración Montt. D. Diego Portales (con mas de 500 documentos inéditos)*. 2 vols. Valparaíso, 1863.

Vicuña Mackenna, Benjamín. *Vida de O'Higgins*. 1936. Obras Completas, vol. V.

Vicuña Mackenna, Benjamín. (ed.). *Historia jeneral de la República de Chile desde su independencia hasta nuestros días*. 5 vols. 1866–82.

Vicuña Mackenna, Carlos. (ed.), *Papeles de don Vicente Claro*. 2 vols. 1917.

Villalobos R., Sergio. 'El bajo pueblo en el pensamiento de los precursores de 1810', *AUC*, no. 120, 1960, p. 36.

Villalobos R., Sergio. 'El comercio extranjero a fines de ladominacion española', *Journal of Inter-American Studies*, IV, Gainesville, Fla., 1962, p. 517.

Villalobos R., Sergio. *Tradición y reforma en 1810*. 1961.

Vivanco Cabezon, Raúl. *Las constituciones de O'Higgins y sus antecedentes históricos, políticos, económicos y sociales*. Valparaíso, 1945.

Walton, William. *An Exposé of the Dissentions of Spanish America*. London, 1814.

Webster, C. K. (ed.), *Britain and the Independence of Latin America*. 2 vols. London, 1938.

Sources

Will, Robert M. 'The Introduction of Classical Economics into Chile', *HAHR*, XLIV (1964), p. 1.

Wolff, Inge. 'Algunas consideraciones sobre causas económicas de la emancipación chilena', *Anuario de Estudios Americanos*, XI, Seville, 1954, p. 169.

Yrarrázaval Larraín, José Miguel, 'Portales "tirano" y "dictador"', *BACH*, año 4, no. 8, 1937, p. 11.

Yrarrázaval Larraín, José Miguel. 'San Martín y los proyectos monárquicos sobre Chile en 1817 y 1818', *BACH*, año 18, no. 44, 1951, p. 5.

Zapiola, José. *Recuerdos de treinta años, 1810–1840.* 5th edn. 1902.